Cavaliers, Clubs,
and Literary Culture

The Sucklingtonian Faction (London, 1641). By permission of the British Library.

Cavaliers, Clubs, and Literary Culture

Sir John Mennes, James Smith, and the Order of the Fancy

Timothy Raylor

DELAWARE

Newark: University of Delaware Press
London and Toronto: Associated University Presses

Associated University Presses
440 Forsgate Drive
Cranbury, NJ 08512

Associated University Presses
25 Sicilian Avenue
London WC1A 2QH, England

Associated University Presses
P.O. Box 338, Port Credit
Mississauga, Ontario
Canada L5G 4L8

The paper used in this publication meets the requirements
of the American National Standard for Permanence of Paper
for Printed Library Materials Z39.48-1984.

Library of Congress Cataloging-in-Publication Data

Raylor, Timothy.
    Cavaliers, clubs, and literary culture : Sir John Mennes, James
Smith, and the Order of the Fancy / Timothy Raylor.
        p.   cm.
    Includes bibliographical references and index.
    ISBN 0-87413-523-0 (alk. paper)
    1. Mennes, John, Sir, 1599–1671.   2. English poetry—Early modern,
1500–1700—History and criticism.   3. London (England)—Social life
and customs—17th century.   4. Poets, English—Early modern,
1500–1700—Biography.   5. Humorous poetry, English—History and
criticism.   6. Royalists—Great Britain—History—17th century.
7. Clubs—England—London—History—17th century.   8. Order of the
Fancy (Group of writers)   9. Smith, James 1605–1667.   10. Burlesque
(Literature)   I. Title.
PR2308.Z5R39   1994
821'.409—dc20   93-37277
                                                                          CIP

To the memory
of
Barry Daniel
(1944–1986)

Contents

List of Illustrations

Abbreviations and Sigla

"Achievement"	Timothy John Raylor. "The Achievement of Sir John Mennes and Dr. James Smith." D. Phil. diss., University of Oxford, 1986.
Alumni	Joseph Foster. *Alumni Oxonienses, 1500–1714*. 4 vols. Oxford, 1891–92.
Athenae	Anthony Wood. *Athenae Oxonienses*. Edited by Philip Bliss. 4 vols. London, 1813–20.
Aubrey	John Aubrey. *"Brief Lives," chiefly of Contemporaries, set down by John Aubrey, between the Years 1669 & 1696*. Edited by Andrew Clark. 2 vols. Oxford, 1898.
Bentley	Gerald Eades Bentley. *The Jacobean and Caroline Stage*. 7 vols. Oxford: Clarendon Press, 1941–68.
BL	British Library, London.
Bodl.	Bodleian Library, Oxford.
CCAM	*Calendar of the Proceedings of the Committee for Advance of Money, 1642–1656*. Edited by Mary Anne Everett Green. 3 vols. London, 1888.
CCC	*Calendar of the Proceedings of the Committee for Compounding, 1643–1660*. Edited by Mary Anne Everett Green. 5 vols. London, 1889–92.
Clarendon	Clarendon, Edward Hyde, Earl of. *The History of the Rebellion and Civil Wars in England*. Edited by W. Dunn Macray. 6 vols. Oxford, 1857.
CSPD	*Calendar of State Papers, Domestic Series*.
DNB	*Dictionary of National Biography*.
EHR	*English Historical Review*.
EIC	*Essays in Criticism*.
ELH	*English Literary History*.
ELR	*English Literary Renaissance*.

11

Facetiae	*Facetiae, "Musarum Deliciae"* . . . *"Wit Restor'd"* . . . *"Wits Recreations."* Edited by J. C. Hotten. 2 vols. London, [1874].
Firth & Rait	*Acts and Ordinances of the Interregnum, 1646–1660.* Edited by C. H. Firth and R. S. Rait. 3 vols. London: HMSO, 1911.
Gardiner	Samuel Rawson Gardiner. *History of England from the Accession of James I. to the Outbreak of the Civil War 1603–1642*. 10 vols. London, 1883–84.
GLRO	Greater London Record Office.
Herrick	Robert Herrick. *The Poetical Works of Robert Herrick*. Edited by L. C. Martin. Oxford: Clarendon Press, 1956.
HL	*The Loves of Hero and Leander*. London, 1651.
HLB	*Harvard Library Bulletin*.
HLQ	*Huntington Library Quarterly*.
HMC	Historical Manuscripts Commission.
Hudibras	Samuel Butler. *Hudibras*. Edited by John Wilders. Oxford: Clarendon Press, 1967.
Ben Jonson	Ben Jonson, *Ben Jonson*. Edited by C. H. Herford and Percy and Evelyn Simpson. 11 vols. Oxford: Clarendon Press, 1925–52.
MD	*Musarum Deliciae*. London, 1655.
MD&WR	*"Musarum Deliciae" (1655) and "Wit Restor'd" (1658)*. Introduction by Tim Raylor. Delmar, N. Y.: Scholars' Facsimiles and Reprints, 1985.
MLR	*Modern Language Review*.
MP	*Modern Philology*.
N&Q	*Notes & Queries*.
OED	*Oxford English Dictionary*.
ODEP	*The Oxford Dictionary of English Proverbs*. 3d edition, revised by F. P. Wilson. Oxford: Clarendon Press, 1970.
P&P	*Past and Present*.
Pepys	Samuel Pepys. *The Diary of Samuel Pepys*. Edited by Robert Latham and William Matthews. 11 vols. London: Bell and Hyman, 1970–83.
PRO	Public Record Office, London.

PRO SP	Public Record Office, London. State Papers.
RES	*Review of English Studies.*
SEL	*Studies in English Literature.*
SP	*Studies in Philology.*
STC	A. W. Pollard and G. R. Redgrave. *A Short-Title Catalogue of Books Printed in England, Scotland, & Ireland . . . 1475–1640.* 2d edition, revised by W. A. Jackson, F. S. Ferguson, and Katharine F. Pantzer. 3 vols. London: Bibliographical Society, 1976–91.
Stokes	Joseph Morgan Stokes. "*Wit and Drollery* 1656." Ph.D. diss., Yale University, 1935.
Suckling	John Suckling. *The Works of Sir John Suckling: The Non-Dramatic Works.* Edited by Thomas Clayton. Oxford: Clarendon Press, 1971.
Tilley	Morris Palmer Tilley. *A Dictionary of the Proverbs in England in the Sixteenth and Seventeenth Centuries.* Ann Arbor: University of Michigan Press, 1950.
TLS	*Times Literary Supplement.*
WD	*Wit and Drollery.* London, 1656.
WD1682	*Wit and Drollery.* London, 1682.
Wing	Donald F. Wing. *Short-Title Catalogue of Books Printed in England, Scotland, Ireland, Wales, and British America . . . 1641–1700.* 2d edition. 3 vols. New York: MLA, 1972–88.
WR	*Wit Restor'd.* London, 1658.
YES	*Yearbook of English Studies.*

Textual Note

In dealing with seventeenth-century texts (printed or manuscript), I have not modernized spelling. In transcriptions of manuscript material, the following conventions apply. Conventional contractions are expanded silently, except "&," which is not expanded. Superscripts are silently regularized and deletions are not shown. Insertions are indicated only in a few cases where this was deemed significant. In such cases the inserted material is placed in pointed brackets <thus>. Expansions where scribal authority is lacking or the reading is dubious are indicated in square brackets [thus]. Editorial comments are placed in italics within such brackets.

In references to books where pagination is inconsistent or problematic for some reason, signatures and occasionally also the number signed on the page are given. In the case of anonymous books, or titles which may be hard to track down, I have given *STC* or Wing numbers.

To avoid confusions over dating, I have given dates as both old and new style, indicating doubts where those exist.

Acknowledgments

A book like this incurs many debts, and now it is a pleasant task to thank those who have helped it along the way.

Institutional debts to the universities of Newcastle upon Tyne and Oxford, where I was respectively an undergraduate and a graduate student, and to the British Academy for funding my research during the writing of the D.Phil. thesis, which underlies this book, can be acknowledged briefly. They are no less important for that.

I have benefited greatly from the kindness of the many librarians in whose institutions I have worked. Chief amongst these are, in England, the Bodleian Library, Oxford; Worcester College Library, Oxford; Sheffield University Library; the British Library; and the Public Record Office; and, in the United States, the Henry E. Huntington Library, San Marino, California. I have also profited from correspondence with or visits to: Bedfordshire Country Record Office; the Beinecke Library, Yale University; the Brotherton Library, University of Leeds; Canterbury Cathedral Archives; Exeter Cathedral Library; the Folger Shakespeare Library, Washington, D.C.; the Greater London Record Office; the Guildhall Library, London; the Houghton and Widener Libraries at Harvard University; Lambeth Palace Library; Lincolnshire Archives Office; Lincoln College, Oxford; the Library of Congress, Washington, D.C.; Nottingham University Library; and Trinity College, Cambridge.

Personal debts are of course the greatest pleasure to acknowledge. I have been lucky in having a supportive family and very patient friends. I owe special thanks to three remarkable English teachers, Peter Gardiner, David Hughes, and Ian Lowe, who first initiated me to the delights and intricacies of Renaissance poetry. Ken Robinson of the University of Newcastle upon Tyne—a model scholar-teacher—encouraged me to explore the field of Restoration burlesque and travesty: were it not for his encouragement I would not have attempted this work. At Oxford, John Wilders offered companionship and hospitality for three years; to him and Benedikte I am immensely grateful. As a supervisor, Michael Gearin-Tosh offered encouragement and good-humoured criticism at all stages. And my external examiner, Peter Thomas of University College, Cardiff, gave me an incisive commentary on my dissertation and, subsequently, his friendship and continued support.

The Hartlib Papers Project at Sheffield University is a unique institution. To its enlightened and generous funding bodies, the British Academy and the Leverhulme Trust, I am much indebted. Its directors, associates, and assistants provided a stimulating and congenial working environment during my four years as research associate. To its leading director, Michael Leslie, I am grateful for friendship and many kindnesses.

Particular scholarly debts are acknowledged in the footnotes. Prime among the friends and colleagues who have helped me, either by supplying information or by commenting on parts of the book, are Kenneth R. Andrews, Sarah Barber, Peter Beal, the late Harold Brooks, the late John Buxton, T. G. S. Cain, Bernard Capp, Stephen Clucas, Kirk Combe, Colin Gibson, Alison Gill, Sarah Hutton, Hilton Kelliher, Julie Macdonald, Sir Oliver Millar, David Norbrook, and Margarita Stocker, Thomas O. Calhoun and Lois Potter read the entire manuscript for the University of Delaware Press and offered some helpful suggestions, and my copy editor, Richard Jones, carefully converted the manuscript from English to American format. Thanks also to Diane Burke for proofreading, Theresa Schaefer for preparing the index, and Carleton College, for funds to cover postage and reproductions.

Vanessa Laird has read more drafts of this book than I can now bear to think about. For her tolerance, encouragement, and endurance I cannot adequately thank her.

Finally, the work on manuscript poetry which underlies so much of this book has been greatly facilitated by the unpublished indexes of manuscript poetry held by the Beinecke, British, Folger, and Huntington Libraries, and by Margaret Crum's invaluable *First-Line Index of English Poetry 1500–1800; In Manuscripts of the Bodleian Library, Oxford*, 2 vols. (Oxford: Clarendon Press, 1969). I am especially grateful to Hilton Kelliher for allowing me to consult the electronic index of manuscript verse in the British Library.

Introduction

Sir John Mennes and James Smith are hardly household names. When they are remembered today, it is generally as the authors of the immortal couplet "He that fights and runs away / May live to fight another day," or as the editors of *Wits Recreations* and other popular seventeenth-century verse miscellanies, such as *Wit and Drollery* (1656) and *Wit Restor'd* (1658). Since they neither wrote this couplet nor edited these or any other collections, a study that attempts to set out what they actually did do has a certain pertinence.[1] But there are other, more pressing justifications for such a study.

While the period leading up to and following the English Civil War has always fascinated historians, the literature of the period has generally been dismissed by critics as too timebound and partisan to be worthy of serious attention.[2] Over the past decade, however, an increasing concern with the political functions of literary texts, and with their existence as objects in society, has facilitated a burgeoning interest in literature of the Civil War period.[3] Although one product of this shift has been a renewed interest in royalist writing, those working in this field are hampered by the lack of basic research tools such as reliable editions or studies of all but a few key figures or genres.[4] Indeed, by contrast with the sophisticated appreciation we now have of the ideological complexities of those traditionally labeled "Puritans," our understanding of cavalier culture appears rather crude, based as it is upon the study of an exclusive courtly elite ("the cavalier poets") and a few courtly modes (the elegant compliment and the public celebration, for example). This sort of study does, of course, present an important aspect of cavalier culture (which was, for sure, fundamentally courtly in flavor),[5] but it does not describe the whole picture, and there have been some noteworthy attempts of late to expand our sense of the social constituency of cavalier poetry into areas beyond the charmed circle of the court.[6]

Without a more detailed mapping of this *terra incognita*, many once prosperous genres will remain ignored, and many traditional fallacies will remain untouched. Thus, for example, the adoption by royalist poets of coarse, native forms such as the ballad as propaganda tools during the Civil War tends to be viewed as an instance of shattering discontinuity.[7] But this development only appears discontinuous if one adopts an over-rigid distinction between elite and popular culture and ignores the extent to which coarse, native forms flourished both at the margins of the court (in the writing of Mennes, Smith, and their circle) and within it (in the ballads of Suckling) during the 1630s. By looking for only what we expect to find, we tend to find only what we are looking for.

Students of Caroline and Civil War literary culture need to imitate the practice of historians of the period, consolidating information and testing hypotheses through a series of local studies—studies of poets now regarded as minor and genres now generally ignored (the burlesque epistle and the classical travesty, for example). In the absence of a more detailed knowledge of the field, attempts at synthesis tend to appear premature.[8] This study of Sir John Mennes, James Smith, and their milieu is a contribution to such a project. It is a case study that highlights the complex interrelations between social and literary practices and religio-political alliances in seventeenth-century England.

The real achievements of Sir John Mennes and James Smith, as opposed to those with which they are wrongly credited, have often been overlooked. They have long been ensconced at the margins of literary history, meriting brief and largely misleading entries in the standard histories.[9] They were, nevertheless, figures of considerable literary importance in their time. Their verse, mainly burlesque epistles and mock-poetry (or travesty), was immensely popular among royalists during the Civil War and Interregnum. Read by the exiled royal family and published widely at home, it made the authors themselves into something like royalist icons, and it set the tone and provided the stylistic model for much Restoration poetry—notably, Samuel Butler's bestselling *Hudibras*. The influence of Mennes and Smith can be traced in the mock-heroic verse of the eighteenth century (Pope, for one, knew their work), and collections containing their verse have been reprinted several times since then (in 1817, 1874, and, most recently, in 1983).[10]

Nor was their importance merely posthumous or page-bound. Among their circle of friends and acquaintances, Mennes and Smith could count some of the leading literary figures of the age: Philip Massinger (who dubbed Smith his poetic son and heir), Robert Herrick (who cited Mennes as "the *True-wit* of a Million"), Sir William Davenant, Sir John Denham, Sir John Suckling, Sir Kenelm Digby, Thomas Pollard (a leading actor), and the bibliophile patron of the group, Edward, Lord Conway. Many of these figures were involved with Mennes and Smith in a forgotten fraternity known as the Order of the Fancy.

Because of the absence of reliable studies of Mennes and Smith, this book is necessarily structured around parallel biographies of the two men and is based upon a newly established canon of their verse (presented here as Appendix 1).[11] This biographical backbone has its own interest, and it forms the point of departure for the exploration of two related areas of social and literary history, the traditions of clubbing and of burlesque writing in seventeenth-century England.

The first part of the book recounts the attempts of Mennes and Smith, younger sons from moderately prosperous gentry backgrounds, to break into courtly circles via their ability to turn witty verses. They contributed occasional poems on some of the key events of the period, including the assassination of Buckingham and the controversial Cotswold Games. Poetry was to Mennes and Smith an avocation, and I attempt to establish its place in their lives. Their experiences reveal problems endemic to younger sons of the gentry at this time, telling us much about the operation of both national and provincial patronage networks and about the social context of literature in Caroline England.

These themes are more fully explored in part 2, which opens up for further study the clubs and fraternities in which many budding wits and writers were at this time involved. I am primarily concerned with the fraternity in which Mennes, Smith, and many of their circle were involved in the 1620s and 1630s, the Order of the Fancy. I examine the heritage of the Order (tracing its derivation from earlier bodies such as Ben Jonson's Mermaid Club and a wild gang known as the Tityre-tu, in which Thomas Carew may have been involved). I plot its social and political coordinates, locating it in relation to other, rival groups. The Order of the Fancy was a subcourtly body, centered around the Blackfriars Theatre. Its members engaged in excessive drinking and riotous behavior and in the ritual persecution of the urban middle class. They spoke nonsense, engaged in competitive composition or "wit-combats," and composed burlesque or drolling verses, often travestying the classical works they had read at school. Despite its anarchic appearance and certain loose oppositional tendencies, the group was not subversive in any self-conscious or ideologically coherent fashion. It was composed largely of younger sons from well-to-do families who were anxious about their social status and were keen to make their names within available channels of advancement—the court and the professions. Their club acted as both mutual support group and pressure valve, releasing their social frustrations within a safely enclosed arena.

The third part of the book is concerned with the verse of Mennes and Smith, which mainly took the form of burlesque epistles and mock-poems, much of which was published in the "drolleries" (verse miscellanies with a royalist bias) *Musarum Deliciae* (1655), *Wit and Drollery* (1656), and *Wit Restor'd* (1658). Such poetry has generally perplexed modern critics, to whom its origins and purposes are obscure. While there are clear difficulties for us in attempting to understand and discuss verse that is designed to appear extempore and humorously shoddy, such productions were a vital part of the courtly and would-be courtly culture of the age: to ignore them because they do not square with our concepts of literary value is to distort our picture of the seventeenth century. In this section, I argue that the rationale of burlesque and mock-poetry can be more readily understood if we look behind Butler's *Hudibras*, the traditional starting point for such study, and consider the extent to which such verse flourished within clubs like the Order of the Fancy. Within the context of the clubs, the apparently arbitrary destructiveness of such verse appears less subversive than festive or "carnivalesque," being closely related to the licensed buffoonery of the court jester.

The conservatism of clubs like the Order of the Fancy does not, however, provide evidence for a revisionist reading that might seek to deny the existence of fundamental cultural conflicts in early Stuart England. On the contrary, it confirms the extent to which the social and cultural divisions of the Civil War were apparent to contemporaries at least as early as the 1630s, despite the Stuart rhetoric of order, harmony, and consensus. By the later 1630s there was an increasing willingness to deploy the techniques of burlesque and mock-poetry for tendentious or satiric purposes. In an important poem, which reveals the increasing ideological tension between country, court, and city, Smith employs such techniques to attack an urban, middle-class print culture. The attack was part of a forgotten paper scuffle, involving some clearly recognizable contemporaries, including Wye Saltonstall, a professional writer of Puritan sympathies, whose translation of Ovid into a bourgeois idiom provoked concern and derision, and the much-maligned figure of John Taylor the Water Poet. The scuffle underlines the close interconnection of literary and sociopolitical allegiances in the 1630s.

Part 4 returns to, and concludes, the biographical narrative begun in part 1. The responses of Mennes and Smith to the events of the later seventeenth century are documented by a remarkable series of comic verse epistles. Since the techniques of such verse depended upon an unquestioned social stability that could be ritually inverted, the breakdown of social order in the middle of the century led to generic breakdowns and attempted reconstitutions, which are traced in these chapters. Despite the war there were recurrent attempts to preserve the ethos of the clubs through the establishment of new groups by royalist exiles on the continent and by the exchange of verses through royalist conspiracy networks at home and abroad. It is even possible that such networks may have been involved in the publication of verse by Mennes and Smith in the popular "drolleries" of the 1650s.

Mennes and Smith remained loyal to the Stuart cause throughout the Interregnum, and they were both rewarded for this after the Restoration. The concluding chapter of the book examines their post-Restoration careers and considers why it was that, despite the ubiquity of the modes and genres they had popularized, they were so swiftly erased from the canon of comic writers.

Cavaliers, Clubs,
and Literary Culture

Part 1
Early Lives, 1599–1639

Introduction to Part 1

This section of the book narrates the early lives of Sir John Mennes and James Smith. It emphasizes the similarities between their backgrounds, focusing in particular on the social anxieties arising from their status as younger sons of minor gentry and on their attempts to construct gentlemanly credentials. It traces the vicissitudes of their quests for preferment through the exploitation of courtly and subcourtly patronage networks, and it sketches out their place in the social and literary milieu of Caroline London before it was shattered by the outbreak of the Scots troubles in 1639.

1

John Mennes:
"Markt for the True-wit of a Million"

During the early seventeenth century Kent was fast becoming one of the most important and influential counties in England. The Kentish gentry were wealthier than those of other counties, they had close connections with the court, and they possessed a keen awareness of their status and their heritage. They were favored by the existing social structure, which they had every reason to wish to preserve. Their conservatism manifests itself in a number of ways. Intellectually, it is significant that Sir Robert Filmer's *Patriarcha*, a defense of Stuart-style absolutism, was first circulated in manuscript among Kentish gentlemen. These gentlemen were not mere fair-weather friends to the monarchy: throughout the civil war period they were a reliable source of support for the crown.[1]

The family of Mennes (pronounced "Mince" or "Minz") had commanded a prominent position in the ancient port of Sandwich, and indeed in Kent, since at least the middle of the sixteenth century.[2] The family provided a succession of mayors of Sandwich. Thomas (John's great-uncle) was mayor on several occasions and was, for a time, a member of Parliament. Matthew (John's grandfather) was mayor five times and was also one of the chief contributors to the grammar school founded at Sandwich by Sir Roger Manwood in 1563.[3] By the end of the sixteenth century the Mennes family had established themselves as an influential force in Sandwich and were well known outside Kent.[4]

There is some evidence that the influence and status of the Mennes family declined, along with that of their home town, during the life of John's father, Andrew. He held no public office, and very little is known about him. Born in September 1566, he married Elizabeth Warham, a local woman, in 1591. They had three children.[5] Presumably she died young, for on 22 August 1596 John's father married again. His new wife, Jane, was the daughter of a local gentleman, John Blechenden. This marriage produced five offspring, including John, the poet.[6] Andrew Mennes was probably dead by 1621, for by that time the eldest son, Matthew, seems to have taken over the management of the family estates—a task he fulfilled with ruthless efficiency.[7]

John Mennes was christened in the parish of Sandwich St Peter on 11 March 1598/9.[8] Little is recorded of his early life, but a likely outline can be inferred. He was probably educated at Roger Manwood's grammar school in Sandwich, the only school in the area at the time and with which the Mennes family had strong connections.[9] A good deal is known about the Manwood school from its statutes. Central to the school's humanist curriculum was the Erasmian notion of imitative composition. In the Erasmian system boys imitated the grammatical, theoretical, and logical correctness of the best classical writers. By doing so they would, so the theory went, be led into correct modes of thought and perception.[10] The equation of stylistic and moral values was made clear at an early age.

The traditional age for grammar school entrance was seven. There, provided that he was able "to write competently and to read perfectlie both englishe and lattyne," as the statutes required, John would have paid his six pence for books and started school in 1606 or 1607. In common with the practice of the age, the routine at Manwood's school was austere, the school day running from seven until five o'clock or later, depending upon the time of year. There was little respite. Pupils were normally allowed to play just once a week, and even this privilege depended upon the completion, in their spare time, of a Latin exercise.[11] The school was organized along the so-called "Winchester system," being divided into six forms, under an usher and master. The usher's role was to give the boys a grasp of Latin grammar and to teach them the rudiments of translation. The pupils were then handed over to the master and were introduced to the rules of rhetoric and to a range of classical authors.[12] Although who taught Mennes is not known, it is possible that his schoolmaster was Richard Knolles, best remembered for his *Generall Historie of the Turks* (1603).[13] Mennes's fascination with travel—inspired in part no doubt by growing up in a town so near the sea—may have been fired by the old scholar's work on a distant, exotic culture.

The statutes of the Manwood school give interesting details of the texts and teaching methods used there. In every aspect of their schooling the Manwood boys were familiarized with the classics: not only did their weekly playtime depend upon the satisfactory completion of a Latin exercise, but they were expected to learn such exercises by heart. Emphasis was placed on the depth, rather than the breadth, of their classical learning. In the fourth form, Mennes would have read Terence, Cicero's epistles, and Apthonius's rhetoric manual, the *Progymnasta*. Having been introduced to a number of different authors and styles, his sense of decorum—his ability to choose a style appropriate to the matter in hand—was tested by exercises in "varieng of latine," in which the sentiment of a given piece of Latin was reexpressed in a different manner. In the fifth form the boys were introduced to Sallust, Cicero's *Offices*, and Virgil's *Eclogues*; and in the sixth form they read Cicero's *Orations*, Horace's *Epistles* and "certen of his chaste odes," and the *Aeneid*. In this form Mennes would have been taught to write his own Latin verses.[14] Wherever he was schooled, Mennes would have gained a knowledge of classical writing and rhetoric and a set of assumptions about literature that informed his poetry.

It may have been in his boyhood that Mennes developed a taste— unusual for his age—for Chaucer and other early English poets. Such poetry was a lifelong love, and Mennes has been regarded as instrumental in keeping Chaucer's reputation alive in the seventeenth century. What Mennes prized in Chaucer was presumably the coarse, facetious, grotesque vein of earthy humor, which seemed to correspond to his own mode of drollery.[15] In his later years, given the opportunity, Mennes would while away whole afternoons entertaining his colleagues at the Navy Office by reading from Chaucer and other early English poets. On one occasion, he recited "many fine expressions of Chaucer, which he dotes on mightily," and, on another occasion, he entertained Samuel Pepys by "reading a book of scolding very prettily."[16]

During his boyhood in Sandwich Mennes acquired a strong sense of family pride. He was much concerned with his family's history and would draw on it in later life for anecdotes, such as the macabre story he related to Pepys of "the discovery of his own great-grandfather, fifteen years after he was murdered."[17] This concern with his family is perhaps evidence of anxiety about its declining status. Any such anxiety would have been aggravated by John's position as a younger brother, a pitiful stock-type of the age.[18] Brought up in an environment of some affluence and gentility, John was unlikely to inherit his family's estates. He would need a career to support himself.[19]

II

John Mennes would have left school around 1611, aged about twelve. Although he may have gone straight on to university, there is no evidence that he did so: in fact, there is no firm information about him until the mid-1620s.[20] It would not have been unusual for him to have gone more or less straight to sea for, despite a certain stigma, the Navy was an increasingly fashionable option for the younger sons of gentlemen. The early Stuarts urged young noblemen to pursue careers in the Navy, securing them posts and creating a body of unpopular, dilettante gentleman officers.[21] Mennes was not one of these court cronies, but he naturally used such patronage as he could muster. Although it is not known how he secured his first position—perhaps with Sir William Monson in the English Channel fleet—he was soon on the ladder of preferment that led inevitably to the Lord Admiral, the hated duke of Buckingham.

In spite of the official encouragement given to gentlemen and courtiers in the Navy and despite the king's personal interest in the Navy, James I's policy of European peace gave him little use for it.[22] Under the aged earl of Nottingham and the venal Robert Mansell, the Navy was a morass of corruption and mismanagement, and its ships did little but patrol the channel. The competition for posts on ships must have been intense.[23] Mennes was lucky enough to receive the support of the respected veteran, Sir Alexander Brett (who was also, usefully, a kinsman of Buckingham).[24] Brett wrote to Secretary Nicholas on 15 April 1626 recommending Mennes for a new command on the strength of his previous record:

> This Gentleman Captaine Mennes, was recommended by me vnto my lord duke [*Buckingham*], for the command of a shipp, whoe hath beene, diuers times at sea, first in the narrow seaes with Sir William Monson, in the late kinges service, and afterwards with his father in law, Captaine Chester into the west Indies with a smale shipp called the Margat and Iohn of london whear they weare assalted by two of the kinges of spaines galleones, and after along and bluddie fight with the loss of a great part of theire men, came ofe with honner, likwise to Virginia, and since he commanded the seahorse in his Maiesties service which imployments with his owne industrie haue made him fitt for command in his kinges and Cuntries seruice.[25]

Since Mennes served "diuers times" under Sir William Monson, he must have entered the Navy before 1616, when Monson was removed.[26] This letter offers the first real facts about Mennes's early manhood. After serving under Monson in the English Channel ("the narrow seaes"), he accompanied an expedition to the New World on which he was involved in a naval battle. He was subsequently given command of a ship, the *Seahorse*. (Brett's note that Mennes sailed to the West Indies under his "father in law, Captaine Chester," is rather puzzling; there is no evidence that Mennes was ever married to Chester's daughter.[27])

The battle referred to by Brett took place off the coast of Dominica in 1620/1 and is documented in a number of accounts that testify to a considerable contemporary interest.[28] It appealed to that English taste for military encounters in which a powerful foreign aggressor is driven off by a small body of underequipped Englishmen. The *Margaret and John*, or (as it was also known) the *Black Hodge*, reached Dominica in the West Indies toward the end of March 1620/1, having been at sea since early

February. On 20 March the ship pulled into Nevis to stock up with water and found two ships flying Dutch flags already at anchor.[29] The *Margaret and John* anchored nearby and sent out a boat to hail them:

> as sone as our ankor was downe our capten cased the boote to bee maned and then his soneinlay mr: Iohn Mines and I and Iames Iorland went into the boot to gooe a bord of them thinking they had bin hollanderes and soe wee wente . . . [the *MS unclear*] boot and wee did see them send of from them to the shoor som boots and being a shoor wee did perseiue agreat manie of ther men comining ronning out of the wodes to there boots and wee draing somthing nier them did perseiue them to bee spannards and soe wee came backe A gaine and tould our capten an[d *MS torn*] hee was angrie that wee did not speack to them and soe hee ca[sed *MS torn*] the boote to be maned againe [and *MS torn*] bid mee gooe and hayl them. . . .[30]

The boat was sent out again, partly to gather more information and partly to buy time: the *Margaret and John* was laden with passengers and luggage and was unprepared for military action. The Spanish insisted that the crew of the boat come aboard; they refused, and the Spanish opened fire, first on the boat and then on the ship. The leading Spanish ship then approached the *Margaret and John* and, after a brief verbal exchange, opened fire. During the ensuing battle the English were boarded twice; but they succeeded in fighting off the attackers. Mennes carried himself bravely during the battle, picking off a particularly dangerous sniper:

> the moste hurte which wee receued from them was out of ther maine tops for ther they had 3 or 4 men which plyed ther smale shot agreat will befor they wear espied by vs and had kylled atthe leste 3 or 4 of our men and then mr: william Burd being shot [from *MS unclear*] thence called to mr: Iohn mines and bid him haue acaer of the maine tops and hee presently mad a shot vp at them and made one of them sinck dow[n *MS torn*]. . . .

Eventually, after losing a number of men, the Spanish ships withdrew to a safe distance. The English waited throughout the night and the next morning for a second assault, but it did not come: the Spaniards decided not to risk another attack and sailed off, leaving the English to continue on their way to Virginia. The popular appeal of this encounter was ensured by the emphasis placed upon the fact that the aggressors vastly outweighed the English in both size of vessel and armaments.[31]

The encounter gave Mennes the opportunity to demonstrate the courage, or "fortus," which was central to his character.[32] There was, however, an unfortunate concomitant of this quality, a streak of hotheadedness that got him into trouble on more than one occasion. Shortly after his return from Virginia he was involved in some kind of brawl in Sandwich: on 5 April 1624 he was bound over to keep the peace after a quarrel with Sir William Barnes.[33] This caution was to be no impediment to his naval career.

III

The prospects for career seamen had been improved by the appointment of Buckingham as Lord Admiral in 1618. The duke was keen to reform, rebuild, and expand the Navy, and, were he judged solely for this contribution, his posthumous reputation would be substantially higher than it now stands. Buckingham restructured the Navy's administrative system and attempted to revitalize the dismally corrupt mechanism for paying seamen and suppliers. He had some success, particularly with respect to wages. But the Navy still lacked the essential commodity that would allow continued efficiency: money. Without it, the Navy continued to be plagued by incompetence and corruption on a barely imaginable scale. The provision of supplies remained an intractable problem.[34] Mennes benefited from the reforms to the extent that, throughout the late 1620s and 1630s, he was employed with some regularity, but the continued inefficiency and impecuniousness of the Navy Office was inescapable. As G. E. Aylmer has noted: "Breakdowns, shortages, and deficiences were chronic in almost all kinds of munitions and supplies, in masts and cordage, in victuals and clothing, in powder and shot, in entrenching tools and swords, and above all in pay."[35] Mennes was constantly beset by such problems. A letter to Secretary Nicholas of 18 February [1625/6], illustrates the kind of frustration faced by those in the naval service:

> According to commands I am at Douer, whear my shipp rides, I find a company of discontented people which through want are almost growne desperat, and readie to forsake the service, I know not wheare the fault lieth but betwixt the owners and the commisioners, there is a greate deal of time, pay, and victualls spent to noe purpose, the shipp being now ready, the sailes readie made in the towne, will not be deliuered with out money, and ere they be had our victualls will be spent. . . .[36]

Lack of money meant that Mennes could pay neither his men nor the sailmakers. Without sails he could not leave Dover Road. The longer he remained there the more supplies he consumed (supplies he could not, without money, replenish), and the more disgruntled grew his men.

Mennes did his best to balance the irreconcilable forces at work in the administration, carrying out his duties for the crown, paying his men, and attempting to ensure his own solvency. In 1627 he commanded a ship on Buckingham's disastrous expedition to relieve the beleaguered French Protestants at La Rochelle.[37] Mennes was given command of the *Conver-*

tine, a large ship of 360 tons.[38] It is tempting to infer from Mennes's engagement in this gesture toward international Protestantism something of his own political and religious complexion, but this is problematic. For a seaman under the king's commission, the expedition was primarily a job of work, not a statement of support for either pan-Protestantism or the duke of Buckingham's faction. Mennes's attitude to Buckingham was ambiguous: while evidently hostile to him, he was nevertheless dependent on him for advancement. His aggressively nationalistic attitude to foreign policy was motivated by economic rather than religious concerns. Like many of his contemporaries in the Navy and in Parliament, he wished to see England regain the respect she had once commanded on the seas and thus viewed with equal suspicion Protestant and Catholic nations that comprised a threat to her maritime sovereignty. He consistently advocated a tough line against the arrogant and affluent Dutch and was perceived by the crown as a trustworthy agent in the controversial peace negotiations with Spain (without being in any sense pro-Spanish). Mennes would therefore have sympathized with what may have been an underlying motive for the expedition, the establishment of a naval base on the French coast.[39]

Mennes's presence on this expedition may have brought him, for the first time, to the acquaintance of a group of wits who were to play an important part in his life. Robert Herrick, James Smith, William Davenant, John Weeks, and Sir John Suckling were all probably present on the expedition.[40] Although there is no firm evidence that this group did meet on the expedition, it would be highly appropriate, given what is known about the formation of other fraternities at this time, for their club to have been conceived during a military expedition.[41]

The expedition to La Rochelle was a desultory failure. The invasion force had tried to secure St. Martin's, the principal fort on the Isle of Rhé, which controlled La Rochelle's harbor, but the island was too strongly defended, and the English force too ill-equipped to succeed. Buckingham laid siege to St. Martin's, and a relief force was promised, but, because of a combination of bad luck and mismanagement back home, it never arrived.[42] The siege became a blockade, and Buckingham was forced to retreat. In doing so his men sustained horrific casualties.

The return to England left the irksome task of consolidating the wreckage of the expedition. Meetings were long and tempers short. At a meeting of Buckingham's management group, the principal officers of the Navy in March 1627/8, Mennes's hotheadedness surfaced again, in a manner that might have jeopardized his career. The outburst points to his sensitivity about status—a sense of being undervalued—and, perhaps, to a fear of being regarded as an outsider. Although Mennes came from a gentle background, his family were gentry of the lower order.[43] Any dissatisfaction Mennes felt about his social status would have been aggravated by his family's decline during the life of his father and by his own marginal position within the family—that of a younger half-brother. He was, like many younger sons, something of a malcontent. A mere naval captain—would he have been considered a gentleman by his peers?[44] At the meeting in question it seems that urgent naval business had been interrupted by Mennes: "Wee were so vncivilly pressed to dispatch a particular Busines brought vnto Vs by one Captain Mintz, that Wee cannot but acquaint your Grace with his Carriadge to Vs."[45] The disturbance was described in some detail:

> Being told that We had busines in hand for his Majestie by your Graces Commaund, which could admitt no delay, and being desired to forbeare till Wee had brought itt to some Conclusion; he brake out into this Language; He would not attend; He was our equall, and as good as Wee; And that Wee should know it if Wee were out of the place; That he would further interrupt Vs, and send all his men to make a Clamour; With many other vncivill and mutinous words, vpon no ground or Cause att all, vnfitt to be vttered by such a person.

There is, beneath the bravado, a defensive quality to Mennes's protestations. He was their equal and as good as they, but they didn't know this—his business could wait.[46] Mennes does not seem to have been punished for this outburst. Perhaps he was lucky, for within five months the duke was dead.

The duke of Buckingham was assassinated at Portsmouth on 23 August by John Felton, an embittered veteran of the Rhé fiasco who saw himself as the enactor of divine judgement on the duke.[47] Mennes was one of the first to interrogate the assassin. James Howell describes these events in a letter to Lady Scroop, countess of Sunderland:

> *Jack Stamford* would have run at him [*Felton*], but he was kept off by Mr. *Nicholas*; so being carry'd up to a Tower, Capt. *Mince* tore off his Spurs, and asking how he durst attempt such an Act, making him believe the Duke was not dead, he answer'd boldly, that he knew he was dispatch'd, for 'twas not he, but the hand of Heaven that gave the stroke; and tho' his whole body had been cover'd over with Armour of Proof, he could not have avoided it.[48]

Mennes's fierce reaction, if not a creation of Howell's fertile imagination, can probably be attributed less to love for the duke than to his short temper, his concern for his career (he was dependent on Buckingham for patronage), and his gentlemanly fear of social disorder. Mennes was amazed by Felton's presumption, by his hubris in attempting to murder a duke. The assassin's claim to have been an agent of God would have impressed upon him the dangers of religious fanaticism and claims to inspiration.

Mennes was presumably to have been employed on the second expedition to La Rochelle, which Buckingham was at Portsmouth in order to lead.[49] But when the fleet returned after the fall of La Rochelle in late October, he was given a fresh command. On 23 November 1628 he was given charge of the *Adventure* "during her present employment."[50] This employment represented another weak gesture of support for European Protestantism. Mennes was to escort a group of supply ships to Gluckstadt in order to bring provisions for Christian IV of Denmark and the band of English troops serving under him in his struggle against the Hapsburg emperor—a struggle effectively doomed by England's failure to provide the support it had promised in 1625.[51] The journey was hazardous; in a letter of 6 December 1628, the Puritan gentleman, Sir Thomas Barrington, wrote anxiously of the difficulties that Mennes would encounter in his passage up the Elbe: "in all probabillytye those cold seas have frozen them all fast by this time and the way is impassable."[52] Barrington's fears were well founded. Mennes was to account for his escape with uncharacteristic piety: "he that directs all, mercifully saued all."[53]

The provisions Mennes brought were too few and too late. Christian was exhausted by defeats and was soon forced to sue for peace.[54] Mennes did not, however, return empty-handed. In addition to capturing a barque bound for Calais, he arrested a ship carrying herring around 23 January 1628/9.[55] The capture of prize ships was one of the perks of naval service. If a captured ship was proven "prize" (being taken in an act of war or while engaged in some illegal activity), a proportion of the ship's goods reverted to the captor. Small wonder then if the King's seamen diligently brought in any ship that appeared remotely suspicious.

In April 1629 Mennes captured a ship from Hamburg in an audacious action.[56] His bravery did not go unnoticed: in a letter of 20 April the Lords Commissioners of the Admiralty wrote approving his "discreete and stoute carriage, and moderacion in that busines."[57] On examining the ship, Mennes found a large quantity of forbidden goods (including copper and lead) hidden on board. Unfortunately, the Lords Commissioners decided that the ship must be released on the grounds that it did not constitute legal prize because it was bound for France with which, at this time, England was negotiating peace.[58] At least two of the ships Mennes had taken during the last three months had now been released.[59]

Despite such local failures, Mennes's continued good service had begun to win him recognition at court. It was clearly an acknowledgment of his good service and his cultured demeanor that in May 1629 he was chosen to convey the painter and ambassador Peter Paul Rubens to England on a secret mission to negotiate peace between England and Spain.[60] By the end of the 1620s, with a decade of naval service behind him, Mennes was regarded as a discreet and trustworthy servant of the crown.

IV

After the termination of Mennes's commission as captain of the *Adventure* early in November 1629, there began one of the long periods of inactivity that punctuated his naval career.[61] During these periods Mennes immersed himself in a wide range of intellectual pursuits. He studied chemistry and medicine, perhaps in league with such aristocratic virtuosi as Sir Kenelm Digby and Edward, viscount Conway and Killultagh.[62] He was an active member of the literary and theatrical milieu centered on the King's Company and its winter base of the Blackfriars Theatre.[63] Various members of this group, including Mennes, the actor Thomas Pollard, the playwright Philip Massinger, his close friend James Smith, and perhaps Robert Herrick and John Weeks, formed themselves into a drinking club known as the Order of the Fancy. The club met in taverns where its members indulged in "wit combats" and in furious bouts of drinking: no doubt Mennes's talent for mimicry marked him out for success in such company.[64] They composed songs, ballads, and humorous verses that circulated around town and at court among those who, like viscount Conway, were keen to pick up the latest songs, squibs, and burlesques.[65]

Moving in such circles, it is no surprise that Mennes turned his hand to writing lyrics, two of which were set by the court musician, Henry Lawes. One of these, the unpublished lyric "What Man may sojourne heere," is a free imitation of a popular piece from *The Greek Anthology*:[66]

> What Man would sojourne heere
> if ought wee choisely prise
> A thousand hasards rise
> to make the purchase deare
> and when with paine and care tis gott
> wee hold itt and wee hold it not.[67]

Rather more successful than this modish pursuit of antithesis and paradox is Mennes's lyric "Active Love." It is an incisive and lively piece attacking the fashionable Platonism of the Queen's court in a manner reminiscent of Suckling: "Tell me no more tis love your passions move in a phantasticke sphear." Such claims, Mennes argues, "confine what is divine":

> Tis Love the sence informs
> And cold blood warms,
> Nor gives the soule a Throne
> To us alone,
>
> But bids them bend
> Both to one end,

> And then tis Love when thus design'd,
> They make another of their kind.[68]

The final line inserts a surprising twist to the conventional anti-Platonic stance by insisting not merely on the need for consummation, but on the need for procreation. The circulation of such lyrics must have helped to bring the young sea captain to the attention of many potential patrons.

Mennes's patrons at this time may have included Endymion Porter, a connoisseur who attracted many budding poets from Mennes's circle of friends, including Robert Herrick and William Davenant.[69] Porter may have been instrumental in securing Mennes's employment on the Rubens mission, for he was a friend of the painter and was deeply involved in negotiations with Spain, having spent much of his youth there.[70] Mennes shared Porter's interest in the visual arts: he fancied himself as something of a connoisseur and, in mimicry of his courtly associates and patrons, had his own portrait painted in the manner of Van Dyck around 1640 (figure 1).[71] Over Whitsun 1630 Mennes may have accompanied Porter and Davenant on a visit to Robert Dover's "Cotswold Games," an excursion charted in Davenant's poem "A Journey into Worcestershire."[72] The journey involved Davenant, Porter, and an unnamed "Captain," who has been variously identified as Mennes, Robert Dover himself, and John Bond (an associate of Porter).[73] It may be that Davenant is describing Mennes when he writes of the laughing, swearing captain who attempts to spur on his recalcitrant steed:

> More cruell than Shrove-Prentices when they
> (Drunk in a Brothell House) are bid to pay;
> Or than the Bawd at Sessions, to that vilde
> Indicted Rout which first her house until'de,
> Is now the Captaine; who laughing swore. . . .[74]

This description draws attention to the captain's bawdy jocularity by means of apposite analogy.[75]

The suggestion that Mennes accompanied Davenant and Porter to the Cotswold Games in 1630 would help to explain Mennes's connection with Dover and his games, for Mennes contributed a poem that appeared in *Annalia Dubrensia. Upon the yeerely celebration of Mr. Robert Dovers Olimpick games upon Cotswold-Hills* (1636). This poem and its context reveals much about Mennes's religious and political concerns in the 1630s.

Although some sort of rural games traditionally took place at Whitsuntide in the area of Weston-sub-Edge, at some point in the early seventeenth century, Robert Dover, a lawyer from Warwickshire, moved to the area and took over their organization. He grafted onto the traditional

Portrait of Sir John Mennes (ca. 1640), School of Van Dyck. (By permission of Lord Clarendon.)

rustic pursuits a classical, Olympic framework, apparently finding modern equivalents for each Olympic game. It is clear from the engraved frontispiece to *Annalia Dubrensia* that the activities included dancing, hare coursing, stick fighting, hammer hurling, and spear throwing. Dover rendered the proceedings respectable and attracted spectators from the local gentry. Endymion Porter (whose family home was nearby) secured for Dover "some of the king's old cloaths, with a hat and feather and ruff, purposely to grace him and consequently the solemnity."[76] The games were not, however, universally popular. During the early part of the century, Puritanism was growing in the area, and the games came under increasing scrutiny after James I's issue of the *Declaration of Sports* in 1618, which insisted on the lawfulness of such recreations on Sundays and holy days. It was as a response to the howl of Puritan opposition that greeted Charles I's reissue of the *Declaration* in 1633 that the poems of *Annalia Dubrensia* were written and collected. The thirty-three contributors included Dover's friends and relatives, established poets such as Ben Jonson and Michael Drayton, and younger poets like Thomas Randolph and Shakerley Marmion.[77] As Peter Stallybrass has shown, the poems in *Annalia Dubrensia* are permeated by the language of the *Declaration of Sports*; they seek to neutralize Puritan opposition by a strategy of depoliticization, by which the games are located in a timeless tradition of harmless rural pastimes.[78]

Mennes's poem "To the Youth of Cotswold, on Mr. Robert Dover, his annuall meetings" is typical of the collection. It reveals Mennes's conservatism, his classicism, and his concern with order.

> Come all you lively Swaines,
> Come all that haunt the plaines
> Of *Cotswold*, let us bring
> Some timely offering:
>   First *Dovers* Statue fix,
> Then Maides, and young-men mix,
> And whilst you daunce a round,
> Let Eccho's shrill resound,
> With lowd shouts, *This is Hee*
> *Renues* our *Iollitie*.
> Then let a Virgin led,
> With two Lads, crowne his head:
> And when the wreath is fitt,
> All once more, circle it.
> And sollemnlie protest:
>   To keepe his yearely Feast.[79]

Like the games, the poem controls and legitimizes peasant energies by incorporating them into a framework of tradition and ritual (the dance and the crowning). The concluding image, with its concentric circles of wreath (a classical detail), dance, and year (symbols of perfection) argues that Dover's ceremony is the microcosmic expression of universal harmony. But there is also in this image, and in the poem as a whole, an anxious note, indicating a sense of concern about the harmony here asserted. There is a defensive quality in this drawing of circle after circle, a quality reminiscent of the strategy of drawing "magic circles" to keep out discordant elements—a strategy isolated by Warren Chernaik as typical of cavalier verse.[80] But Mennes's poem includes, confronts, and suppresses such elements in a more aggressive strategy of containment than the quietism and retreat typically emphasized by critics of cavalier verse. The word "haunt" is revealing in this respect. In the first place, it means, neutrally, "The act or practice of frequenting or habitually resorting to a place" (OED, 2), but there is, obliquely, a more sinister meaning. In the seventeenth century, the verb "haunt" was used "Of unseen or immaterial visitants" (OED, 5), such as diseases "as causes of distraction or trouble" (OED, 5b). The liveliness of the swains is thus a potential source of malignancy, distraction, or discontent, which must be neutralized by strategies of containment. This is why the poem instructs and guides their activities through rituals of praise: "First Dovers Statue fix, / Then Maides, and young-men mix." The swains are instructed to "protest," an ambivalent term, the meaning of which is carefully controlled in the poem. They are permitted to "affirm asseverate, or assert in formal or solemn terms" (OED, 2), to pay their dues to Dover and the established order; the possibility of other kinds of protest ("To give formal expression to objection, dissent or disapproval" [OED, 7]) is introduced and excluded. The sounds of rustic revelry are orchestrated from above. So explicit are these directions that the poem has the appearance of a masque lyric, although there is no evidence that it was ever performed. Mennes's poem, like the volume as a whole, provides a ringing endorsement of royal policy.

Although Mennes's Dover poem does not exhibit a major talent at work, it shows an increasing metrical and syntactical sophistication and an abandonment of conceit and antithesis in favor of metrical smoothness, clarity, and classical reference:

> Come all you lively Swaines,
> Come all that haunt the plaines
> Of *Cotswold*, let us bring
> Some timely offering:
>
> . . . .
> And when the wreath is fitt,
> All once more, circle it.

This change in style derives in part from the change in subject, but it also derives from the influence of another contributor to the Dover collection, a leading light in the world of literary London that Mennes was so keen to enter, Ben Jonson. One might detect a bid for Jonson's attention in Mennes's casting of his contribution in the form of a masque lyric.

The precise nature of the allegiance of Mennes and his circle to Jonson is difficult to pin down, and it will be discussed further in the pages that follow. Mennes was judged by his associates according to Jonsonian values, Jonsonian standards of wit: Herrick, in his epigram on Mennes, alludes to him as "the *True-wit* of a Million," an allusion to the clubbable Truewit of *Epicoene*.[81] An insight into the form of this allegiance in the late 1620s and early 1630s can be inferred from Mennes's ballad on Alexander Gill, son of the Master of St. Paul's, which embodies a matrix of interrelated social, political, religious, and literary values.[82] Although it is not known exactly when it was written, the immediate occasion for the ballad was the pardon issued to Gill in November 1630 for his libeling of the king in 1628. Gill had been arrested in September 1628 for drinking a health to Buckingham's murderer in the buttery of Trinity College, Oxford. Incriminating documents were found in his possession, including a satire that made lewd innuendos about King Charles's relationship with the duke. He was fined, stripped of his divinity degree, and condemned to have his ears clipped (one in Oxford and one in London). It was only through the intercession of his father, the Master of St. Paul's School, that a pardon was secured.[83] Although Mennes may well have shared Gill's animosity toward Buckingham, Gill had extended his criticism beyond a mere courtier to the monarch himself. This unprecedented threat to order forms the climax of Mennes's ballad:

> But now remains the vilest thing,
> The Ale house barking 'gainst the K.
> And all his brave and Noble Peers,
> For which thou ventredst for thy ears. . . .[84]

In addition to hitting at Gill's political unsoundness, the ballad swipes at his Puritanism, citing a notorious outburst of enthusiasm while at Oxford:

> Next for the offence that thou didst give,
> When as in *Trinity* thou didst live,
> And had thy Arse in *Wadham* Coll. *mult*
> For bidding sing, *Quincunque vult*. . . .

When he was Clark in Wadham, *and being by his place to begin a Psalm he flung out of Church, bidding the people sing to the praise and Glory of God* Quicunque vult.[85]

Mennes's attack on a Puritan critic of the monarch involved an urgent social and literary dimension: it was an intervention in a battle that was currently raging between the Gills and a loose faction of Jonsonian poets.

David Norbrook has shown that Gill the elder was the champion of a Spenserian tradition of poetry, a Protestant, prophetic, and loosely "opposition" tradition, very much at odds with the urbane classicism of Jonson and his imitators. In his rhetorical treatise, *Logonomia Anglica* (1619), the elder Gill cried up the young poet George Wither and virtually ignored Jonson.[86] Hurt pride may well have prompted Jonson's animosity, and he vilified Gill and Wither in his masque *Time Vindicated* (1623), associating them with bad verse, political and religious faction, and social disorder.[87] The conflict escalated. The younger Gill was to write some verses scoffing at Jonson's *The Magnetick Lady* (a notable flop for the King's Company at Blackfriars in 1632), and Jonson responded with routine disdainfulness in "An Answer to Alexander Gill"—an answer that dwelt on Gill's recent arraignment for disloyalty.[88] This was a prudent move since Jonson, like Gill, had been under suspicion for writing satiric verses against Buckingham. (Jonson thus dissociates himself from Gill by establishing such metrical disloyalty as the distinguishing feature.) Battle lines formed: Jonsonians rushed to defend the literary reputation of their master and to dissociate both him and themselves from Gill.[89] Mennes's ballad should, it would seem, be read in this context as strategy for self-defense that establishes the author's loyalty by attacking Gill. Perhaps he, like his friend, Smith, had written against Buckingham? Perhaps he was under suspicion, or thought he might be? Although Mennes makes no reference to Jonson in his ballad, the significance of an attack on Gill for his political and religious heterodoxy at this time is a clear statement of his allegiance both to the court and to Jonson and his circle.[90]

Mennes's ballad reveals a degree of generic and structural sophistication. Mennes draws on a tradition of ballads against Gill the elder, but transforms this tradition by deploying the ballad against a second satiric target, Gill's son.[91] By placing the critique of Gill junior in the mouth of his father, Mennes effects a double-edged attack: while enumerating the faults of his son the grammarian incriminates himself, revealing his pedantry and his love of thrashing offenders:

> Sir, did you me this Epistle send,
> Which is so vile and lewdly pen'd;
> In which no line I can espy
> Of sense, or true Orthography,
>   So slovenly it goes,
>   In verse and Prose,
> For which I must pull down your Hose. . . .[92]

The ballad is wittily constructed in a satisfactorily formal *narratio* that examines the younger Gill's offenses in an order at once chronological and
incremental, with a stanza for each offense.[93] Mennes was using the
coarse, popular form of the street ballad in an unusually sophisticated
fashion. This colonization, as it were, of a popular mode of expression is
a feature of the verse of Mennes and Smith during the 1630s, a fact that
underlines the point that the ballad form was being employed by metropolitan wits long before its use as a propaganda weapon during the Civil
War.

Mennes's literary activities helped to establish his reputation as an unusually civilized sea captain, a reputation that, in turn, improved his employment prospects. In September 1630, Sir Henry Mervin wrote to
Secretary Nicholas to beg that Mennes be given charge of a ship under his
command: "I could allso wishe that Mints had her that I might once haue
some Captaines with mee that had past there a.b.c."[94] Mennes became
much sought after for prestige tasks such as the ferrying of diplomats between England and the Continent. At the end of December 1630 he took
the duchess de la Tremouille from England to France; in January he was
instructed to bring home Sir Henry Vane, ambassador to the United Provinces; and in February he took the Spanish ambassador, Don Carlos de
Coloma, back to the Continent, after the successful conclusion of peace
negotiations.[95] The close involvement of Mennes's poetic and professional reputations underlies one of the most serious flaws in the Navy under
the early Stuarts: the persistent dominance of a courtly, humanist system
of patronage. While the ability to turn an elegant verse may have been a
suitable qualification for a state post involving delicate negotiation, it
hardly fitted a man to command a ship.[96] One wonders how many competent officers were passed over for commands in favor of those with
humanist credentials.[97] Mervin's despairing plea for literate officers implies that where the Navy was free of effete courtiers, it was afflicted with
ignorant and illiterate seamen.[98]

V

The 1630s were marked by the king's attempt to build up the Navy as a
means of restoring English power and prestige. There was grave concern
at all levels about incursions by Dutch and French shipping and about
piratical activity in English waters: there was little that the pathetically
small and ill-equipped channel fleet could do to prevent such intrusions.
The Dutch were a particular focus for resentment because of their control
of the cloth trade and their blatant fishing of waters close to the British
coast. English pride was piqued by the frequent sight of heavily laden

"fluitschips" lumbering past the Kentish coast fat with spoil. Further, the Dutch behaved in an arrogant and insolent fashion, refusing to strike their sails for ships of the royal fleet (the habitual mark of respect) and even shouting insults at English seamen.[99] To Englishmen like Mennes, who must have looked back with pride to the great days of Elizabeth, the parlous state of the King's Navy was nothing short of a scandal, a national humiliation. The building up of the Navy was thus a project that might have been expected to unite the country but that, for a complex of reasons, created only discontent and division.[100]

It was early in the decade that Charles set up a commission to investigate the organization of the Navy. During the summer of 1631, the king himself was seen clambering around the holds of ships.[101] It was presumably in connection with this investigation that Mennes, a constant advocate of a tough stance against the Dutch and French, wrote in March 1630/1 to Secretary Nicholas to explain his views on coastal policing, enclosing a transcription of some notes he had obtained from the retired admiral, Sir William Monson, concerning Dutch incursions in 1616.[102] Mennes sent Nicholas his synopsis of Monson's work in the hope that it would assist the Lords Commissioners in their determination of a policy, "the times nowstanding in some sorte as then they did."[103] This intervention reveals a tough nationalism and an anxiousness over the current lack of a coherent naval policy.[104]

In the early years of the decade a program of cautious expansion began to take place, with several ships being built or refitted. Naval administration remained a mess, however, and the pace of expansion was slow.[105] It was not enough to ensure the regular employment of officers: in March 1630 Mennes failed to gain a lieutenantship for his brother, Andrew.[106] Even Mennes himself, by now one of the most respected of naval captains, seems to have been unemployed for almost four years, from late 1631 until 1635.[107] During these years he was embroiled with his friends in the literary life of London—drinking, theatregoing, and competing in the production of witty verse. At some point around the middle of the decade, he wrote some lines in praise of James Smith's "Mock-Poem" *The Innovation of Penelope and Ulysses*. He was forced, like many talented officers, to consider private employment: in the autumn of 1633 he was rumored to be planning an ambitious voyage to the East Indies in league with Lord Denbigh.[108] The scheme, if it existed, seems to have come to nothing.

The middle years of the decade witnessed a substantial improvement in the condition of the Navy. In 1635 the first of the new Ship Money fleets set sail. Here, at last, was a fleet of which Englishmen might not be embarrassed: while deficient in many areas (the design of ships remained resolutely old-fashioned), it was a force to be reckoned with.[109] The expansion of the fleet improved employment opportunities. In March 1635 Mennes was given command of the *Red Lion*, perhaps the largest vessel he had yet commanded, weighing 650 tons. He even managed to secure the post of lieutenant for his brother.[110] The fleet's role was to police English coastal waters. A series of letters from Edward, viscount Conway, then aboard the *Merhonour*, to Secretary Coke reveals the need for such a force. All around the coast a string of infringements and insults by foreign ships took place. On one occasion a Dutch ship at anchor in English waters (and thus under the protection of the king) was attacked by two Dunkirk privateers and had to be rescued by an English merchantman. On another occasion a French warship passing an English ship struck his flag according to the required protocol but, as the ship passed, one sailor bellowed "Amain; you English dogs!" The English were swift to respond to such affronts. The *Rainbow* shot through a Dutchman that had the temerity to raise its flag while still in cannon range.[111] While nothing is known of Mennes's contribution to the fleet, he evidently continued to impress his superiors. In October he was transferred to the refurbished *Vanguard* and raised to the position of vice admiral, his most important post to date.[112] The fleet turned in for the winter after a year that had done much to restore English self-respect, but had yielded little of tangible value.[113]

Part of the Navy's continued problem lay in its administrative culture: the lack of decisive leadership (from the king downward) and the continued prevalence of an atmosphere of courtly amateurism. This condition is illustrated by the presence in the fleet of Edward, Lord Conway, who was associated with Mennes's literary club. Conway was a man with no naval experience who had joined the fleet merely to ingratiate himself with the latest royal fad.[114] His presence in the fleet warns against erecting a division between Mennes's professional employment in the Navy and his literary activities: there was almost no distinction between the two worlds. Throughout the summer Conway's agent, George Garrard (an erstwhile member of the Mermaid Club), kept him in touch with the latest lampoons: "There is an excellent song, which privately passes about, of all the Lord and Ladies in the town; 'twill please you, and I am promised a copy of it." Conway responded in kind and conducted similar exchanges of verses with other contacts such as George Radcliffe in Ireland and Kenelm Digby in France.[115] Conway's letters confirm the impression that, to senior courtiers, the policing of English waters was regarded as little more than a pleasure cruise.[116]

In May 1636 Charles issued a new proclamation, in the wake of John Selden's *Mare Clausum*, again insisting on English sovereignty over coastal waters. The implementation of sovereignty was a prime concern of the augmented fleet of that year.[117] Mennes's instructions as captain of the

Convertine made his priorities clear: "It must bee your principall care to preserve his Majesties honour Coasts Iurisdiccions Territories and Subiects . . . that noe nacion or people whatsoever intrude thereon or iniure any of them." Should any foreign ship refuse to pay their respects captains were instructed "to force them therevnto not sufferinge in any wise any dishonour to bee done to his Majestie or derogation to his power or Soveraignity in those Seas."[118] On 30 May the fleet, under its dynamic new commander, Algernon Percy, earl of Northumberland, set out to intercept a number of Dutch men-of-war sighted off the Lizard, and battle instructions were issued. No encounter took place, largely because, despite the grand intentions of his proclamation, the king checked any attempt by Northumberland to enforce it, being timorous of the possible consequences of engaging with a foreign fleet.[119] Indeed, the instructions issued to Mennes are almost risible in their vagueness, being characteristic, in their lack of clear aims and procedures, of the weaknesses of Charles's personal rule.[120]

The conscientious Northumberland was appalled by the inefficiency of the Navy. After the fleet had retired for the winter, he compiled a scathing report drawing attention to its gross mismanagement and generally parlous state. His report drew on the testimony of respected commanders like Mennes, who again criticized the system of supply that had equipped him with bad cordage and rotten fish.[121] The report, of course, had little effect: there were too many vested interests at stake and too little interest on the part of the king to set about the overhaul of the corrupt supply system. The situation would have been little different when in March 1636/7 Mennes was once again given command of the *Vanguard*.[122]

Sixteen thirty-seven was another frustrating year of indecision and inaction. After complaints from the Low Countries about the collection of tolls for fishing in English waters, the king instructed Northumberland not to pursue any Dutch ships who tried to avoid payment, thus undermining the very purpose of the fleet he had built at such expense.[123] Licensing being effectively abandoned, the fleet was left without a role. It sailed aimlessly up and down the coast, and was again reduced to a glorified taxi service for dignitaries traveling to and from the Continent. In mid-July Mennes was carrying back to Holland some members of the elector Palatine's party, after their unsuccessful attempt to secure the king's support for a Protestant offensive in Europe.[124] The fleet of 1638 was similarly uneventful. In April Mennes was given charge of the *Nonsuch*, a large vessel of the second rate, in which he apparently patrolled the coast until the fleet was recalled in the autumn.[125] Despite these professional frustrations, Mennes's loyal service during the past two decades did not go unrewarded. In November 1637 he was given command (for life) of Walmer Castle in his native Kent.[126]

The final year of the decade was a troubled time for England. After his disastrous attempt to impose his episcopalian prayer book on Scotland, Charles found himself faced with a major insurrection in the north. Such domestic concerns naturally took priority over the occasional incursions of marauding Dutchmen. Instead of a full fleet only a small squadron was assembled.[127] Mennes was by now an important enough commander to be guaranteed a post on this fleet: in March 1638/9 he was given charge of the *Victory*.[128] It was another hopeless expedition. Admiral Pennington was instructed to enforce England's territorial claims, but was not provided with any specific instructions: he was forced to issue his officers with an almost verbatim copy of the instructions employed in 1636.[129] The Scots crisis presumably exacerbated the monarch's habitual mixture of indecision and indolence. Charles was eventually prevailed upon to concur that, in the event of any conflict, the squadron should flee or, if this was impossible, side with whomever seemed most likely to win.[130] This was not the kind of leadership that would gain the respect of naval officers, whose near unanimous support for Parliament during the Civil War comes as no surprise.[131] The patrol was uneventful. The appearance of a vast fleet of 140 ships off Dover caused a brief scare in June—on Mennes's investigation they turned out to be harmless salt ships bound for Holland. On another occasion the Dutch fleet under Van Tromp chased a Spanish squadron right into Dover Road and destroyed them under the noses of the English Navy, who peered impotently on.[132]

The *Victory* was Mennes's last naval command for some time. After the customary winter break, he was given command not of a ship, but of a troop of carbineers destined for the Scottish border. This appointment marks a turning point in his career and—although he did not know it at the time and consistently refused to acknowledge it in the years that followed—the end of his riotous, metropolitan lifestyle. It would be many years before he could again spend the winter months in the congenial company of his London club and his literary friends. It is the closest of these friends, James Smith, who is now considered.

2

James Smith:
"A man much given to excessive drinking"

I

James Smith was baptized at Marston Moretaine, Bedfordshire, on 25 July 1605.[1] His father, Thomas Smith, was parson of Marston and a man of some means. He owned lands and houses in Oxford, Berkshire, and Bedfordshire, and his parish was one of the largest in the county.[2] He regarded himself as a gentleman, habitually signing himself "Gent."[3] Until his death in 1619, Thomas Smith provided a stable, if unillustrious, background for his children, of which he and his wife, Mary, had a number.[4] With the exception of James's elder brother, Thomas, little is known about these children.

Thomas Smith matriculated from Lincoln College, Oxford, in 1619, at the age of seventeen and went on to become a physician.[5] He was a riotous character, even a bit of a thug. In 1635 he was asked to leave Lincoln College for keeping dogs in his room and for beating up a colleague with a cudgel, an instrument he claimed to carry with him in case he was attacked in the city (town and gown relations were then, as now, sometimes strained, but the cudgel seemed an excessive precaution).[6] The motive for this attack is obscure, but Thomas seems to have avoided dismissal by offering a timely apology to all concerned.[7] This was not to be the only occasion on which members of the Smith family were castigated for loutish behavior.

James Smith, like John Mennes, was one of a large family. He was apparently the third son and so had little hope of inheriting his family's estate, which was probably insufficient, in any case, to generate a comfortable income. Like Mennes he needed a career. Although it is not known when he made the decision to follow his father into the church, this was not an unusual choice to make: the disgruntled younger son entering the ministry against his will was a stereotype of the age.[8] Smith's aptitude for scholarship must have been evident early on, probably while he was at grammar school. Although there are no records for this period he may have gone to the Free School at Bedford—a school better known for its possible connection with John Bunyan.[9] Whether or not he went to school in Bedford, James Smith's early education would have been fundamentally similar, in its rigorous, humanist classicism, to that of John Mennes.

Smith matriculated at Christ Church, Oxford, in March 1622/3 at the relatively advanced age of eighteen. Entry to Oxford was Smith's opportunity to make contacts and gain access to the learned professions. A sociable character, he made full use of the opportunity to make friends. One of his early contacts may have been John Weeks, a Cambridge friend of Robert Herrick's, who was studying for his B.D. (a graduate divinity degree) at Exeter College at this time (he was ordained in April 1633). For some reason Smith soon moved to his brother's old college, Lincoln: perhaps its fees were lower than those of the prestigious Christ Church.[10] Despite his move to Lincoln, Smith's connections with Christ Church were strong enough for him to fall under the influence of its charismatic dean, Richard Corbett. Corbett's love of tavern society and popular culture—his taste for drink, ballads and buffoonery—was imbibed by the young Smith. One manifestation of this influence is Smith's imitation of Corbett's poem on the aging Oxford harpy, Mistress Mallett.[11]

Smith's poem "Upon Madam Mallett" reveals something of his literary temper and talent. Smith's invective, like Corbett's, derives from the Renaissance tradition of praising the unlaudable, the most famous example of which is Erasmus's *Praise of Folly*.[12] The tradition had its origins in scholastic rhetorical training, in which the student would be asked to defend such indefensible positions as "black is white" or "bad is good." During the early seventeenth century, the praise of a deformed mistress became a popular genre in its own right, being practiced by Sir Philip Sidney, John Donne, Thomas Carew, Robert Herrick, and Thomas Randolph, among others.[13] Despite the potential for skepticism latent in this paradoxical tradition—a potential exploited to a certain extent in Donne's juvenile *Paradoxes and Problemes*, and more profoundly in the Earl of Rochester's "Upon Nothing"—such pieces derive at base from the assumption that the world is fundamentally ordered and meaningful.[14] In Smith's poem, as in Corbett's, Mallett is attacked as a grotesque exception to a standard of orderliness. She is discordant—"thy Lute-string veynes / Make such a discord"—and is perceived to be a freak—"Thow art thy owne fine foole, the Peoples Iest."[15] Smith's poem is the product of a conservative, not that of a relativist or a skeptic. While it draws on learned forms the poem is not an exercise in arid scholasticism; it is immersed in a lively, popular tradition. This is most apparent in its rough, harsh style, which is not merely the result of metrical incompetence. The opening lines make it quite clear that the poet is adopting a role:

> Skelton some rimes; good Elderton a ballett
> Heere's theame enough for all, Madam Mallett
> Whome Poetts all do scorne; but driuing Muse
> Makes choyse of this occasion; & doth chuse
> To write of her whom all the Towne admires
> For going, speaking, looking, strange attires. . . .

(lines 1–6)

These allusions to the Tudor laureate John Skelton (whose verses were now considered rather uncouth) and the prolific contemporary ballad-monger William Elderton locate the poem in a coarse, native tradition of invective that demands an emphatic, repetitious, even pugilistic style. The spirit of Skelton's "flytings" informs the poem. Skelton's clattering aggregation of insults against Garnesche—

> Thou tode, thow scorpyon,
> Thow bawdy babyone,
> Thow bere, thow brystlyd bore,
> Thou Moryshe mantycore,
> Thou rammysche, stynkyng gote,
> Thou fowle, chorlyshe parote. . . .[16]

is echoed in Smith's alliterative exclamation:

> Ah thow Queane!
> Thow Citterne-head! oh thow painted Post!
> Thow Puppett! Baby! Baggage!

(lines 40–42)

Similarly, while both poets are concerned to establish and destroy a target, there inheres in both extracts a sense of sheer delight in the linguistic performance that spills over in an undirected, almost carnivalesque laughter.[17] Smith's use of the term "Baby" illustrates this. The dubious pertinence (Mallett is supposed to be an old hag) and the limited power of such an insult mark a point of overspill—a point at which the satirist/ target dichotomy breaks down, and the free play of wit begins. But the poem's relation to the carnivalesque must not be overstated. There is not in the poem a prolonged or sustained escape from closure, from univalency, but a tension between such momentary leakage and a controlled and orchestrated satire. The term "Baby" is not entirely free from satiric connotation (it works ironically); it is simply less forceful and more delightful in its arbitrariness than the surrounding insults.

While "Upon Madam Mallett" cannot be said to exhibit much in the way of organization, poems of this sort do not require it: they work on the logic of the incantation, on the repetition of insults and curses, which were traditionally felt to have a direct physical effect on their victims, causing illness or death. Such poems, as Rochester argued in defense of his satires, are supposed to be composed in a fury and should not, in consequence, appear too finely tuned.[18] Smith takes care to point out that he is writing under the inspiration of a "driuing Muse," and the presence of clear structural divisions would detract from the impression of off-the-cuff venom created by, for instance, this breakdown of syntax:

> Come Goody fiddle strings, must yow have a Man?
> A handsome husband? with some Lutheran?
> Noe some old Fidler, who after two yeares space
> Shall strip thy skin off, for his fiddle Case
> Or to a Carryer, that may Scrape thy hide
> Which yett, with Scabbs & Itch is fortifide
> Ah, thow old Glew-pott! hast not yett enough?
> Is not thy Taper yet burnt owt? Noe, there's a snuff
> Foh! owt with it, for it stinkes I sweare
> Worse then burnt Partridge feathers, or Goates hayre
> What! are yow prowd? & must yow needs ingender
> Gett thee a Baboone, or Ape, & with them blender.
>
> (lines 23–34)

The search for an appropriate match for Mallett slides (via a pun on Lutheran), before a verb can be introduced to complete the sentence, into a digression about her complexion. This is halted by an apostrophe to Mallett herself that, by readdressing the question of the match from a different angle, introduces the required verb "blender" almost imperceptibly, to define another noun. This deformed syntax mirrors Mallett's own deformity, but it also, perhaps more importantly, points back toward the poet, suggesting the agility and copiousness of his fancy, which cannot be restrained in its search for absurd and outrageous comparisons. There is, in other words, a strong element of self-display in the poem. It is not impossible to imagine Smith following Corbett's lead in the hope of gaining the dean's patronage and being brought, in turn, to the attention of Corbett's powerful patrons, Buckingham and Laud, and his influential literary friend Ben Jonson. Smith may have been attempting to wheedle his way into an emerging Christ Church circle that, under the tutorship of Brian Duppa (another friend of Jonson), later included such budding wits as William Cartwright and Jasper Mayne.[19] If so, this course appears to have been blocked to him, perhaps because his unruly nature ruled him out of serious consideration by this donnish group.

In reading the coarse poem on Mallett one should be wary of mistaking rudeness for crudeness. Smith, like Skelton and Corbett before him, was a learned man self-consciously adopting (and, one might argue, appropriating on behalf of an elite culture) a popular mode of expression.[20] John

Aubrey's anecdote about Corbett, a senior Oxford clergyman, singing ballads "at the Crosse at Abingdon on a market-day" affords a telling illustration of the scholar's adoption—apparently without self-consciousness or irony—of a popular role: "The ballad singer complaynd, he had no custome, he could not put-off his ballades. The jolly Doctor putts-off his gowne, and putts-on the ballad singer's leathern jacket, and being a handsome man, and had a rare full voice, he presently vended a great many, and had a great audience."[21] While wearing his academic gown, Smith would have read widely in classical and neo-Latin authors, but there is no evidence that his learning was extraordinary. His exercises in mock-erudition, "Ad Johannuelem Leporem, Lepidissimum, Carmen Heroicum" and *The Innovation of Penelope and Ulysses*, reveal that he was conversant with the standard classical authors as well as medieval and contemporary writers like Johannes Goropius Becanus, Conrad Gesner, Guidus Pancirolus, and Polydore Vergil.[22]

II

Smith seems to have left Oxford for London by the middle of the 1620s. In 1626 he was married to an unidentified Elizabeth.[23] He had clearly left Oxford for good by late 1627, when he became chaplain at sea to Henry Rich, earl of Holland, then in command of the relief force for Rhé.[24] Like Mennes, Smith was probably motivated to join the expedition by concern for his career rather than by sympathy for the Huguenots. Indeed, almost everything known about Smith points to his reliance on a wittily unillusioned and self-serving pragmatism. He appears at this point very much the archetypal younger son and university wit, lacking an estate but equipped with an education and a ready intelligence, forced into the ministry, as John Earle put it in his character of "A Younger Brother," "as a profession hee is condemn'd to by his ill fortune."[25] For if ever a man were temperamentally unsuited for the cloth, it was the boorish, drunken Smith. The post of chaplain to the admiral must have appeared a relatively secure, even perhaps rather dashing appointment. It was, at any rate, a job, and in the highly competitive context of the early-seventeenth-century church, it was an enviable one.[26]

If Smith's decision to enter the church looks out of character, his appointment as chaplain to the earl of Holland, the patron of radical Puritans, looks at first sight even more bizarre. Rich was a complex, slippery character who seems (despite the defense of a recent biographer) to have been something of a carpet knight. His patronage of Puritan preachers and projects should not be taken as an expression of a deep personal sympathy for their views. In fact, it seems unlikely that he held any strong religious beliefs at all: he flirted with Puritanism to consolidate his family's position at the center of a Puritan faction at court (he even toyed at one time with the idea of converting to Catholicism to ingratiate himself with the queen). Rich probably appointed Smith on the basis of his ready wit and his ability to turn a verse, rather than out of any respect for the young cleric's doctrinal position. It was a happy appointment for Smith. He had attached himself to a man who had consolidated a prosperous family background by befriending the most powerful courtier in the land, the duke of Buckingham.[27] In the short run, however, Smith may have been disappointed with his new post for, due to a mixture of bad luck and mismanagement, Holland's force never reached Rhé, and Buckingham's shattered troop returned, defeated, by mid-November. The adventure was over, and Smith would have spent most of it kicking his heels in Portsmouth harbor.[28] There may have been compensations: it is likely that after the expedition returned he met Robert Herrick, John Mennes, William Davenant, John Weeks, and Sir John Suckling, all of whom seem to have served on the expedition, and all of whom became friends of Smith. In fact, given the possibility that Smith had known Weeks for several years, and the fact that Weeks knew Herrick from Cambridge, it is tempting to posit some sort of group enlistment in the expedition.

In spite of Smith's involvement in Buckingham's expedition he was attached to the duke only by the demands of a rather distant clientage. Once that demand was removed, he was quick to join the chorus of poets who celebrated Buckingham's assassin—a fact that prevents any easy association of court poets (or would-be court poets) with Buckinghamites.[29] Unlike his poem on Mallett, Smith's poem on John Felton displays a control of a range of tones and an ability to organize material; it also offers a further illustration of his whimsical imagination. It is divided into two sections: the first consists of a series of apostrophes to the "Antient Lawes of Right," to the "late tonguety'd Iudges of the land," and to the country as a whole to spare Felton because he has been the instrument of their deliverance from Buckingham's tyranny. There is a straining in the first part of the poem for a language fit to account for Felton's act (a murder, but a necessary, even a laudable one) and for conceits to master or nullify the paraphernalia of imprisonment—and this strain is enacted in the troubled texture of the verse:

> But O his Countrie, what can you verdict on
> If guiltie, 'tis of your Redemption
> And if there cann be Honor in A sinne
> His well complotting starrs, haue wrought him in
> Thy Fetters (Ransom'd England) and thy feares
> Triumphant Trophie=like stout Felton weares

> On him like seemely Ornaments they decke
> His Armes and wrests; and hange about his neck
> Like gingeling braceletts, and as riche they bee
> Soe much the cause cann alter miserie.[30]

An unnatural stress is forced by the meter onto the first syllable of "verdict on," while the ensuing rhyme "Redemption" doesn't quite work.[31] This sense of unease is rapidly dispelled with the turn of the poem to its second part, in which the inevitability of Felton's sentence is accepted and his impending death embraced:

> But wherefore liu'st thou in thy doomes suspence
> The Tyrant Lawe, hath doubld violence:
> For all thy fellowe Saints haue waited long
> And weared Tyme with expectation
> It is thy end that must beginn thy glorie
> Noe Finis shalbe period to thy storie
> die brauely then; for till thy death bee writt
> Thy Honor wants A seale to perfect it
> With peacefull prayers to heauen weele waft thy soule
> While euery bell thy funerall shall toule

The sanctification of a murderer is a feat of considerable audacity, and Smith manages to carry it off with the minimum incongruity: he even achieves (in the final couplet quoted) a certain elegaic grace. This grace should be remembered when one considers some of his more raucous productions: the burlesque style was not simply the result of incompetence.

Placed alongside the poem on Madam Mallett, the Felton elegy displays an increased assurance (it lacks the gaucheness of parts of the Mallett poem), but it also reveals an interesting continuity. In the first poem, Smith aligned himself with Corbett; in this piece he probably aligned himself with Ben Jonson, a friend of Corbett and the central figure in the London circle with which Corbett was associated.[32] As noted above, Jonson himself may have written in praise of Felton and was strongly suspected of having done so. It is likely that, having gone down from Oxford, Smith turned his attention to the world of literary London, to the mentors of his own mentor. This may have been a common move. The attacks on Jonson's enemy, Alexander Gill, by Mennes and Townley may be traces of a group of young wits seeking Jonson's support in the late 1620s.

Smith evidently used the Rhé expedition to extend his network of patrons. Soon after it he became domestic chaplain to Thomas Wentworth, fourth baron of Nettleshead and first earl of Cleveland.[33] Wentworth had also been at Rhé and, like Holland, had been a client of Buckingham.

Portrait of the Wentworths of Nettleshead, Anthony Van Dyck. (By permission of Mr. Julian Byng, who retains copyright.)

The earl was a brave man, zealous in his support of the crown during the Civil War and Interregnum (he is probably best remembered for the heroic street charge he led at the Battle of Worcester). He was a popular courtier, noted for his wit, intelligence and urbanity, all of which are qualities apparent in the portrait of himself and his family painted by Van Dyck around 1637 (figure 2).[34] He was, on paper, an extremely wealthy man, possessed of considerable estates, including a fine Tudor mansion at Toddington, Bedfordshire.[35] But despite his wealth he fell into financial difficulties and was forced to sell the leases of many lands to settle his debts.[36] It is probably an indication of the state to which he was reduced that in 1639 he was forced to lease some land to John Mennes's rapacious brother, Matthew.[37]

What caused Cleveland's financial crisis? The upkeep of his estates must have been a constant drain, as was the extravagance of his lifestyle. There is some evidence that the Wentworths of Nettleshead participated in that large-scale drift by the aristocracy from their country seats to houses nearer the pleasures of the court and the capital.[38] This much was implied by Robert Reyce who, in his 1618 "Breviary of Suffolk," appears to rebuke the Wentworths for abandoning Nettleshead, their modest, traditional seat, for "other shires where nearer the court they are furnished with houses of greater state and acceptation."[39] Reyce's carefully pointed remark invokes the seductive myth of the gentry's abandonment of traditional, country values for empty, courtly ostentation: the houses to which the Wentworths have moved are not better than the old, only showier (surely an allusion to the manor at Toddington, built around a prodigious courtyard some eighty feet wide).[40] Wentworth, however, was no court flunkey.[41] He spent much of his time in Bedfordshire in the 1630s, where he was a conscientious lord lieutenant (an archetypal "country" office), and where he adopted a defiantly oppositional posture toward the levy of ship money.[42]

Cleveland's wit and extravagant lifestyle made him a suitable patron for Smith, whom he regarded highly, having (according to Anthony Wood) "an especial respect for him for his ingenuity and excellent parts."[43] His service must have given Smith a welcome degree of security, access to potential patrons, and contact with other aspiring poets, for it seems that Smith's career was moving in similar channels to those of other literary friends and Rhé veterans.

The Wentworths of Nettleshead had been closely related to the Crofts family of Saxham since the early sixteenth century. Despite their move from Suffolk, this relationship remained extremely close. Smith's patron married Anne Crofts, daughter of Sir John Crofts of Saxham, in 1611. The couple set up house at Toddington Manor along with their aunt and several members of the Crofts family.[44] Given this proximity it is not surprising to find the burgeoning court poet, Thomas Carew, writing pieces for both families. More than one poem celebrates the Crofts's seat of Saxham, and poems for the Wentworths were occasioned by a family bereavement in 1632/3 and a marriage in 1638.[45] At least two of Smith's friends, Robert Herrick and William Davenant, wrote poems for the younger John Crofts, and it is argued at the end of this chapter that Smith may have been involved with Crofts in a club.[46] Since both Herrick and Davenant were concurrently currying favor with Endymion Porter (along with Mennes, perhaps), it seems that a group of budding poets, all of whom had served on the Rhé expedition, were seeking advancement in much the same circles in the early 1630s.

Through the service of Cleveland, Smith may have gained access to a group of riotous young courtiers with which Cleveland's son, Thomas (later fifth lord) Wentworth, was associated. Thomas was a cavalier rake, very much a prototype of the Restoration court wits. He appears at the center of Van Dyck's family portrait (figure 2), a strange mixture of sophisticate and thug—a fulcrum between the masculine (his father on his right) and the feminine (his mother and sister on his left). His armor-clad body inclines toward his father, while his sensitive, almost wistful eyes, gaze toward and beyond his sister. He leans casually on a stick with his head cocked, a louche contrast to the rigid postures of the two women. His sophistication no doubt derived in part from the European tour he undertook as a young man. After his return in 1631, he hung around at court and attracted trouble. In 1636 he was thrown into the Tower for dueling and using unseemly language: the precise nature of the outrage is not known, but it may have had something to do with his attachment to a group of hard-drinking court wits associated with the king's and queen's bedchambers. This group was headed by William Murray, nephew of the king's tutor, and included several of the tearaways later involved in the Army Plot (a bungled attempt by members of the queen's faction to rescue the earl of Strafford from the Tower). Although he was not a member of the bedchamber, Wentworth liked to associate himself with it. He may even have posed as a member to avoid paying his debts—a ruse that was rumbled in 1639.[47] He is mentioned in a ballad as a member of Murray's circle of wits, along with Henry Wilmot (later first earl of Rochester), Hugh Pollard, and George Goring. One cannot be sure of Smith's involvement with this circle, but (as is argued below) he may have been the cleric involved in Peter Apsley's rival group.

III

How long Smith remained in Cleveland's service is not known, but by the late 1620s he had either been dismissed or was moonlighting as a lecturer in London. Paul S. Seaver has drawn attention to the presence of an unidentified "Mr. Smith" as an unlicensed curate and lecturer at St. Michael le Querne in 1628, suggesting that this figure may be identical with the "Mr. Smith" who was preaching the Sunday afternoon lecture at St. Botolph's Billingsgate in 1629.[48] It can be shown that the Smith who delivered the lecture on "Sundayes in the afternoones" at St. Botolph's was the James Smith of this study.[49] The main source of this information comes from a brief of 1633, relating to a case in the High Court of Delegates, which is extensively concerned with the life and character of a James Smith who is said to have been turned out of the cure or lectureship of St. Botolph's Billingsgate within the preceding year. This James Smith is said to have been involved with a club called the "Order" or "Family of the Fancy."[50] It is clear that James Smith the poet was involved with this club because "The Black-Smith," the ballad that follows his poem *The Innovation of Penelope and Ulysses* in *Wit Restor'd* (1658), is there attributed to the Order of the Fancy: it is described as being "*collected out of* Homer, Virgill *and* Ovid, *by some of the Modern Familie of the Fancies*," an obvious reference to the order.[51] Given that James Smith wrote *The Innovation* and was involved with the order, it follows that he was the lecturer at St. Botolph's in 1629.[52]

The brief in question contains fascinating information about James Smith and his milieu, but this information is by no means authoritative. It is important to be aware of the dubious status of the document. The brief, dated 3 June 1633, was compiled for the case of Lewis against Warner in the High Court of Delegates, "on the behalfe of Samuell Newman, Iohn Lewis and Abigall Lewis Children of Abigall Lewis the only sister of Iohn Busby deceased."[53] The case concerned the will of John Busby of St. Alban Wood Street, dated 12 January 1625/6. Busby's sister, Abigail, claimed that her mother, Margaret, had forced the dying man to make a will, that he had refused (adding that, if he did, he would leave nothing to his mother anyway), that he died "vtterly bereft of reason" (he "talked of boylinge blood, and that all the souldiers would be starved and all the fishes in the sea would be blood"), that his hand had been held in order to force him to sign the will, and that one of the witnesses, James Smith, had never seen the will and was, in any case, completely untrustworthy (fols. 3–18). It is clear from the probate of Busby's will that Margaret Busby inherited her son's estate.[54] She apparently married Warner, the defendant, and then died. Abigail Lewis was attempting to claim back some of her brother's estate from her mother's widower. Since Abigail's case rested to a great extent upon Smith's unreliability as a witness, the depositions concerning his character should be treated with caution.

The principal deponents as to Smith's character are William Hawkins and Stephen Church, figures about whom nothing seems to be known. Their depositions are similar, and they both give important information about Smith. As they have never been printed, it is worth quoting from them at length. The anonymous lawyer asserts, on the authority of Hawkins,

> That for 4 yeares last past Iames Smith hath bin a Common and ordinary frequenter of tavernes alehouses playhouses, and players Companye, and hath professed that he should gett more by players then by preachinge the word of God, and was within these twelve monethes turned out of his Cure or lecture in St Bottolphes Billingsgate for keepinge excessive Companye with players, and he with them and others stiled themselves of <u>the order of the fancye</u> whose practise was to drinke excessively, and to speake non sence, and is not a man to be beleeved vpon his oath. (fol. 13)

Stephen Church backs this up in his statement:

> that he hath knowne Smith very well these 4 or 5 yeares togeather, and that he soiourned with the dep[onen]t about a yeare togeather, in which time he

observed him to be a man much given to excessive drinkinge, and hath often seene him Come home much distempered and overtaken with drinke, and knowne him frequently goe to tavernes and alehouses vpon sundayes when he should haue gone to Church, and hath knowne him sundry times lye whole nightes and days abrode drinkinge and keepinge of ill Company.

. . . that for all the said time hee hath bin from time to tyme an ordinary frequenter of alehouses play houses and boulinge alleys.

. . . that he hath heard him extoll the society of players and theire facultyes, and saied that he loved the Company of players above all, and that hee thought there might be as much good many times done by a man in hearinge a play as in hearinge a sermon, and that he thought it a Credditt to keepe them Companye, and hoped to gett good meanes by them, with many other such like speeches, which the dep[onen]t Cannot now Cast to mynde

. . . That he heard Iames Smith say and affirme, (and as if it had bin a Credditt to him) bragge that he was one of the Cheifest and first founders of that societye, and that he of that Company that Could speake best non sence was Counted the best man, which was him selfe, and for which Cause he vsually had the Cheifest place at the meetings of that Companye.

. . . That he beleeveth that the said Smith for money and reward may be drawne to sweare any thinge wheather true or false, and the reasons inducing this condemnator soe to beleeve, are his bad life, and Conversacion, and naughty qualityes. (fols. 13–15)

The lawyer then points out, on the authority of Church and Hawkins, that "Iames Smith for these 4 yeares last past hath bin a poore and needy person livinge by Coseninge and Cheatinge, much indebted, and hath often bin arrested and imprisoned, and hath fled beyond seas to avoyd his Creditors and to escape imprisonment" (fol. 15). He goes on to establish the nature of Smith's involvement with Warner and with Busby's will, suggesting that "Iames Smith expected some moneyes (as hee saied) in reward from mr Warner" on the basis of Hawkins's claim,

That the dep[onen]t beinge earnest with Iames Smith for moneys due to him on a time happeninge about a yeare since, hee the said Smith talkinge of the auctoritate Warner told this dep[onen]t that hee was to speake with the said mr Warner for money, and that he made no question but that he said mr Warner would furnish him with soe much money as would pay this dep[onen]t and that he hoped to gett as much money by mr Warner as hee Could gett in a whole yeare by his place, meaning or speakinge of his Curateshippe or lecture addinge moreover these or the like wordes in effect, If I had as much witt as I should haue had, I might haue gotten as much money by mr Warner as would haue paid all my debts, or discharged me from all men. (fols. 15–16)

Stephen Church adds to this his claim,

That the Dep[onen]t Iames Smith: and two of his brothers beinge in a taverne togeather neare B[isho]ppsgate they fell into talke with the dep[onen]t touchinge this busines, questioninge the dep[onen]t what he should gett by it,

Where vpon the dep[onen]t replyed to this effect: Tis you mr Smith that looke
to gett by it, meaninge this busines, I for my part doe not expect any thinge,
Wherevnto hee the saied Smith in the presence of his said bretheren, replyed
againe I haue gotten nothinge as yet, I know not what I may, imitatinge by his
speeches as this dep[onen]t did apprehend that he was to haue some thinge
from mr Warner touchinge this busines. (fol. 16)

The lawyer also asserts that on his own admission Smith never heard the
will read (Hawkins claims to have met Smith at the Boar's Head tavern
near Cripplegate as he was on his way to Mrs Busby's house to sign the
document, without knowing what it was) and that he had lied about the
length of the deceased's illness (fols. 16–17). Finally, the lawyer concludes his traduction of Smith's character by referring to Stephen
Church's claim that "It was vsuall with Iames Smith to sweare and Curse
bitterly and fearefully" (fols. 17–18). A note is subscribed to the brief
stating that judgement was passed in the High Court of Delegates on 16
July 1633, but the outcome is not specified, and the docket books record-
ing it have not survived.

The fact that Smith witnessed Busby's will on 12 January 1625/6 determines his presence in London at that time (Busby was a resident of St.
Alban Wood Street) and confirms the earlier surmise that he left Oxford
around 1625/6.[55] Although there is no firm evidence that Smith was permanently based in London—Church and Hawkins only claim to have
known him for four or five years (since 1628/9 if the depositions are contemporary with the brief)—two facts suggest that he was not just passing
through London in 1625/6: first, he was known to Warner as a man likely
to witness a bogus will in return for money, and second, he had spent
time in the Wood Street Counter (a debtor's prison).

The James Smith who emerges from these depositions is a colorful, unsavory character: a foul-mouthed, drunken braggart, a denizen of the
London underworld. Even if one allows for exaggeration on the part of
the deponents—and one is skeptical of Church's claim that he kept a
written record of his conversation with Smith—a clear picture emerges.
Smith was a rogue. He kept dubious company and led a debauched life,
haunting taverns, playhouses, and bowling alleys. (Bowling alleys were
notorious at the time for the kind of bad language attributed to Smith.)[56]
He was even incarcerated in a debtor's prison. There is, however, no evidence that he ever fled the country to escape his creditors, unless this was
the motive underlying his involvement with the Rhé expedition.

The brief draws attention to Smith's involvement with players, whose
company he extolled and by whom he hoped to "get good meanes." Just
what did Smith hope to gain from hanging around in taverns and theatres
with actors? To answer this question one must first realize that Smith can
be clearly connected with a particular theatre and acting company, the

King's Company at Blackfriars. In the mid-1630s Philip Massinger, who was from 1625 until his death in 1639, effectively the resident playwright for the King's Company, wrote a poem in praise of Smith's *Innovation of Penelope and Ulysses*, in which he acknowledges a close, even paternal relationship with the poet. In 1639 Smith wrote a verse epistle from the north to "Tom Pollard," probably the comic actor who was a member of the King's Company from 1623 to 1647.[57] Finally, Smith's haunts seem to have been around the Blackfriars area: his lectureship was in Billingsgate, he drank at a tavern in Bishopsgate and at the Boar's Head near Cripplegate, and he was once committed to the Wood Street Counter. The knowledge that Smith was involved in particular with the King's Company and the Blackfriars milieu assists the development of an understanding of his remark that he hoped to "get good meanes" by the players. There are two ways in which he may have done this. He might have hoped to gain financially from associating with the most prestigious troupe in the country (patented members of the company like Pollard were wealthy men).[58] More likely he hoped to gain preferment by associating with the company, who performed at court more frequently than any other troupe and by frequenting the Blackfriars Theatre, which was the resort of wealthy and influential members of the aristocracy and gentry (even the queen visited the theatre on one occasion in 1634).[59] As Martin Butler has shown, the private theatres were social melting pots where different classes mingled together in an informal, affable environment and around which a literary network developed, with a whole variety of clubs and circles.[60] It may have been through his involvement with the King's Company that Smith gained the patronage of Edward, second viscount Conway, who was deeply involved in the Blackfriars milieu.

Smith's frequenting of theatres obviously laid him open to criticism, and he had a ready justification for his behavior: he is reported to have claimed that "there might be as much good many times done by a man in hearinge a play as in hearinge a sermon." This has the feel of a stock response, and it seems clear that Smith's interest in the theatre was in large part social rather than moral, but his attitude does bear some scrutiny. In his studies Smith would have imbibed the classical dictum about the instructive value of art, embodied in Horace's maxim, "utile e dulce." But it seems likely that he shared with many conservative thinkers a belief in the didactic value of popular culture.[61] Although he clearly spent time with the King's Company, his theatrical interests encompassed the outmoded Marlovian moralities that were the staple of the downmarket, public theatres.[62] His interest in the popular drama as an instrument for social instruction and control parallels Mennes's celebration of traditional rural pastimes in his poem on the Cotswold Games.

A taste for popular drama was not the extent of Smith's involvement with popular culture. From Corbett he had picked up an interest in ballads, and his time in London, the center of publishing, consolidated this interest. He even wrote a number of ballads himself, which reveals a willingness to engage in popular forms, to employ them for humorous or didactic ends, while preserving an air of sophisticated detachment. "The Miller and the King's Daughter" is Smith's tongue-in-cheek version of a traditional ballad. It is a macabre tale about a princess murdered by her sister, whose body is discovered by a miller and turned into a viol that, when played, identifies the murderess. The heart of Smith's version is a series of absurd appropriations of parts of the corpse by the miller: "What did he doe with her nose-ridge? . . . Unto his Violl he made him a bridge"; "What did he doe with her two shinnes? . . . Unto the violl they danc't *Moll Syms*."[63] Through these comic details, Smith adds to the story a burlesque twist that casts an ironic glance at the operating conventions of the ballad. Smith also employed the ballad form for didactic purposes. "Dr. Smiths Ballet," written some time after 1631, is a savage attack on women, whose pride, duplicity, and lechery were thought to be threatening the fabric of society. The ballad is a forgotten contribution to a debate that had been running since the early 1620s, and it responds to an earlier ballad by Will Bagnall, one of Smith's associates in London.[64] Women are attacked by Smith for their monstrous and unnatural behavior—for their wearing of fashionable patches, for example, and for their adoption of masculine dress. Although the ballad has the appearance of a piece of normative propaganda aimed at a broad popular audience (it circulated widely, eliciting many replies, and was even printed up as a broadside in the 1650s), this appearance is in part deceptive.[65] Even in the midst of a satiric attack, Smith insists on reminding the reader of his superiority to the medium by subverting it. Toward the end of the penultimate stanza, he throws in a metrically mistaken line and, lest one fail to notice the humor of this, points it out with an authorial aside:

> Nay, now I have got them within my Clutches,
>   I'le neither favour Lady nor Dutches,
> Although they may thinke this over-much is,
>   They are no more to me, then those that goe on crutches
> *I made this staffe too long.*[66]

This act of gratuitous comedy severely undermines the normative force of the ballad and reveals profoundly mixed motives on the part of the poet, caught between the desire to sermonize, the attempt to play the clown, and the need to assert his sophisticated detachment from the culture of the ballad.

With his advocacy of the moral instructiveness of playhouses and his refusal to retain a serious stance even on those questions of order that concerned him, James Smith must have cut a strange figure among the godly parishioners of St. Botoloph's, which perhaps helps to explain why he did not remain there long. The Lewis-Warner brief, dated 3 June 1633, states that he had been removed from his lectureship within the preceding twelve months.[67] Given the widespread religious radicalism associated with the lecturers and the City of London at this time, his expulsion is no surprise. What might seem more surprising is the fact of his appointment in the first place, but Seaver has observed that ambitious Anglican clergymen habitually used London lectureships as the first rung on the ladder of preferment, and Smith seems to have been no exception.[68] His career was not damaged by his expulsion. He was given an Oxford B.D. at the same time as his B.A. on 3 April 1633, without completing the statutory fourteen years of study (he had matriculated only ten years earlier), and he was installed as rector of Wainfleet All Saints, Lincolnshire on 27 May 1634, having been presented to the living by the king.[69] This appointment may, however, have been due less to a royal regard for Smith's abilities than to problems in Lincolnshire at the time.

IV

In the 1630s Archbishop Laud began an attack on the insubordinate John Williams and his diocese of Lincoln.[70] In 1631 Laud began to use the Court of Ecclesiastical High Commission to curb the nonconformity he felt Williams was conniving at. Many Lincolnshire ministers fled rather than face this fearsome body. It may have been that Smith, a man temperamentally disinclined to Puritanism, if not a supporter of Laudianism, was appointed as a corrective after the flight of such a minister.[71] Laud's official enquiry into misdemeanors in the Lincoln diocese was much concerned with the spread of Puritanism. The visitors were to ask such questions as "Doth your minister 'preach standing and with his hat off?'" The parishioners of Wainfleet would not have been afflicted by such unseemly behavior after the appointment of Smith, who appears to have done no preaching at all. Indeed, a report sent by Williams's chancellor to Laud on 14 July 1634—some two months after Smith's appointment—suggests that it would have been difficult for Smith and his flock to get into the church: "At waynfleet there is one of their churches a very fayre one vtterly deserted, it being suncke downe into the marishe grownd 4 or 5 yards deepe, soe that half the windows stand within the earth." (The decay of church buildings was another central concern of Laud's investigation.) In spite of information about the valuable contents and pleasant prospect of the church (it contained materials valued at £1500 and stood within a mile of the sea), Wainfleet All Saints does not sound a benefice of which to be proud. In fact, the chancellor's note offers a further explanation for Smith's nonresidence: it states that the corporation of Lincoln "starve their poore Curats allowing not aboue 20^{li} per annum to him that hath most."[72]

Smith's view that players would bring him more money than the church becomes increasingly tenable when one considers the evidence about Wainfleet. He probably spent little time there, choosing rather to remain in London until the end of the decade, where he frequented the theatre, met with his club, furthered his reputation as a writer of novel and witty verses, and perhaps mingled with a subcourtly circle of wits centered on Peter Apsley.[73] This seems to have been the period when he composed his burlesque masterpiece, *The Innovation of Penelope and Ulysses*, a piece that is discussed at length below (part 3, chapter 9).

During this period Smith may have been associated with a cavalier drinking circle, along with the son of his erstwhile patron, Thomas Wentworth. Evidence about this group appears in two linked ballads, "The Gallants of the Times. Supposed to be made by Mr. William Murrey of His Majesties Bed-chamber," and "The Answer, By Mr. Peter Apsley."[74] In the first ballad, Murray (later earl of Dysart) extols the praises of his group of gallants, "the maddest of the Land," who meet at "the Bear at the Bridge-foot" in order to let drink and wit run riot. This group included young courtiers like Henry Wilmot and George Goring, in addition to Murray, Wentworth, and Hugh Pollard—a wild young man from a notable Devonshire family.[75] There was an element of reaction in their meetings against the austerity and cheerlessness of Charles's court and against the Platonic affectations of the queen's circle. The ballad indicates a desire to marry courtly refinement and contemplation to sensuality and action:

> Tis pleasure to drink among these men
>   For they have witt and valour good store,
> They all can handle a sword and a pen
>   Can court a lady and tickle a whore,
> And in the middle of all their wine,
>   Discourse of *Plato*, and *Arretine*.[76]

Plato provided the model for the spiritual love pursued by the court, while Aretine was the author of a notorious collection of pornographic sonnets, *I Modi*. Closely related to Murray's circle was a rival group, perhaps a slightly downmarket version of Murray's, that included men who had served as professional soldiers in Holland ("som Holland blades") and was centered on Peter Apsley (a would-be courtier who spent most of his time fighting brawls and duels). This group included William Crofts (another inveterate dueller) and one of the Killigrew family (probably Thomas), both of whom were related to Wentworth and were involved with the queen's circle.[77] It also included an anonymous cleric who may well have been Smith:

> There is a joviall Parson
>   Who to these men doth preach:
> On the week days he does learn of them,
>   And on Sundays does them teach.
> Of books and of good company
>   Hee takes his share of each. . . .[78]

There are obviously strong similarities between Smith and this clubbable cleric. The identification of him with this "joviall Parson" would help to explain his failure to deliver the Sunday afternoon lectures at St. Botolphs, when he would "goe to tavernes and alehouses"—he was preaching in taverns to Apsley's circle.[79] The Murray and Apsley groups were closely connected, but, without further evidence, Smith's involvement remains conjectural.[80]

Through the Order of the Fancy and through the Blackfriars milieu, Smith had established a network of contacts and potential patrons. On 17 July 1639 he was presented to the rectorship of Kings Nympton, Devon, a living worth almost £30 per year.[81] The living was held by Hugh Pollard's father, Sir Lewis, a civil and military leader in the county.[82] Smith's appointment to the benefice of King's Nympton may have been the result of his association with Pollard's son, but it may also illustrate the operation of a small patronage network among the gentry of Devon. Smith's friend John Weeks had been rector of Shirwell, near Barnstaple in Devon, since 1627. This living was held by the Chichester family, who had close, long-standing associations with the Pollards.[83]

The new post was a mixed blessing for Smith. He no doubt shared some of his friend Herrick's misgivings about being thrust out of the metropolis into the backwaters of "dull Devonshire."[84] But this disappointment would have been mitigated by the proximity of his friends, Herrick and Weeks. Whatever his initial reaction, his sojourn in Devonshire was to be long and troublesome.

Part 2
The Order of the Fancy

Introduction to Part 2

"Man is said to be a Sociable Animal," wrote Joseph Addison, "and, as an instance of it, we may observe, that we take all Occasions and Pretences of forming our selves into those little Nocturnal Assemblies, which are commonly known by the Name of *Clubs*."[1] It is a commonplace of literary history that many wits in the eighteenth century formed themselves into societies like the Kit-Cat, Scriblerus, and Nonsense clubs. Although the existence of clubs in the early and late seventeenth centuries has been noted, historians have come across little evidence of clubbing in the midcentury, much less of any continuity throughout the century.[2] Recent studies have, however, contributed to an understanding of the complex social and literary networks of Caroline London, especially as they converged on centers such as the Blackfriars Theatre and Gray's Inn.[3] Evidence is now hard to come by, but such networks seem to have contained numerous clubs. This section of the book attempts to establish the existence of a tradition or, rather, two distinct traditions of clubbing in the early part of the century. It is intended to show that the club in which Mennes and Smith were involved, the Order of the Fancy, derived from a fusion of these two traditions. The composition, activities, and character of the Order of the Fancy will be examined thereby to shed new light on the social and literary practices of the seventeenth century. This survey offers a fresh perspective on some well-known writers, as well as establishing the contemporary significance of a number of figures now regarded as marginal.

The specific use of the term "club" should be explained briefly. The earliest use of the word to refer to a social meeting or assembly, as opposed to a thick stick, seems to date from 1627 and appears in "The Vision of Ben Jonson, On the Muses of his Friend M. Drayton."[4] The *Oxford English Dictionary* suggests that the term did not, however, come to describe the highly formal gatherings now associated with it until the end of the seventeenth century.[5] The word "club," along with the terms favored earlier in the seventeenth century, such as "society," "fraternity," and "order," are used here to refer to assemblies whose meetings are marked by some degree of regularity and formality and that may therefore be distinguished from the casual encounters of a loose circle of acquaintances.

3

Precursors

I

The term "club" may date from the seventeenth century, but the concept of clubbing is ancient. Two related institutions flourished in ancient Greece: the *symposium*, a drinking group or session, and the *hetaireia*, a club of men with shared interests (religious, occupational or political). Although these groups underwent many transformations, a brief summary provides the context necessary for an understanding of the English clubs of the seventeenth century, most of which looked back to classical models.

The *symposium* seems to have been an organization designed to contain excessive competition between rival members and to strengthen bonds of loyalty between them in a world in which clan and kinship ties were not dominant. The very term *symposium* ("drinking together") emphasizes the importance of sharing.[1] It began as the communal feasting of a warrior elite in order to ensure the community's continued protection. This led to the development of a leisured class of aristocrats that continued to hold *symposia*, although these no longer reflected—and were even opposed to—the interests of the community at large. The *symposium* is associated with both moderation and excess. On the one hand, leaders were often elected to draw up rules to regulate behavior, but, on the other hand, the need for such rules is telling, as is the fact that *symposia* would frequently conclude with a *komos*, a drunken procession through the streets in which the group displayed its power by beating up passing citizens. The *komos* was itself a ritualized form of degenerate behavior. The main activity of the *symposia* (of the later ones at least) appears to have been the competitive composition of verses on set themes or the parodying of serious activities.

The other major classical associations, the *hetaireia* were, like the *symposia*, formed by young aristocrats in order to strengthen social and political ties. They gave themselves obscene nicknames ("the wankers," "the erections"), held *symposia*, and frequently engaged in acts of vandalism and assault. Such groups were regarded as a threat to Athenian democracy. Oswyn Murray has shown that such suspicions were largely justified by examining the ritual profanation of the Eleusinian mysteries by Alcibiades's club. Both *symposia* and *hetaireia* were functions of an aristocratic society that had survived, incongruously, in the age of the *polis*.[2]

The Greek traditions of *symposia* and *hetaireia* were continued and refined in Roman times. The Roman *convivium* was, according to Cicero at least, a more civilized affair than the Greek *symposium*, involving not merely a drinking, but a "living together." Indeed, the *convivium* appears to have placed more emphasis on quality of food than on quantity of drink. In Augustan Rome there was much discussion of the moderation essential to a successful *convivium*, a moderation celebrated famously by Horace. Participation in *convivia* and membership of clubs were important parts of Roman life. In the period of the middle republic, lavish *convivia* were held by upwardly mobile groups to reinforce their sense of status and to expand their social contacts, with club membership affording a sense of group security. Despite occasional brushes with the authorities for outrageous behavior, the Roman clubs were not generally perceived as politically sensitive (due, perhaps, to the oligarchic character of Roman government).[3]

The chief characteristics of these classical groups are, then, a tension between competition and bonding within the group, the strengthening of social ties through sharing, the assertion of power (individual or group) through displays of wit, wealth, or violence, a philosophy of moderation, and potential subversiveness. Most of these characteristics are found in the clubs and fraternities of early seventeenth-century England.

II

Apart from a fifteenth-century society known as "La Court de Bone Compaignie," which had literary inclinations and valued moderation, it is not until the early seventeenth century that evidence of the existence of clubs in England begins to appear.[4] Groups involving Ben Jonson were based at the Mermaid and at the Devil and St. Dunstan taverns, and a group centered on John Hoskyns met at the Mitre in Fleet Street. These groups seem to have flourished contemporaneously. Jonson was involved with the Mermaid group by 1604, and it still met in 1616. Hoskyns's involvement in the Mitre group dates from the period 1608–12.[5] There was a degree of overlap in membership between these clubs. In addition to Hoskyns and Jonson, Thomas Coryate, John Donne, Richard Martin, Christopher Brooke, George Garrard, Inigo Jones, and Hugh Holland were involved in the Mermaid group: they are all mentioned (with the exception of Garrard and Jonson) in "Convivium Philosophicum," a poetic account of a meeting at the Mitre generally assigned to Hoskyns.[6] In addition to these figures, Richard Corbett's involvement in the Mermaid group has been posited.[7] Almost all the members of these clubs were, like their classical predecessors, well connected and of relatively high social standing. Their number includes courtiers, members of Parliament, lawyers, and diplomats. Ben Jonson is conspicuous as the only professional writer in the group.[8]

The fact that these groups were formalized clubs is implied by their association with particular taverns and by the fact that they were governed by behavioral conventions. Jonson drew up his "Leges Convivales" for the group that met in the Apollo Room of the Devil and St. Dunstan, while the Mermaid group had a formalized hierarchy, with a "High Seneschall," a "Clerk of the Purse," a "Beadle," and various degrees of fellows, brothers, and probationers.[9] Evidence that the Mitre group constituted a club is contained in the "Convivium Philosophicum" from which it is clear that certain conventions, if not conditions, governed its meetings. The assembly was convened with a some formality:

> Whosoever is contented
> That a number be convented
> Enough but not too many;
> The *Miter* is the place decreed,
> For witty jests and cleanly feed,
> The betterest of any.[10]

It seems, moreover, that different members were assigned different roles. Coryate, who had adopted the role of fool in order to gain the patronage of the young prince Henry, found that he was forced to play a similar part as comic butt for the Mitre group:[11]

> But yet the number is not ri[gh]ted;
> If *Coriate* bee not invited,
> The jeast will want a tiller.
>
> For wittily on him, they say,
> As hammers on an anvil play,
> Each man his jeast may breake.[12]

Coryate's adoption of this role has classical antecedents in the figures of the Greek parasite or the Roman *scurra*, self-styled comics who were admitted to *symposia* or *convivia* because of their buffoonery. Coryate's adoption of a classical role is symptomatic of the pervading flavor of these clubs.

That the classical models for these societies appear to be predominantly Roman is not surprising given the primacy accorded to the Latin language and Roman culture in the English educational system. The very title "Convivium Philosophicum" emphasizes its Roman basis, while Jonson anchors his "Leges Convivales" in an Augustan (or, more specifically, Horatian) tradition of moderate banqueting.[13]

The clubs were playgrounds for cultured men, courtiers and aspiring professionals, and it is no surprise that (as in the *symposia*) light-hearted literary production formed an important part of club life. The most celebrated production of this kind was "The Fart Censured," a poem on a fart let by Sir Henry Ludlow in Parliament, which is generally attributed to Hoskyns and his club and dated to 1607. The poem is an uneven production, listing the responses of various members of Parliament to Ludlow's breach of decorum. There are intermittent attempts to tailor responses to speakers (Robert Cotton's antiquarian interests are invoked, for example), but there is little consistency of tone or wit. The poem's coarse list structure indicates its composition by a group: indeed, verses were continually added to it, introducing new members.[14] One couplet is enough to give an impression of the poem: "Quoth Sir *Henry Pool*, 'Tis an audacious trick, / To Fart in the Face of the body Politick."[15]

In addition to group composition, membership of a club encouraged its members to send one another informal epistles in verse. An epistle, supposedly sent by Francis Beaumont from the country to Jonson in the town between 1610 and 1613, discusses the Mermaid Club:

> What things haue wee seene
> Done at the Mermaide? heard words that haue beene
> soe nimble, & soe full of subtill flame
> as if that euery one from whom they came
> had meant to putt his whole witt in a Ieast
> and had resolu'd to liue a foole the rest
> of his dull life. . . .[16]

The sending of verse epistles may have been something of a convention, because, in his poem "On the Muses of his Friend M. Drayton," Jonson denies that this, his first poem to Drayton, marks an intent to "raise a riming club / About the towne," implying that such an intent might be construed merely from the evidence of one poem (although the poem is not, formally, an epistle).[17] In addition to writing epistles, many members of the clubs contributed to the "Panegyricke Verses" that prefaced *Coryats Crudities* (1611), debunking Coryate's work with nonsense, rhetorical buffoonery, and displays of mock-learning: there are, for example, poems by Donne, Martin, Holland, Brooke, Hoskyns, and Jones; Jonson contributed a number of pieces that appear elsewhere in the *Crudities*.

It is not clear how long these clubs continued to flourish, but it is likely that during the 1620s and 1630s younger wits like Robert Herrick and Alexander Brome were admitted to their meetings, thereby ensuring their continuation. Evidence for Herrick's involvement with Jonson appears in one of his poems on Jonson, "An Ode for him":

> Ah *Ben*!
> Say how, or when
> Shall we thy Guests
> Meet at those *Lyrick* Feasts,
> Made at the *Sun*,
> The *Dog*, the triple *Tunne*?
> Where we such clusters had,
> As made us nobly wild, not mad;
> And yet each Verse of thine
> Out-did the meate, out-did the frolick wine.[18]

It is clear from Herrick's poem that, if the locations of the club meetings were variables, the preeminence (in theory, at least) of poetic composition and moderate behavior were not.[19]

III

The early seventeenth-century clubs are distinctive for their concern with poetry and for their advocacy of Augustan moderation. There was, however, another tradition of fraternizing in early seventeenth-century England, a tradition that eschewed moderation—the roistering gangs of young blades known as "Tityre-tus" that sprang up in the early 1620s.[20] The Tityre-tus were not simply clubs that met on convivial occasions: such organizations can best be described, as they were by contemporaries, as fraternities, fellowships, or societies. Although they met in taverns, they were bound together outside the confines of the tavern by oaths and rules of conduct. Such groups were often known as "orders" and had names such as the Order of the Bugle and the Order of the Blue, mimicking such contemporary chivalrous orders as the Garter and the Golden Fleece. These "orders" have a remote classical antecedent in the Greek *hetaireia*, but their direct origins are obscure. They share structural characteristics with the youth groups that flourished in early modern Europe in that they were fraternities of young men with similar professional backgrounds who engaged in a kind of organized misrule.[21]

The immediate origin of the fraternities seems to have been the bonding effected by military service. The Tityre-tu was formed by a group of blades in the regiment raised by Lord Vaux in 1622 for Spanish use in the Low Countries. Both this regiment and the Tityre-tu included men of Catholic sympathies.[22] John Chamberlain registered his concern about the fraternity's combination of Catholicism, soldiers, and secrecy to Sir Dudley Carleton on 6 December 1623:

> There is a knot of such kind of people [*papists*] discovered who under cover of goode fellowship have made an association and taken certain oaths and orders devised among themselves, specially to be true and faithfull to the societie and to conceale one anothers secrets, but mixed with a number of other ridiculous toyes to disguise the matter, as having a Prince whom they call Ottoman, wearing of blew or yellow ribans in their hatts or elsewhere, having certain nicknames (as Titere-tu and such like) for their severall fraternities. . . . Many of them are young gentlemen who use to flocke to taverns thirty and forty in a companie. This combination began first in the Low Countries in the Lord Vaulx his regiment, and hath since spread yt self here to the number of eight score alredy knowne. What mischeife may lurke under this maske God knowes, but sure they were very confident and presumed much of themselves to carrie yt soopenly.[23]

Other fraternities of young rakes soon sprang up, taking oaths of loyalty and wearing "bugles" (tubular glass beads, frequently black, sewn on to one's clothing) or colored ribbons to identify themselves.[24] They caused something of a storm, and there are frequent references to them in writings of the period.[25] Walter Yonge noted in his diary that,

> The beginning of December, 1623, there was a great number in London, haunting taverns and other debauched places, who swore themselves in a brotherhood, and named themselves *Tytere tues*. The oath they gave in this manner: he that was to be sworn, did put his dagger into a pottle of wine, and held his hand upon the pommel thereof, and then was to make oath that he would aid and assist all other of his fellowship, and not disclose their council. There were divers knights, some young noblemen, and gentlemen of this brotherhood, and they were to know one the other by a black bugle which they wore, and their followers to be known by a blue ribbond.[26]

This seems to hark back to the world of the subversive aristocratic *hetaireia*. The orders are comprised of young noblemen and gentlemen, and they are perceived as a threat to society. The very choice of the name "Tityre-tu" parallels, even if it does not consciously imitate, the phallic nicknames favored by the *hetaireia*. On one level the name is an allusion to the opening line of Virgil's first *Eclogue*, the significance of which will be discussed shortly, but Walton B. McDaniel has shown that there is another, obscene level of meaning here. The word "tityros" was not only a conventional term for a shepherd, it also referred to satyrs, particularly to those endowed with enormous penises.[27]

In trying to define the character of these fraternities one has to treat contemporary records with caution, since they exhibit that prevailing Protestant paranoia through which recent history was interpreted as a succession of increasingly sinister attempts to reestablish Catholicism in England. Fears of popery were currently at fever pitch: in the summer of 1624 Thomas Middleton's anti-Spanish satire *A Game at Chesse* played at the Blackfriars Theatre for an unprecedented nine days before being closed after a complaint by the Spanish ambassador.[28] Such was the prevalence of anti-Catholic feeling at this time that one scholar has recently concluded that the Tityre-tus were themselves an expression of radical Protestantism.[29] Several factors, however, suggest that contemporary observers like Chamberlain were right to regard the Tityre-tus as sympathetic toward Catholicism. It has been noted that the society originated in a regiment used by the Hapsburgs. It is possible that, in addition, some evidence of anti-Protestant feeling inheres in the sartorial signatures adopted by the fraternities. While the bugle was presumably a neutral device (it was a common enough flourish to be easily obtainable, but distinctive enough to be easily spotted by other members), the blue ribbon may travesty the blue ribbon worn by the knights of the Garter, an order perceived at this time as a locus of pan-Protestant sentiment.[30] Further evidence appears in the official examinations of those involved.

Parliament was naturally alert to the subversive potential of secret societies of whatever persuasion, and a number of those involved were arrested and interrogated. The only surviving examination appears to be that of Michael Constable, a Catholic who had once been arrested trying to enter the country with a packet of letters from Douai stuffed inside his boot.[31] Constable was examined on 19 December 1623 at the command of the House of Lords, and, since he was a founder member of the Order of the Bugle, his statement affords a unique insight into the origins, practices and composition of the fraternities:

This examinant being examined where and vppon what occasion this Order of the Bugle beganne saythe that this examinant with foure five or six others of the Retynu of the Admirall, Vice Admirall & Rere Admirall, viz: Raphe marshe, Robert knaplock, Mr Sudburie, & Thomas Mannors, went a shoare in the Isle of weight, and to the Towne of newport and lay at the signe of the Bugle, from tuesday vntill satterdaie; where they did Combyne themselves in a league of Amitie, but att that tyme tooke noe name, nor gave any signes nor made any Articles neither made any societie amongst themselves; but after theire retorne out of Spayne, takeing knowlege att Sea of a Socyetie that did call themselves by the name of (Tittere tu) to which Societie they were invyted, after theire Commyng to London to a Supper att the Boares head neere Creplegate & haveing a weeks warnyng did gyve themselves the name of the Bugle, and added more to theire Company such as were desyrous thereof to the number of fortie or thereabouts, and made Choyce of a Rybbond of Orendge Tornye Colour, as thother Company of the (tittertu) did wetched [*i.e. watchet, tawny*] Coloure Rybond; And att that tyme made no other associacion but onelie to be merrye, and droncke wyne and toake Tobaccoe, and called each other Brùthers without either Articles or other Agreementhe.[32]

One is again presented with a locus for Catholicism. The reference to the return from Spain surely implies that these men served on the fleet that collected Prince Charles and the duke of Buckingham after their unfortunate attempt to cut through diplomatic red tape and negotiate a Spanish marriage in person. While the general mood in England was one of jubilation at their failure, the expedition attracted Catholics like Constable who were presumably disappointed. Perhaps they hoped, like Charles himself, that the threat of the prince's departure would force an agreement and that the return voyage might bring back the Infanta to England in triumph.[33] Perhaps some of these men had also served for a time in Vaux's regiment, which would explain how Constable came to find out about the Tityre-tu on the voyage.

There are some other questionable points in the examination. Despite Constable's claim that firm articles were not drawn up, he admits that a number of officers were appointed: he was himself elected president, one "mr. Marshe" was appointed treasurer and "Sir. wm. Wyndsor" secretary.[34] The degree of formality in the organization of the fraternities is suggested by the arrangements made by members of the Bugle for a return supper for the Tityre-tu: "this ex[aminant] and his Company did make the like supper for those of the (Tittere tu) att the miter in Fleetestreete, before which tyme they did agree of the Charge and made a Colleccion of some thirtie poundes by Contribucion." Parliamentary suspicions about the degree of secrecy in the orders must have been confirmed by Constable's admission that they used a password, despite his attempt to play this down:

> they did vse in merryment one to another the word Oatemeale, thereby to call one an other out of theire lodgeinges to meete which they onelie did in the night tyme as they passed the streete by any man's lodgeing of theire Companye, and yf any of the Company heard they would answere by the like word Oatmeale, and would come out and for orders there were none other but such as he hath in wryting deliuered vnto the Lords

The evidence is suggestive of subversiveness without being conclusive.

The final piece of evidence contained in Constable's interrogation points away from subversive Catholicism and toward simple good fellowship. Appended to Constable's examination is a list of "Names of the orders of Titire tu. and the Bugles." This list is divided into those who attended the feast (presumably either that at the Boar's Head or the Mitre) and those who could not attend:

Thos that weare at the supper	The names that weare not at the supper but of the culler
Sir. Francis Fulgam	Mr: Tho: Russell
Mr: Glouer	sir: Rich: Brookes
Captayne <?> Alline	sir: walter waller
Captayne <?> Tho: Harbert	Sir: Hary Leegh
Captayne <?> Webbe	Mr: Iohn Sauidge
Mr: Ld: Colles <?>	Mr: Will: Warmistrye
Captayne <?> Blaby	Mr: Antho: Penridocke
Mr: Dix: Hickman	Mr: Will: Riuett
Mr: Tho: Humfrevild	Mr: Will: Wasborne
Mr: Ed: Askew	Mr: Phill: Garrowaye
Mr: Tho: Windesor	Mr: Gauill <?>
Mr: Will: Dansye	Mr: Barnefild
Mr: Fran: Hewes	Mr: Ig: Windesor
Mr: Gorge chambers	Mr: Samuell Bidges
Mr: Ha: Cundall <?>	Mr: Tho: Carew <?>
Mr: Ro: Meeringe	Mr: Iohn Vndrill
	Mr: Iems Wackline
	Mr:—Buttler
	Mr: Tho: freeman
	Mr: Iohn folken
	Mr: Iohn Horsye
	Mr: I <?> Phillpott

3 admitted at the globe
Tauern that I know not
there names[35]

These names bear witness to the military and naval origins of the fraternities rather more than to their Catholicism. The list includes men who served on several contemporary expeditions, some of which were decidedly pro-Protestant ventures. "Captayne <?> Tho: Harbert" was probably Thomas Herbert (the brother of Lord Herbert of Cherbury) who commanded the ship on which Prince Charles returned from Spain.[36] Several figures subsequently served in the desultory force raised at Buckingham's behest in 1624 by Count Mansfeld (a continental mercenary) to assist in a European Protestant offensive with the impractical aim of recapturing the Palatinate.[37] On 11 December 1624 a Mr. Blaby was appointed captain in the regiment raised for Mansfeld by the earl of Lincoln.[38] One "Phil. Garway" (probably "Mr: Phill: Garrowaye") is referred to as an officer in Mansfeld's force on 14 December; and on 22 January a number of soldiers were delivered to Sir Walter Waller and a Captain "Thos. Webb."[39] Walter Waller was the younger brother of the Parliamentarian general, Sir William Waller: he made his career as a professional soldier, serving on Mansfeld's force and later on Buckingham's expedition to Cadiz in 1625.[40] This pattern of service was not untypical.

John Underhill ("Mr: Iohn Vndrill") was probably the professional soldier who served in the Netherlands and on the Cadiz expedition before emigrating to achieve some notoriety as a military adviser in New England.[41]

The name on this list most interesting to literary historians is that of "Mr. Tho: Carew." It is quite possible that this was the poet Thomas Carew, but until recently no commentator on Carew seems to have been aware of the list.[42] Carew accompanied Lord Herbert of Cherbury on his trip to France in 1619, but it is not clear how long he remained there (Herbert was recalled temporarily in 1621 and permanently in 1624).[43] There is no evidence to prove that the Carew mentioned by Constable is the poet, but the involvement of Lord Herbert's brother in the fraternities establishes a connection between Carew and these groups. If Carew were involved with the fraternities it is likely—since nothing suggests that he served in Lord Vaux's regiment—that he was in England when they became fashionable in late 1623.

If the poet Carew was involved with a band of crypto-Catholics in the 1620s (and, given some of his known connections, this is not implausible: he was a good friend of Sir Edward Sherburne, a staunch Catholic), this involvement might afford a point of departure for a radical reassessment of his work.[44] A sympathy with Catholicism would add a sinister undertone to the strategy of retirement from the cause of European Protestantism celebrated in his "answer of an Elegiacall Letter upon the death of the King of Sweden from Aurelian Townsend," a text generally regarded as crucial to an understanding of his work.[45] But one need not posit a closet collusion with Hapsburg interests to make this argument (English Catholics were not, as Protestant propagandists would have it, Spaniards in English clothes): Carew's poem distances England from the Protestant cause by suppressing the religious dimension of the European war and presenting it as a purely national affair:

> what though the German Drum
> Bellow for freedome and revenge, the noyse
> Concernes not us, nor should divert our joyes[46]

The war drum here is alien, German; it is intrusive, inharmonious, and best ignored. Despite Sharpe's impressive attempt to uncover a profound ambiguity in Carew's attitude toward English isolationism (and one cannot ignore Carew's substantial praise of Gustavus Adolphus), the noise made by the drum remains recalcitrantly discordant.[47] Were Carew really hinting at the necessity of English involvement, the drum should sound a harmony of European Protestantism with which England is out of tune. But any revisionist reading of Carew's work would require more evidence for his religious position than that which can presently be offered. His membership of the fraternities is not proven and, even if it were, need not imply Catholic sympathies.

The precise character of the Tityre-tu and the orders of the Bugle and the Blue are difficult to establish. Although little remaining poetry can be associated with them, they were, like the clubs, clearly associated with literary men—Ben Jonson alludes to Skelton as the "*Tityre tu* of those times."[48] Parliament apparently found little ground for its fears of papist conspiracy, although at least two members (George Chambers and Andrew Windsor) were imprisoned for a time.[49] The orders did include Catholics and men who had fought for the Hapsburg Empress in Vaux's regiment, but many of these men were clearly professional soldiers who also fought in the anti-Hapsburg forces of Mansfeld and Buckingham. That their primary interest was conviviality rather than conspiracy is suggested by their adoption of buffooning identities, akin to those adopted by apprentices in their initiation rituals, which point to a concern with drink, food, and wit.[50] On the recto of the leaf containing the list of members appears a list headed "The names of the Giants belonging to the order of the blew." This list includes such comic nomenclatures as "Giant. Asdriasdust," "Giant. Tossacan," "Giant. Drunckzadoge," "Giant Drinkittupall," "Giant: Neuersober," "Giones: Lady: Linauele," and "Giant: Legomitton."[51] It is hard to concur with Chamberlain that such "ridiculous toyes" were really a cover for serious subversion.

If there were no specific religious or political agenda implied in the orders, they do seem to have been symptomatic of a general sense of discontent and perhaps, in the loosest sense, a degree of opposition. This discontent might be located in several areas. Firstly there is the perennial discontent of youth, caused to some extent by exclusion from positions of power and influence. The violent behavior of the fraternities (inscribed in nicknames like "the roisterers" or "roaring boys") underlines this sense of their being comprised of "angry young men."[52] More specifically, discontent might be located in the presence in the groups of younger sons of the nobility and gentry. Men like Waller and Herbert came from powerful, wealthy families, but were excluded from the full stretch of these benefits by the prevalent custom of primogeniture: they were forced to find careers for themselves.[53] Their pursuit of military careers would have bred further discontent. The life of the soldier and the sailor at this time involved, as has been seen in the career of John Mennes, ill-treatment, poor payment (or nonpayment), and frequent bouts of hunger and disease. Such men were accordingly feared and despised by the populace. A sense of the unfairness of their lot is embodied in the punning allusion in the very title of the fraternities to the opening line of Virgil's first *Eclogue* ("Tityre, tu patulae recubans sub tegmine fagi") with its implicit contrast between the otiose and luxurious life-style of Tityros and that of the exiled and hard-pressed Meliboeus.[54] In its context the allusion establishes a distinction between the lives of foreign military service led by members of the fraternities and the lives of leisure and affluence enjoyed by others (older brothers, perhaps) at home.

There may have been a more explicitly political dimension to the societies. Their members' firsthand experience of the gross mismanagement of the military must have led them to question the abilities and even the policy decisions of their leaders (it is no coincidence that Buckingham was murdered by a disgruntled soldier).[55] Because the discussion of policy decisions was so zealously prohibited by the early Stuarts, a degree of conscious or unconscious opposition may have been involved.[56] Clubs were certainly associated with incursions into state affairs at the time.[57] There is at least one instance of a youthful confederacy with explicitly opposition tendencies being founded at this time. A stir was caused at Christmas in 1622 when various members of the Middle Temple took oaths on their swords and, passing round a cup of wine, vowed to live and die in the service of Elizabeth of Bohemia (a controversial gesture striking at James's failure to provide any meaningful support for her).[58] In a more general sense, the very structure of these fraternities was oppositional in that they established, through their oaths of allegiance, bonds of loyalty that rivaled, even if they did not actually subvert, those of the state. The implication is that these men found the social structures provided by the family and the state inadequate: they were unhappy with their position within both, and they formed their own mutual assistance associations to improve their lot. These suggestions will be explored further when the Order of the Fancy is considered. Before turning to that subject, however, this chapter is concluded by a summary of the characteristics of the fraternities and the clubs that have been examined.

Some of the differences between the fraternities and the clubs can be illustrated by contrasting a ballad attributed to George Chambers (one of the revelers mentioned in Constable's list), with Herrick's ode for Ben Jonson. The ballad in question, "The Tytre-Tues, or A Mock-Songe to the tune of Chive-Chase. By Mr George Chambers," alludes to the arrest of Chambers and Andrew Windsor in late 1623 or early 1624. They were exposed for suspected "papistrie" and conspiracy by the vigorously anti-Catholic Archbishop Abbot ("My Lord of *Canterburie's* grace / This treason brought to light"):

> Two madcaps were committed late,
> For treason, as some say;
> It was the wisdom of the State,
> Admire it all you may.

Brave *Andrew Windsor* was the prince
  George Chambers favorite.
These two bred this unknowne offence
  I wo'd they had bine be—

They call themselves the Tytere-tues
  And wore a blew Rib—bin,
And when a drie, would not refuse,
  To drink—O fearefull sinn![59]

The fraternities did not share the same ideals and aspirations as the clubs. The difference between them is inherent in the verse forms chosen by each poet. Chambers[?] writes a pastiche of a ballad—an unsophisticated popular form designed for drunken singing (it is set to the traditional tune of "Chevy-Chase"); Herrick writes an ode—a sophisticated classical vehicle for lyric inspiration. Chambers[?] refers to himself and Windsor as "madcaps"; Herrick's club engage in temperate feasts that make them "nobly wild, not mad." Herrick's club grow wild with poetic fury; Chambers[?]'s with drink. In Herrick's poem drinking is sanctioned by its resonant classical context; in Chambers[?]'s ballad it is simply something one does "when a drie." The different characters of the poems can be explained in part by reference to the types of men involved in each group. While there seems to be no appreciable difference in social status between the two groups, the clubs were largely comprised of highly educated professional men (members of Parliament, lawyers, and clergymen), while the fraternities were formed by professional soldiers. These men were not, of course, illiterates—an easy classicism underlies the very name "Tityre-tu," but there is a difference of emphasis and, perhaps, of classical models. The clubs consciously adopted the ideals of moderation associated with Augustan *convivia*, while the orders, like the Greek *hetaireia*, indulged in debauched behavior (although there is no evidence that this was a conscious imitation). It is, perhaps, the difference between the senior common room and the locker room.

4

Membership

I

This chapter offers the first published account of the Order or Family of the Fancy. It will attempt to establish the membership of the club, to trace its derivation from the clubs and fraternities outlined above, and to infer something about its activities and its character.

The proceedings of the Order of the Fancy were not documented in a systematic or considered fashion (given the bibulous character of such groups it would be surprising if they were). There are, it seems, only two explicit references to the order. The most fertile source of information is the Lewis-Warner brief on the character of James Smith, which gives a number of details about the club. The brief states that Smith was a founder of the club, that it was known as the Order of the Fancy, that it included players, that its members drank to excess, that its members spoke nonsense and graded it (presumably by its wittiness), and that these gradations were reflected in the seating plan at its meetings. The only other direct reference to the order found thus far appears in the title of the ballad that follows Smith's *Innovation* in *Wit Restor'd*, "The Black-Smith." This ballad is described as a corporate production by the order, being "*collected out* of Homer, Virgill, *and* Ovid, *by some of the Modern Familie of the Fancies.*"[1] These references provide a point from which to begin building an account of the Order of the Fancy.

Although when the order was founded is not known, it was flourishing by the time the Lewis-Warner brief was drawn up (3 June 1633). Sixteen twenty-six may, perhaps, be taken as a *terminus a quo*: Smith, a founder of the society, probably moved to London around this time. The outbreak of the Civil War in 1642, in which so many members of the order seem to have been involved, surely put an end to its meetings. It is also clear that the group was referred to as both "Order" and "Family." The former term is generally employed here, to emphasize the derivation of the club from the earlier "Orders."

In attempting to establish the membership of the Order of the Fancy four criteria will be loosely applied. These are not infallible touchstones, the fulfillment of which determines membership (just as the absence of evidence for these criteria does not discount involvement). They are intended to be rough guidelines and are handled with caution since there is a degree of circularity in their formation (they are to an extent drawn from a search for common characteristics among personalities who are *likely* to have been involved). Bearing in mind these caveats, the working criteria are: first, knowledge of, or some clear connection with, Mennes, Smith, or someone whose membership in the order appears probable; second, the composition of verse epistles or mock-poetry in doggerel (preferably octosyllabic) verse (these forms and styles being almost invariably associated with Mennes and Smith in the 1630s); third, proven involvement in clubs; and fourth, congruence on social, political, and literary grounds with other members.

II

It seems safe to assume that both Smith and Mennes were members of the Order of the Fancy: Smith on the basis of the Lewis-Warner brief and Mennes because of both his close friendship with Smith and his allusion to being part of some kind of social club. In a verse epistle to Smith of January 1640/1, Mennes alludes to a fellowship from which he is absent, complaining that he hears how "fellowes nine in *London*, / Get cash, carouse, while I am undon."[2] I take this fellowship to be the Order of the Fancy, which, given Mennes's absence, must have contained ten members. But ten members need not have been the full quota of the club: other members may also have been absent, and the quota may have fluctuated. In the account that follows a dozen likely members of the Order are suggested, and attention is drawn to a further four figures who may have been loosely associated with it.

Information about the composition of the Order of the Fancy is provided by the text of Smith's *Innovation of Penelope and Ulysses*, which appears in *Wit Restor'd*. This is prefaced by a battery of commendatory poems by Smith's friends (including one by Smith himself). It is reasonable to assume, given the association of this poem with the order (the accompanying ballad is assigned to "*the Modern Familie of the Fancies*"), that the friends identified as James Atkins, Philip Massinger, and J[ohn] M[ennes] were members of the order.[3] Massinger's involvement in the order has been posited by Martin Butler on the basis of his commendatory poem.[4] James Atkins may have been the Scottish bishop who was in England between 1637 and 1638, when he studied divinity at Oxford under John Prideaux of Exeter College. Atkins may have become involved with Smith and his London club through the Oxford Divinity Faculty, where Smith had earlier studied.[5]

More evidence about possible members of the order is afforded by Smith's verse epistle of 5 July 1640, "Mr. Smith, to Tom Pollard, and Mr. Mering."[6] Strong circumstantial evidence suggests that the Tom Pollard mentioned here was the comic actor of that name. It is known that players were involved in the club and that Pollard was not only a player but, between 1623 and 1647, a member of the King's Company. There are therefore clear connections between the King's Company and the order since Massinger was effectively the resident playwright for the King's Company after 1625.[7] The other addressee of the poem, the Mr. Mering who is referred to in the text as "Robbin," was probably the "Mr Ro: Meeringe" named by Michael Constable as one of those present at the feast given for the Tityre-tus by the Order of the Bugle. "Robin" Mering thus provides a direct link between the earlier fraternities and the Order of the Fancy.

Having posited the involvement of Massinger, Pollard, and Mering, the possible involvement of other men associated with them can be examined. It is likely that the minor poet William Bagnall was involved in some way because he is connected with both Massinger and Smith. At some point in the early 1630s, Smith wrote a response to "Will Bagnalls Ballet"—an antifeminist diatribe that focused on a threat to social order in the current female fashion for masculine dress. In his response Smith aligned himself with Bagnall.[8] Further evidence for Bagnall's involvement appears in his association with Massinger and the King's Company. In November 1624 Bagnall and Massinger opened a lawsuit against Thomas Smith and Tristram Horner after an attempt by Smith and Horner to dupe them out of some money in an elaborate con-trick.[9] The two men had literary as well as social connections. Bagnall contributed commendatory poems to two of Massinger's plays, *The Duke of Milan* (1623) and *The Bondman* (1624), the former being in the repertory of the King's Company. Further, Bagnall's verse appears along with Massinger's in a manuscript copied by the King's Company scrivener in 1626.[10]

Given the claim in the Lewis-Warner brief that players were involved in the Order of the Fancy and given the association of Massinger and Pollard with the King's Company, this troupe and the milieu that grew up around its base, the Blackfriars Theatre, are obvious places to look for additional members. It seems that Pollard was a close friend of Elliardt Swanston, a member of the company from about 1624, for in 1639 Richard Benfield of Gray's Inn made a bequest "vnto my gossipp Eliardt Swanston and Thomas Pollard" (Benfield may have been a relation of another member of the company, Robert Benfield). Since Benfield and Swanston were friends of Pollard, it is possible that they were also involved with the Order of the Fancy.[11]

The Lewis-Warner brief does not claim that the Order was comprised exclusively of players: it states that Smith, some players "and others" formed the society. There are three other discrete areas in which one might look for other members of the Order: the inns of Court, the church, and the navy. The possibility of the inns of Court providing members is raised by the fact that Benfield was a Gray's Inn lawyer. Philip Edwards and Colin Gibson have used the evidence of commendatory poems to posit a circle of about six admirers of Massinger who were friends at Oxford in the 1620s. In addition to Smith, this group included wits like Robert Harvey and Henry Moody, who went from Oxford to Gray's Inn.[12] But there is no evidence to connect any of these figures with Mennes or Smith.

The search for possible members among Smith's clerical colleagues is more fruitful. There is considerable evidence for the involvement of Robert Herrick and his friend, John Weeks, in the order. Weeks and Herrick were contemporaries at Cambridge. Weeks became a fellow of St. John's in 1613, the year of Herrick's matriculation there as a rather mature undergraduate (he was twenty-two). Weeks may have met Smith after transferring to Oxford to study for a B.D. in 1617. Despite this transfer, Weeks retained his Cambridge connections: he was appointed deacon of Peterborough in 1623 (on the same day as Herrick). In 1627 he returned to his native Devon, having obtained the rectorship of Shirwell, and he became vicar of Banwell, Somerset in 1640. He may have served, along with Smith, Herrick, Mennes, and Davenant, on the Rhé expedition.[13] His connections with these men continued in the early 1630s, when he acted as chaplain to Endymion Porter: Herrick, Davenant, and possibly Mennes were all clients of Porter at this time.[14] Because Weeks was, according to Anthony Wood, "a jocular person," he was temperamentally suited for the order.[15] Direct evidence for his involvement is contained in a verse epistle addressed to him by either Mennes or Smith in 1642, "To Parson Weeks. An Invitation to London." In this epistle, the poet recounts the tale of an impoverished parson who undertook an arduous journey to London to visit a single friend, and he uses this point to rebuke Weeks for his laziness:

> One friend? why thou hast thousands here
> Will strive to make thee better chear.
> Ships lately from the Islands came
> With Wines, thou never heardst their name.
> *Montefiasco*, *Frontiniac*,
> *Viatico*, and that old Sack
> Yong *Herric* took to entertaine
> The Muses in a sprightly vein. . . .
>
> . . . .
> Rouze up, and use the meanes, to see
> Those friends, expect thy wit, and thee.
> And though you cannot come in state,
> On Camels back, like *Coryat*:

> Imagine that a pack-horse be
> The Camell, in his book you see.
> I know you have a fancy, can
> Conceive your guide a Caravan. . . .[16]

These references to Weeks's fancy, to Herrick, and to a witty association in London, suggest a connection with the Order of the Fancy. If Weeks was a member, the reference to his fancy is an elegant and apt play on the matter. Such a connection is rendered more plausible by the allusion to the epistle that Coryate sent to his club from Agra: the reference to Coryate riding a camel alludes to the engraving on the title page of *Mr. Thomas Coriate to his Friends sendeth Greeting from Agra* (London, 1618) (figure 3). The poet assumes a shared awareness of the tradition of clubbing and locates his epistle within it. He also alludes to Herrick's use of sack to inspire his muse, implying a knowledge of Herrick's sack poems, which were then circulating in manuscript.

Herrick certainly knew Mennes, Smith, and Weeks. *Hesperides* contains a laudatory poem on Mennes, "To his honored friend, Sir John Mynts," as well as a number of poems dedicated to Weeks.[17] An early draft of one of these pieces, "His Age, dedicated to his peculiar friend M. John Wickes under the name of Posthumus," shows that Herrick knew Smith. In this draft the poet mentions an unspecified "Smith" among a group of friends given to drink and conviviality:

> Hind, Goderiske, Smith
> And Nansagge sonnes of chine and pith
> Such who know well
> To beare the Magicke bowle and spill
> All mighty blood, and can doe more
> Then Jove and Chaos them before. . . .[18]

That this is a reference to James Smith is generally agreed. Herrick's knowledge of Mennes, Weeks, and Smith makes it likely that he was involved in the order, as does his clear interest in clubs and fraternities. He was involved in one of Jonson's clubs and was possibly a member of Thomas Stanley's Order of the Black Ribband; he even alludes to the Tityre-tu in one of his poems.[19] The fact that he and Weeks held benefices in Devon in the 1630s must mean that they could not have played active roles in a London club during this period. But Weeks spent time away from his benefice in Porter's service, and, in 1640, Herrick was living in Westminster long enough to be reported for nonresidency.[20]

The question that follows from this is whether the other friends mentioned in "His Age" were members of the Order of the Fancy. The facts that Herrick, Weeks, and Nansogg all held Devon benefices in the late

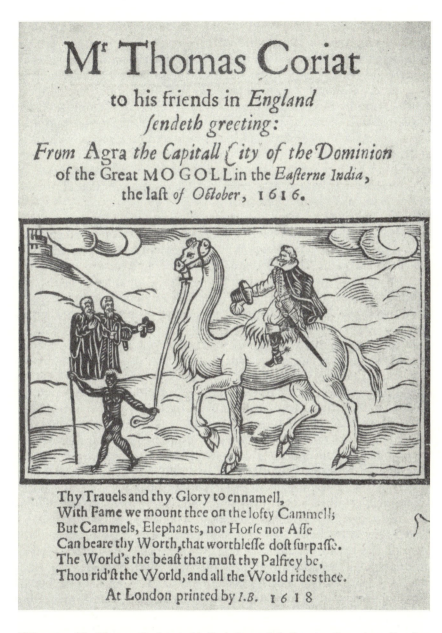

Mʳ Thomas Coriat

to his friends in *England*
ſendeth greeting:
From Agra *the Capitall City of the Dominion*
of the Great MOGOLL in the *Eaſterne India*,
the laſt *of October*, 1616.

Thy Trauels and thy Glory to ennamell,
With Fame we mount thee on the lofty Cammell;
But Cammels, Elephants, nor Horſe nor Aſſe
Can beare thy Worth, that worthleſſe doſt ſurpaſſe.
The World's the béaſt that muſt thy Palfrey be,
Thou rid'ſt the World, and all the World rides thee.

At London printed by *I.B.* 1618

Title page, *Mr. Thomas Coriate to his Freinds sendeth Greeting from Agra* (London, 1618). (By permission of the Folger Shakespeare Library.)

1620s and that Smith held one from the late 1630s suggest that the allusion is to a group of Devonshire clergymen. But this does not explain the references to Hind and Goderiske, the first having no known association with Devon and the second not being satisfactorily identified. In fact, the connection between them seems to be an earlier one: all these figures, with the exception of Smith, were probably at Cambridge in the second decade of the seventeenth century.[21] It is likely that they met during their Cambridge days and that Smith became involved with them in London during the 1620s or 1630s (possibly through Weeks). While they could have been connected with the Order of the Fancy, the absence of any reference to Mennes, Massinger, or Pollard suggests that Herrick is writing about a different group.

In turning to question the possible involvement of Mennes's naval and military colleagues in the Order of the Fancy, figures whose careers took various paths will be considered. William Davenant and Sir John Suckling served briefly on the Rhé expedition before seeking advancement at court (via the inns of Court). Sir Kenelm Digby, on the other hand, had a sporadic naval career punctuated by long periods of study and travel, acting as a privateer in the late 1620s and as a lieutenant in the King's Navy in 1634.[22]

A considerable body of circumstantial evidence points to William Davenant's involvement in the Order of the Fancy. He was a friend of Mennes and probably also of Smith. Along with Herrick and Weeks he sought the patronage of Endymion Porter.[23] Like Massinger he wrote for the King's Company at Blackfriars in the early 1630s, and he even alludes in "The long Vacation," a poem of the mid-1630s, to his involvement in a club.[24] The likelihood that the club in question is the order is increased by the fact that the poem is written in octosyllabic doggerel, a style associated at this time with Mennes and Smith. Further circumstantial literary evidence for his involvement appears in his use of the mock-heroic manner, which was virtually monopolized by Mennes and Smith in the 1630s. In 1630 Davenant composed a mock-poem on the queen's dwarf, Jeffrey Hudson ("Jeffereidos") and wrote a doggerel "*mock* romanza*," travestying the literature of chivalric romance, as the antimasque to *Britannia Triumphans* (1637/8)—this was later printed along with Smith's *Loves of Hero and Leander* in 1651.[25] It would not be out of character for Davenant to become involved in a club like the Order of the Fancy because he was a genial and playful character, a close friend of Sir John Suckling, with whom he made a riotous excursion to Bath in 1637.[26] But, despite his cordial nature, Davenant was a pompous man, obsessed about his status (he was the son of an Oxford vintner) and desperate to make his way at court. In his cups, he used to claim that "he writt with the very spirit that Shakespeare," and he rather liked the idea that he might have been the bard's illegitimate son. In later life he even affected an apostrophe in his surname (to add a specious air of nobility) for which he was mercilessly lampooned.[27] His concern about status and his desire for court preferment may help to explain an otherwise rather problematic (problematic for his possible association with the order) contretemps with Massinger—the notorious Caroline War of the Theatres.

The War of the Theatres was a literary squabble that broke out between two groups of writers associated with the rival King's and Queen's players in 1630. Its immediate occasion was the failure of Davenant's *Just Italian* to attract theatregoers to Blackfriars in late 1629. Davenant's friend Thomas Carew leapt to his defense in a poem published with *The Just Italian* in 1630. With gentlemanly disdain he laid the blame for the play's failure on the fickleness of public taste. In doing so he cast a glance at the Cockpit Theatre, confounding the Queen's players with that most downmarket of all theatres, the Red Bull. The writers of the Cockpit and their friends responded angrily. James Shirley's *The Grateful Servant* was published in 1630 with a battery of supporting poems, including one by Massinger who, despite his association with the King's Company, was currently writing for the Cockpit. Massinger was in the thick of the quarrel. He penned a prologue for a Cockpit performance of *The Maid of Honour* that lambasted Carew (who even attended the theatre to hear it delivered), and he dashed off a withering response to an anonymous libel in defense of Carew, possibly by Davenant, which had made much of Massinger's lowly status as a professional hack (Massinger attacked the author as a court toady, clinging to Carew's coat tails).[28] Battle lines appear then to have been drawn over three issues: dramatic style, social status, and playhouse affiliation. On one side were courtiers like Carew and would-be courtiers like Davenant, associated with the King's Company, who favored a heavily conceited, fanciful style; on the other hand were professional writers like Shirley and Massinger, associated with the Queen's players, who preferred a plainer, smoother style.[29] Such an array sits somewhat uncomfortably with the contention that Massinger and Davenant were at about this time allied in the Order of the Fancy. But the intensely personal acrimony of the exchange between Massinger and the author identified as Davenant suggests that this was a fight between friends, with the latter carefully asserting his courtly credentials at the expense of the former.[30] The War of the Theatres does not discount the possibility of Davenant's involvement with the Order of the Fancy, which remains likely but unproven.

Another figure whose possible involvement with the Order of the Fancy ought to be considered is Sir Kenelm Digby. This seems a rather implausible suggestion given Digby's serious and reclusive temperament, but both Mennes and Smith knew him. Mennes may have met him at sea, either on the Rhé expedition or in 1634, when Digby served as lieutenant of the *Garland* (although Mennes is not known to have had a commission in this year). The two men may have been drawn together by their interests in experimental chemistry and medicine—interests they shared with Edward, viscount Conway, who seems to have acted as a patron of the group. Digby corresponded regularly with Conway during the 1630s, procuring books and other luxuries for him.[31] Conway, in fact, provides an explicit link between Digby on the one hand, and Smith and Mennes on the other. In December 1640 and January 1640/1 Smith and Digby were both staying at Conway's house at Queen Street, Covent Garden (Smith was currently acting as Conway's chaplain).[32] Digby was certainly in England between 1625 and 1635, when the order flourished, and he was at this time involved with the circles of Jonson and Hyde. He was also something of a poetaster. But he was perhaps too sombre a character—especially after the death of his wife in 1633—to have been attracted by the debauchery and frivolity of Smith and his friends.[33]

Digby's residence with Smith at Conway's house raises the possibility that Thomas Pope, second earl of Downe, was an associate of Smith and a member of the order. It is clear from the verse letters mentioned above that Downe was also resident at Conway's house in December 1640. Smith signs his letter of 27 December 1640 "From house of Viscount *Conway*, where / *Kenelme* hath food, and *Down's* Count Lare," and, in a reply of 1 January 1640/1, Mennes sends his greetings "To noble Kenelm . . . / And unto Lord of *Downe*."[34] This connection is important because, in January 1641 Digby, a prominent Catholic, was hauled in front of the House of Commons accused of trying to convert the earl of Downe to Catholicism. In his defense, Digby protested his innocence, claiming that he had, in fact, attempted to release Downe from "such hazards of ryott and dissolution as his great youth and unlucky breeding, formerly, did too much expose him vnto with that stock of acquaintance he yet had."[35] Is it possible that the bad company referred to by Digby was the Order of the Fancy? This, given his friendship with Mennes and Smith, might seem unlikely, but Digby was on trial at the time and thus had every reason to portray himself as a model of virtue. Smith, furthermore, was exactly the kind of trickster one might expect to find duping a gullible young nobleman out of his inheritance. Perhaps, however, the reference is more generally to a circle of dubious acquaintances that may have included Smith.

Sir John Suckling is in many ways an obvious candidate for membership of the order. It has generally been assumed that he and Mennes were acquainted and, although some of the evidence for it might be questioned, this is a reasonable assumption.[36] Both men served on the Rhé expedition (Suckling was probably a horseman under Edward Conway), and they both commanded troops of carbineers under Conway in the Second Scots War.[37] Suckling moved in similar circles to other members of the order. He was a close friend of Davenant, and he frequented the same playhouses and taverns as other members of the group. Like many young courtiers, he was deeply involved with the King's Company and the Blackfriars milieu. Three of his plays were performed by the company in the late 1630s and early 1640s, and he had been a visitor to Blackfriars throughout the 1630s. In 1634 he and a group of cronies attempted to beat up Sir Kenelm Digby's brother, John, outside the Blackfriars Theatre (a fracas that resulted in ignominy for Suckling).[38] He and his associates also seem to have frequented the same tavern as Smith and his friends. In his epistle "The Wine-drinkers to the Water-drinkers," he states that his group of wine-drinkers have had "divers meetings at the *Bear* at the *Bridge*-foot," and the letter is dated from there. The Bear was at the Southwark end of London bridge and was evidently a favorite haunt of young courtiers and wits. Smith claims that he received the inspiration for *The Innovation of Penelope and Ulysses*, a travesty associated with the Order of the Fancy, while drinking there.[39] Suckling was also associated by contemporaries with the tradition of fraternizing from which the order developed: an anonymous broadside of 1641 attacks "the debaucht Gallants of these lascivious and loose-living times" who comprise the "Sucklingtonian faction," alluding to them as "*Titere tris*, or joviall roaring Boyes."[40]

There is a little literary evidence for suggesting Suckling's involvement with the order. It seems possible that the water drinkers of this epistle were Mennes and the party who made a trip to Epsom wells in the 1630s. Suckling's letter was written in response to a communication from some travelers who had gone to "take the waters." It is tempting to suggest that this communication may have been Mennes's poem "To a friend upon a journey to Epsam Well," or another epistle from the same journey, because there are clear thematic parallels between the pieces: both dilate upon the laxative effects of the waters.[41] But this is not surprising (it is an obvious subject to discuss) and Suckling alludes to certain difficulties not apparent in Mennes's poem. More evidence for Suckling's connection with the order appears in his composition in the 1630s of light verse epistles in octosyllabic meter, forms associated with Mennes and Smith. Suckling composed at least two poems in this form. One of these is an invitation to John Hales, the Cambridge divine, to come to London.[42] It is similar enough to Mennes or Smith's "To Parson Weeks. An Invitation to London" to suggest that the invitation poem in octosyllabic doggerel was recognized within the clubs—and perhaps beyond—as a distinct subgenre of the invitation poem.[43] Like "To Parson Weeks" it entices a friend to come to London by any means (Hales is urged to pinch the college horse), it emphasizes the wine, wit, and good company to be had there, it is written in octosyllabics, and it employs comic double rhymes—"Leave *Socinus* and the Schoolmen / (Which *Jack Bond* swears do but fool men)."[44] The other epistle is, significantly, to William Davenant. Although "To Mr. Davenant for Absence" does not exhibit quite the same degree of crafted roughness in its verse form, it does share the reductive wit and casual intimacy of these poems: "Persinda's eyes great mischief do, / So does (we know) the Canon too."[45] Wood's claim that Mennes assisted Suckling in the composition of some of his poetry does not seem at all implausible when these epistles are considered.[46]

This search for the members of the Order of the Fancy can be concluded by considering two figures who do not easily fit into any of the preceding categories—Sir John Denham and Edward, viscount Conway. Denham is a figure whose possible involvement must be considered, although the evidence for it is not convincing. Denham certainly knew Mennes in exile during the Interregnum when he wrote his ballad "To Sir John Mennes Being Invited from Calice to Bologne to Eat a Pig." Like other members of the order he was a *bon viveur* and a prankster. His involvement might be deemed unlikely on account of his youth: he was only about eleven years old when the society was formed (if 1626 is the correct date for its formation). On the other hand, however, Denham was a precocious youth whose early literary activities provide two pieces of circumstantial evidence for associating him with the order. First, Aubrey attributes to him a burlesque of Virgil's *Aeneid* that may date from the mid-1630s (he later burnt it, "sayeing that 'twas not fitt that the best poet should be so abused"). At this time James Smith's travesties of Ovid (which were circulating in manuscript) seem to have been the prime models for classical travesties of this sort. Second, Denham may have been associated with the King's Company: the title page of his play *The Sophy* (1642) claims that it was performed by the company at the Blackfriars Theatre. But this claim has been questioned by a recent scholar, leaving no firm evidence to connect Denham with members of the order prior to the 1650s.[47]

It seems possible, finally, that Edward, viscount Conway, might have been involved to some extent as a patron of the order. Although there is no evidence that he actually attended their meetings, Conway was closely connected with members of the Order of the Fancy, and he shared many of their tastes and interests. Mennes served with him at Rhé, in the fleets of the 1630s, and in the Second Scots War and shared his interests in chemistry and poetry. Smith, Davenant, and Suckling also served in the Rhé expedition, and all served under Conway in the Scots wars. As is noted below, during the Second Scots War Smith acted as his chaplain, and Mennes sought his assistance in gaining military preferment. Conway is a fascinating character whose wide-ranging intellectual interests would repay further study. The poet and diplomat George Rudolph Weckerlin described him to Samuel Hartlib as "A very learned man and very curious for all manner of rareties."[48] Clarendon offers a rounded and judicious portrait of him:

> He had been born a soldier, in his father's garrison of the Brill when he was governor there, and bred up under the particular care of the lord Vere, whose nephew he was, in several commands; and though he was married young, when his father was Secretary of State, there was no action of the English either at sea or land in which he had not a considerable command; and always preserved a more than ordinary reputation, in spite of some great infirmities which use to be a great allay to the credit of active men; for he was a voluptuous man in eating and drinking, and of great license in all other excesses, and yet was very acceptable to the strictest and gravest men of all conditions. And, which was stranger than all this, he had always from his pleasure, to which his nature excessively inclined him, and from his profession, in which he was diligent enough, reserved so much time for his books and study that he was well versed in all parts of learning, at least appeared like such a one in all occasions and in the best companies. He was of a very pleasant and inoffensive conversation, which made him generally very acceptable: so that the Court being at that time full of faction . . . he alone was even domestic with all, and not suspected by either of the lords' or ladies' factions.[49]

Like the members of the Order of the Fancy, Conway was, as Clarendon observes, devoted to pleasure: in one of his witty, allusive, and often ribald letters to George Garrard he describes his life with the court at Newmarket in 1637:

> When we do not hunt we hawke, and in both these Mukkle Jhon and Jefferey are great actors, the rest of the time is spent in tennis, chesse, and dice, and in a worde we eat and drink and rise up to play; and this is to live like a gentleman, for what is a gentleman but his pleasure.[50]

Although one must allow for a certain license in such self-presentations, Conway was addicted to pleasure: to exotic food and drink, to fine clothes, and to the fine arts. He despatched sumptuous shopping lists to friends and agents throughout England and the Continent, urging them to procure him walnuts from Warwickshire, linen from London, Bologna sausages, and paintings from Italy—and from France, Frontignac wine (an exotic wine favored by the Order of the Fancy), anchovies, "angelott cheeses," capers, caviar, olives, sardines, "Dryed Apricocks, Citrons, and other Dryed Sweat=meats, and dryed Cherryes, and Apricocks, without sugar, and other choyce plummes, as Pomgranates. Peaches, etc." (the agitated syntax reveals the barely controlled relish of a gourmand). His love of luxuries was so conspicuous that one of his servants was forced to warn him "that he may one day be told that he had more regard to the making of a Bologna sausage, or the covering of his table, or the training of a horse, than to the worship of Almighty God" (Bologna sausages were obviously a favorite delicacy). It is in the context of this gentlemanly pursuit of pleasure that one must view his extensive literary interests.[51]

Conway collected books and manuscripts with the same delight and excess that he sought other luxuries, obtaining from his agents in Europe details of the latest books published in France, Spain, Italy, and Germany. He owned an enormous library that presented a formidable task to the servants who tried to catalogue it by placing the books "in their several faculties alphabetically."[52] A list prepared in 1637 of those books that were defective, or of which he had duplicates, contains almost five hundred titles. The range of his interests is equally remarkable, covering alchemy, architecture, chemistry, medicine, poetry, politics, romances, theology, travel, and warfare. With bemused detachment he kept himself abreast of the religious debates of the 1630s, and he read avidly in texts on military strategy for precepts he could apply in his commands. In 1643 his great library, then comprised of over 4,700 titles, was seized by the Committee for Sequestrations; it was not recovered until 1647.[53] Conway then retreated to a life of study and contemplation at Petworth, the home of his close friend, Algernon Percy. Here he turned his energies once more to his collections, procuring more books and manuscripts (Sir Walter Ralegh's son, Carew, provided him with some of his father's manuscripts); from here he dispensed advice to friends and relatives on what to read, what cures to take, and even on how to make red ink or lamprey pies.[54] Occasional excursions took him up to London, where he imbibed with literary friends like John Denham and Bishop Brian Duppa.[55]

Conway was especially interested in drama and poetry and was an active member of the Blackfriars circle.[56] A list of titles purchased from the stationer Humphrey Moseley shows that he bought copies of 37 percent of all plays published in England between 1634 and 1640: the list naturally includes Suckling's *Aglaura*, a text he was at pains to procure even before its publication, though not (perhaps significantly) Milton's tendentious *Maske Presented at Ludlow Castle*.[57] While he was not directly connected with other clubs, he was intimate with members of Hyde's and Jonson's circles, men like Sir Kenelm Digby, George Garrard, and John Selden.[58] He was a drinking companion of some of the more riotous courtiers in the Murray-Apsley circle, like George Goring, and possibly Henry Wilmot and Will Crofts.[59] His collection of poetry was as wide ranging as his acquaintance, including classical poets like Catullus, Tibullus, and Propertius, moderns like Francis Beaumont, Michael Drayton, and Ben Jonson, and the popular miscellany, *Wits Recreations* (1640).[60] He was a keen collector of the latest songs, lampoons, and complimentary verses:

in 1640, while commanding the northern army, he found the time to write to Elizabeth, countess of Devonshire, advising her on how best to respond to some verses sent to her by Lord Herbert of Cherbury.[61]

In addition to sharing with men like Mennes a love of fine wine and good fellowship, a penchant for the theatre, and an interest in chemistry and medicine, certain of his tastes in poetry mark him out as a potential patron of the Order of the Fancy. Not only did he share with Mennes and Smith an appreciation of earlier English poetry unusual in the Caroline period (he possessed a copy of Skelton's works), he was also interested in burlesque verse, a mode popularized in England by members of the order. One of the earliest English discussions of the classical travesty occurs in a letter written to Conway by the physician, Theodore Turquet de Mayerne, and this discussion may have been prompted by Conway's gift to Mayerne of a copy of Smith's newly published *Loves of Hero and Leander* (1651).[62] As early as the 1630s, Conway was collecting burlesque poems. He owned a copy of R[obert] S[peed]'s raucous account of a bun fight in the Wood Street prison, *The Counter Scuffle* (1621); in 1640 he purchased a copy of Richard Braithwait's marital satire *Ar't Asleepe Husband? A Boulster Lecture*, and in the 1640s he assembled a manuscript of cavalier songs and satires, many of which were later published after the Restoration in *Rump* (1662).[63] Some interest in the order seems likely, even if it amounted to no more than his recorded patronage of certain individual members.

Despite the sparse documentation of the Order of the Fancy, it seems likely that in addition to Mennes and Smith the group included some of the following—Massinger, Pollard, Mering, Bagnall, Benfield, Swanston, Atkins, Herrick, Weeks, and Davenant. It seems possible that Digby, Denham, Suckling, and Conway may have been involved in some way. Many of these men may have met on the Rhé expedition in the late 1620s. Having established the probable members of the Order of the Fancy, it is possible to build up a hypothetical account of its character.

5

Character

I

In this chapter the character and activities of the Order or Family of the Fancy are considered, and some suggestions are made about the motives underlying its formation. It is intended to show that the order drew upon and fused the two distinct traditions of clubbing and fraternizing that flourished in early seventeenth-century England.

The order, like the earlier fraternities, was a meeting place for a number of budding wits who were concerned with bettering their status (social and financial), many of whom felt seriously discontented with their lots. By terming their association an "Order," members of the Order of the Fancy emphasized the connection between their group and fraternities such as the orders of the Bugle and the Blue. This connection is evident in several ways. First, there are continuities of personnel. Robin Mering (or Meering) was involved in both the Order of the Fancy and one of the earlier groups. Thomas Carew was possibly involved in the earlier fraternities and was later associated with Davenant and possibly with the Blackfriars Theatre. John Mennes may also have been associated with the early fraternities: the Order of the Bugle was founded by members of the king's fleet in 1623, on which Mennes may have served.[1] The fraternities undoubtedly influenced the literary activities of the order. The only literary work attributed to the order as a group ("The Black-Smith") is, like that associated with the Tityre-tu, a street ballad, designed to be sung in taverns.[2] It is, however, in their social practices—their intemperate drinking and the debauched conduct that followed it—that the members of the order seem most like the fraternities. It seems likely that Mennes's habit of riding home after a night of hard drinking on the back of an unfortunate citizen derived from the riotous practices of the fraternities (and ultimately, perhaps, from the drunken *komos* and the ritual humiliation of the lower classes practiced by the Greek *hetaireia*).

In addition to mimicking the practices of the fraternities, the Order of the Fancy drew on those of the literary clubs of early seventeenth-century London. Smith may have been conversant with these practices

98

through his literary mentor, Corbett, or through the players whose company he kept—a group that would almost certainly have absorbed the influence of Jonson. The spirit of Jonson and the earlier clubs is apparent in the structure of the Order of the Fancy. Philip Massinger's reference to Smith as his son and to himself as Smith's father—"*Thou art my son, in that my choyse is spoke*: / *Thine with thy fathers muse strikes equall stroke*"—suggests that the order was organized after the model of Jonson's "tribe" with Massinger playing the paternal, Jonsonian role.[3] There is no necessary conflict between this suggestion and the claim in the Lewis-Warner brief that the "Chiefest place" at meetings of the order was given to the best speaker of nonsense, rather than to a senior member: Massinger may have occupied an extraordinary place of honor. Indeed, the singling out of the best speaker of nonsense provides further evidence that the order was influenced by the earlier clubs since it seems possible this practice derived from the focal position accorded to the self-styled fool Coryate at meetings of the Mitre group. The literature associated with the Order of the Fancy also reflects the influence of the clubs. Although there is no evidence that in his role of fool Coryate spoke nonsense, there was a tradition of written nonsense associated with Coryate. The Order of the Fancy—Smith, at least—was influenced by this tradition.

Nonsense poems were written by at least two members of the earlier clubs, Hoskyns and Corbett. Hoskyns contributed some "Cabalisticall verses, which by transpo*sition of words, syllables, and letters, make ex*cellent sense, otherwise none" to *Coryats Crudities*. These begin:

> Euen as the waues of brainlesse butter'd fish,
> With bugle horne writ in the Hebrew tongue,
> Fuming vp flounders like a chafing-dish,
> That lookes asquint vpon a Three-mans song. . . .[4]

Corbett seems to have been responsible for two nonsense poems, "Epilogus Incerti Authoris" and "A Non sequitur," the first of which was clearly influenced by Hoskyns's "Cabalisticall verses." It begins:

> Like to the thund'ring tone of unspoke speeches,
> Or like a lobster clad in logick breeches,
> Or like the gray freeze of a crimson cat,
> Or like a moon-calf in a slipshoo hat. . . .

The second poem employs many of the same elements as these two pieces:

> *Saturne* craules much like an *Iron Catt*
> To see the naked moone in a slippshott hatt
>
> . . . .
>
> The putrid skyes
> Eat mulsacke pies,
> Backed up in logicke breches.
>
> Munday trenchers make good hay,
> The Lobster weares no dagger. . . .[5]

This congruence of detail among these three poems suggests that a tradition of nonsense verse with a stock of conventional material flourished among members of literary clubs. Smith later drew on this tradition in his poem "Ad Johannuelem Leporem, Lepidissimum, Carmen Heroicum." His line "And to the butter'd Flownders cry'd out, *Holla*" alludes to Hoskyns's "waues of brainlesse butter'd fish . . . Fuming vp flounders"; and his line "And mounting straight upon a Lobsters thigh" alludes to the lobsters that appear in both of [Corbett?]'s pieces—"And like a lobster clad in logick breeches" and "The Lobster weares no dagger."[6]

Evidence that the Order of the Fancy was influenced by the literary traditions of the earlier clubs appears not only in their shared partiality to nonsense. It can be found also in their writing of humorous, informal verse epistles, examples of which (by Beaumont and Coryate) have been quoted. A correspondence between friends is nothing remarkable, but the allusion in an epistle to John Weeks to one of Coryate's epistles to *his* club suggests that the Order of the Fancy was conscious of drawing on an epistolary tradition associated with the clubs. Further evidence for continuity appears in James Atkins's commendatory poem on Smith's *Innovation of Penelope and Ulysses*. Atkins alludes, in his contribution, to "*the scribe; / Famous in water-works*," John Taylor the Water Poet, an allusion that might suggest that the order inherited Coryate's much-publicized feud with Taylor.[7]

The literary concerns of the order appear to locate it midway between the clubs and the fraternities. This position is best illustrated by considering "The Black-Smith." On the one hand, "The Black-Smith" betrays in its coarse ballad form the influence of the fraternities, but, in its group composition and its witty classicism, it shows the influence of the clubs. Like "The Fart Censured" it is a loosely connected collage of witticisms that were transposed and added to with ease. The versions of the ballad that appear in *Wit and Drollery* (1656) and *Wit Restor'd* (1658) differ greatly in their stanzaic layout, and the *Wit Restor'd* version includes a number of additional stanzas.[8] Indeed, a description of "The Black-Smith" as a witty street ballad fails to account for the fact that it displays a greater level of sophistication than one tends to attribute to the form. Part of its wit lies in the fact that its claim to classical authority—"*collected out of* Homer, Virgill, *and* Ovid"—is actually justified: the ballad does draw on these poets, albeit in a wittily anachronistic manner. Its second stanza alludes to Virgil's description in the *Aeneid* of Vulcan's cave, in which the first, half-finished thunderbolt is described:

> The first that ever thunderbolt made,
> Was a Cyclops of the *Blacksmiths* trade,
> As in a learned author is sayd. . . .[9]

A quarter of the way through the ballad there is an allusion to Ovid's account in the *Metamorphoses* of the fine net woven by Vulcan in order to trap Venus and Mars *in flagrante delicto*. The ballad playfully associates this with Paul's Chain, an alley that existed during the seventeenth century on the South side of St. Paul's Churchyard:

> At last *he made a Nett or traine,   *Vulcan.
> In which the God of warre was t'ane,
> Which ever since was called Pauls-chaine. . . .[10]

Finally, four stanzas before the end of the poem, there is an allusion to Homer's tale of the wanderings of Ulysses, which is the opportunity for a pun:

> Though Ulysses himselfe has gon many miles
> And in the warre has all the craft & the wiles,
> Yet your Smith can sooner double his files. . . .[11]

The point is not that these references are particularly erudite (they are not), but that their inclusion exhibits a greater degree of sophistication than is found in a true street ballad. In fact, "The Black-Smith" problematizes the category of a "true" street ballad because (like others of Smith's ballads) it later entered the popular market as a broadside, where it was embellished and rewritten.[12] Both the earlier clubs and the Order of the Fancy were exploring ways—very different ways, admittedly—of deploying classical literature in the taverns and on the streets of contemporary London, of mingling popular and elite culture.

Although there is ample evidence to connect the Order of the Fancy with the earlier clubs and, as in the preceding accounts of Mennes and Smith, to associate its members with Ben Jonson, it would be a mistake to see the club simply as a new litter of the ubiquitous "Sons of Ben," for, not only is Jonson himself too incongruous and contradictory a figure to provide a mould for subsequent poets, the lines of allegiance exhibited in the Order of the Fancy are more complex than the traditional division of Caroline literary culture into Metaphysicals and Sons of Ben will allow.[13] None of the central members of the Order of the Fancy were among the loyal followers who contributed poems to Jonson's tumulary collection, *Jonsonus Virbius* (1638)—one possible member (Suckling, in *The Goblins*) even attacked Jonson for his lumbering classicism. Members of the order valued easy urbanity over laborious learning and gentlemanly dilettantism over earnest professionalism or laureateship. One may, of course, say the same for many of the courtiers who followed Jonson's lead and may note the incongruity that the father of the order, Massinger, was a mere professional playwright (albeit a reluctant one). The ambiguous relationship between Jonson and Mennes and Smith may be explained in part by reference to the demands of the patronage system. Mennes and Smith marked themselves out as Jonsonians when, in the 1620s, the poet's star was waxing. As it began to wane in the 1630s, they switched their allegiance to Massinger, the dependable resident dramatist of the King's Company.

II

While there is a reasonable amount of evidence to build up an account of the origins of the Order of the Fancy, a discussion of the activities of the club requires a degree of circumspect inference. The general tenor of their gatherings can be deduced from biographical fragments, from the Lewis-Warner brief, which points to their engagement in intemperate drinking and nonsense contests, and from the verse associated with the group. Mennes's well-documented taste for puns, anecdotes, bawdy jokes, and self-mockery and his aptitude for mimicry and the competitive composition of humorous verses probably reflects something of the ambience of the order.[14] Massinger's poem to Smith points to the existence of a paternal relationship with the younger poet, and the verse epistles exchanged by members of the group afford an insight into their relations. From these fragments one may perceive the outline of a group of ambitious young malcontents, anxious about their status within society, keen to better themselves within the available social channels, and determined also to seek psychological release from the place in society to which they were consigned. Such release was achieved by the deployment of a variety of "social creativity strategies." Through fraternal bonding, the members of the order created an alternative society that would favor qualities they possessed but which were ignored by society at large. They publicly abused other social groups in order to establish comparisons in which they would appear favorably.[15] They sought to escape from social restrictions through drunkenness, through imagination, and through the use of nonsense.

The Order or Family of the Fancy appears to have been a focus for disgruntled younger sons of gentlemen and aspiring middle-class wits or "alienated intellectuals," all of whom had reason to feel dissatisfied with their families and with their position in society: the only notable exceptions are Suckling and Denham, both of whom were first sons who inherited considerable estates.[16] Mennes, the second son of a family of moderately important although perhaps declining gentry, was forced to pursue a career he probably regarded as demeaning—he was beset by fears of social exclusion. Smith, the son of a very minor gentleman-cleric, was forced, against his temperament, to enter the church. Davenant and Herrick came from the respectable middle classes, but for Davenant at least this was not enough—he entertained fantasies of noble descent.[17] Massinger had aspirations to serve, like his father, in a noble household. Throughout his career as a dramatist he tirelessly petitioned the Herbert family with poems and dedications in the hope of obtaining the administrative post he felt he deserved.[18] All of these men were exceedingly ambitious: Davenant and Suckling made highly successful careers for themselves at court. All of them had reason to feel that their families ought to have provided them with a better living than they actually had. This feeling of being inadequately supported by their own families—or, in the case of younger sons like Mennes, actually done out of an inheritance they deserved—led them to form their own version of a family, the "*Familie of the Fancies*," that could provide them with some of the support they lacked.

There are several ways in which the Family of the Fancy may have served to alleviate the discontents of ambitious young men attempting to make their way in a highly competitive world.[19] In a practical sense it acted as a kind of mutual support group. Its structure established strong fraternal—and paternal—bonds of loyalty between members who sought opportunities to assist one another: Weeks probably pressed for Smith's admission to a benefice in Devon, and Massinger, as the group's "father," gave literary support to the endeavors of his "sons" (in his commendatory poem to Smith's *Innovation*, for example).[20] On a more general level the Family of the Fancy constituted a kind of surrogate family in which privileges of birth and the unjust system of primogeniture were exchanged for a system of intellectual meritocracy in which one stood or fell on one's own abilities. Massinger may have had a paternal role, but it was the wittiest "son" (the member who spoke the best nonsense) not the eldest, who was given the best seat at meetings. While the group thrived on internal competition, the fraternal bonds it established would have served, as they did in the classical sodalities, to *contain* excessive competition between members, who were, after all, seeking much the same channels of preferment (the vitriolic War of the Theatres may illustrate a temporary breakdown of this function).[21] Such bonds had the advantage over real fraternal bonds of being largely free of what Montrose has termed "the material conflicts of kinship."[22] The use of nonsense as a medium of competition helped to prevent such competition from endangering group solidarity by providing a harmless, nonsemantic field in which such urges could be released and nullified.

Despite the superficially subversive quality of the constitution of an alternative society, linked up by strong internal bonds, the Order of the Fancy was less radical than it might at first appear. In structural terms it was highly conservative. In response to their subordination, members of the order did not, as Gerrard Winstanley or John Lilburne would later do, posit a radical vision of a more just society; rather, they established their own version of the very structure that currently ignored them. They established a paternal hierarchy buttressed by fraternal bonds that mimicked those of the family and, in Stuart ideology, the state.[23] Dissent was thus limited by the structure through which it was articulated. This containment of rebelliousness can be traced throughout the activities of the club.

The social conservatism of the order is reflected in its acts of aggression against those perceived as a threat to the traditional social order. The order cemented its internal bonds by acts of violence against outsiders. These acts served both to assert the identity of the group, and to define and constitute it in contradistinction to the abused. Smith recalls this use of violence in a nostalgic epistle to Mennes written during the Interregnum:

> And now I call to mind the tale,
> How mounted in thy nights of ale
> Thou rod'st home duely to thy Den
> On back of resty Cittizen. . . .[24]

That this is an act of class aggression is suggested by the collocation "resty Cittizen." The term "Cittizen" carries a snobbish disdain, emphasized by its position at the close of the couplet. It is a supercilious sneer against mere "citizens"—the bourgeoisie or "middling sort," as opposed to the nobility or the gentry.[25] In this context the adjective "resty" refers to more than just the recalcitrance of Mennes's human steed; it implies a general restyness of a kind frequently associated with the ambitious "middling sort" who were, in the eyes of conservatives, undermining the traditional fabric of society: the "factious citizen" was a stock type of the age.[26] This interpretation is confirmed by a couplet that explains the

significance of the anecdote. With the abolition of monarchical government the world has been turned upside down, and these citizens are now,
unnaturally, in command: "Now 'tis their time, and thou art ore- / Ridden
by them, thou roadst before."[27] Ritual humiliation of this sort may function, as it did in the case of the youth groups discussed by Davis and
Capp, as a social control mechanism.[28] In the case of the order such
humiliations are an extreme method of proclaiming superiority, expressing a need to enact dominance, rather than simply assert it.[29] Such acts
betray an element of anxiety about the social status of those involved.
One recalls that Davenant (a probable member of the order) was actually
from the prosperous middle classes, but was seeking to establish an aristocratic identity at court, and that Mennes and Smith were from families
whose gentle status was marginal and whose status within those families,
as younger sons, was uncomfortable.

In addition to strategies designed to constitute alternative identities,
members of the order also pursued strategies of escape from their actual
identities. Their drinking, nonsense-speaking, and pursuit of fancy all
functioned as means of release from the constraints of reality, from a
world that appeared to undervalue them. Nonsense-speaking and drinking have been connected in this way by Freud. In *Jokes and their Relation
to the Unconscious* Freud depicts nonsense (the free-play of language
without the constraint of meaning) as a source of infantile pleasure that is
engaged in by children with alacrity, but that the developing rational and
critical faculties attempt to quash. In later life, he suggests, a narcotic
stimulus is often required for the release of nonsense, as in the student's
tavern "Bierschewefel": such behavior is a "rebellion against the com-
pulsion of logic and reality."[30] The use of nonsense can also, of course,
be considered in Bakhtinian terms as a "carnivalesque" liberation, as a
temporary suspension of social order and hierarchy.[31] Despite their apparent subversiveness, it is increasingly recognized that such liberations are
fundamentally ambivalent in that they are circumscribed by the special
circumstances that permit them and are thus, to a significant extent, *contained* by society: the uproar of festival days lasts—in theory, at least—
only as long as the festival, which ultimately serves, as a safety valve, to
reinforce social order.[32] The same ambivalence appears to inform the
nonsense of the Order of the Fancy. Nonsense, almost by definition, pro-
hibits a cogent critique of society. But while it might be perceived, in
functional terms, as a safely enclosed arena in which angry young men,
like the members of the order, could release their frustrations in a truly
meaningless and thus unthreatening manner, there are signs that nonsense was used by members of the order, at least on occasion, in a polemical fashion—signs that will be discussed below.[33]

The pursuit of fancy fulfilled a similarly liberating and constraining function for the order as nonsense-speaking and drunkenness. Fancy was regarded in seventeenth-century England as a liberation from reason and order, and some of the central concerns of the group can be inferred from its use of the title "Order of the Fancy." While various uses of the term "fancy" were current, the most common was probably the creative process known, since Coleridge, as the imagination. This sense of the fancy as a faculty appears to have been conflated with other meanings of the term like wit and fantasticalness.[34]

Fancy was a dominant ideal in Caroline aesthetic vocabulary, at least among the elite audiences of the private playhouses that were the breeding ground of the Order of the Fancy. In his study of these audiences, Michael Neill has argued that the fancy was perceived, in something approximating mannerist terms, as "a kind of self-conscious formalism," involving both bravura displays and "the control of emotion by witty self-awareness."[35] Such qualities—the self-conscious (and often apparently arbitrary) shifts of tone, the sense of self-display, and the wry ironic humor—can be seen to inform the verse of Mennes and Smith (discussed at length in the next section). But in the seventeenth century, the faculty of fancy had other, less positive, connotations. It was regarded as a disordering, anarchic force, as a threat to mental, and thus to social and political, order. The lunatics in Middleton and Rowley's *The Changeling* (1622) are presented as creatures who lack the restraining power of reason:

> They act their fantasies in any shapes
> Suiting their present thoughts. . . .
> . . . .
> Sometimes they imitate the beasts and birds,
> Singing, or howling, braying, barking; all
> As their wild fancies prompt'em.[36]

As a threat to social order the fancy was frequently construed in political terms. In James Shirley's masque *The Triumph of Peace* (1634), the character of Fancy (adorned with garishly colored feathers and a pair of bat's wings) presents the antimasques and is driven off by the forces of peace and order.[37] In his unfinished epic "The Civill Warre," Abraham Cowley attributed the outbreak of war to an excess of fancy among Puritan thinkers, while Sir William Davenant registered concern about inspiration for similar reasons in his preface to *Gondibert* (1650). Davenant's dismissal of fancy as a delusion mistaken by young sparks (who lack sober judgement) for true wit might express some embarrassment about his own youthful involvement in the Order of the Fancy.[38]

By assigning value to the faculty of fancy, the order were engaged in a strategy of redefinition.[39] In pre-Romantic psychology the faculty was feared as a threat to order or was, at best, accorded a marginal literary status as a purveyor of pleasing fictions (even here it was usually presented as an immature or feminine faculty, subordinated, in gendered terms, to "manly" judgement). The order's valuation of the fancy thus afforded a sense of status for men who excelled in imaginative copiousness, but who found that this alone was not enough to gain them preferment at court or advancement in the professions. It is perhaps significant in this respect that one of the most important female writers of the age, Margaret Cavendish, duchess of Newcastle, deliberately eschewed a "masculine" style, heavy with judgement, choosing instead to write imaginative (often fantastical) pieces she termed "fancies."[40]

A clearer sense of the nature of the group's concern with fancy may be illustrated by reference to a verse epistle from Mennes or Smith to the cleric John Weeks, in which the parson is urged to employ his imagination to escape his straightened circumstances—to escape from a dismal reality:

> And though you cannot come in state,
> On Camels back, like *Coryat*:
> Imagine that a pack-horse be
> The Camell, in his book you see.
> I know you have a fancy, can
> Conceive your guide a Caravan.[41]

An epistle to Mennes, in which Smith alludes to his own use of the imagination as an escape from reality embodies a degree of fantasticalness. This is mingled, however, with a knowing sense of the delusoriness of such escapism:

> Mee thinkes I fancie Prester *James*
> In Cope envellop't without seames.
> With silke and golde embroydred ore,
> And brestplat like a belt before:
> As Pedler ha's to bear his pack,
> Or Creeple with a childe at's back.[42]

The passage exhibits the fantasticalness that seems to have been a part of the order's conception of the fancy. The outrageously inappropriate similes of the pedlar and the cripple undermine, rather than reinforce, Smith's vision; they have such a bathetic effect that their employment can only be regarded as a self-conscious display of wit, of fantasticalness. Their studied inappropriateness contains a further level of wit, for the vehicle of each simile emphasizes the very problems of penury and discomfort that the poet is attempting to evade. The terms of the escape show it to be a no more than a delusion.

This sense of the limitation of the fancy should warn against interpreting the order's concern with it as a prefigurement of romantic concepts of the transcendental imagination. The Order of the Fancy may have employed the imagination, but it did so in a playful manner that recognized that the faculty was only allowed free rein within a carefully controlled and enclosed arena and without attributing to it the capacity for revealing higher truths. The strictness and clarity with which the fancy is circumscribed in Smith's poem embodies the same containment of rebellion found in the group's structure and its use of nonsense.

III

The preceding pages have attempted to show that the Order of the Fancy was a focus for malcontents of various casts and that it formed an outlet for the frustrations of members about their place in society. The question remains as to whether the discontent of the members of the order represented anything more than a general unease about their position—whether it was an opposition group in a specific, political sense, possessing a clear ideology and agenda.

The very existence of any opposition with this degree of coherence has been called into question by the so-called "revisionist" historians. Earlier historians, such as Zagorin and Stone, sought to explain the political and social tensions that led to civil war in terms of a conflict between ideologically coherent "court" and "country" parties. To simplify the case to the point of travesty, the court was felt to represent sophistication, high church tendencies at home and support for Catholic alliances abroad, while the country stood for old-fashioned Englishness and honesty, for Puritanism at home and an aggressive anti-Catholic foreign policy.[43] "Revisionist" historians like Sharpe have made the important point that the court and the country were contesting ideologies, rather than distinct political parties. They were not mutually exclusive: the ideals of the court and the country could and did coexist in individual minds. Through the work of Sharpe and Smuts, one can see that the court itself was a more diverse group than has previous been acknowledged, involving a wide range of opinions and personal styles.[44] Sharpe and the revisionists have reinterpreted the broad constitutional and political struggles of the early seventeenth century in terms of factionalism—in terms of the competition for power among different factions of courtiers rather than among adherents of clear, ideologically demarcated parties. While these factions may not be interpretable in the tempting terms provided by modern parliamentary democracy, the fact remains that some such factions were possessed of certain shared ideological assumptions.[45] In an influential essay entitled "The Puritan Followers of Henrietta Maria in the 1630s," Smuts has outlined a group he terms "the queen's faction"—a loose and not entirely happy alliance of more or less Puritan peers who sought the support of Charles's French (and staunchly anti-Spanish) queen in the urging of "an aggressive [*broadly pro-Protestant*] foreign policy and an alliance between the crown and great landed families."[46] This is not so far removed from the "country" creed outlined by Zagorin.

There is some evidence to associate members of the Order of the Fancy with members of the queen's faction. The involvement of many members of the order in the Rhé expedition may have been an early expression of the ideals of Protestant internationalism (although there were, as has been suggested, other, more mundane, motives for their involvement, such as their need of Buckingham's patronage). Massinger sought the patronage of the Herbert family, who were at the center of a "loyal," Puritan opposition to what they perceived as a pro-Catholic, pro-Spanish crown policy.[47] Smith is connected with two leaders of the queen's faction, the earls of Holland and Northumberland: he served as chaplain to Holland and was associated with Northumberland through his service of Conway, a close friend of the earl.[48] In the mid-1630s, Davenant was effectively the queen's poet, and Suckling was one of a group of young courtiers from the queen's circle who mounted a reckless plot to spring the earl of Strafford from the Tower in 1641.[49]

The writings of these likely members of the Order of the Fancy exhibit a tendency to criticize the king's policy and court, practices that may be consonant with sympathy with the queen's faction and, to some extent, with a Puritan, country ideology. That such criticism appears even in the work of those writers who are, like Davenant, traditionally regarded simply as "court" poets, is now clearer, thanks to the work of scholars like Butler, Parker, and Sharpe.[50] Philip Massinger appears to have used the public stage as a vehicle for some alarmingly outspoken assessments of royal policy during the 1620s and 1630s: his play *The King and the Subject* contained a passage glancing at arbitrary taxation, which the king himself struck out of the manuscript.[51] William Davenant displayed concern about the potential consequences of the fashionable Platonism he was, as the queen's poet, involved in promoting.[52] Even Sir John Suckling—the archetypal cavalier courtier—takes up a stance of old-fashioned, unaffected Englishness against the continental affectations of the court in his merciless debunking of Platonism and in his adoption of coarse, native modes of literary expression, like the ballad: an adoption that is, in a loose sense, a stance of country opposition to the court.[53] One also finds country values and critiques of the court in Suckling's little-studied plays. As mentioned above, *The Goblins* (1637) attacks the classicism of poets like Jonson and Carew, and *Brennoralt* (before 1641) offers what can only be interpreted as a withering critique of the court's fudging of the First Scots War.[54]

There is not enough evidence to cast the Order of the Fancy as a self-conscious and coherent "opposition" group. Such evidence as there is applies to individuals who may have been members, and not necessarily to the order as a group. The evidence is in many cases ambiguous. Smith did not serve Northumberland but Conway, a character who flitted easily between different factions. Massinger may even have been a Catholic.[55] Davenant, moreover, is an exceptionally mercurial figure. Nor is there evidence that the Order of the Fancy engaged as a group in any of the major social or political crises of the age, either domestic or foreign. It lacked the religious extremism of the earlier fraternities (which may have contained an element of pro-Catholicism), nor does it seem that it was ever subject to government investigation. There is no sense in which the group or its members can be construed as sympathetic to Puritanism, and, despite a degree of antisocial behavior in the order, this does not appear to stem from any deeply radical impulse. In this respect it is worth bearing in mind, despite the anachronism inherent in this observation, that almost all the likely members of the order were staunch supporters of the king during the Civil War.[56] The Order of the Fancy appears to have consisted of angry young men who, by the time war broke out, had little left to be angry about: no longer "alienated" and certainly not potentially revolutionary freethinkers, their careers were well consolidated within the existing regime.[57] Mennes was a successful naval commander; Smith had gained a useful benefice and a patron; Davenant and Suckling had made their names at court.

The Order of the Fancy illustrates the existence of groups of disgruntled younger sons and intellectuals in early Stuart London. Despite its oppositional character, it does not provide evidence for any easy association of such groups with revolutionary Puritanism or even a coherent opposition: indeed, the available historical evidence does not suggest that the Order of the Fancy possessed a coherent political position. The sense is that its members were primarily concerned with their exclusion from positions of power and wealth, rather than with larger political, social, or religious questions. This concern with self-advancement within the available channels of courtly patronage is apparent in the verse of Mennes and Smith. It is this verse that will be examined next.

Part 3
Burlesque and Mock-Poetry

Introduction to Part 3

In this section of the book the early burlesques and mock-poems of Mennes and Smith are considered—those written before the outbreak of the Second Scots War in 1640 brought about the breakdown of the social order, on the continued and stable existence of which (it is argued) such verse was predicated. It is intended to show that this poetry grew out of Mennes and Smith's involvement in the tradition of literary clubbing outlined in the previous chapter and thereby to reassess the literary and social implications of such writing. It is argued that, far from being coarse or subversive, as is generally assumed, the burlesque was a conservative mode employed by cultivated gentlemen and by those who wished to be regarded as such. A careful analysis of the early burlesque verse of Mennes and Smith reveals their commitment to an ideology of courtliness and their opposition to the rising bourgeois ethic of urban commerce.

6
Critical Contexts

The verse of Mennes and Smith is generally regarded as an important source for the burlesque of Samuel Butler.[1] The tendency to view their writing in the light of *Hudibras* has led to some unfortunate misconceptions about their verse and, more generally, about the character and the development of the burlesque mode. Butler's bizarre creation transformed an existing tradition so successfully that no subsequent poem in the tradition could escape its influence. But to base a definition of the burlesque on *Hudibras* is comparable to taking *Hamlet* as the archetype of the Jacobean revenge tragedy.

The burlesque is now generally defined as a genre of imitation or caricature.[2] An imitative definition underlies the major modern studies by Richmond P. Bond and John Jump.[3] Bond offers an elegant four-part classification, defining burlesque as a method of incongruous imitation in which a dignified subject may be debunked by a low style (if a specific text is imitated, the term "travesty" is used; if the incongruity is more general, he adopts the description "Hudibrastic"), or in which an undignified subject may be ludicrously inflated by the application of a high style (again, if there is a particular text involved, it is a "parody"; if not, it is a "mock-poem").[4] But the term "burlesque" did not always possess such a tidy generic definition.

In the early seventeenth century the word "burlesque" was used loosely to describe a comic style or mode rather than a specific genre.[5] The word derived from the Italian "burla," meaning "ridicule, mockery," via the French "burlesque," which Cotgrave translates in his *Dictionarie of the French and English Tongues* (1611) as "Jeasting, or in ieast; not serious; also, mocking, flouting." The earliest English citation offered by the *Oxford English Dictionary* is the definition in Thomas Blount's *Glossographia* (1656): "drolish, merry, pleasant."[6] The adjective "drolish" requires a gloss because it seems at this time to have been synonymous with and to have preceded the term "burlesque." "Drollery" is, for instance, the term Smith employs to describe his style in 1640.[7] It is also used in this manner by Henry Herringman, in his preface to *Musarum Deliciae*,

113

an anthology built around the verse of Mennes, Smith, and their circle: "*Plaine* Poetry *is now disesteem'd, it must be* Drollery *or it will not please*" (sig. A3r). In seventeenth-century usage, "droll" could, substantively, describe a facetious, buffooning fellow, a jester (Cotgrave translates the French "drole" as "a good fellow, boone companion . . . one that cares not which end goes forward, or how the world goes"). The adjectival form "droll" describes the manner of such a fellow and often implies elements of fantasticalness, caricature, and grotesqueness. The term "drollery" was used at this time to describe a style of painting based on just these qualities—a style that might be recognised as that of Brueghel or Callot.[8] Connections between Brueghel, Callot, drollery, and the burlesque were noted by contemporaries: Richard Flecknoe, for instance, noted that "your Burlesque, or Drolling Poem" corresponds to "a *Brughel*, and (in his kinde) *Callot*, representing Grotesque & fantastick figures."[9]

Drollery was clearly a fashionable subject in the later 1630s because *Salmacida Spolia*, the masque prepared by Davenant and Inigo Jones in January 1639/40 includes in its antimasque "*Four grotesques or drollities, in the most fantastical shapes that could be devised*"; Jones's sketches for these figures depict bizarrely dressed, physically deformed, and even obscene figures (one of them is equipped with an enormous erect penis—a feature, it will be recalled, associated with the Titrye-tus) (figure 4).[10] As these examples show, nothing in Blount's definition of burlesque demands imitation in the narrow sense: the term was being used by 1656 to describe a comic spirit, a buffooning, fantastical, even grotesque manner, which did not necessarily involve incongruous imitation—a point that later critics have occasionally noted.[11]

This definition of burlesque as a style or manner was prevalent in seventeenth-century England and also, it has recently been shown, in seventeenth-century France.[12] During the latter part of the century the vogue for incongruous imitations of specific texts, which had spread from Italy into France, crossed the channel along with returning royalist exiles. The new manner (not, perhaps, so very different from the native manner of Mennes and Smith) was embodied in travesties like Charles Cotton's best-selling *Scarronides, or, Virgile Travestie* (1664) and the imitations it spawned.[13] In response to this influx, the term "burlesque" came increasingly to refer to a specific genre of incongruous imitation. One can, of course, point to exceptions that do not observe this chronology,[14] but, broadly speaking, the semantic shift of the term "burlesque" from a broad description of a style to a precise description of an imitative genre mirrors the shift that took place in contemporary France after the success of Scarron's imitative *Virgile Travesti*.[15]

While Bond's classification might therefore be appropriate for his own purpose—that of describing eighteenth-century productions involving

Sketches for *"grotesques or drollities"*, **for** *Salmacida Spolia* **(1639/40), Inigo Jones.** **(Devonshire Collection, Chatsworth. Reproduced by permission of the Chatsworth Settlement Trustees.)**

imitation—it fails to account for many earlier works that were nevertheless regarded as "burlesques" by contemporaries. Even if such poems
meet Bond's criteria, it is anachronistic to use the classification "Hudibrastic" of poems that predate *Hudibras*. These confusions are typified by
the fact that Bond's classification ultimately fails, on his own admission,
to account for *Hudibras* itself—a poem that is, paradoxically, one of the
bases of his classificatory system. One might wish to jettison Bond's system, but it remains difficult to account for *Hudibras* in generic terms as
long as incongruous imitation is taken as the defining feature of burlesque. As Ian Jack points out, to a great extent Butler's poem exhibits
"not incongruity but rather a perfect aptness: the style matches the characters and action."[16]

The changing connotations of the term "burlesque" are mirrored in critical discussions of the mode. Whereas modern critics tend to structure
their discussions of the burlesque around the generic issue of imitation,
earlier commentators usually focused on the question of style and its implications. Sir William Temple offers a brief discussion of the character
and history of burlesque or, as he terms it, "ridicule" in his essay "Upon
Poetry" (1690):

> It began first in Verse with an *Italian* Poem, called *La Secchia Rapita*, was pur-
> sued by *Scarron* in *French* with his *Virgil* Travesty, and in *English* by *Sir John
> Mince*, *Hudibras*, and *Cotton*, and with greater height of *Burlesque* in the
> *English* than, I think, in any other Language. But let the Execution be what it
> will, the Design, the Custom, and Example are very pernicious to Poetry,
> and indeed to all Virtue and Good Qualities among Men, which must be dis-
> heartened by finding how unjustly and undistinguish't they fall under the lash
> of Raillery, and this Vein of Ridiculing the Good as well as the Ill, the Guilty
> and the Innocent together.[17]

While acknowledging that the burlesque may be effective in its own
terms, Temple objects to the style on moral and social grounds. It is an
instrument for indiscriminate ridicule: it makes no distinction between
good and bad, it destroys those things that ought to be celebrated, and its
lack of clear standards undermines its authority to judge of anything.
Underlying this critique is a sense that the style ought to be used for
morally improving satire. It is interesting in this respect that Temple
associates the rise of the style with the adoption by young wits of the
licensed, uncritical mockery of the professional fool. "Ridiculing" was, he
writes, "Encouraged by finding Conversation run so much into the same
Vein, and the Wits in Vogue to take up with that Part of it which was
formerly left to those that were called Fools, and were used in great
Families only to make the Company Laugh."[18] (This point will be considered again.)

Temple's assumption that the burlesque was a style is shared, along with his reservations about it, by many of his contemporaries. In "A Discourse concerning the Original and Progress of Satire" (1693), John Dryden begins his discussion of satiric versification by considering Butler's use of "The sort of verse which is called *burlesque*, consisting of eight syllables, or four feet," which employs double rhymes. While he tersely acknowledges the success of *Hudibras* ("The worth of his poem is too well known to need my commendation, and he is above my censure"), Dryden expresses grave reservations about the burlesque mode.[19] Like Temple, his objections are moral and social:

> The choice of his numbers is suitable enough to his design, as he has managed it; but in any other hand, the shortness of his verse, and the quick returns of rhyme, had debased the dignity of style. And besides, the double rhyme (a necessary companion of burlesque writing) is not so proper for manly satire; for it turns earnest too much to jest, and gives us a boyish kind of pleasure. It tickles awkwardly with a kind of pain, to the best sort of readers: we are pleased ungratefully and, if I may say so, against our liking. We thank him not for giving us that unseasonable delight, when we know he could have given us a better, and more solid. . . . 'Tis, indeed, below so great a master to make use of such a little instrument. But his good sense is perpetually shining through all he writes; it affords us not the time of finding faults.[20]

To Dryden the burlesque style is ungentlemanly, morally insubstantial, and ill mannered: Butler's good sense is apparent in spite of it, although considerable critical acrobatics were required to distance the master from his chosen mode.[21] This view of burlesque as destructive, morally dubious, and vulgar became something of a critical commonplace in late seventeenth-century English criticism, and—it may be added—in that of contemporary France.[22]

II

The anxieties of early critics about the moral or social implications of the burlesque are not entirely absent from recent discussions.[23] Indeed, the most interesting work on burlesque in recent years has, taking its lead from Mikhail Bakhtin, privileged those very elements of vulgarity and moral subversiveness that so distressed seventeenth-century commentators. This subversiveness has been located in the burlesque's tendency to undermine authority and social hierarchy by debunking specific classical texts (in mock-poems and travesties), by shattering the purity of linguistic registers (through its heteroglossic mingling of coarse and elevated diction), and by undermining the status of language as a mode of representation (through playing on the gap between signifier and signified). The burlesque, in this view, is an essentially radical, subversive, and contestatory style.[24] It is no surprise to find such emphasis in studies of the function of burlesque in France, a country in which the relationship of political and linguistic authority was concretized in the foundation by Cardinal Richelieu of the Académie Française. But similar comments are often made with regard to England. Michael McKeon, for instance, has described the mock-heroic as "a profoundly unstable form that flourishes especially in periods of radical cultural crisis."[25]

There are, however, alternative views about the origins and purposes of burlesque and travesty. Bakhtin himself has argued that the parodies and travesties that flourished in classical and medieval times were, "in some cases, just as sanctioned by tradition and just as canonized as their elevated models."[26] The ritual parodying by an institutionally appointed *Terrae Filius* of the ceremonial Act (the public defense of a thesis) at Oxford University in the sixteenth and seventeenth centuries is but one example of the continued presence of such institutionalized subversion in early modern culture, albeit in an attenuated and increasingly threatened form. There were several unsuccessful attempts to suppress the *Terrae Filii* during periods of unusual authoritarianism—first under Laud and again under the Protectorate—and a number of *Filii* were expelled for overstepping their license, but the institution itself survived into the eighteenth century.[27] Examples of the survival of such practices into more recent times might also be provided.[28] Burlesque verse is, it would seem, another example of this survival.

Studies of the burlesque based on seventeenth-century accounts have tended to the view that the burlesque poet transgresses the norms of good usage not out of ignorance or ideological opposition, but in a spirit of playfulness and pleasantry—"par affectation et gentillesse d'esprit," as Gabriel Naudé put it. According to this view the burlesque is not so much subversive as marginal, a diversion rather than an inversion.[29] These polarized responses reflect two different ways of looking at the burlesque and, indeed, at laughter. The chaotic, anarchic laughter of burlesque may be used subversively, but it may equally be (and may derive at root from) a conservative response, designed to legitimate, by playful inversions, an existing social hierarchy.[30] Interpretation of laughter and the burlesque, then, require a careful analysis of its contexts and occasions. But such attention has rarely been paid to English burlesque.

In modern Anglo-American discussions of the burlesque Mennes and Smith frequently figure as footnotes—as the sources of Butler's octosyllabic doggerel style, or as the authors of the earliest English travesties to employ classical models. In 1919, Sturgis E. Leavitt made the important observation that Smith's *Innovation of Penelope and Ulysses* predated

Paul Scarron's French travesties by several years and that subsequent English travesties, such as Cotton's *Scarronides*, owed more to Smith's coarse knockabout style than to Scarron's subtle and incisive wit.[31] Later genealogists of the genre have focused on post-Butlerian traditions and add little to an understanding of the earlier period.[32] There are, however, two notable exceptions, Douglas Bush and David Farley-Hills, both of whom include brief discussions of Mennes and Smith in their broad-ranging accounts of burlesque and travesty. Both attempt to offer explanations for the causes and motives of such works.

In *Mythology and the Renaissance Tradition in English Poetry* (1932), Bush connects the rise of travesty with the Renaissance revival of classical learning, and he is surely right to do so. But one has doubts about his assumption that such travesties express a modernist revolt against the ancients and represent an heroic stance against tyrannical humanist notions of imitation.[33] Does a work that gains comic capital by incongruously dressing Virgil or Ovid in modern clothing necessarily represent a claim for the greater genius of modern poets? The incongruity may easily cut the other way. Recent work on Paul Scarron and Charles Cotton has clarified the extent to which travesty may be a means of celebrating, rather than demolishing, a classical text.[34] Bush's discussion suggests that he does not find, in Smith's travesty at least, any earnest destructiveness: "The poem's chief merit is the light-heartedness characteristic of its author's unclerical muse" (p. 289).

A less genial quality has been found in the verse of Mennes and Smith by David Farley-Hills. In his discussion of burlesque and travesty in *Rochester's Poetry* (1978), Farley-Hills characterizes the habitual style of Mennes and Smith as one of "deriding negativity."[35] He comments on the "boisterous and coarse method" of *The Innovation*, drawing attention to "The excruciatingly bad rhymes, the deliberate use of vulgarisms, the irregularities of metre," which create an atmosphere of gleeful vandalism, and he observes a tendency toward self-mockery through their adoption in verse epistles of "the role of clown" or "comic butt" (pp. 95–96). Farley-Hills regards these procedures as essentially destructive (they offer "no positive viewpoint," no clear alternatives to what is destroyed), and, as such, he considers them typical of the burlesque (pp. 91–92). The burlesque is thus a confused response to a world in which standards for judgement were no longer clear, a world in which the position of the poet in society—and, indeed, that of humanity in the cosmos—was no longer secure, a world that was losing coherence. Despite the fact that the impetus behind most burlesque was pure entertainment, the form teeters on the brink of complete philosophical skepticism (p. 101). It is telling that this definition of burlesque appears in a study of the work of the profoundly skeptical Rochester. One wonders whether, even in Farley-Hills's reading of it, the verse of Mennes and Smith can sustain such assumptions.[36]

Criticism of the burlesque has thus been hampered by the tendency to approach the mode through *Hudibras*, its best-known but most untypical example.[37] The concern here is not with the mode as a whole, but with the verse of Mennes and Smith and, specifically, with the sources, methods, and social purposes of that verse. The next two chapters intend to show that their verse arose out of a tradition of burlesque writing that flourished in the clubs and fraternities of the early seventeenth century. Rather than being negative, skeptical, or subversive, the burlesque mode employed by Mennes and Smith is, at base, deeply conservative in impulse, embodying most of the values it has been supposed to subvert (although this is not to imply that it was never used for subversive purposes). It is argued that far from being a coarse, popular style, burlesque was used by those with pretensions to gentle status as an instrument for establishing gentlemanly credentials. A reading of the verse of Mennes and Smith is offered in which the distorting glass of *Hudibras* is as far as possible removed. This should allow for a more accurate assessment of these early writers and, ultimately, for a deeper understanding of Butler's achievement.

In the following discussion the term "burlesque" is used in its early seventeenth-century sense, to describe a style: "Droll in look, manner or speech; jocular, odd, grotesque." In literary terms this usually involves the use of a number of conventional devices: a rollicking doggerel meter, often, though not always, of octosyllabic quantity; comic double rhymes, or rhymes that fail to work; and infelicitous diction. Works involving incongruous imitation can be adequately described by the phrase "mock-poem" since this is how contemporaries referred to them (both Smith's *Loves of Hero and Leander* and his *Innovation of Penelope and Ulysses* are so defined in their subtitles).[38] Finally, there is no problem in retaining the term "travesty" to describe poems that imitate a particular source. No attempt is made to establish rigid distinctions between works that inflate and those which deflate, since many of the classificatory problems examined derive from the fact that successful works often deploy both strategies.

7

Sources

Although there are classical precedents for the writing of burlesques and travesties (in works like the pseudo-Homeric *Battle of the Frogs and Mice* and Virgil's *Culex*), it is often assumed that Mennes and Smith were the first English poets to write classical travesties and employ octosyllabic doggerel for comic purposes. It will be shown here that a number of English burlesques, mock-poems, and travesties predate those of Mennes and Smith and that a tradition of such writing flourished in the early-seventeenth-century literary clubs.

Native travesties began to appear in England by the end of the sixteenth century in renderings of the tale of *Hero and Leander* by Marlowe, Nashe, and Jonson.[1] Although there is disagreement as to the extent of its effect, there is clearly a burlesque spirit at work in Marlowe's *Hero and Leander* (1598). Marlowe took his cue from the urbane irreverence with which Ovid had handled gods and goddesses, drawing on Ovid's version of the Hero and Leander story in the *Heroides*.[2] But Marlowe went further. Brian Gibbons finds in *Hero and Leander* an increasing tendency towards "the full burlesque"—a tendency manifested in the poet's invention of Neptune's attempt to seduce Leander.[3] Gibbons's argument is contentious, but, whatever Marlowe's intentions, the story of Hero and Leander was subsequently regarded as an appropriate model for travesty—an appropriateness that may reflect the tale's move downmarket, perhaps through the popularizing medium of the street ballad.[4] Nashe includes a coarse prose version of the story as told by Marlowe and Chapman in his *Lenten Stuffe* (1599)—a version that translates the tale into a popular idiom: Hero becomes a homely creature, "a pretty pinckany," while Sestos and Abidos are compared to Yarmouth and Lowestoft. The tale ends with a comic version of Chapman's metamorphoses, the lovers being turned into fish.[5] Jonson takes the reductive modernization of the tale one stage further in the version acted out by puppets in *Bartholomew Fair* (1614). He places the tale in contemporary London and relates it in appalling homespun couplets. Leander, for instance, becomes an apprentice dyer from Puddle Wharf, "*Which place wee'll make bold with, to call it our* Abidus, / *As the Banke-side is our* Sestos; *and let it*

not be deny'd vs."[6] These travesties, brief though they are, predate by
some years the Continental poems that are usually assumed to have been
the source of the form in England—works such as Alessandro Tassoni's
La Secchia Rapita (1622), Giambattista Lalli's *L'Eneide Travestita* (1633),
and Paul Scarron's *Virgile Travesti* (1648).

Alongside classical travesty, both mock-poetry and octosyllabic doggerel flourished in early seventeenth-century England. Much of this work
is associated with the Mermaid and Mitre clubs. The ironic "Panegyricke
Verses" contributed by Coryate's friends to his *Crudities* (1611)—an account of his European perambulation—represent an important, yet
ignored source for the burlesque. Many of the "Panegyricke Verses" employ mock-poetic contrasts between "high" and "low" elements, the most
interesting aspect of which is the temporal dimension, so frequently introduced, by which "high" elements are associated with the classical past and
"low" elements with the present. There are recurrent comic comparisons
between the itinerant Coryate and the epic wanderers Ulysses and
Aeneas.[7] Hugh Holland, for instance, locates his *"parallel betweene Don
Vlysses of* Ithaca *and Don* Coryate *of* Odcombe" in a Plutarchan
tradition.[8] Such comparisons are not, as Bush might argue, satirical
attacks on the classical epic or, as Farley-Hills might suggest, expressions
of epistemological confusion. The allusions to classical heroes serve the
unambiguous purpose of mocking Coryate by their disparity. The style,
structure, and rhetorical strategies of these poems tend toward this end.
The Renaissance notion of decorum demanded that Coryate, the professional buffoon, should be written of in a buffooning manner. The poems
thus deploy a range of ludicrous figures and infelicities for maximum
absurdity. The Latin poem of "Glareanus Vadianus," the most sustained
mock-poem in the collection, opens with an inflated travesty of the beginning of the *Aeneid*:

> Ἀ'ρμα virumque cano, *nostris qui raptus ab oris*
> Armoricosq; *sinus rostratis nauibus intrans,*
> *Multa tulit fecitque miser.* . . .
>
> (sig. g6v)

These opening lines contain the figure of *paronomasia* (punning) and
the vice of *soriasmus* (an absurd mixing of languages). Vadianus puns the
Greek homophone "αρμα"—"burden, load" on the original Latin
"arma," rendering the bathetic opening, "I sing the man and his burden,
who was carried violently from our country to Northern France, where
entering the bays in beaked ships he did much and endured many things,
the wretch." A witty reference to Coryate's seasickness on his crossing

to France is implicit in the alternative meaning of "αρμα"—"Food."[9]
Vadianus enlivens his text with mock-learned footnotes similar to those of
"Mr. *Primrose Silke-worme, student in Gastrologia and Tuff-moccado,*"
which accompany his English contribution (sig. 11r). (Bush could reasonably detect a glance at the pedantic excesses of humanist textual scholarship here.) Thus, for instance, the opening hemistich is falsely glossed:
"*hoc sic Anglice reddendum censent Critici, viz.* (I sing the harmelesse
ma[n]) *vt ille olim, (Oratio pro Archia poeta)* A praier for the Arch-Poet"
(sig. g6v). The hemistich is mistranslated by means of another pun on
"αρμα" with "harmelesse," a kind of *cacozelia* ("vulgar error through an
attempt to seem learned").[10] This misinterpretation is then justified by a
bogus allusion to Cicero's defense of Archias ("Pro Archia Poeta"), the
title of which is also humorously mistranslated (Cicero's argument was
that Archias had done no one any harm). When one reflects on the
learned buffoonery of this poem and on Coryate's adoption of the role of
fool in order to gain preferment, one is close to concurring with Sir William Temple that the origins of burlesque are to be found in the adoption
by wits of the discourse of professional folly.

In addition to mock-poetry, the "Panegyricke Verses" contain a number of pieces written in octosyllabic doggerel. John Hoskyns is responsible for one such poem, which exhibits the qualities generally associated
with the burlesque style: an octosyllabic verse form (with the occasional
addition of an unstressed final syllable), comic double rhymes, and a
grotesque, shambling style that mixes languages and jumbles classical
learning with colloquial informality:

> No more but so, I heard the crie,
> And like an old hound in came I
>
> . . . .
> Greater than the Stymphalides
> That hid the Sunne from *Hercules.*
> And if fames wings chance not to freeze,
> It may passe North ninetie degrees;
>
> . . . .
> When all haue talked, and time hath tried him,
> Yet *Coryate* will be *semper idem.*

(sig. e7)

Hoskyns's use of this style was not fortuitous. It seems that the style was
formalized to some degree and regarded as appropriate for buffoonery
because other contributors also employ it. Hugh Holland's "Epilogue of
the Parallel" is one example, Thomas Bastard's poem is another, and
William Austin's contribution even includes the notorious "inviron"/
"iron" rhyme later used by Butler: "Hee'l guard him selfe if foes inuiron,

/ As well with verses as old yron."[11] It is worth digressing for a moment to consider the origins and purposes of this style.

It seems likely that the origins of this doggerel style can be traced back to a coarse, vernacular tradition of rough-hewn verse that was frequently used for lampoons and broadsides. This tradition may have had its origins in the Latin verse of medieval wandering clerics, but it was fundamentally anticlassical in spirit.[12] Throughout the seventeenth century, octosyllabic meter was regularly employed in such verse.[13] A warning against establishing too rigid a distinction between elite and popular culture appears in the fact that this rustic verse appealed to men of scholarly bent: Skelton's doggerel style probably derives from this tradition, and the humanist scholar Gabriel Harvey wrote poems in this manner in the 1570s.[14] One of these productions, "A Milk Maid's Letter," is a homespun epistle supposedly written by "an honeste cuntrye mayde" in response to "a Miller's vayne letter." It begins:

> My soveraigne joye,
> And pretty pigges nye,
> I receivd yesternight.
> By candlelighte,
> A litle before bedd,
> Your soverayne toye[15]

While this piece is not written in octosyllabics (one of the defining features of this species of doggerel is the lack of any quantitative regularity), it shares with the burlesque the use of forced or double rhymes, a rollicking rhythm, a familiar style, and demotic diction.

It is significant that the poem is a familiar epistle and that it is supposed to be written by "an honeste cuntrye mayde," for by the later sixteenth century the style was employed in octosyllabic verses in order to establish the author's honesty, unaffectedness, and integrity. The derivation of this style from an old-fashioned, country tradition clearly enabled this association; it was felt to be free from urban fashion or courtly duplicity. Nicholas Breton employed the style for the communication of sound moral advice in *Honest Counsaile* (1605), a monologue supposedly delivered by a father to his son.[16] The style was regularly used for this purpose in libels and invectives. The Arundel-Harington Manuscript of Tudor verse contains an anonymous "Copie of a Libell. Written against Bashe," which lambasts the upwardly mobile Edward Bashe by focusing on the hypocrisy, corruption, and gluttony of this "new made squier." The poet takes pains to clarify his procedure and establish his own rustic honesty and indignation: he states that he is to write in "ryding ryme" and explains that the infelicities of style and meter are to be attributed to the extremity of his rage (they are, that is, adjuncts of his chosen style):

> my Witte is dull my speech is plaine
> For I must call a knave a knave
> and though he thinke I raile & rave
> yet when I speake of such a slave
> let him be sure I will not spare
> to ryme a little out of square[17]

Libels in this style were often written against unpopular courtiers, and the duke of Buckingham was a favorite target.[18] The scabrous attack on Buckingham attributed to Alexander Gill gains a deal of force from the apparently unaffected honesty of its homely style, adorned with colloquial (yet pious) oaths:

> And now, just God! I humbly pray,
> That thou will take that slime away,
> That keeps my Sovereign's eyes from viewing
> The things that will be our undoing.
> Then let him hear, good God! the sounds
> As well of men as of his hounds[19]

This glance at the king's obsession with hunting marks the oppositional potency of such a style. It is, in both its origins and its employment, a country mode, standing for unaffected plainness against courtly hypocrisy. Yet Sharpe's warning against associating the rhetoric of the country with a coherent party is well taken here.[20] King James I himself had written a response to an octosyllabic oppositional libel—a "Libell called the Comons teares"—in the same blend of doggerel and homely diction as the assailant, appropriating for himself the values associated with the style.[21]

By the early seventeenth century, this unsophisticated doggerel manner was being employed, often in octosyllabics, as a grotesque, clownish, parodic medium. It is employed, for instance, in such comic productions as the anonymous *Pimlyco. Or, Runne Red-Cap* (1609), a comic work recounting the discovery and reading of a book of Skelton's poems.[22] Ben Jonson, who figures so frequently in the prehistory of *Hudibras*, employs it in *Volpone* for the song of the dwarf, Nano: "Had old Hippocrates, or Galen, / That to their books put med'cines all in."[23] The use of this manner in the ironic panegyrics on Coryate is therefore entirely decorous: it is suitable for familiar banter with a degree of lampooning, and its clownish flavor is appropriate for discussing the "Odcombian" buffoon.

The "Panegyricke Verses" on Coryate were clearly associated with the early seventeenth-century clubs. Many of the contributors were members—men like Hoskyns, Donne, Holland, Brooke, and Martin—while Jonson provided verses that appear elsewhere in the *Crudities*.[24] The involvement of these contributors shows that the burlesque mode, mock-poetry, and octosyllabic doggerel flourished in the early seven-teenth-century clubs. But the style was not exclusive to the clubs, and it is clear that by the early 1620s the burlesque mode and mock-poetry were being widely deployed.

One of the most popular and influential mock-poems of this period was R[obert] S[peed]'s *Counter Scuffle* (1621), a poem that went through no less than nineteen editions by the end of the century.[25] The *Counter Scuffle* employs octosyllabic triplets with intermittent trisyllabic lines and numerous doggerel tricks.[26] It relates the story of a food fight during a lent supper in the Wood Street Counter (a debtor's prison where James Smith once spent some time) in a raucous, mock-heroic style. Its proem places it in a classical tradition of mock-poetry by invoking "those who tell of Mice and Frogges" (an allusion to the pseudo-Homeric *Battle of the Frogs and Mice*).[27] After the participants have resolved their differences the prisonkeeper is discovered cowering under a table, his clothes and codpiece stuffed with food—"Somwhat it held of every thing, / *Smelts, Flounders, Rochets*, and of Ling / A Broad piece"—a passage that may well be a source for Butler's description of Hudibras's breeches, stuffed with victuals.[28]

Speed's poem spawned a number of imitations. One of these was David Lloyd's *Legend of Captaine Iones* (1631), which was popular enough to prompt Lloyd to publish a second part in 1648. Lloyd, like James Smith, was a witty, royalist cleric, and his poem casts an ironic and half-affec-tionate glance at the forms and conventions of popular culture.[29] *Captaine Iones* is a mock-poem that recounts the improbable adventures of its larger-than-life hero, a Welsh braggart (Welshman were then, as now, comic butts), in heroic couplets and in a style that mixes doggerel with bombast, coarseness with classical allusion.[30] "The Invocation" establishes its mock-heroic quality: "I sing thy Armes (*Bellona*,) and the Mans / Whose mighty deeds out-did great *Tamerlane's*."[31] Having been raised on "Mares milk" and "Goats flesh," Jones joins a ship bound for the East Indies. After various improbable adventures, such as the slaugh-ter of the giant "Asdriasdust" (a name adopted, perhaps significantly, by a member of the near-contemporary fraternities) and the conversion of a Jesuit, Jones returns to great applause.[32] Lloyd's poem parodies the tales of derring-do that formed the basis of much contemporary popular literature.[33]

Who read the mock-poems of Speed and Lloyd? Their knockabout humor and commercial success suggests a large, popular audience, but the irony with which popular conventions are pastiched suggests a bid for the sophisticated reader. A copy of *The Counter Scuffle* was one of a number of mock-poems owned by Edward, lord Conway.[34] If such mock-poems were consumed by all sections of society, it should warn against the erection of rigid distinctions between elite and popular culture.[35] In the case of these productions, at least, what distinguishes elite from popular culture is not origin or form, but mode of consumption: a reader like Conway would have read *The Counter Scuffle* in a very different way (perhaps making of it a different text) from the unsophisticated readers who must have made a large proportion of its market. The irony with which popular forms are handled by Speed implies the existence of a sophisticated audience equipped with a developing sense of their own superiority from such forms.[36] Lloyd's ironic adoption of popular forms contrasts markedly with Corbett's naïve adoption of the ballad-monger's gown in Abingdon market.

It seems that during the 1620s the doggerel style was also being used for familiar epistles, and this may indicate a continuation of the tradition that seems to have given rise to the burlesque style—a tradition that may have developed independently of the influence of the clubs. At least one unpublished poem of this sort survives. Its author was Thomas Morton, and it was written from the Netherlands in 1624, where Morton was serving on the English expeditionary force.[37] The fact that members of the Tityre-tu and the Bugle served on these expeditions opens up the possibility of a connection between burlesque epistles and the fraternities, but there is no evidence to confirm such an association. Morton's poem is a response to an epistle by Sir Ferdinando Carey, which had evidently informed Morton of his comfortable condition. Morton's bantering reply exhibits the familiar, shambling style of the early doggerel, with its metrical irregularity (it employs lines ranging between four and six feet) and its appalling rhymes:

> Then thinke what 'tis, your selfe be Arbitratour
> To make your friend's teeth so to runne a-water.
> This cruelty is Like to that of Tantalus
> To name good meate in such a place, as scant a Louse
> Can breake his fast. . . .[38]

At times the poem appears close to the octosyllabic burlesque of the verses on Coryate. It is dated:

> From Breda as I remember
> The three & twentieth of Nouember
> Sixteene hundred, foure & twenty
> Oldest style this Letter sent I.

> (fol. 175r)

But Morton's uneasiness about how to define his style—"my verse, my Ballett / My poetry, my Rime, or what you'le call yt" (fol. 175r)—renders it unlikely that he was aware of following a coherent tradition of such writing, although his dismissiveness should not be taken too literally: it is in part an affectation of gentlemanly unconcern.

This survey is concluded by considering one more source for the tone and verse form popularized in the 1630s by Mennes and Smith. It seems reasonable to imagine that Mennes and Smith were familiar with the fairy poems composed in a spirit of playful competition by Robert Herrick and his circle of Cambridge college friends in the middle 1620s.[39] Mennes and Smith were familiar with Herrick's sack poems, and it has been suggested above that they came into contact with Herrick and members of his circle on the Rhé expedition in 1627, by which time a number of the fairy poems were circulating.[40] The fairy poems are well known and exhibit many features found in earlier travesties and burlesques as well as in the drolling manner of Mennes and Smith: these features include competitive composition, the use of comic octosyllabics with absurd rhymes, the debunking of mythology through the filter of rustic domesticity, the juxtaposition of the charming and the grotesque, and a tone of knowing and playful irony. It is therefore significant that one of these fairy poems ("King Oberon's Apparell") was later printed alongside poems by Mennes and Smith in *Musarum Deliciae*, a collection that was, in broad terms, an anthology of verse associated with the Mennes-Smith circle.[41]

It is clear, then, that when Mennes and Smith adopted the burlesque style and employed it for mock-poetry and epistles in the mid-1630s there was a body of mock-poetry and travesty (the latter on a small scale) and a native tradition of comic doggerel (some of it octosyllabic, some of it epistolary) on which they could draw. This verse had popular origins but flourished in the sophisticated ambience of the Mermaid and Mitre clubs in the 1610s and among Herrick's circle in the 1620s.

8

John Mennes and the Burlesque Verse Epistle

The discovery that burlesque and mock-poetry flourished in the early seventeenth-century clubs gives a new insight into the tradition. The purposes and techniques of this verse, which have previously been rather perplexing, can be readily understood if they are considered in the context of club life. The atmosphere of cultured wit and urbane banter that pervaded the Mermaid and Mitre groups gave rise to the burlesques and mock-poems on the ubiquitous butt, Coryate. It will now be shown that the competitive fantasticalness of the Order of the Fancy and their adoption of the conventions of clubbing gave rise to the mock-poems and burlesques of John Mennes and James Smith. These poems embody the same values that are found in the nonburlesque productions of these poets: a commitment to traditional concepts of order and an espousal of classicism, good-fellowship, and wit. These were the qualities that contemporary readers found in their verse. Mennes, for instance, was praised by his friend Robert Herrick for his "civill, cleane, and circumcised wit, / And for the comely carriage of it"—a delicately resonant set of terms, suggesting qualities of orderliness, seemliness, brevity, neatness, and clarity, rather than the more restricted moral implications of modern usage, although there is probably an element of hortatory irony in Herrick's decision to use terms that carried a moral load, without privileging those implications.[1]

If the Order of the Fancy was more excessive in its behavior, in its pursuit of debauchery, than the earlier clubs, this excessiveness is paralleled by the burlesque verse associated with it. Indeed, the concept of excess might be regarded as the key to this verse, which exhibits a continued attempt to outdo all previous productions of this kind in wit, in absurdity, and in obscenity. This competitive edge, encouraging experiment and innovation, no doubt contributed to the transformation of the burlesque from a mode of pure play into a tool that could fulfill other purposes, like the social satire of Butler. This examination will begin, however, by examining a poem by Mennes that exhibits, in a remarkably pure form, the procedures and purposes of his early burlesque and mock-poetry.

Mennes's epistle "To a friend upon a journey to Epsam Well" is a poem that, at first glance, appears to confirm the view that burlesque and mock-poetry represent a destructive attitude to the classics and a generalized skeptical pessimism. A closer analysis shows that the poem depends upon a belief in the value of classical literature and an optimism about human potential for rational behavior.

The poem is a comic account of a trip to take the medicinal waters of Epsom (a trip that probably took place in 1639 or 1640), and it does so in coarse, doggerel octosyllabics. It is part of a clear genre of burlesque "journey" poems that goes back to Horace's "Journey to Brindisi" (*Satire* 1.5). The burlesque poem on a journey to the wells seems to have been a recognized subgenre of this tradition in the seventeenth century—a subgenre possibly instigated by Mennes's poem.[2] Mennes may have been influenced by such recent efforts as Corbett's "Iter Boreale" (Corbett seems to have had an influence on Smith, and may have been involved in the Mermaid and Mitre groups), but other than the shared burlesque style there are no close parallels.[3] Mennes rather draws directly on Horace, whose satire he would have read at school. The poem is not a close travesty of Horace, since Mennes has his own story to tell, but it establishes a Horatian ethos by employing a self-mocking style and including details that parallel the opening of Horace's satire—a stop at a tavern, a boat journey, and an upset stomach.[4] The upset stomach (a minor inconvenience in Horace) is expanded by Mennes into the comic core of his poem, and the thematic proximity of Mennes's epistle to Smith's undated poem, "Mr. Smith's taking a Purge," suggests that the composition of witty poems on scatological subjects flourished among members of the Order of the Fancy, perhaps as a variant of the oration on the barren theme.

Mennes and his friends had made their journey in order to avail themselves of the purgative properties of the well, and the sight that greets them on arrival offers a grisly confirmation of the efficacy of the waters:

> Close by the Well, you may discerne
> Small shrubs of *Eglantin* and *Fern*,
> Which shew the businesse of the place;
> For here old *Ops* her upper face
> Is yellow, not with heat of Summer,
> But safroniz'd with mortall scumber.
> But then the pity to behold
> Those antient Authors, which of old
> Wrote down for us, Philosophy,
> Physick, Musick, and Poetry,
> Now to no other purpose tend,
> But to defend the fingers end.
> Here lies *Romes Naso* torn and rent,

New reeking from the Fundament:
Galens old rules could not suffice,
Nor yet *Hippocrates* the wise.
Not teaching, how to clense, can doe,
Themselves must come and wipe it too.
Here did lye *Virgil*, there lay *Horace*,
Which newly had wip'd his, or her Arse.
Anacreon reeled too and fro,
Vex'd, that they used his papers so.
And *Tully* with his Offices,
Was forc'd to doe such works as these.[5]

The wit of this passage derives from the assumption that the reader will be struck by its outrageousness rather than by its appropriateness. Whether the modern reader finds it funny or not is irrelevant. It is a piece of innocent comedy, the structure of which establishes a disjunction between the assumed value of the classics and their actual employment. In structure it is akin to Pope's or Dryden's mock-heroic, but it involves none of the tendentiousness of the Augustan poets. The text itself invites no concern that literary or social values are being seriously threatened by this deployment of the classics: it assumes that such values are stable and that this is a comic aberration (it is comic precisely because it is an aberration). The passage is not complicated by a questioning of these values: the allusions to Hippocrates and Galen involve no hint of progressive Paracelsian disdain for classical medical authorities (although Mennes may have been interested in Paracelsian iatrochemistry). The passage is an excuse for the display of wit: the allusion to Cicero, for instance, affords the opportunity for a pun on the defecatory connotation of "offices."

This sense of display informs the central event of the poem, a shitting contest. On arrival at the wells Mennes is informed by the old hermit who stands guard of "The vigour of our Ancestors, / Whose shiting far exceeded ours" (p. 6). Determined not to be outdone, Mennes prepares to fire:

. . . my head I straightway put,
Between my knees, and mounting scut,
At chiefest randome, forty five,
With Lyons face, dung forth I drive,
The ayre's divided, and it flyes,
Like *Draco volans* through the skies.
Or who had seen a Conduit break,
And at the hole with fury reak:
Had he but hither took the Paine
To come, had seen it once againe.

(pp. 6–7)

The event is framed by an epic structure. It is explicitly contrasted with
the Olympic games ("Here no Olympick games they use, / No wrestling
here, Limbs to abuse"; p. 6), it involves an epic-style libation ("The good
old father takes a cup, / When five times washed he fills it up"; p. 5), and
the quoted passage contains an absurd parody of an epic simile (the allusion to a shooting star probably has a specific source in the funeral games
of Virgil's *Aeneid*, in which an arrow shot by Alcestes ignites in mid-air;
5.525–28). While this poem may have influenced Pope (who knew the
work of Mennes), the contest contains none of the sinister undertones of
the pissing contest in *The Dunciad* (2.153–82).[6] It is an exercise in mere
fantasticalness, in grotesque humor, and the resulting tone is festive in an
almost carnivalesque fashion. Like the carnivalesque—and like the joke
in Freud's conception of it—it affords an area of contained release from
social and rational restraints, a fantasy world of pure play (the simile in-
habits the far reaches of absurdity), but it does not transgress those limits.
The epic may be toyed with, but it is not seriously subverted. Indeed, an
endorsement of epic values underlies the comedy, which relies on an incongruity between grand classical models, which are assumed to possess a
continued validity, and the coarse events of the poem.

In this context Mennes's allusion to the theory of universal decay is no
more than an allusion and cannot be treated as a despairing subscription
to any such belief.[7] Even those who wish to interpret the vogue for
travesty as an attack on the ancients would be hard-pressed to argue that
Mennes's success in out-shitting his ancestors is evidence of the superiority of the moderns. If anything, the grotesqueness of the allusion cuts the
other way, implying that this is the only activity at which the moderns are
unparalleled. But the festive comedy of the poem renders such assertions
dubious. Mennes may have believed that his ancestors were stronger,
taller, and in every way superior to him, but this poem does not afford
evidence for such a belief. The idea is deployed in a purely frolic fashion,
as a comic topos for witty improvisation.

One of the most striking things about Mennes's poem is the proximity
of its coarse form, style, and subject matter to the tradition of burlesque
verse outlined in the previous chapter. It seems reasonable to assume that
Mennes came into contact with this tradition through his involvement
with a club that derived from the Mermaid and Mitre groups, with whom
this style was often associated. But the style would have possessed an
added attraction for Mennes because of its presumed congruity with the
manner of his beloved Chaucer. For Chaucer's verse was often prized by
its seventeenth-century admirers (of whom there were few and of whom
Mennes is one of the most notable) for its coarseness and facetiousness,
for its grotesqueness and quaintness. His verse form was regularly mis-
understood by Elizabethan commentators as a rough "riding rhyme"

(Dryden later argued that it was, at times, an octosyllabic meter). To many at this time, the work of the medieval poet was "a kind of drollery," a prototype of the burlesque style.[8]

While the example of Chaucer and the practice of the earlier clubs may account for Mennes's adoption of such a style, there is a rhetorical basis for its employment. The key here is the poem's title: it is an epistle to a friend. The writing of familiar epistles in Latin formed an important part of the humanist ethos, being dinned into boys in the school curriculum. Although Cicero had distinguished letters into intimate and jocular on the one hand and austere and serious on the other, Erasmus applied the divisions of classical rhetoric to epistolary art, adding to the traditional trinity of deliberative, panegyric, and forensic epistles a fourth variety, the familiar epistle, appropriate for the conveying of news, congratulation, commiseration, and so forth.[9] In his letter-writing manual *Modus Conscribendi Epistolas*, Erasmus advocated that the epistle ought to emulate "the mutual conversation of absent friends."[10] He further recommended the employment of commonplaces, proverbs, and fables: the story of Tantalus could, for example, dissuade a man from greed.[11] The use of this very example by Morton in his epistle to Carey reveals the extent to which authors of the period were conversant with such conventions.[12] In *The English Secretorie* (1586), Angel Day followed Erasmus in subdividing the familiar epistle into such categories as narratory or nunciatory (conveying news to distant friends), jocatory (expressing witty conceits), and remunatory (offering thanks for courtesies).[13] An acute awareness of such divisions and subdivisions was common among Renaissance letter writers.[14]

The ideal of the familiar epistle underlies Mennes's use of vulgar subject matter and a coarse style. His epistle might even be classed, in Day's terms, as both narratory and jocatory, for this epistle was a private piece, addressed "To a friend," and was intended for coterie circulation, not for wide dissemination either in manuscript or in printed form: indeed, the paucity of manuscripts of the verse of Mennes and Smith is striking. As Thomas Sprat noted toward the end of the seventeenth century, "In such Letters the Souls of Men should appear undress'd: And in that negligent habit they may be fit to be seen by one or two in a Chamber, but not to go abroad into the Streets."[15] The conversation of close friends might (and, in the Order of the Fancy, did) involve scurrility and laxity (Smith, one recalls, was an inveterate swearer), and the conventions of the familiar epistle recommended a preservation or representation of this conversational style.[16]

The scatological humor of the poem creates an impression of easy intimacy and mutual frankness and perhaps registers a note of disdain for the platonic preciosities popularized by the queen's court. The octosyl-

The Picture of an English Antick **(London, 1646). (By permission of the British Library.)**

labic verse form contributes to this relaxed impression through its apparent carelessness and artlessness: it never aspires to become a formal or public utterance. The "negligent habit" commented upon by Sprat appears also in what might be regarded as the poem's stylistic infelicities; the use of such offbeat rhythms as the "*Horace*"/"her Arse" rhyme (which forces an unusual suppression of the noun), or such half-rhymes as "Offices"/ "works as these." This looseness is not mere ineptitude (it has been seen that Mennes was a competent versifier), nor is it an expression of skepticism about poetry or the order of the universe; it is the literary equivalent of the gentleman's negligent dress, the cavalier's affected insouciance. Contrivedly louche, such devices create a swearing, swaggering, roistering persona that contemporaries would have recognized as "cavalier" in the colloquial sense.[17]

A useful illustration of the kind of personae these devices are designed to present is afforded by a Civil War polemic, which attacks such characters, who were by then a political stereotype. *The Picture of an English Antick* (1646) stresses in its text as in its engraving the flashily "undressed" quality of the cavalier's appearance (figure 5): "A long wasted-dubblet unbuttoned half way," "His breeches unbuttoned half way," "His breeches unhooked, ready to drop off," "His shirt hanging out." It also mentions his adornment with bright flourishes that have a similar purpose to the flamboyant rhymes and absurd similes of Mennes's poem—"His codpeece open, tied at the top with a great bunch of riband."[18] It was not by coincidence that Herrick chose a metaphor of deportment to praise Mennes's verse for its "comely carriage."[19]

Rather than being a piece of considered literary vandalism or an excursion into philosophical pessimism, Mennes's epistle "To a friend upon a journey to Epsam Well" is firmly planted in a tradition of epistolary burlesque, deriving from the literary experiments of the Mermaid and Mitre groups. It is entirely congruent with Mennes's defense of classical traditions and communal pastimes in his poem on the Cotswold Games, and, like most cavalier verse, it is predicated upon a commitment to concepts of ceremony, classicism, good-fellowship, and social order.

9

James Smith and the Mock-Poem

The Loves of Hero and Leander

Although James Smith's earliest surviving mock-poem, *The Loves of Hero and Leander*, was not published until 1651, it almost certainly dates from the early or mid-1630s. It may have involved a parody of Nicholas Lanier's grandiloquent and novel recitative on the subject, which was apparently circulating in manuscript at this time.[1] To the modern reader the poem is obscure in its humor, relentless in its obscenity, and unaccountably long. One wonders why Smith wasted his time composing a poem of over eight hundred lines in order only to make a few dirty jokes. But it is worth trying to understand the poem not only because Smith's contemporaries evidently considered it the acme of wit, buying it in such quantities that it was reprinted at least eleven times by 1705, but also because it occupies something of a seminal position in the history of English travesty and might therefore help in interpreting this problematic genre.[2] While one cannot hope to offer a full explanation of the poem—the point of many of its jokes are probably lost forever—it is possible to offer some general comments about its purposes and techniques.

The Loves of Hero and Leander, like Mennes's epistle, can best be understood as an extended exercise in gratuitous wit. Sir William Temple's connection of the fool with the burlesque is helpful here. The important point about the jester's mockery is, in Temple's view, that it was not critical: it was deployed "only to make the Company Laugh." It was, in Freudian terms, "innocent" rather than "tendentious."[3] The fool might make fun of the master, but his role was only given meaning by his place in a stable hierarchical order. The mockery of the jester is similar to the temporary inversion of carnival or to the comic subplot in Renaissance drama in that it "strengthens rather than weakens the very officials and institutions it attacks."[4] Or this, at least, is what those who appoint jesters or allow carnivals to take place hope it will do. It would be too much to claim that in the early modern period hierarchical containment was strong enough to prohibit the use of such mockery for tendentious purposes, but those known instances of tendentious folly tend to represent

136

aberrations. When Charles I's fool, Archy Armstrong, scoffed at Arch-bishop Laud's failed attempt to introduce the prayer book into Scotland (by enquiring of the prelate "Whea's feule now?"), he was symbolically divested of his office (his coat was pulled over his head) and dis-missed—a clear illustration of the existence of boundaries beyond which a fool was not expected to stray.[5] Such boundaries may have been sur-prisingly broad (it is amazing that Archy was not castigated for celebrat-ing the death of Buckingham), but they did exist.[6] Like the jester and like the comic subplot, Smith's mock-poem invests in the very values it appears to subvert. His poem assumes in its reader good sense, a familiar-ity with the classical and contemporary sources that are humorously altered, a sound grasp of the principles of rhetoric that are wittily flouted, and a commitment to a rational order that is temporarily overturned.

The motives underlying the poem are further illuminated by Temple's comment that the kind of buffoonery that had traditionally been the pro-vince of professional jesters became increasingly adopted by wits. Tem-ple's explanation for this shift is vague: the discourse of folly became fashionable. But, in the case of Coryate, a clear economic motive for such behavior, the need for preferment, has been seen. During the 1620s and 1630s members of the Order of the Fancy were, it is argued, engaged in a similar pursuit, hoping by displays of wit to gain the attention and patron-age of courtiers involved in the Blackfriars milieu (one recalls Smith's claim that he would "gett more by players then by preachinge the word of God"). Smith's *Loves of Hero and Leander* is one such display.[7] Although there is no evidence that it was presented to a prospective pat-ron, it is significant that Edward, Lord Conway, who had a taste for such productions, may well have sent a copy of this poem to his friend, the physician Mayerne.[8] Smith's prologue reveals the context of competition and self-display underlying the poem:

> *The famous Greek and Asian Story,*
> *Of honour'd Male and Female glory.*
> *Know all, I value this rich Gem,*
> *With any piece of* C.J.M.
> *Nay more then so, Ile goe no lesse.*
> *Then any script of friends,* J.S.[9]

Smith's claim that his poem outdoes anything written by Mennes ("C.J.M." presumably stands for Captain John Mennes), or other friends makes it reasonable to posit the existence of a body of verse, similar in its aims and methods, that never found its way into print.

The prologue implies that the poem is to recount the Greek version of the Asian story of Hero and Leander, that of Musaeus the Grammarian. This claim is slightly misleading because Smith's narrative owes less to

Musaeus's text than to the modern version of the story by Christopher Marlowe and George Chapman—and less to this than to his own fancy. Smith takes the framework of his poem from Marlowe and Chapman. On to this he grafts the coarseness of the Nashe and Jonson travesties of the story, the mock-learned notes of Glareanus Vadianus, and the octosyllabic doggerel of Hoskyns and Speed. Even if he was familiar with Contintental travesties like those of Tassoni or Lalli, his poem can be explained entirely by reference to a native tradition.

Smith's poem opens with Leander setting out on a bright spring morning. He has not gone far before he stops to remove a stone from his shoe, whereupon he sings a lewd song, which concludes with what may have been a popular refrain:

> *Oh would I had my Love in Bed,*
> *Though shee were nere so fell;*
> *I'de fright her with my Adders head,*
> *VVntill I made her swell.*
> *Oh, Hero, Hero, pitty me,*
> *With a dildo, dildo, dildo dee.*
>
>   (p. 3)[10]

(The inclusion of this song adds some weight to the notion that the poem involves a debunking of Lanier.) He answers one call of nature by rubbing himself against a tree and another by squatting behind it. Hero, who has witnessed the scene, is most impressed by Leander's considerable endowments and sends her maid to summon him. Unperturbed by the enormous fart he lets fly, she invites him to her tower and, by way of enticement, seduces him. Her maid, meanwhile, is bent on her own gratification (she is assisted here by a branch and a passing weaver). This scene of amorous dalliance is interrupted by the arrival of a servant who takes Hero back to the tower, while Leander returns home (pp. 3–12). Night falls, and Hero gazes from her window, awaiting the approach of her lover. Leander strips off and plunges into the water. The god Neptune, who is swimming in the area, is taken by the young boy's charms and tries to persuade him to stay by offering him large supplies of seafood, in a close parody of Marlowe ("I am as great a God as *Mammon*, / Thou shalt have Ling, Poor John, and Sammon"; pp. 13–18). There then begins a most bizarre subplot. Leander is washed up on the shore and is mistaken by some passing watchmen for a merman. One of the watchmen, attempting to investigate more closely, lodges his nose in Leander's backside. Leander leaps up, breaking off the watchman's nose (pp. 18–21). He rushes to the tower where a night of passion begins, during which he regales his mistress with the tale of the marriage of King Cophetua and the beggar-girl (a favorite story for contemporary ballads, which parodies Marlowe's tale within a tale; pp. 21–29).[11] Having exhausted both his story and himself, he gets up to leave, whereupon the nose flies out of his arse and makes such a thud that Hero's father is awakened. The father rushes into the room while Leander makes for the window. Catching himself momentarily on a hook (it is not difficult to imagine what gets caught), Hero's father strikes at him, but he escapes and falls into the water below. The jealous Neptune immediately transforms him into a crab. The watchmen arrive at the tower and are greeted by Hero's father with the nose stuck in his hatband as a trophy (he imagines he has cut it off the intruder). They give chase to him and are turned into a series of birds (the noseless fellow is transformed into an owl "Because his Face did seem to scowle"). Hero's father goes mad and dies, and the grief-stricken Hero falls down "flat as Flownder, / Her Floodgates ope't and her own water drown'd her." The poem concludes with a comically sententious couplet: "*They both were drown'd, whilst Love and Fate contended; / And thus they both pure Flesh, like pure Fish ended*" (pp. 30–37).

That Smith's poem is not designed to demolish a classical original appears from the fact that it bears little relation to Musaeus's text. There is no festival of Adonis, no meeting in the Temple of Venus, and the action is compressed into a single day: only the swim, the tower, the rendezvous, and the deaths remain.[12] From the Marlowe-Chapman version, Smith retains the Neptune episode and the tale within a tale; while the metamorphoses of the lovers could derive from either Chapman or Nashe.[13] If anything is mocked in the travesty it is the Marlowe-Chapman version. But mockery is the wrong word here: the earlier text is not mocked, it is exceeded. The burlesque aspects of the earlier poem are seized on and exaggerated beyond all proportion.

The relation of Smith's text to Marlowe's is made explicit on its title page, which borrows the epigraph "*Ut Nectar Ingenium*" from the second edition of the Marlowe-Chapman poem (sig. A2r).[14] This epigraph denotes the concern of both poems with wittiness and ingenuity. The Elizabethan epillyon was generally conceived of as a loose narrative on which a series of witticisms, rhetorical effects, and *sententiae* could be displayed.[15] Smith's poem is a coarser, more extreme version of the same phenomenon. What this brief description omits is, in an important sense, the heart of the poem—the series of jokes, puns, proverbs, colloquialisms, comic misapplications, and rhetorical infelicities that motivate it. A number of these travesty the "beauties" of Marlowe and Chapman. The lines "He tooke him to a trusty rock, / And stript him to the ebon nock" are a coarse version of Marlowe's "he stripp'd him to the ivory skin," with a glance at Chapman's "Admired Teras with the ebon thigh."[16] Similarly, the learned *sententiae* that adorn the Marlowe-Chapman version are replaced by commonplace proverbs and idiomatic expressions. When

Leander is turned into a crab, Smith comments that he "made the Proverb, sure 'twas so, / That love must creep where't cannot go" (p. 32). But these reductions do not amount to a full-scale demolition of Marlowe and Chapman. Most of Smith's witticisms have no specific source, and proverbs are not inherently negative: in the Renaissance they were often regarded (by Erasmus, for instance) as embodiments of a living tradition of useful wisdom.[17] Smith uses them with a gently ironic affection, revealing again that developing awareness among the elite of a distinction between their own and popular culture.[18]

The bulk of Smith's humorous devices rely upon the reader's sense of rhetorical or poetic correctness, a sense that is continually thwarted. There is, for instance, no logical purpose for the comic chiasmus, "Her Cheek on hand her Arme on stump, / Her Leg on grasse, on mole-hill rump," or for the meaningless antithesis, "My Father's rich and yet hee's bald" (pp. 4 and 5). The frequent use of bad rhymes is likewise gratuitously comic. It is interesting that Smith deploys the same "inviron" / "iron" rhyme used earlier by Austin and later by Butler: "Then round about they him inviron, / And up they lift their rusty Iron" (p. 33). This sort of playfulness is the literary equivalent of the clown's juggling act.

The Loves of Hero and Leander is an extended collage of proverbs, ballads, idioms, and colloquialisms—a texture derived perhaps from the folk flavor of the fairy poems composed by the Herrick circle.[19] There is barely a line in the poem that does not contain some such expression. The poem has the air of an attempt to create a coarse, rural version of the epyllion: a version that might be related by the unaffected, inarticulate rustic persona implied by its homely doggerel style. Smith's concern to establish such a persona is indicated by the proverbs, idioms, and narratorial asides that appeal to common experience, and by the narrator's frequent admissions that he is not quite in control of his story. Thus, when Leander wipes his arse with his thumb, a marginal note appeals to the shared experience of the reader, "*As it may be Reader thy self hast done*" (p. 4). Similarly, when offering an *effictio* (a head-to-toe description) of Hero, the narrator (like Donne in the "Elegie: To His Mistris Going to Bed") fails to observe the correct order: he begins with her foot and points out his error with embarrassment: "Her foot shee washt, O pretty foot, / (But yet I am not come unto't)" (p. 14). It is in this context that most of the rhetorical infelicities should be considered. The poem's false antitheses and awful rhymes contribute to the characterization of its narrator as an amusing bumpkin.

Despite the depiction of narrator as buffoon, he is not assaulted by authorial satire. The values he embodies are, to a limited extent, celebrated. The opening of the poem, with its account of Leander setting out on a spring morning, illustrates the genial tone of the work:

> *LEANDER* being fresh and gay,
> As is the Leek, or green Popey;
> Upon a morne both cleere and bright,
> When *Phoebus* rose and had bedight
> Himselfe with all his Golden rayes,
> And pretty Birds did pearch on sprayes:
> When Marigolds did spread their leaves,
> And men begin to button sleeves:)
> Then young *Leander* all forlorne,
> As from the Oak drops the Acorne;
> So from his weary Bed he slipt,
> Or like a Schoole-boy newly whipt;
> But with a look as blithe to see,
> As Cherry ripe on top of Tree:
> So, forth he goes and makes no stand,
> With Crab-tree Cudgell in his hand.

(pp. 1–2)

The opening *chronographia* (description of a time) employs a formal framework of similes, the homeliness of which undermine the dignity of the structure. The account of Leander, involving *characterismus* ("description of body or mind") and *effiguration* ("elaborate description of an object or event") is undercut by the vice of *systrophe* ("heaping up of descriptions of a thing without defining it"): the narrator becomes carried away by his similes, which are piled upon one another, hindering the movement of the narrative. Perhaps Smith had in mind an allusion to the self-consciously naïve description of a spring morning in *Pimlyco. Or, Runne a Red Cap* (1609), but inordinately long and complex descriptions of spring were commonplace.[20] The resulting tone is not negative. The vehicles of the similes are positive in a homely, familiar fashion (pretty birds and ripe cherries). The ironic treatment of them—the inept style and the comic inappropriateness (fresh as a leek?)—does not completely undermine this positive quality. The gaucheness entails a charming, comic naïveté that is not unworthy of comparison with Charles Cotton's much-admired "Quatrains."

Despite these similarities, the comparison with Cotton should not be pushed too far. While Cotton probably took his cue for the rural charm of his *Scarronides, or, Virgile Travestie* from Smith, he is consistent in his creation of a rustic narrator and setting, whereas Smith is not. There is, in Smith's poem, no attempt to find rustic equivalents for epic devices in the way that Cotton, for example, converts the Temple of Juno into a fine country church.[21] Even Smith's narratorial persona is not, like Cotton's, consistently employed: there are too many examples of extreme absurdity and fantasticalness that are inconsistent with the narrator's rustic simplicity. The comic business with the watchman's nose is a useful example of this extremity—useful because it also allows the problem of the poem's obscenity to be tackled. This obscenity, whether sexual or excremental, is generally light-hearted—an excuse for the play of wit. The anal humor, for example, is harmless—Leander lets out an embarrassing fart—or absurd—the watchman fixing his nose in Leander's naked backside triggers off a series of farcical actions and affords the excuse for a dreadful simile and a marginal pun (pp. 5 and 30–33):

> *Oh who hath seen an Archer good,
> Poaking for arrow-head with wood;
> So far'd this Clot-pole nose to finde. . . .
>
> **This I commend to thee for a searching Simile.*
>
> (p. 20)

This sort of humor is crude, tasteless, and not very amusing, but it is far removed in tone from the lingering disgust of Swift's deranged Strephon in "The Lady's Dressing Room." Its main point is the strangeness of the simile, which, despite being an appeal to everyday rustic experience, is in this context just too bizarre to be contained by the persona of the plain, honest narrator. This slippage is significant because it underlines the fact that the purpose of the poem is to offer a sustained display of wit, of fancy, and that the narrator's persona is only one, expendable device for achieving this purpose. It would be a violation of the dominant tone of the poem to argue that the narrator is constructed to embody a coherent and genuine popular voice.

The Loves of Hero and Leander was Smith's first mock-poem. It illustrates his use of the doggerel style and mock-poem format for the gratuitous pursuit of wit. An audience, familiar with the earlier versions of the story and conversant with the principles of rhetoric, is invited to applaud the wittiness of the alterations, the extent to which the earlier versions are outdone in burlesque, the aptness of the stylistic errors, and ultimately the copiousness and facility of the poet's fancy. The poem entails neither seriousness nor destruction and is best understood as an example of the kind of competitive fantasticalness encouraged by the Order of the Fancy. Nothing is destroyed in it because nothing is attacked. In his next mock-poem, *The Innovation of Penelope and Ulysses*, Smith would find a target.

The Innovation of Penelope and Ulysses

The Innovation of Penelope and Ulysses, which probably dates from the mid to late 1630s, is Smith's most ambitious mock-poem: it marks a critical moment in his development as a poet. While it is only a fraction of the length of *The Loves of Hero and Leander*, it was regarded as important enough to circulate as a manuscript pamphlet among Smith's associates in the 1630s. Although no copies have survived, the text printed in *Wit Restor'd* seems to derive from such a pamphlet: it is embellished with a separate title page, a dedicatory epistle addressed "*to the Reader*," a preface, and six commendatory poems, including contributions by James Atkins, Philip Massinger, J[ohn] M[ennes], an anonymous author, and, humorously, two by Smith himself.[22] Smith's title and the commendatory poems laud the poem as an innovation, a new kind of writing.[23]

The Innovation is a loose adaptation of the opening epistle of Ovid's *Heroides*, "Penelope Ulixi." Smith's poem is not a close imitation of Ovid's because Penelope's epistle forms only a small part of it. Penelope's letter is compressed to a mere twelve lines (from Ovid's one hundred and fifteen) and is framed by a narrative that outlines the reasons for its composition (Ulysses's absence in the Trojan War) and its supposed consequences (Ulysses's return and a celebratory banquet at which the ballad "The Black-Smith" is sung). The poem is adorned with a series of burlesque footnotes similar in character to, but more sophisticated than, those of *Hero and Leander*.

Modern discussions of the poem have focused on its imitative aspect: it is cited by Bush, for example, as "the first real Travesty."[24] As a travesty, however, the poem is not particularly original. Smith had already attempted this kind of loose improvisation in *Hero and Leander*, a point he makes in his prefatory poem:

> This History deserves a grave translation;
> And if comparisons be free from slanders,
> I say, as well as *Hero* and *Leanders*.

> (p. 148)

The originality of *The Innovation* lies not in its travesty of Ovid, but in its introduction of a tendentious, satiric dimension to what had previously been a playful, innocent mode. The burlesque devices that served in *Hero and Leander* a purely comic purpose are converted to embody stylistic and social misvalues. The coarse style, the absurdities and infelicities, and the narratorial persona are employed in *The Innovation* as satiric tools to mock "*the garish rabble*" of "*pamphleteers*," "*Dunces*," and "*Scriblers*" who have brought the name of poetry into ill repute (pp. 139, 143; sigs. K8, L2).

This satiric purpose is repeatedly and anxiously stressed by Smith and his friends in their prefatory writings. James Atkins relates a fable in which Thalia ("*Guide ore the Comick straynes of poetry*") summons a convocation of all the poets "*That since old* Chaucer *had tane leave to call, | Upon her name in print*" (sig. K8r). Thalia announces her intention to withdraw her protection of poets because of

> *A crue of Scriblers that with brazen face*
> *Prostitute art and worke unto disgrace*
> *My patronage, each calling out on mee*
> *For midwife to his bastard progenie.*
>
> (p. 140; sig. K8v)

Casting her eye over the assembled hordes in search of a champion, "*One to distinguish by a different style, | Dull* Latmus *from Diviner* Pindus *soyle*," Thalia seizes on Smith:

> *Then was this worke, presented to her eare.*
> *She smiled at it, and was pleas d to heare*
> *Dunces so well traduc'd; and by this rule,*
> *Discoverd all that nere were of the schoole*
> *Of noble poesie, and them she threw*
> *Farre from her care and her aquantance too;*
> *Thus were they found and lost, and this the test,*
> *They writ in earnest what's here meant in jest.*
>
> (p. 140; sig. K8v)

The Innovation is to serve as a sort of inverted Arnoldian touchstone, exhibiting in a comic form the vices of bad verse. The danger of this approach is that the poem may be mistaken by the undiscerning for an example of the very verse it attacks. Philip Massinger is especially concerned by this problem, warning that

> . . . *such as read and do not apprehend*
> *And with applause the purpose and the end*
> *Of this neat Poem, in themselves confesse*
> *A dull stupiditie and barrennesse.*
>
> (p. 142)

The implication is that stupidity and barrenness are to be found, in an ironic form, in Smith's poem. Details of the precise stylistic vices that are attacked are enumerated by M[ennes]:

> *Blush, Blush, for shame, yee wood-be-poets all,*
> *Here see your faces, let this glasse recall*
> *Your faults to your remembrance, numbers, rym*
> *Your long parentheses, and verse that clime*
> *Up to the elbow. . . .*
>
> (p. 143)

Inept rhythms, false rhymes, inordinately long digressions, and over-full lines: these are the characteristic devices of the burlesque style. In *The Innovation*, unlike *The Loves of Hero and Leander*, they are put to work for a satiric purpose.

The conversion of the buffooning burlesque style to an instrument for satire is effected through the persona of the poet. By a relatively slight shift of emphasis the plain, homely, unaffected narrator of the earlier burlesque becomes a vain, bombastic, pedantic pot-poet—a poetic enthusiast who mistakes his drunken stupor for a state of inspiration. Smith establishes this persona in "The Epistle Dedicatory:"

> Courteous Reader, I had not gone my full time, when by a sudden flight occasioned by the Beare and Wheel-barrow on the Bank-side, I fell in a travaile, and therefore cannot call this, a timely Issue, but a Mischance, which I must put out to the world to nurse; hoping it will be fostered with the greater care, because of its own innocency. The reasons why the Dedication is so generall, is to avoid Carps in the Fishpond of this world, for now no man may reade it, but must patronize it.
>
> And must protect what he would greet perchance,
> If he were not the Patron with def-iance.
>
> You see here I have much adoe to hold in my muse from her jumping meeter: 'tis time to let slip. (sig. K7)

This depiction of the poet, pregnant with inspiration and barely in control of his wits, is part of a strategic directing of the reader to prevent the poem being mistaken for a purely comic display. The poetic persona even goes as far as to define the style he is adopting: he announces at the end of his preface that his style is to be one of "strong lines," the (by now) old-fashioned style of "elliptical syntax and abstruse thought" associated with poets like Donne (p. 149).[25] The opening lines are a parody of such verse:

> O All ye (1) Cliptick Spirits of the Sphæres
> That have or (2) sense to hear or (3) use of eares,
> And you in number (4) twelve Cælestiall Signes
> That Poets have made use of in their lines,
> And by which men doe know what Seasons good
> To gueld their Bore-Piggs, and let Horses blood;
> List to my dolefull glee, o (5) list I say,
> Unto the complaint of Penelopay.

(1.) The harder the word is, the easier it is to be understood.
(2.) (3.) In varying the use of the senses, the Author shewes himselfe to be in his wits.

(4.) There the Author shewes himselfe to be well versed in the Almanack.
(5.) Being twice repeated, it argues an elegant fancy in the Poet.

(sig. L5r)

The opening line is bombastic and obscure. This obscurity is compounded by the omission of the initial syllable of "ecliptic" (the technique of *aphæresis*). The second line, with its supposedly elegant double application of the concept of sense, is syntactically tortuous to the point of incomprehensibility. The invocation of the celestial houses is also syntactically dubious. The rusticity of the ensuing exempla and the appalling rhyme "I say"/"Penelopay" bring the poet crashing to earth with a gross breach of decorum. In *Hero and Leander* this might have possessed a charming unaffectedness, but in this context of bombastic pretension the effect is destructive. The notes to these lines, unlike the witty asides and appeals to common experience of *Hero and Leander*, compound the poet's pretentiousness by embodying pedantry, obscurity, and false learning. But stylistic misvalues represent only one aspect of Smith's concern.

Smith's attack on strong-lined obscurity and inspirational, "vatic" notions of poetry possesses social dimensions. To a mind like Smith's, trained through the imitation of classical authors, good style was expressive of correct modes of thought. A corollary of this is the belief that bad style is indicative of incorrect modes of thought—of irrationality, or even of madness. During the trial for libel of William Prynne over the *Histriomastix* outrage, for example, the House of Lords were urged to "obserue the particulars and stile" of his writings on the grounds that "the very stile doth declare the intent of the man," which was "to worke a discontent and dislike in the kings people against the Church and government, and a disobedience to our gratious soueraigne the kinge."[26] The persona adopted by Smith in *The Innovation* is significant in this respect. His portrait of the swelling poet, pregnant with inspiration, exhibits a metonymic concern about the religious enthusiasts whose increasing influence in London so disturbed the church authorities in the 1630s.[27] This was a milieu in which Smith had been reluctantly moving as a lecturer in Billingsgate, a parish in the heart of the restive city, and a profession infested with religious radicalism.[28] In assaulting such errors the poem represents the beginnings of a move toward Restoration rationalism (a movement with which cavalier poetry of the Civil War period is often associated).[29] It exhibits many of the social and intellectual concerns of the Restoration theorists of style: the fear of inspiration as a subversive force and the desire to silence nonconformist or vulgar discourse.[30]

An examination of the context of the poem suggests that Smith had in mind a composite target that might be loosely defined as the city: the bourgeois, mercantile metropolis, a center of opposition to crown policy in the 1630s, a hotbed of religious extremism, and the home of "factious Citizens."[31] It is a literary expression of the antagonism toward the "middling sort" that led members of the Order of the Fancy to ride home from their meetings on the backs of "resty" citizens. The commendatory poems afford an orientation here, confirming the direction of Smith's attack. To the anonymous contributor, the scope of the attack is no less than the age itself: "*this stupid age, wherein each mate / That can but ryme, is poet laureat*" (p. 141). James Atkins is a little more specific, singling out John Taylor the Water Poet in the midst of a sweeping censure:

> *But O the rabble*
> *Of pamphleteers even from the court toth' stable,*
> *Knights, and discarded Captaines, with the scribe;*
> *Famous in water-works*

> (sig. K8r)

Taylor is attacked not simply for being a bad poet, but for not being a gentleman. Firstly, he was, as Atkins emphasizes, a mere Thames waterman, and secondly he was a prolific pamphleteer—an exponent of the rising bourgeois medium of print: his collected *Workes* had appeared, in mimicry of Jonson's, in 1630.[32] Despite the apparent broadness of the attack (the court is not excluded from this sketch), Atkins distinguishes between bourgeois hacks who "*Prostitute art*" (not merely by being bad writers but, the prostitution metaphor entails, by reducing art to the level of the marketplace) and those gentlemanly writers "*the schoole / Of noble poesie*," who presumably do not print their works. "M[ennes]" likewise distinguishes Smith and himself from vulgar pens with the snobbish admonition, "*Nor let the garish rabble look a squint, / As though I were one of their tribe in print*" (p. 143). (It is ironic that the only existing text of Mennes's poem is a printed one, which may even have been published with his connivance.) Despite Ben Jonson's attempts to give the printed book the legitimacy of a classic text, an appearance in print was still widely regarded as an unseemly act, not fit for gentlemen or would-be gentlemen.[33] Such attempts notwithstanding, Jonson himself regularly inveighed against the medium, most notably in *The Staple of News* (first performed in 1626). To appear in print was appropriate only for professionals or artisans like John Taylor, who was well aware of the instability of his own position as a mere sculler in a system that equated social with literary values, and who was himself to attack Parliamentarians for their lack of breeding in his Civil War satires.[34]

If one looks back at *The Loves of Hero and Leander*, it seems possible that Smith's poem may have involved some mockery of Taylor and his clumsy style, without this becoming a full-fledged and coherent satiric attack. The persona of the narrator is not far removed from the literary persona of the bluff waterman constructed by Taylor: there may even be some attempt in the poem to render the story as Taylor might do it.[35] There is even more likelihood that *The Innovation* parodies Taylor's crude, lumbering style, and the scholarly footnotes of which he was so fond.[36] But the poem has a broader base. If the context of *The Innovation* is considered, it becomes clear that the poem is a general attack on bourgeois print culture, of which Taylor is only one exponent, for Smith's poem appears to have been a direct response to a recent translation of Ovid's *Heroides*—a translation that exhibits many of the social and literary vices satirized in *The Innovation*.

In 1636 the first new translation of the *Heroides* since that of George Turberville in the previous century was published.[37] Both its author and its circumstances would have antagonized Smith. Its author was the prolific pamphleteer, Wye Saltonstall, who came from a powerful family of London merchants, a family with strong Puritan leanings. Saltonstall himself, after a spell at Oxford and possibly Gray's Inn, tried to eke out a living as a writer of pamphlets, translations, and journalism—a career uncomfortably close to that of Smith himself.[38] In addition to his translation of the *Heroides*, he published versions of Ovid's *Tristia* (1633) and *De Ponto* (1639). His original compositions include *Picturae Loquentes* (1631) (a collection of characters), *Clavis ad Portam* (1634) (an index to Comenius's linguistic textbook, *Porta Linguaram*), a jest-book entitled *A Description of the Times* (1638), and a satire against the Scots, *The Complaint of Time* (1639).[39] It is likely that he was known to Smith since he was an energetic and indiscriminate solicitor of patronage, dedicating works to members of Smith's circle like Sir Kenelm Digby and Sir John Suckling.[40] Despite his attempts to gain their patronage, Saltonstall appears to have been a part of a militantly ascetic Puritan culture very much at odds with the convivial classicism of Suckling and the Order of the Fancy.[41] In *Picturae Loquentes* (1631), for instance, he makes much of the virtue of the solitary, brooding, ascetic "Melancholy Man"—a figure remarkably similar to Milton's "Il Penseroso".[42] In an addition to the 1635 edition of *Picturae Loquentes*, he intervenes in the controversy over the *Declaration of Sports*, alluding with disdain to the Sunday dances, which the *Declaration of Sports* (reissued in 1633) had deemed legal and which Mennes and his circle had so vigorously defended.[43] Saltonstall's militant Puritan milieu is further illustrated by the fact that his translation of the *Heroides* was published, like several of his writings, by the radical bookseller, Michael Sparke, the publisher of Prynne's notorious attack on stage plays, *Histriomastix* (1633).[44] Saltonstall's career and background are therefore typical of Atkins's "*rabble / Of Pamphleteers*" who write for the marketplace. His translation of the *Heroides*, furthermore, exhibits the unlearned mediocrity (both social and literary) and the religious enthusiasm that are satirized in Smith's mock-poem.

Saltonstall makes it clear in his dedication that his translation is aimed at an unlearned audience, for which one might read a bourgeois audience, but Saltonstall retains an upmarket aura by targeting the ladies and gentlewomen of England, who (unlike their husbands) do not have access to the original Latin.[45] His translation itself is a clumsy, long-winded affair. The opening epistle "Penelope to Ulysses" sprawls over one hundred and sixty-eight lines (compared with Ovid's one hundred and fifteen) and exhibits some shoddy metrics and poor rhymes. These are its opening lines:

> My deare *Vlysses*, thy Penelope
> Doth send this Letter to complaine of thee,
> Who dost so long from me unkindly stay,
> Write nothing backe, but come thy selfe away.
> For *Troy* now levell with the ground is layd;
> Which was envy'd by every Grecian mayd. . . .
>
> (p. 2)

It takes four lines for Saltonstall to render Ovid's first couplet. The initial rhyme is graceless, the final line is metrically unsound (forcing an unhappy stress on the first syllable of "envy'd"), and the overall tone is so far from Ovid's urbanity as to approach unintentional burlesque. This problem of decorum derives in part from Ovid himself, who incorporated a mock-heroic dimension into his poem, subverting the traditional picture of Penelope as a paragon of feminine virtue by turning her into something of a homely shrew.[46] Saltonstall may be attempting to recreate this aspect of the poem, but his style is not stable enough to sustain an Ovidian balance between dignity and mockery.

This tonal problem is compounded by Saltonstall's remarkable attempt to translate Ovid's language into a bourgeois idiom, reducing the heroic and stylized Latin to the level of colloquial English. Saltonstall replaces Ovid's rhetorical allusiveness with literal explication. Where Ovid's Penelope employs delicate circumlocution to refer to the manner in which "the son of Menoetius fell in armour not his own" ("Menoetiaden falsis cecidisse sub armis"), Saltonstall's letter writer spells out these allusions: "that brave *Patroclus* clad / In *Vlysses* Armour such ill fortune had" (p. 3).[47] Ovid's grandiloquence is rejected in favor of an attempt to catch the cadences of everyday speech, as in Penelope's lament:

> For I do feare thy fancy loves to rove,
> And that thou hast some Sweet-heart thou dost love.

In forraine Countries; nay, and it may be
That thou dost wooe her by disgracing me,
Telling her that thy Wife's a countrey Ioane,
That knoweth only how to spinne at home.[48]

It is a measure of Saltonstall's success in translating Ovid into a bourgeois idiom that, despite its shortcomings, his version of the *Heroides* was a roaring success, going through eleven editions by 1695.[49]

The likelihood that Smith had Saltonstall in mind as part of a composite target of bourgeois scribblers is given added credibility by the existence of another contemporary translation of the *Heroides* that shares many of Smith's concerns, John Sherburne's *Ovids Heroical Epistles* (1639). Sherburne was a member of a prominent family of Lancashire Catholics.[50] Quite possibly he knew Smith through his brother, Edward (a notable poet in his day). In later life, Edward informed Anthony Wood that in his youth he had been steeped in the literary world of London: "I had . . . the familiar Acquaintance of Tho: May, Tho: Randol, James Shirley, Ro: Herrick and some other Contemporary Witts."[51] Herrick, at least, was a friend of Smith. Even if they were not acquainted, Sherburne's preface reveals a congruity with the values of Smith and his friends: he expresses concern about the dire effects of incompetent and voluminous scribbling, and he is anxious to distance himself from the printed medium in which he appears. He inveighs against the ignorant hacks of "*this* Papirivous *Age, wherein that* Scripturientum Pruritus, *doth every where, so more then abundantly raigne; the swarming issues of whose petulant braines, have induced such a nauseousnes, and utter loathing of the Muses banquets. . . .*" Sherburne is at pains to excuse his own translation on the grounds that it was not written for the marketplace. He classifies it as "*my recreation, my sport*" rather than as a piece of work or labor, and claims that it was published not out of a desire for praise (or, by implication, profit), "*But an humble, and modest hope, of rectifying the wrongs our Author hath sustained through the rude attempts of a too-too busie pen.*"[52] The "*rude attempts*" and the busyness point to the crude and hastily conceived appearance of Saltonstall's translation, while the *synecdoche*, which implies a busy man through his busy pen, suggests, with gentlemanly disdain, the frantic activity of Saltonstall's career in print ("business" as well as "busyness") and involves a sideswipe at Puritanism, the epithet being widely applied to Puritans on account of their devotion to earnest spiritual and economic endeavor.[53] There is almost certainly a specific allusion to Saltonstall here, but the picture is designed to be a stereotypical one.

Sherburne's translation is an attempt to regain control over Ovid's text, an attempt to wrest it from the demystifying, bourgeois clutches of Saltonstall. Sherburne is concerned above all to restore Ovid's dignity and status as a classic author and thereby to reaffirm traditional lines of authority and respect for individual property.[54] He claims to imitate Ovid's characteristic *"sweetnesse"* through *"the genuine, sweet, and fluent statelines of the English* Decasyllable" and to handle Ovid's meaning with *"a respective care."*[55] The extent to which Sherburne actually achieved these aims is not important here;[56] of some pertinence, however, is the contemporary reception of his translation. When John Aubrey was compiling his *Brief Lives* in the last decade of the century, Sherburne's translation was cited by his brother, Sir Edward, as "better . . . than any we have in print."[57] This was pointed praise, for Sherburne's translation had never been reprinted, while Saltonstall's was still going through regular reissues. That Sir Edward's praise involved more than just filial loyalty is revealed in the manuscript notes he compiled on his brother's version of the "Penelope Ulixi" epistle. These annotations begin with a lengthy demonstration that the *Heroides* are so called because they concern heroes, and heroes are defined, on the authority of numerous commentators, as superhuman, semidivine beings.[58] Sherburne would, therefore, expect to find in a translation of the *Heroides* exactly that aura of grandeur and mystique that Saltonstall had been at pains to remove. The commercial success of Saltonstall's version and the failure of Sherburne's to gain more than the praise of a narrow circle of elite readers reveal much about the qualities demanded by an emergent, middle-class market in its versions of the classics.[59]

While Smith's poem is not a full-blown parody of Saltonstall's version of "Penelope Ulixi," its clumsy rhythms, hopeless rhymes, coarse imagery, and comically ignorant footnotes scoff at the milieu of the translation and at the attempt, in particular, to bring the urbane Ovid down to earth—a cardinal sin in a translator, who was (according to the royalist poet Richard Flecknoe) expected "to *indue and put* on *the person of the* Author, as to imagine himself him."[60] One might suggest that there is, in the opening of Smith's version of the letter, a travesty of the opening of Saltonstall's: *"My pretty Duck, my Pigsnie, my* Ulysses, / *Thy poor* Penelope *sends a thousand Kisses"* (p. 151). The style is low (incorporating idiomatic endearments), the rhythm is clumsy (demanding the suppression of the final syllable of Penelope's name), and the rhyming of *"Kisses"* with "Ulysses" is bathetic. In addition to scoffing at such ignorance, Smith quietly implies as his readership an elite community of learned gentlemen who can see exactly where Saltonstall has erred and can appreciate the wit of his own transformations. Smith plays upon such a reader's familiarity with the *Heroides*, even to the extent of undermining his satiric persona. His preface, for example, contains an unannounced allusion to another epistle, "Canace Macareo": the line "My pen in one hand, Pen-knife in the other" (p. 148), travesties Ovid's "dextra tenet calamum, strictum tenet altera ferrum" ("My right hand holds the pen, a drawn blade the other holds").[61] This travesty does not express disrespect for Ovid; its purpose is to suggest the existence of an exclusive body of cultured readers drawn together through an intimate knowledge of the classics and, by implication, shared, gentlemanly values. The bad rhymes, appalling rhythms, and false learning fulfill a similar function. Smith therefore attacks Saltonstall for attempting to demystify Ovid, and his mock-poem represents an attempt to reassert the literary and social authority of his implied readers.

In his use of the frolic devices of mock-poetry for a serious satiric purpose, Smith adds a level of sophistication absent from earlier mock-poetry and travesty and points the way, via Butler's *Hudibras*, toward the full seriousness of Pope's *Dunciad*. One can see in Smith's poetic persona, with his stylistic, intellectual, and social misvalues (bourgeois Puritanism and enthusiasm), the not so distant ancestor of Sir Hudibras. Unlike Pope and like Butler, Smith is not consistent in his satire. At times the impulse toward innocent comedy inherent in the drolling style spills over and weakens the attack—a phenomenon that has long perplexed students of *Hudibras*.[62] Just as the bluff rustic narrator of *Hero and Leander* is dropped on occasions in order to allow a greater play of wit, so the deranged persona of the pot-poet is not consistently maintained. The allusion to another Ovid epistle operates at a level behind the persona, appealing to an exclusive cognoscenti. If one looks back at the poet's dedicatory epistle, it is clear that the "perchance" / "def-iance" rhyme is too awful to be contained by the persona (sig. K7r). It signals the presence of the clown and prevents satiric seriousness from dominating the piece. Similarly, the mock-poem's rustic elements—the homely fare provided at the feast ("Pyes, and Capons, Rabbits, Larkes, and Fruit") and the proverbial asides ("Better once done then never")—have a limitedly positive effect, serving as a homely antidote to the pot-poet's bombast and pedantry (indeed, the satire is directed in part at his attempt to rise above his "natural" level of discourse; pp. 150 and 155). This inconsistency (the wavering between gratuitous buffoonery and the preservation of a satiric mask) is not just ineptness. It is in part the result of a carnivalesque pull toward the pure play for which the drolling style had habitually been employed. But it is also an adjunct of the poem's expression of gentlemanly values. It establishes a tone of confident insouciance, a refusal to regard dunces, hacks, and scribblers as a serious threat to good sense and order. The resulting clash of tones is, nevertheless, frequently confusing for the reader.

In *The Innovation of Penelope and Ulysses*, Smith uses the clowning, burlesque style to represent a matrix of poetic, social, and intellectual vices. His attack is explicitly focused on the culture of print, but this culture is located in a social context of urban, bourgeois mercantilism and religious enthusiasm. At the center of this matrix is the city, London, and its "factious Citizens."[63] Although the empirical evidence for the rise of an urban middle class during the Renaissance may have been severely questioned, the literary evidence examined here suggests that, if the rise of the middle class is a myth, it is, nevertheless, a myth that contemporaries recognized and feared.[64] The City of London is only one of three perspectives presented in the poem—perspectives familiar from contemporary accounts as well as from modern scholarship. Smith's poem mirrors and serves to construct the political tensions of the 1630s in that it revolves around the competing ideologies of court, country, and city. Smith's own position is partially obscured by the irony of his poem. The traditional association of the burlesque style with country values (in the broad sense) and the oppositional tendencies of many members of the Order of the Fancy might lead one to expect a clear alignment with the ideology of the country. It is true that Smith milks the bucolic associations of the burlesque through rustic details and by reconstructing, in a somewhat inconsistent fashion, the narrating bumpkin of *Hero and Leander*. The narrator is a tool for exposing urban vices, and the charming rustic details of the poem act as a corrective for such vices. But Smith does not combine these elements into an explicitly coherent ideology because (as in the earlier poem) he refuses to align himself fully with the narrator's world. He retains a superior, amused detachment from which rustic coarseness is perceived as charming but laughable. Through acts of ironic distancing and through his display of contempt for professional hacks from a posture of gentlemanly amateurism, Smith hints that while he may ironically celebrate rustic simplicity, his true perspective is that of the court. He does not make this perspective explicit, but, in such a context, how could he? He was a minor cleric, perhaps at this point an unemployed one; the attempt would have been absurd.

Smith's poem thus mirrors the social situation of himself and of his club. They aspire toward the court without actually being part of it, and they express disdain for those they perceive or wish to display as social inferiors through acts of aggression both physical (the riding of citizens) and literary (the lampooning of them).[65] These acts express the anxiety of their position, since they serve to construct a distinction that might not otherwise be perceived between themselves and the likes of Saltonstall and Taylor—a distinction between gentlemen and "the middling sort."

Part 4
Later Lives, 1640–1671

Introduction to Part 4

In this section the careers of Mennes and Smith during the Second Scots War, the Civil War, and Interregnum, up until their deaths after the Restoration, are considered. The verse they composed during these periods is examined in some detail, and the continuities and differences between Caroline and Restoration poetic forms are emphasized.

The verse composed by Mennes and Smith during the Civil War and Interregnum reveals, in a refreshingly candid fashion, the responses of two minor gentlemen to the tumultuous events of the age. Mennes and Smith attempted to accommodate the climactic events of these years within established literary practices. The conventions of genres such as the familiar epistle and the mock-poem and of modes such as the burlesque or drolling manner are frequently buckled under the strain of such manipulations. At times these conventions crack, on occasions they are successfully reconstituted; but there is little evidence of gradual generic development in the period. On the contrary, these poems represent a fundamentally disparate, occasionally confused, response to the crises of the period in which can be detected an intermittent fear that the natural order of society has been fundamentally shattered, a dogged refusal to face up to the implications of such change, and an attempt to preserve social and literary practices even in the face of such fears.

10

War with Scotland

I

The Order of the Fancy flourished during the years of Charles I's personal rule—years in which the country enjoyed a peace and prosperity that was, so the royal propaganda never tired of insisting, the envy of Europe. But the calm facade of Stuart rule obscured a host of problems and a cancerous discontent. The ill-defined dissatisfaction of groups like the Order of the Fancy has been considered in the preceding chapters. There were, however, more clearly focused forms of discontent. There was political agitation: large sections of the gentry were aggrieved at the king's attempt to rule without their consent through Parliament. There was religious dissent: moderate Calvinists objected to the rise of Archbishop Laud's personal brand of Arminianism, which (together with the king's refusal to intervene on behalf of the European protestant states) often seemed to be leading England down the highroad to popery. To many minds these problems were one and the same. Sir Cheney Culpeper, a Kentish gentleman of radical political views, saw Stuart England as a battleground "between Protestancy and liberty on the one side & Popery & tiranny on the other," confounding Charles's rule as one of "Ciuill Popery."[1] But it was not discontent in England that brought an end to the king's halcyon years. An unwise decision to foist Laud's Anglican prayerbook on the staunchly Calvinist Scots led to disobedience and, in 1638, to outright rebellion, thus forcing Charles to summon a Parliament and opening the way to war.

When the Scots rose in 1638 the king had no army to quell them, and he lacked the means to raise one. The expeditionary force he gathered to suppress the Scots was very much a do-it-yourself affair, paid for by the loans and private donations of courtiers and noblemen. Suckling and Davenant, now established at court, were quick to assist. Suckling raised a troop of one hundred horsemen, equipping them at his own expense in dazzling outfits: "white doubletts and scarlett breeches, and scarlet coates, hatts, and . . . feathers."[2] Davenant, more modestly, supplied carrier pigeons for the troops.[3] Suckling's doomed attempt to banish disorder with spectacle recalls the last, poignant court masque, Davenant's *Salmacida Spolia*. The contrast between the splendor of his troop and their ignominious conduct in the face of the enemy was the subject of several lampoons—including at least one traditionally attributed to Mennes.[4] The king's support in the north crumbled quickly, and a treaty was hurriedly made. The Scots were paid a handsome due, buying the king time to raise a more substantial force.

Back in London Charles summoned a council of war. Northumberland was given command of the army, and his friend Conway that of the horse.[5] With characteristic vigor Northumberland attempted to reform the army, replacing court toadies with experienced soldiers.[6] Tried and tested commanders were at a premium—especially those who could be relied upon to support a royal intervention that many felt to be against the interests of the reformed religion. Given the priorities of the new regime and its network of clients, it is not surprising that Smith, Mennes, and many members of their circle were shortly given army appointments. On 22 February 1639/40 Mennes was appointed captain of a troop of carbineers, which he was ordered to raise.[7] Suckling was issued with a commission to raise a troop on the same day, and the two men were among the first commanders to reach the rendezvous at Newcastle in late April.[8]

At about this time Smith was appointed as Conway's chaplain, probably through the good offices of his patron, Sir Hugh Pollard.[9] Pollard wrote to Conway on 6 May, informing him that "your Lordship's Chaplayne is heare" and promising to "bringe him downe with me" to Newcastle. But Pollard would not allow a state of national emergency to interfere with his amours: he lingered for a while in London, delayed by a mistress "in an honest way."[10] Smith, however, was anxious to get to Newcastle to join his friends and his new employer. On 2 July, Pollard wrote to Conway from Thirsk in Yorkshire apologizing for his delay and noting that "your chaplain, Mr Smith, impatient of my slow march, though late, hastens to you."[11] Smith hastened, reaching Newcastle in less than three days. On 5 July he sent a verse epistle from Newcastle to two members of his London club, Thomas Pollard and Robert Mering, to inform them of his health and to outline the state of the preparations for war.

James Smith's epistle from Newcastle marks a turning point in the use of the burlesque mode, the doggerel verse form, and the convention of the familiar epistle by members of the Order of the Fancy. In Smith's poem, and in the numerous verse epistles exchanged by Mennes and himself over the next three months, one can witness a series of attempts to incorporate serious matters of state into a mode and genre antithetical to such material. As a familiar epistle, Smith's verse letter of 5 July had to communicate greetings and convey news to friends in an appropriately humorous fashion. For comparison, it may help to recall Mennes's epistle from Epsom Wells, which embodies, in its scatological theme and frolic manner, the familiar epistle as a means of humorous and intimate communication eschewing serious subjects. Smith's epistle attempts to deploy the same drolling mode and epistolary genre, but can hardly (if any news is to be given) avoid the serious subject of what he and the army are doing in Newcastle. The familiar epistle does not readily allow such intrusions, and the result is a marked tension between theme and genre, which gives the poem its peculiarly unstable tone. The opening lines establish the identities of the epistle's recipients and construct an intimate, jocular, and bantering tone of address:

> My hearty commendations first remembred
> To *Tom*, & *Robbin* tall men, and well timberd
> Hoping of both your welfares, and your blisse
> Such as my selfe enjoy'd when I wrote this;
> These are to let you understand and know,
> That love will creepe there where it cannot go[12]

The easy civility of the verse is enhanced by the uncharacteristic use of a relatively stately, decasyllabic line. The tone shifts neatly from the comparative dignity of the opening address to the humorous informality of the second line, with its affectionate diminutives ("*Tom*" and "*Robbin*") and idioms ("tall men and well timberd"). The use of the proverb ("love will creep where it cannot go"; Tilley K49)—a conventional accessory of the Erasmian familiar epistle—helps to establish a sense of shared values and traditions. These values are reinforced in the lines that follow:

> And that each morning I doe drink your healths
> After our Generalls, & the Commonwealths;
> For nothing is more fatall then disorder
> Especially now *Lesly's* on the Border   (p. 54)

These lines effect a substantial shift. While the first line continues to establish the tavern camaraderie and good fellowship that, Smith insists, is preserved even in his absence from his friends, the second line introduces a public dimension to the poem (the general and the state)—a dimension that leads to a registration of concern. The poet's insistence that he drinks the health of his friends only after toasting the general and the commonwealth is presented as a comic qualification rather than a serious endorsement of Stuart notions of hierarchy. The jaunty rhythm and tone of the line assert a half-mocking acknowledgment of the triviality of issues such as the order of toasting. This jauntiness appears to be compounded in the pompous *sententia* that follows it, the resounding claim that "nothing is more fatall then disorder"—a resonance that is emphasized by the heavy stress pattern, which underlines the three key words, and by the extra syllable, which lengthens and draws attention to the line. But the line is given too much weight, and the assertion is too ponderous to be implied by the instance of disorder Smith has in mind. In the line that concludes the couplet that jauntiness and playfulness, embodied in the verse form with its introduction of a comic double rhyme ("disorder"/ "Border"), is threatened by the chilling intrusion of the Scottish general, Leslie. What began as a private epistle, a light-hearted toast to absent friends, is forced to broaden its perspective and take into account public figures and national crisis.

The poem then moves to its most interesting attempt to handle national problems within the generic restrictions of the familiar epistle and the drolling manner:

> That done we gather into *Rankes* and files,
> That a farre off we look like greeat wood piles;
> And then we practise over all our knacks
> With as much ease as men make Almanacks,
> Size all our bulletts to a dram, we hate
> To kill a foe with waste unto the State,
> And for our carriage heere, it hath been such
> Declar't I cannot, but Ile give a touch:
> Here is noe outrage done, not one that Robbs
> Perhaps you think it strange *Tom*, so does *Nobbs*
> But tis as true as steele, for on my word;
> Their worst is drinking Ale, browne as their sword.
>
> (pp. 54–55)

The significant point about these lines, with their celebration of order in the army, is the inappropriateness of the similes. The army looks like a pile of wood—unthreatening and inert. The drill is performed as easily as the writing of almanacs—texts scorned by genteel wits as bogus and vulgar.[13] Smith's expression of surprise about the unprecedented orderliness of the troops (a denial of the well-founded rumors of mutiny and murder in the camps that were currently circulating) becomes a cause for concern when the lines that follow it introduce a more profound dislocation of order in the metaphoric association of swords with ale: such things ought to be associated through the pledging of loyal oaths, not through their rusty appearance.[14] The overriding impression is one of order gone askew, of a world in which linguistic tropes prompt unexpected and undesired associations and in which language itself keeps sliding out of control. As such, it is appropriately unclear how far Smith is using a metaphoric code, and how far he is simply describing a meteorological phenomenon when he signs off with the excuse that "More I could write deare friends, but bad's the weather" (p. 55). Bad weather was to become the classic cavalier code for the Civil War, reducing it to the status of an inevitable but temporary natural phenomenon.[15] Smith delicately encodes in the figurative language of his verse a sense of doubt and misgiving about the preparedness of the English force that is at odds with the poem's tone of jaunty bravura. This disguising of his concern was in part, no doubt, a prudent strategy for avoiding punishment in the case of the interception of his mail (private letters were regularly opened, and discussion of public affairs was prohibited).[16] But it is also a more profound instance of self-censorship: Smith registers concerns, but he does so in terms and in a style that refuses to accede to their pessimistic conclusions. In this way he manages (barely) to fulfill the conventional expectations of the familiar epistle.

His doubts were justified. On 28 August the Scots army crossed into England at Newburn Ford, brushing aside the English force with its untrained, ill-disciplined men, and washing over its feeble fortifications.[17] It is not clear what part, if any, Mennes and Smith played in the battle. They may have been among the band of men left by Conway to defend Newcastle, and they presumably retreated south shortly after the battle, when Newcastle was abandoned, meeting at York in early September.[18]

II

The Newburn debacle left the north of England in the hands of the Scots, who made extravagant demands for money to support their army while negotiations for a settlement were undertaken. In October they demanded £40,000 per month until the conclusion of negotiations.[19] On 8 December Sir John Conyers wrote from York to inform Conway that £20,000 was to be taken to the Scots at Croft Bridge, Durham, and to bemoan the fact that only a handful of captains were discreet enough to be trusted with this mission. It is indicative of Mennes's reputation as a loyal and competent commander that he was chosen by Conyers to convey the money.[20] On 16 December he was instructed to take two troops of Sir Henry Wilmot's regiment of horse to collect the money at Ripon and to take it to the Scots at Croft Bridge.[21] Mennes set off a few days later with about one hundred and forty horsemen. In his report to Conway, Conyers relates an incident prior to Mennes's departure that says much for the latter's astuteness as a leader: "When Captaine Mynce receaued my order to march with two Troopes to convoy the monies, he came presently to me, to tell me that could not be done without monies to discharge the

Quarters; for a whole troope leavinge theire lodginge without payment they would thinke all was lost, & without question some mischance would fall out. . . ."[22] To solve the problem, Conyers ordered Mennes to take twenty-five men from each troop and borrowed £100 to feed them on the journey.

Smith, meanwhile, had returned to London with the disgraced Conway. He seems to have entered into an agreement to provide Mennes with a weekly newsletter on behalf of the Order of the Fancy, for Mennes alludes to those "Who weekly think upon *J. M.*" in a letter to Smith at this time.[23] The first surviving example of these epistles is dated 21 December 1640 from Conway's house in Queen Street, Lincoln's Inn Fields, where Smith was lodging. This epistle is remarkable for its open admission of doubts and tensions that only a few months before had been carefully submerged. The result is a thorough violation of generic conventions.

The opening of the epistle is appropriately Janus-faced, it looks back, with ironic overestimation, on Mennes's poetic triumph, the epistle from Epsom Wells, and contrasts his past effusiveness with the current costiveness of his muse. But this good-natured joshing slides almost imperceptibly into a serious expression of concern:

> Why what (a good year) means my *John*?
> So staunch a Muse as thine ner'e won
> The Grecian prize; how did she earne?
> The bayes she brought from *Epsom* Fearne?
> There teem'd she freely as the hipps,
> The Hermit kist with trembling lipps.
> And can she be thus costive now
> While things are carried (heaven knowes how)[24]

The casual colloquialness of the exclamation "(heaven knowes how)" disguises a serious appeal to providence for terms in which the unprecedented events of 1640 (the open conflict of king and Parliament; the impeachment of leading ministers of church and state) can be accommodated. The text registers an admission of disorder while insisting on the possibility that things can be righted. Thus the contrast established between the current costiveness of Mennes's muse and her past copiousness is presented primarily in geographic rather than temporal terms. It is a contrast between now and there, rather than now and then. The implication of this logical subterfuge is that a mere geographical relocation would resolve the problem (which is in one sense true: Mennes was only in the north because of the Scottish trouble). Again the text refuses to admit the possibility of fundamental, unalterable change.

The admission and denial of problems continues in the following lines:

> While Church and State with fury parch,
> Or zeal as mad as hare in March?
> While birds of *Amsterdam* do flutter
> And stick as close as bread and butter:
> As straw to Jett, or burre to squall,
> Or something else unto a wall.

The seriousness of the problems in church and state introduced in the first three lines is undermined by the increasingly coarse and trivial similes of the next three lines. The poet goes on to employ the meteorological analogy that registers concern about social disorder while reducing it to the status of a natural and temporary event: "Can such a dreadfull tempest be, / And yet not shake the North and thee?" But Smith's ruses are insufficient to keep seriousness at bay or defend against the intrusion of an open rebuke:

> Where is thy sense, of publicke feares?
> Wil't sit unmov'd as Roman Peeres,
> Till some bold Gaule pluck thee by th'beard,
> Thou and thy Muse (I think) are sear'd,
> As I have heard Divines to tell
> The conscience is that's mark't for hell.
>
> (pp. 1–2)

The lines allude to Livy's account of the massacre of the Roman nobles by the invading Gauls (5.41). Despite the superficial humorousness of the allusion and its latent optimism (the Gauls were eventually defeated), Smith admits here a gravity of tone and subject that are alien to the familiar epistle and the drolling style. Smith recognizes this and steps outside the operating convention of the epistle to justify his breach of generic decorum:

> Ah Noble friend, this rough, harsh way
> May pinch where I intended play.
> But blame me not, the present times
> So serious are, that even my Rymes
> In the same hurry rapt, are so,
> Indeed whether I will or no.
> And otherwise my Numbers flie
> Than meant, in spight of Drollerie:
> Tis good to end when words do nipp
> And thus out of their harnesse slipp.
>
> (pp. 1–2)

These are striking lines. Events have forced a violation of generic boundaries and, in the current climate, even language itself cannot be controlled. Smith's harness metaphor lays claim to the existence of a deep, un-spoken turbulence beneath the surface of the verse—a turbulence that should not be expressed in "Drollerie," but that can no longer be com-fortably excluded. In order to prevent another incursion, Smith devotes the remaining lines of the poem to an inordinately long signing-off, a witty quibble on the date of composition and on the locations of ad-dresser and addressee:

> From *London* where the snow hath bin
> As white as milke, and high as shin
> From Viscount *Conwaies* house in street
> Of woman Royall, where we meet:
> The day too cold for wine and Burrage
> The fourth precedent to Plum-porrage
> December moneth, and yeare of grace
> Sixteene hundred and forty to an Ace.
>
> (p. 2)

Only on such trivial matters dare Smith allow his wit a free rein. In this respect it is significant that the epistle has related absolutely nothing by way of concrete news: its silence speaks volumes.

III

Throughout the next two months, Smith remained in London and Mennes in the north. Little is known of Smith's activities. He clearly spent some time at Conway's house and may have gained an additional or alternative employment. In a letter of late January, signed as usual from Conway's house in Queen Street, he alludes to himself as "once of *Lin-colne*-Colledge / But now of Bromely Hall neere Bow," as if this were some sort of institutional association.[25] The same epistle insists on the poet's enforced sobriety ("I must bee sober as the Bee / That often sip-pes, yet doth not stray"), as if this were to be explained by his new posi-tion. An epistle of February 1640/1 is dated from Bromley.[26] He may have been acting as chaplain to the Ferrers family, who seem to have owned the Hall at this time.[27] Whatever his official employment, Smith spent the winter months engaged in the time-honored pursuit of evading creditors. Despite this, he found time for a certain amount of socializing with those of his friends still in London, including Sir Kenelm Digby and Thomas Pope, earl of Downe, and possibly a clerical friend, Dr. Edward Layfield, vicar of All Hallows, Barking.[28]

Mennes, meanwhile, was stranded in the north and desperate to return to London. He wrote to Conway on 1 January 1640/1 pleading for his release on the grounds that he had "a long depending, and concerning cause to be heard in the chequer." But so few officers had remained with the northern troop that he could not be spared. He was forced to remain and make another humiliating journey to the Scots with their payment. Mennes hoped that his loyalty would be rewarded with a suitable promotion. He urged Conway that "since I must be the druge I hope your Lordshipp will thinke me fitt some recompence."[29] He clearly had in mind the post of serjeant major under Henry Wilmot, commander of the Commissary regiment of horse, but, as Smith explained to him later in the month, despite Conway's efforts, Sir John Berkeley was given the post.[30] In the king's army, loyalty and competence were clearly insufficient recommendations for preferment.

Mennes's northern sojourn, however, was not entirely fruitless. By 9 February, he had married a wealthy widow, Jane Anderson of Newcastle, and had set up house with her at York.[31] Jane Anderson was a member of the wealthy Liddell family of Ravensworth Castle in Durham, a prominent family of merchants with whom the king had stayed on his visit to Newcastle in 1639. Other than the pious platitudes of her funeral monument in Nonnington Church, Kent, little is known about her.[32] She was born around 1602; her first husband had been the Newcastle merchant, Robert Anderson, a man with considerable lands and mining interests in the area.[33] Mennes presumably met her in Newcastle, and the death of her husband in early May 1640 must have rendered her an attractive prospect for the impecunious officer.

The newly married Mennes did not remain long in the north. By 13 February, he had gone to London, perhaps in order to hear his exchequer case. But he was back in the north by 21 June, when he was given instructions as commander of Wilmot's commissary regiment—a post he now seemed to hold in an acting capacity, at least. He spent part of the summer inspecting his new estates in Northumberland and Durham. On 4 August, he was ordered to repair to Doncaster, where the king intended to review the northern regiments. One can only guess at Mennes's reaction when, in the middle of August 1641, he received instructions for disbanding the army.[34] This was not the end of hostilities; it was the calm before the storm.

IV

During the winter of 1640–41 Mennes and Smith exchanged a series of around a dozen verse epistles. Smith kept Mennes supplied with news of domestic occurrences and state affairs, while Mennes responded with humorous accounts of his northern exploits. Despite their drolling manner, these epistles are consistent in the uncertainty of their tone, which teeters uneasily between serious reflection and comic relativism. These epistles exhibit frequent, sometimes shocking, breaches of generic decorum and tonal consistency and a typically cavalier tendency to turn away from problems by retreating into fantasy or by grasping at dubious consolations. There are also recurrent registrations of doubts about the present and fears for the future.

The difficulty of preserving an appropriate tone is well illustrated in an epistle of January 1641 in which Smith was forced to inform Mennes of the death of his beloved landlady. A lengthy comic *notatio* establishes her worthy character by outlining the good offices she has performed over the years, but this is debunked at its climax by an ungainly change in direction:

> This Landladie in grave is pent
> Now shedd thy moysture, man of Kent:
> Two rings shee left, for thee tone, to'ther
> For *Andrew* that does call thee brother.
> This dries thy teares that were a brewing;
> Now li'st to newes of State ensuing.[35]

The crunching shift from tongue-in-cheek sentimentality to cynical insouciance goes beyond the bounds of appropriate flippancy. It is a self-consciously vulgar move that reveals an inability to comprehend profound emotions within the operating conventions of the drolling epistle and is symptomatic of a general cavalier incapacity to handle elegiac subjects without sliding off into comic indirection or satiric invective—an incapacity admirably illustrated in John Cleveland's "Elegy on the Archbishop of Canterbury."[36] Even the further shift to a discussion of public affairs fails to provide tonal resolution. The merry-go-round of appointments following the flight of leading government officers is presented, in the manner of "The Fart Censured," as an exercise in untendentious comedy:

> Iudge *Littleton* is made Lord Keeper.
> And feeds on chick and pigeon peeper,
> The kings Attourney, *Sr Iohn Bancks*
> Succeds him, but may spare his thankes
>
> . . . .
> And St *Johns* one that's sharp and wittie
> Is made winde-instrument o'th'Citty.

(pp. 8–9)

Smith's off-hand treatment exhibits the prudent caution of the Renaissance letter writer, but it also reveals a failure of nerve consequent upon confusion about the status of such events. While Smith follows "The Fart Censured" in providing each statesman with a witty tag, he lacks either the information or the confidence to imbue them with the aptness or bite of those of "The Fart" (the quibbling pun of "winde-instrument" for "recorder" is a good—or bad—example of this loss of nerve). This sense of confusion is typified by Smith's mistake: Oliver St. John was actually appointed solicitor general, not recorder of the City.[37] The flippant tone of the lines is not convincing: they lack the requisite arrogance. The adoption of the mode of "The Fart Censured" seems, in itself, to embody a failure—or a refusal—to come to terms with events themselves.[38] Shocking changes can be made to appear less shocking by wrapping them in the mantle of an old comic poem.

Reliance on the directionless, untendentious comedy of "drollery" is a recurrent stratagem of these winter epistles. Refuge is sought in the free play of fancy. Smith imagines himself as a fabulously wealthy "prester *James*," the impecunious Mennes portrays himself as a wandering knight-errant, and Alderman Abell's loss of his monopoly on wine occasions a vision of a fantasyworld of drink and debauchery on a scale worthy of Sir Epicure Mammon.[39] But these imaginative constructs invariably self-destruct in the act of presentation, being destroyed by the very tropes that establish them (Smith's metaphoric undermining of the "prester *James*" vision has been discussed at length above, chapter 5).

In addition to escape through fantasy, Mennes and Smith tend to rely on extended, epic-style similes to provide safe havens for the play of wit. At times these similes threaten to consume entire epistles. This is true of Smith's account of his visit to the Catholic priest, John Goodman. The case of Goodman, condemned by Parliament but reprieved by the king, was a sticking point for financial negotiations in January 1640/1: Parliament refused to vote funds for the northern forces until Goodman was executed.[40] Mennes jokingly asked Smith to intercede with the priest on his behalf: "*What is't for him to hang an houre, / To give an Army strength and power?*"[41] Smith's (presumably fictitious) account of his reception is largely taken over by an extended simile that compares his action on Mennes's behalf to that of the sleeping puppy whose paw is employed by the wily ape to pick chestnuts from the fire. The simile, a miniature narrative or *parabola*, is drawn out at inordinate length (it takes up one third of the epistle) and with a care that its parabolic significance appears not to warrant. Smith's account of the dog awakening, for instance, appears quite gratuitous:

> The Cur awakes, and finds his thumbs
> In paine, but knows not whence it comes,
> He takes it first to be some Cramp,

> And now he spreads, now licks his vamp;
> Both are in vaine, no ease appeares,
> What should he doe? he shakes his eares,
> And hobling on three legs he goes,
> Whining away with aking toes.
>
> (p. 64)

This loving attention to visual detail recalls the association of literary drollery with the genre of grotesque and humorous painting also known as drollery. It is the kind of scene one might expect to find played out in a corner of one of Brueghel's crowded canvases, like the "Netherlandish Proverbs."[42] Unlike the epic simile or the *parabola* proper, Smith's simile is applied to events in only the most cursory fashion. Its detail appears more important than its application, which is dismissed in a curiously off-hand manner: "Not in much better case perhaps, / I might have been to serve thy chaps" (p. 64). Like Smith's excursions into fantasies of wealth and power, the parable represents another form of imaginative escape from the troubled public stage, this time into a scene of simple domesticity—and, like those excursions, the consolation it affords is seriously questioned.

Strategies of consolation are common in these winter epistles, as they were to become in so much cavalier poetry of defeat. Such consolations are not simply escapist or isolationist, like Thomas Carew's advocacy of retreat from the northern troubles in "To my Friend G.N. from Wrest."[43] Many of them directly engage with both national turmoil and personal discomfort, but they do so with the characteristic self-irony of the burlesque mode, which prevents them from achieving a state of untroubled optimism. Mennes's current lack of ready money, for example, (a direct result of the crown's inability to provide regular pay for its northern forces, and a situation apparently not immediately alleviated by Mennes's marriage) is treated by Smith in various ways. Proverbial wisdom is invoked, in Erasmian fashion, to offer commonsensical advice from the perspective of everyday rustic experience:

> There is a Proverb to thy comfort,
> Known, as the ready way to *Rumford*,
> That, when the pot ore fire you heat,
> A Lowse is better then no meat;
> So, in your Pocket by your favour,
> Something, you know, will have some savour.[44]

Classical precedents are offered: a battery of impecunious Roman poets is assembled to mitigate Mennes's current situation and convince him that poetry need not be dependent upon "good Wine and ease." Elsewhere, stoic self-reliance and vegetarianism are invoked in a pseudo-Horatian paean in praise of country living:

> O happy Captain, that may'st houze
> In Quarter free, and uncheckt brouze
> On teeming hedge, when purse is light,
> Or on the wholsom Sallat bite:[45]

Despite a recent attempt to emphasize the centrality of stoicism in cavalier poetry, such consolations in Smith's poetry are tried on and flippantly discarded.[46] The drolling tone of the verse inhibits seriousness, as do the terms in which such consolations are embodied. In the Horatian allusion (a reference to the second *Epode*), Mennes is envied for being able to browse at a hedgerow, like a goat. Even the invocation of a "wholsom Sallat" (to modern eyes a less equivocal notion) embodies an ironic glance at the growing fashion for salads from the perspective of a traditional gentlemanly suspicion of vegetables as a vulgar dish.[47]

Escapism and consolation were by no means the only responses of Mennes and Smith during the winter of 1640–41. Doubts and fears about the times were regularly, if obliquely registered. Such registrations range from the vague foreboding of Mennes's allusion to the month of January staring, "with face double," "on the pass'd, and coming trouble," to more specific admissions of the existence of disorder.[48] In an epistle of late December 1640, Smith responds to Mennes's humiliating journey to the Scots with their payoff by means of a natural analogy:

> So sillie Bee with wearie thighes
> Home to her master's storehouse hie's;
> Whence (her rich fraught unladed) shee
> Againe returne's an emptie Bee.[49]

In the Renaissance the image of the bee bringing honey to the hive was a commonplace for public-spirited endeavor, and the beehive was frequently invoked as a model of the perfect commonweal.[50] The appearance of such an analogy seems, therefore, to offer the promise of consolation for Mennes's predicament by reference to a validating natural order. But the analogy is misshapen and refuses to deliver this payoff. Its internal logic subverts the traditional association of the hive with commonweal and insists instead that this bee would have no benefit from her labors. Instead of going out empty and returning laden with food, she goes out laden and "returns" empty, carrying her honey to an alien "storehouse"—a clear inversion of the natural order. The application of the analogy prompts a recognition of a miscarriage of nature in the state. The simile demands that Mennes is a bee and that his master is Scotland, whereas the reader recognizes that his master *ought* to be King Charles. This disjunction underlines a parallel disjunction between ideal and actual order in the state: in the Britain of 1640, the Scots had effectively become masters of the king. The analogy thus fails to provide consolation, implying instead that relations between the two nations represent a natural aberration. While such a figure registers disorder, it is not entirely bleak, for it also insists on the possible restoration of order through a potential correction of the analogy.

V

The spring and summer of 1641 witnessed a shift in the mood of the nation from confusion to confrontation, causing a rapid escalation of tension. Typical of this shift (and instrumental in effecting it) was the creation in late March of a secret discussion group by a number of army officers intent on assisting the king to secure money (and possibly Strafford's safety) through the threat of military action. This group was formed, with the king's connivance, by a merger of two separate cliques. It involved many of the courtiers who had earlier been members of the clubs of Caroline London: its members were Henry Wilmot and Hugh Pollard (members of William Murray's group), George Goring (who may have been in Peter Apsley's group), Suckling and Davenant (possibly members of the Order of the Fancy), and others, including Henry Percy, Henry Jermyn, Daniel O'Neill, and William Ashburnham.[51] It is impossible to establish exactly what was discussed at the group's meetings. According to Pollard there was little agreement between the more moderate members like himself and extremists like Suckling and Jermyn with their "wilde extravagant discourses."[52] News of a horrid plot, involving papist forces and designed, amongst other things, to free the earl of Strafford (who was currently awaiting execution) broke in early May. Suckling and several others fled the country—an action that appeared to confirm the worst suspicions of those who lived in fear of a papist insurrection. The officers who remained were hauled in and interrogated by a Parliamentary committee.

It is not clear whether James Smith was involved with his patron, Hugh Pollard, in the plot. He prudently displays incredulous ignorance of it in his epistle to Mennes of June 1641. This epistle marks a notable shift from the escapism and barely balanced tone of the winter months, to an increased assuredness. The epistle successfully incorporates serious matters of state without forfeiting the lighthearted, drolling manner of the familiar epistle, the conventions of which are in some sense redefined in the process. Smith foregoes strategies of escape and attempts to make comedy out of actual events. He makes great play, for instance, of the predicament of Davenant. Davenant was apprehended at Dover after his attempt to escape to France was foiled on account of his distinctive appearance (he lacked a nose, having contracted syphilis some years earlier):

> You heard of late, what Chevaliers
> (Who durst not tarry for their eares)
> Prescribed were, for such a plot
> As might have ruin'd Heaven knows what:
> Suspected for the same's *Will D'avenant*,
> Whether he have been in't, or have not,
> He is committed, and, like Sloven,
> Lolls on his Bed, in garden Coven.
> He had been rack'd, as I am told,
> But that his body would not hold.
> Soon as in *Kent* they saw the Bard,
> (As to say truth, it is not hard,
> For *Will* has in his face, the flawes
> Of wounds receiv'd in Countreys cause:)[53]

These are exuberant lines, which succeed in handling Davenant's predicament with exactly the right blend of generous humor and witty detachment.

Smith's poem also illustrates the extent to which the ideological polarities of 1642 were already taking shape. He invests the traditionally neutral term "Chevalier" with the positive, partisan connotation one finds in later royalist propaganda.[54] Elsewhere in the poem, his reflection on Mennes's marriage ceremony from the ironic perspective of a Puritan enthusiast illustrates the extent to which the apparatus of cultural conflict was already firmly in place:

> Alas poor Soul, thy Marriage vow
> Is as the Rites, unhallowed now,
> Sleighted by Man, ordain'd by Bishop,
> Not one, whom zeal hath scar'd from his shop.
> The Ring prophane, and Surplice foule,
> No better than a Friers Cowl,
> With Poesie vile, and at thy Table
> Fidlers, that were abhominable,
> Who sung, perhaps, a song of *Hymen*,
> And not a Psalm to edifie men.[55]

Smith's Puritan persona perceives an unholy alliance between Laudian church ceremony and pagan ritual—an alliance epitomized in the singing of a pagan song during a Christian marriage ceremony. This blending of classical and Christian traditions was an integral part of the cavalier ethic and had been a religio-political issue of great concern to those associated with the Order of the Fancy since the 1630s. Herrick had composed a pagan "Porch-verse" for the wedding of two Devon parishioners in 1639, and earlier in the decade Mennes and others had celebrated Robert Dover's blend of native and classical traditions in the Cotswold Games.[56] The Puritan persona, with his Hebraism and his celebration of zealous lower-class preachers, personifies the threat posed by Puritan precianism to this royalist myth of a timeless "merrie England." So Smith's poem reflects an ideological conflict that was becoming increasingly explicit as the attack on episcopacy escalated in the months prior to the outbreak of war.

The whereabouts of Mennes and Smith during the summer and winter of 1641 are not known for certain. It seems safe to assume, however, that after the disbanding of the army, Mennes spent some time with his wife in the north. Smith presumably divided his time between Devonshire and London, where there may have been meetings of those members of the Order of the Fancy who were still in the city. He was certainly in Devonshire in mid-October 1641, when he wrote to Lord Conway to bemoan his patron's failure to acquire some payment due to him—presumably the expenses for his trip to the north in 1640. After offering fulsome thanks for his endeavors on Smith's behalf in terms designed to appeal to the nobleman's interest in alchemy, Smith offers a mordant sketch of an increasingly factious Devon: "all our bussines is to pray, and pay, and our cheifest farmers have their loynes girt with a divinity Circingle, and beginne to bristle vp for a Lay=Eldershipp. But let the tymes worke."[57] The reliance on time to heal social problems was to become one of the characteristic strategies of royalists during the Civil War years: it reveals a deep-rooted belief in the naturalness of—if not a clear constitutional definition of—monarchical rule and a confidence that any divergence from it must only be temporary. This belief was to be sorely tested in the years to come.

VI

The emphasis placed here on the evasions, confusions, and concessions inherent in the epistles of 1640 and 1641 should not be pushed too far. What emerges most strongly from these epistles is not despair, but a concerted attempt to retain a posture of arrogant and assured defiance in spite of confusion, personal adversity, and national crisis. Concern with this posture is typified by the final couplet of Smith's poem on the marriage of Mennes. Noting that this is "The day that Bishops, Deans and Prebends, / And all their friends, wear mourning Ribbands" (the eve of the Parliamentary vote to abolish episcopacy) Smith signs off with a flourish:

> If this day smile, they'l ride in Coaches,
> And, if it frown, then *Bonas Noches*.[58]

The recourse to Spanish for that excruciating final rhyme conveys a gentlemanly poise, a cavalier insouciance, and a devil-may-care detachment in the face of potential disaster. The preservation of this tone, the presentation of an unruffled "face," was to become an important weapon in the cavalier armory—eventually, indeed, the only weapon.

11

Civil War

During the winter of 1641 the possibility of agreement between king and Parliament receded. While the queen urged a policy of no compromise, the king negotiated a series of politic concessions in order to strengthen his hand for a direct confrontation with his opponents. Throughout the winter the initiative rested with the sly Parliamentary leader John Pym, whose orchestration of events undermined the king's popular and Parliamentary support. Pym's handling of both city and Parliament was so dextrous that, after a bungled attempt to make an armed arrest of certain key members of Parliament for treason (a group that included Pym himself), the king was forced to flee London, forfeiting control of the capital and his authority in Parliament.

The royal party repaired to Hampton Court, moving south to Dover in late February where a small squadron of ships met to take the queen and Princess Mary to Holland: there they would pawn the crown jewels to raise money for arms and would solicit foreign support. John Mennes was one of the naval officers to whom this delicate maneuver was entrusted, and he was knighted for the occasion.[1] The knighthood ceremony must have been a subdued affair, lightened by the contribution of a much-needed jester. It has been said that the obvious devotion of Mennes and his crew gave the king an ill-founded confidence in the temper of the Navy.[2] There is probably some truth in this, although the king's faith in the Navy was already firmly, if unwisely, founded. He simply could not imagine that the force of which he was so proud, and on which he had lavished so much of his attention over the previous decade, could be anything but loyal. How wrong he was.[3]

The Navy was the most substantial military force in the country and possession of it was critical for both sides since it controlled trade and contacts with Europe. Despite the king's relaxed and dilatory attitude, in the struggle for control of the Navy, Parliament had the edge: not only were the bulk of naval officers unsympathetic to the current regime, but the main naval depot, Chatham, was within easy reach of the capital. In early March 1641/2, the summer fleet was announced by the House of Commons. Mennes was given command of a ship and was appointed rear admiral.[4] Parliament as usual took the initiative by requesting Northumberland, still Lord Admiral, to entrust the fleet to one of their sympathizers, the earl of Warwick. The inscrutable Northumberland concurred, to the chagrin of the king, who desired that Sir John Pennington should, as usual, be given the command. But other than removing Northumberland (an unwise move, Charles felt, given the lack of a competent replacement), there was little he could do. He foolishly urged his most valued officers to refuse to serve in the fleet, thus excluding from it what little support he might have commanded.[5]

For several months Mennes busied himself with pressing men and making short patrols in the channel, until, in early July, the king resolved at last to remove the unreliable Northumberland from his command and appoint the dependable Pennington in his stead. Pennington, who was then with the court at York, was an old man and did not relish the dangerous journey south, fearing that he might be recognized and the scheme discovered. Rather than send Pennington down to the fleet, which was then in the Downs, the king sent letters to each captain, informing them of the removal of Northumberland and Warwick and ordering them to rendezvous at Bridlington Bay on the Yorkshire coast, where they would be given new instructions. After some deliberation, however, Pennington decided to travel down to the fleet himself, sending supplementary instructions ordering the fleet to attend his arrival. It may have been that additional secret instructions were sent to Mennes, ordering him to depose Warwick and bring the fleet to the king—in later life he implied as much to his colleague, Samuel Pepys.[6] Pennington's hesitation was a fatal blunder. Parliament responded swiftly, appointing Warwick admiral. Given the Navy's long-standing discontent with court policy, and the fact that Warwick was already in command, most officers accepted the Parliamentary ordinance. It was thus that the king lost the Navy.[7]

On 2 July Warwick instructed his officers to attend a meeting on board his ship, the *James*, where he announced his intention to continue as admiral under the authority of Parliament.[8] There are various accounts of the events of that day, the most reliable of which is probably Warwick's own report to Parliament:

> having declared to my Captaines at the Counsell of Warre, all of them unanimously and cheerefully tooke the same resolution excepting five, which was the Reare Admirall [*Mennes*], Captaine *Fogge*, Captaine *Burley*, Captaine *Slingsby* and Captaine *Wake*: All which five refused to come upon my Summons, as having no authority over them, and got together round that night to make their defence against mee, onely Captaine *Burley* came in and submitted to me,

whereupon in the morning I weighed my Anchors, and caused the rest of my Ships so to doe, and came to an Anchor round about them, and besieged them, and when I had made all things ready I summoned them, Sir *Iohn Mennes* and Captaine *Fogge* came into me, but Captaine *Slingsby*, and Captain *Wake* stood out, whereupon I let fly a Gun over them, and sent them word I had turned up the Glasse upon them.[9]

Slingsby and Wake were taken by their own men and dragged aboard the *James*, where Warwick attempted to persuade them to submit to him. When it became clear that they would not, he sent them ashore. All, that is, except Mennes, who was the most respected and competent commander of the five. According to Clarendon, Warwick "used all the persuasions he could to sir John Mennes, whom he and every body loved, to induce him to continue his command under his new commission, which he refusing to do, he caused a boat to set him on shore, without permitting him to go to his ship."[10] Mennes and his fellow officers were discharged, branded delinquents and summoned by the Commons "to answer this their Contempt in Parliament." On 10 July Mennes was examined and acquitted by the Lords on the grounds that once he "understood that the Earl of *Warwick* had an Ordinance from both Houses he submitted himself," a claim to which Warwick himself testified. The Commons agreed to release him and even repaid his personal arrears.[11] Mennes parted peacefully with Parliament, but others were not so lucky. Walking in Westminster on 11 July Mennes ran into a colleague and fell into discussion about his clearance by Parliament, noting that they were still "much incensed" with another commander.[12]

It is difficult to know whether to interpret Mennes's justification of his actions as a previously unsuspected commitment to constitutionalism or as a time-serving gesture of accommodation. Mennes was not a fixed member of any particular royalist faction—he flitted easily between moderates and extremists during his years in exile. But his sympathies, and those of his friend Smith, probably lay more toward the absolutism of the army plotters like Smith's patron, Pollard, than toward the cautious constitutionalism of Falkland or Hyde.

After his reconciliation with the Commons Mennes was unemployed, and his movements are, for a time, hazy. There was talk in August that he was in command of the fort of Deal in his native Kent. He may have held this post for a short time but seems to have been in London in September, meeting those of his friends who were still at large. An invitation poem by Mennes in octosyllabic doggerel, "To Parson Weeks. An Invitation to London," dates from this period. The epistle urges Weeks (a friend of Herrick and Smith) to leave his Somerset vicarage to join a convivial gathering of friends in the capital—quite possibly a meeting of the Order of the Fancy.

In this epistle, as so often in the verse of Mennes and Smith, an informal tone disguises a careful structuring. The epistle is underpinned by the
logic of the deliberative oration, urging a particular course of action. To
begin with, a series of possible excuses for Weeks's failure to come to the
capital are anticipated; these are then dismissed by a series of persuasive
exempla and an enumeration of the delights to be found in the capital,
including good fellowship, wit and wine:

> Ships lately from the Islands came
> With Wines, thou never heardst their name.
> *Montefiasco*, *Frontiniac*,
> *Viatico*, and that old Sack
> Young *Herric* took to entertaine
> The Muses in a sprightly vein.[13]

On the basis of these exempla, the penultimate paragraph of the epistle
asserts the course of action to be taken ("Come then") and emphasizes
the parson's obligation to visit his "thousands" of friends: "Rouze up, and
use the meanes, to see / Those friends, expect thy wit, and thee." A coda
warns Weeks of the dire social consequences of remaining in his parish:

> But if besotted with that one
> Thou hast, of ten, stay there alone;
> And, all too late lament and cry,
> Th'hast lost thy friends, among them I.

(p. 3)

The argumentative force of the epistle depends upon its being read in
the context of contemporary events. While the conclusion states that
Weeks's failure to appear will leave him without friends and with only his
tithe (the one-tenth of the parish produce to which, as curate, he was entitled), Weeks's ability, should he choose to stay home, to console himself
with his tithe (and therefore the notion that seeing his friends will force
neglect of his responsibilities to the church) is itself undermined by the
foregrounding at the conclusion of the epistle of tithes, a *synecdoche* for
episcopal authority, currently under attack in both Parliament and the
country (Somerset being a hotbed of such opposition).[14] In the autumn of
1642, in the wake of the recent Parliamentary declaration on church
reform, ecclesiastical authority was not the resource on which a parson
would ideally choose to base his contentment.[15] The ironic undermining
of Weeks's most legitimate motive for remaining in Somerset is designed
to lead the parson to the conclusion that it is not an option worth taking
seriously, thus leaving only the obligation to visit his friends.
    Although the writing of a poem urging such an apparently trivial social

indulgence at a time of national crisis might appear to confirm the traditional caricature of cavalier verse as introspective and escapist, to read
the poem in this way would be to misunderstand the political significance
of the social practices advocated by Mennes. The epistle is predicated on
the assumption, unstated yet implicit throughout, of the importance of
the rituals of friendship. According to Aristotle, friendship is expressive
of concord between men and is therefore the fundamental unit of society.
The bonds of friendship are the building blocks of the political community, which is nothing more than an extended network of friends. Such
bonds may be codified in the rules of social clubs or, at the national level,
in constitutions.[16] Implicit in this view is the assumption, expressed by
Cicero among others, that friendship is essential to the maintenance of
social harmony (*Of Friendship*, 7.23).[17] Thus, rather than marking a retreat into a private space free from and opposed to a public sphere riven
by social disorder, the rituals of friendship invoked by Mennes are deployed as weapons, operating at the boundary between the private and
the public, to counter social fragmentation.

The countering of social disorder is enacted in the epistle in two ways.
First, the poem includes at its margins the marks of public disorder,
threats that are contained through the implied power of friendship. The
poem opens with an allusion to the recent closure of the theatres ("hath
the Bishop, in a rage, / Forbid thy comming on our Stage?"), and it closes
with allusions to treasonable speech, here presented as one means by
which Weeks could guarantee a free trip to the capital.[18] The symptoms
of social breakdown are thus converted in the epistle to excuses for the
play of wit and are thereby rendered humorous and harmless. The second
means by which the poem counters social disorder is by enacting the
meeting that it attempts to arrange. The sending of a familiar epistle is itself a performance of the rituals of friendship, being a physical exchange
of wit and affection between friends. James Howell, for instance, referred
to letters as the threads that bind society together: "*Letters*, like *Gordian*
Knots, do Nations tie, / Else all Commerce, and Love, 'twixt Men would
die."[19] Howell's allusion points to both the importance and the essential
fragility of such threads.

II

In late autumn of 1642 the king and his forces, recently victorious
at Edgehill, repaired to Oxford, which became the center of court life for
the remainder of the Civil War. To Oxford came courtiers, poets, and
painters, like William Dobson, who was to provide so poignant a record
of the last years of the court, and there the Caroline belief in the power

of spectacle thrived in adversity. The trooper who took to shaving in sack only took his cue from a court that insisted on the preservation of appearances and ostentatious display.[20]

The royal propaganda machine was established at Oxford under the lively and rebarbative figure of John Berkenhead, who ran the royalist newsletter, *Mercurius Aulicus*.[21] Despite the control of the royal propaganda by Berkenhead and his Laudian literary mafia (a group with which Mennes seems to have had little contact), it has been quite reasonably suggested that Mennes acted as a propagandist at this time, and he may have intermittently supplied copy for the *Aulicus* or composed the occasional drinking song. No evidence of these activities, however, survives.[22]

Mennes arrived at Oxford sometime in the winter of 1642/3. He must have found the atmosphere congenial: his younger brother, Andrew, was already there, as, no doubt, were many courtiers and wits of his acquaintance.[23] But Mennes's experience marked him out for speedy military employment, and, early in the year, he was dispatched with Lord Capel to Shrewsbury where he was appointed lieutenant colonel and given command of the ordnance.[24]

Shrewsbury was a town of strategic importance where a royal mint and printing press were established.[25] Capel was an unfortunate appointment for so important a commission. He angered local citizens by imposing heavy taxes and was resoundingly defeated near Nantwich by an inferior enemy force in September 1643. In desperation Prince Rupert himself took over the command of Shropshire and its adjacent counties in January 1643/4 and attempted to introduce large-scale administrative reforms. Mennes was diligent in implementing these.[26] His letters from Shrewsbury provide an insight into financial problems that were no doubt typical for royalist officers in the field. In a letter of 2 February he wrote despondently to Rupert:

> I must craue your highness pardon yf I quitt the place for I haue not where withall to subsist any longer, hauing receiued but 22^{li} nowe in eleuen months & liud vppon my owne, without free quartrs for horse or man, the fortune I haue; all in the rebbells hands or in such tennants, as haue forgott to pay. . . .[27]

The most intractable problem, however, was the aggressive neutralism of the local people. Only the presence of the feared prince himself had any effect on the locals, who otherwise remained adamantly uncooperative.[28]

Rupert was evidently impressed by Mennes's performance as a local commander, for in May 1644 he gave him the charge of the counties of Carnaervonshire, Merionethshire, and Anglesey.[29] Mennes took up residence at Beaumaris, Anglesey, and attempted to secure the area for the king, corresponding with the earl of Ormonde in Ireland about the provision of Irish forces for the royal cause. In a letter of 11 May he outlined his situation to Ormonde:

> The Necessity of his Majesty's Affaires would not permitt me to bring any Forces more then my owne Troope to Countenance that power which my Commission gaue, besides the Resolution taken by me in obedience to his Highnes Commands, which was, to deale very gently, & civilly with the Inhabitants, & endeavour to treate with them for a Contribucion, & secure their holdes & other places of Accesse & Landing by their owne People; which though I haue not perfectly done, yet haue I soe farre effected, that the Castles and Holdes are in my power, though not lined with such a strength of Foote as is Necessary in that behalfe, & haue alsoe discouered the Rottennesse of many heere, whoe pretending to his Majesty's Service, Designe Nothing lesse, all thier Ayme being to possesse either the enemy or themselues of that power which should be beneficiall to his Majestie, & is absolutely necessary at this tyme. My humble Suite vnto your Excellence therefore is, to hasten the sending ouer of those 300 foote, which I vnderstand from my Lord Byron, (by his Lordship's letter) are ready to be transported. . . . The Castles here, are without Coeuerings to make them habitable for the want whereof we cannot lodge Souldiers within: May it therefore please your Excellency to cause to be sent out of those partes in Ireland whence it may be well spared such quantitie of Timber as may doe vs some Service in that behalfe. . . .[30]

Ormonde hesitated, however, because a fleet of Irish soldiers was at this time intercepted by Parliamentary ships, and the soldiers drowned.[31] Further support was not forthcoming, and Mennes was left to his own devices. On 14 June he ordered a general muster and set about repairing the island's defenses, levying a tax on coastal trade to raise money.[32]

Mennes's attempt to consolidate the royalist grip on Wales was arduous, and it gained him few friends. He was a stranger to the area, which was witnessing a power struggle among its leading families, and his appointment offended many local dignitaries. Thomas, Lord Bulkeley (resident at Beaumaris) and his crony, John Williams, archishop of York (then in charge of Conway Castle) made life difficult for him by interfering in his affairs, by acting without reference to his authority, and by complaining to his superiors about his unpopularity and inefficiency.[33] Mennes in turn complained to Ormonde about "som ouer busie bishopps" who could "looke better to theire texts, & leaue the millitarie & ciuill discipline to such as haue studdied Cæsar & Ploydon as much as they St Austen & machivill."[34] Others, however, had more respect for the difficulties of Mennes's position. Arthur Trevor wrote to Ormonde describing Wales as "a Dry & hot Country where english Gouernours seldom fayle to gett feauers & troubles & nothing else,"[35] and Daniel O'Neill (a courtier and royalist officer) informed Ormonde that

sir Iohn minnes with his patience, industry & fooling has brought these coun-
tryes to allow off him off ther gouernour, butt ass yett hee has not a man but 2
in the castle of carnaruan & 4 in this, which in sober sadnes iss a sadd story: for
lett mee assure your lordshipp that these 2 castles and tounes are the strongest
places I euer see in Ingland & not to bee taken but by famin or treason
. . . . minnes complaines much off the Bishop off york I feare the prelate in-
terposes to much.[36]

This was not the last occasion on which Mennes's expert foolery, gained
through his experience of the witty club life of Caroline London, was to
be of strategic importance for the royalist cause.

Mennes's Welsh sojourn had apparently ended by the spring of 1645,
when he was rumored to have been appointed admiral of the king's
fleet—a post that would have meant more had the king actually possessed
a fleet—following the death of Sir John Pennington. But Pennington was
not dead, and Mennes's whereabouts until the autumn are unknown.[37] In
the early summer, however, he may have been present at the disastrous
Battle of Naseby.[38] This, at least, is the tentative conclusion that can be
drawn from the evidence of one of the most bizarre and interesting poems
associated with Mennes and Smith and their circle, "Ad Johannuelem
Leporem, Lepidissimum, Carmen Heroicum."

III

"Ad Johannuelem Leporem, Lepidissimum, Carmen Heroicum" (To
witty Johnny, the wittiest, an heroic song) is an exceptionally witty and
complex poem, and possibly the only poem by Mennes or Smith ever to
receive the distinction of being printed in a modern anthology. It was recently reprinted (anonymously) in *The Chatto Book of Nonsense Poetry*
and was singled out for praise by at least one reviewer.[39] First printed
anonymously in the miscellany *Wit Restor'd* (1658), it is so close in manner to Smith's *Innovation* that it seems safe to attribute it to him and to
identify the "witty Johnny" of the title as Mennes.[40]

Structurally, Smith's poem grows out of the tradition of mock-poetry
with which he had been experimenting since the 1630s in works like *The
Loves of Hero and Leander* and *The Innovation of Penelope and Ulysses*.
Its mock-epic framework incorporates an invocation to the muses, burlesque inversions of the beauties of classical epics, and a set of footnotes
that are even more witty and obscure than those of *The Innovation*. It is a
supposedly fragmentary piece consisting of nine iambic quatrains and
twenty-one footnotes, but the concluding "*Cætera desiderantur.*" (the rest
is wanting) is simply another joke, implying the venerable antiquity of the

work. Stylistically, the poem draws on the tradition of composing witty nonsense that flourished in the Order of the Fancy and other clubs, with its stock of conventional material, including lobsters and buttered flounders: "And to the butter'd Flownders cry'd out, *Holla*," "And mounting straight upon a Lobsters thigh . . . " (lobsters, in fact, became a stock comic image in burlesque and satire of the Civil War and Restoration).[41] Thematically, it owes something to the coarse, popular "scuffle" poems of Robert Speed and David Lloyd. Like Speed's *Counter Scuffle*, Smith's poem is a mock-heroic account of a food fight in a tavern, and, like Lloyd's *Captain Iones*, a Welshman is used as a comic butt. The poem debunks Marlovian bombast ("*Holla* you pamper'd Jades, quoth he . . . "), and epic *zeugma*:

> Boots against boots 'gainst (*x*) Sandals, Sandals, fly.
>
> (*x*) This is an imitation of *Lucan*—
>   —*Signis Signa, & pila*—&c.
>   *Pharsalia. lib.* I: *in principio*[42]

The citation of Lucan's *Civil War* "signis / Signa . . . et pila minantia pilis" (1.6–7) is about the only accurate reference given in the footnotes. Smith's travesty of it may be directed at the contemporary translation by the Parliamentary apologist, Thomas May, who rendered it "Piles (*u*) against Piles, 'gainst Eagles Eagles fly," appending a quibbling footnote to justify his retention of the Latin term "pile."[43]

Smith's poem is an oblique and sophisticated production, and it is difficult to know exactly what to make of it. Not only does the presence of nonsense make it disorientating, a modern reader is left feeling that he or she is missing a whole set of private jokes. This is hardly surprising since the piece was written to and for Smith's close friend, Mennes: its addressee and its narratee are one and the same. What is perhaps surprising is that the poem seems to incorporate within its burlesque framework and nonsensical manner a coded account of the Battle of Naseby.

Smith's poem is an example of the employment by royalists of private codes as means of illicit communication and subversion during the Civil War period—a subject discussed at length in a recent book by Lois Potter.[44] Smith's poem opens with a mock-epic invocation, heavily footnoted, not unlike that of *The Innovation*:

> I Sing the furious battails of the Sphæres
> Acted in eight and twenty fathom deep,
> And from that (*a*) time, reckon so many yeares
> You'l find (*b*) *Endimion* fell fast asleep.

(*a*) There began the *Vtopian* accompt of years, *Mor: Lib. I. circa finem.*
(*b*) *Endimion* was a handsome young Welshman, whom one *Luce Moone* lov'd for his sweet breath; and would never hang off his lips: but he not caring for her, eat a bundance of toasted cheese, purposely to make his breath unsavory; upon which, she left him presently, and ever since 'tis proverbially spoken [as inconstant as *Luce Moone.*] The *Vatican* coppy of Hesiod, reades her name, *Mohun*, but contractedly it is *Moone*. *Hesiod. lib. 4. tom. 3.*   (p. 35)

Were the travesty of the legend of Endymion and the moon in footnote "(*b*)" simply a pun on an old proverb (Tilley M1111), Smith's careful addition that "The *Vatican* coppy of Hesiod, reades her name, *Mohun*, but contractedly it is *Moone*" would be redundant. If, however, the poem dates from the mid-1640s, it is unlikely that such a name could be read or written by a royalist without reference to the inconstancy of Lord Mohun, who had notoriously shifted his allegiance from king to Parliament in 1643. A string of similarly coded allusions are littered throughout the poem.

The third stanza opens the account of the battle with a series of allusions to the Roman Civil War:

> (*e*) *Pompey* that once was Tapster of *New-Inne*,
> And fought with (*f*) *Cæesar* on th' (*g*) *Æmathian* plaines,
> First with his dreadfull (*g*) *Myrmidons* came in
> And let them blood in the Hepatick veines.

(*e*) There were two others of these names, Aldermen of *Rome*. *Tit. Liu. hist. lib.* 28.
(*f*) *Æmathia*, is a very faire Common in *Northamptonshire, Strabo. lib.* 321.
(*g*) These *Myrmidons* were *Cornish-men*, and sent by *Bladud*, some times King of this Realme, to ayd *Pompey. Cæsar de bello. civili. lib.* 14.   (p. 36)

The bogus allusion to Caesar's history of the Civil War is more than a learned witticism. The parallel between the Roman civil war, with its conflict between Caesar and Senate, and the English Civil War, with its conflict of king and Parliament, was inevitably perceived in the 1640s: accounts of the Roman wars by Caesar and Lucan provided participants on both sides with analogies and a conceptual framework for understanding the conflict (a framework that was deployed in remarkably different ways). Caesar was generally associated with Charles: the standard raised by the king at Nottingham bore the legend "Give Caesar his due."[45] But in a desperate attempt at revisionist propaganda, Abraham Cowley inverted the Parliamentary claim to defend traditional liberties by associating Charles with Pompey and popular liberty in his unfinished Lucanian epic, "The Civill Warre."[46]

The likelihood that the conflict described by Smith is intended to be read as a code for Naseby is increased by the glossing of the "*Æmathian plaines*" as "a very faire Common in *Northamptonshire*" since such was the site of Naseby field. Not only does Smith's poem include an allusion to the site of Naseby, it also appears to incorporate coded references to many of the leading commanders in the battle. At Naseby the conventional association of Charles and Caesar was reinforced by the royalist battlecry: "*Cæsar or nothing.*"[47] Smith's allusion to Pompey as once "Tapster of *New-Inne*" is a multilayered pun that glances at Cromwell. On one level, this is a literary allusion to Pompey the tapster in *Measure for Measure*, but this character is conflated with Jonson's play *The New Inn.* At another level it seems to be a slur on Cromwell's breeding: he was often accused by royalist propagandists of having been a brewer.[48]

Further circumstantial evidence that the poem alludes to Naseby appears in possible allusions to other prominent figures present at the battle.

> But then an *Antelope* in Sable blew,
> Clad like the (*h*) Prince of *Aurange* in his Cloke,
> Studded with Satyres, on his Army drew,
> And presently (*i*) *Pheanders* Army broke.

(*h*) It seemes not to be meant by *Count Henry*, but his brother *Maurice*, by comparing his picture to the thing here spoken of. *Jansen. de præd. lib.* 22.
(*i*) *Pheander* was so modest, that he was called the Maiden Knight; and yet so valiant, that a French Cavaleer wrote his life, and called his Book, *Pheander* the *Maiden Knight. Hon. d'Vrfee. Tom.* 45. (p. 35)

The "*Antelope* in Sable blew" may be a reference to the arms of Prince Rupert, which depicted a lion rampant on quarters of sable and azure. Smith may have mistaken the lion for an heraldic antelope—a fierce (albeit horned) beast, or he may have been referring to Mennes, whose family arms depicted an antelope.[49] Note "(*h*)" glosses this allusion with a mock-learned quibble over which prince of Orange the antelope is compared with—Maurice or Frederick Henry? Both Rupert and his brother Maurice were present at Naseby, as was Lord Fairfax, whose legendary meekness and modesty could well be the point of the sneering reference to "*Pheander* the *Maiden Knight*." These identifications are given added plausibility by the fact that at Naseby Rupert's cavalry routed the left wing of Fairfax's army—"and presently *Pheanders* Army broke."[50] Finally, the fifth stanza opens with a description of "*Philip*, for hardiness sirnamed *Chub*," a rough and lascivious thug who bears a remarkable similarity to the Parliamentary general, Philip Skippon, whose boorishness was a byword among royalists (p. 37). Skippon's "hardiness" was proven at Naseby, when, after receiving a serious wound, he refused to leave the field.[51]

While the poem appears to incorporate a level of encoded allusion to Naseby, it does so within the generic framework of a mock-poem written in a nonsensical mode. The inclusion of such serious matter in a framework suited for innocent play results in an outlandish and confusing clash of tones. In this respect it is not unlike the verse epistles written by Mennes and Smith during the Scots War, in which serious themes threaten and occasionally overwhelm the generic demands of the familiar epistle. In "Ad Johannuelem," mock-poetic genre and nonsensical mode attempt to neutralize (by rendering absurd or meaningless) the serious elements admitted into the poem—a more aggressive strategy than the typical cavalier response of retreat and exclusion.[52] But the attempt at a magical dissolution of those elements that signify defeat is not entirely successful: allusions to the actors and actions of Naseby field remain resolutely recognizable. Furthermore, the use of minimalization techniques, like the travesty of Lucan, without a clear signaling of targets is a strategy akin to pulling the pin out of a hand grenade and neglecting to throw it. With its fundamentally incommensurable strategies, the poem continually threatens to self-destruct, and it is at this stage in the development of the burlesque mode that the anxieties of late seventeenth-century commentators and modern critics over its confused, despairing, and vandalistic nature begin to make sense.

In its failed attempt to erase defeat and its unfinished form, Smith's poem to Mennes, "Ad Johannuelem Leporem, Lepidissimum, Carmen Heroicum" is in keeping with other royalist responses to the disaster of Naseby—responses that included denial, minimalization, and, finally, silence.[53] The fragmentary piece might well be regarded as a burlesque analogue to Abraham Cowley's unfinished and radically unstable "The Civill Warre," an unsuccessful fusion of Lucanian epic and coarse satire that the poet abandoned soon after the royalist defeat at Newbury in 1643 appeared to collapse the necessary congruity between modern war and epic framework.[54]

IV

At Naseby all hope of a royalist victory was lost. During the autumn and winter of 1645, garrison after royalist garrison fell. In the autumn Mennes was in Bristol with Prince Rupert, where he played a leading role in drawing up the treaty of surrender in September.[55] Under the terms of the treaty, Rupert and his forces were permitted to march toward Oxford, now the last remaining royal garrison. Mennes presumably accompanied him and seems to have been present at Oxford at its fall in June of 1646, when he was hauled before the Committee for Compounding at Goldsmith's Hall and forced—like many others—to adopt the Negative Oath and pay a hefty composition fine.[56] For his part in the surrender of Bristol and for his compounding, Mennes was to be mocked and scoffed at by even his closest friend, James Smith.

Smith apparently saw out the Civil War from his benefice in Kings Nympton, protected from outbursts of local violence by the patronage of the Pollards. Quite how frequently he communicated with Mennes during the war is not known. But two verse epistles of the late 1640s, printed in a cluster of poems by Smith in *Wit Restor'd*, suggest that such communication was irregular, for the letters discuss events that had, in the main, taken place in the mid-1640s—some two years previously.

The first of these epistles is a response to a lost letter from Mennes. "An answer to a Letter from Sr. John Mennis, wherein he jeeres him for falling so quickly to the use of the Directory" is datable to 4 May 1648 and illustrates the difficulty of preserving the light-hearted tone requisite for "drollery" in such troubled times. Smith responds to a letter in which, he claims, Mennes "jeeres," lashes, "upbraidst, and raylst in rime" (railing being a form of bad-tempered abuse, as opposed to the gentler joshing of raillery) with an epistle in which flippancy borders on cynicism.[57] This tendency is illustrated in Smith's emphasis on blaming Mennes for his forced adoption of the Puritan Directory of Worship:

> Freind, thou dost lash me with a story,
> A long one too, of Directory;
> When thou alone deserves the Birch
> That broughtst the bondage on the Church.
> Didst thou not treat for *Bristow* Citty
> And yeld it up? the more's the pitty.
> And saw'st thou not, how right or wrong
> The common prayer-book went along?
> Didst thou not scourse, as if inchanted,
> For Articles *Sir Thomas* granted,
> And barter, as an Author saith,
> The Articles o'th'Christian faith?[58]

The tone is closer to the Skeltonic railing of Smith's poem on Madam Mallett than to the epistolary ideal of good-humored drollery, and it teeters on the brink of outright satire. But through his brusque, no-nonsense manner, Smith manages to preserve an ironic detachment and something of the spirit of "drollery." This tonal instability permeates the poem.

The epistle concludes with a paean for the rituals of the rural church year, including the "churching" of women, and Christmas and holy days, abolished by Parliamentary ordinance in 1647.[59] But rather than the tone of wistful elegy one might expect from Herrick's friend and fellow clergyman, Smith turns the passage into a jibing, half-serious satire on Mennes:

> Thou little thoughtst what geare began
> Wrap't in that Treaty, *Busie Iohn*,
> There lurk'd the fire, that turn'd to cinder
> The Church; her ornaments to tinder.
> There bound up in that Treaty lyes
> The fate of all our Christmas pyes,
> Our holy-dayes there went to wrack
> Our Wakes were layd upon their back;
> Our Gossips spoones away were lurch'd
> Our feasts and fees for woemen church'd
>
> (p. 48)

It is the flip irony of such passages that served as a model for the characteristic style of *Hudibras*. One can compare with this, for instance, Butler's description of Sir Hudibras as the kind of Puritan who would

> Quarrel with *minc'd Pies*, and disparage
> Their best and dearest friend, *Plum-porredge*;
> Fat *Pig* and *Goose* itself oppose,
> And blaspheme *Custard* through the *nose*.[60]

The striking similarity helps to reveal something of the nature of Butler's style, which, far from being miraculously *sui generis*, was the result of a lengthy process of generic transmutation, as the gentlemanly drolling style of the 1630s was applied to the horrific events of the 1640s. The recognition that the style of *Hudibras* is a hybrid dissolves many of the classificatory problems that have dogged interpretation of Butler's poem and the burlesque mode.

Smith's epistle also illustrates the complex deployment of coded language by royalist poets during the revolutionary period. Smith offers a classical parallel for Mennes's action at Bristol:

> Imagine freind, *Bochus* the King,
> Engraven on *Sylla's* Signet ring,
> Delivering up into his hands
> *Fugurth*, and with him all his Lands,
> Whom *Sylla* tooke and sent to Rome
> There to abide the Senate's doome,
>   In the same posture, I suppose,
> *Iohn* standing in's doublet and hose,
> Delivering up, amidst the throng,

> The common-prayer and wisedom's song
> To hands of *Fairfax* to be sent
> A sacrifice to the Parliament:

(pp. 46–47)

The appeal to the visual imagination is a familiar ploy of the Order of the Fancy, and the visualization of Sulla's signet ring is pregnant with significance. Smith alludes to the betrayal of Jugurth by Bocchus (his father-in-law) to the Roman commander, Sulla, a coup that concluded the Jugurthine War and consolidated Sulla's reputation at Rome. The story was familiar to Renaissance schoolboys through its rendition in Plutarch's *Lives* ("Sulla," 3; "Marius," 10). Smith's vignette thus seeks to establish Mennes as Bocchus, the Church of England as Jugurth, and Fairfax as Sulla. It seems at first a rather slapdash analogy, with only the most fleeting pertinence to its subject. But the point of the analogy lies as much in what it does not say as in what it does, for its significance is less the parallel between Mennes and Bocchus than that implied between Fairfax and Sulla. The pertinence of this emerges only when the reader supplies the Roman context for the episode: after the incident, Sulla went on to win a civil war and set himself up as a ruthless dictator. The parallel is thus predictive and embodies a warning that was in essence prophetic (although it was Cromwell and not Fairfax who became the Sulla of later royalist propaganda).[61] Smith's parallel is therefore a kind of code, the full significance of which eludes the casual peruser.

Smith's choice of an analogue drawn from Plutarch's parallels of Romans and Greeks is a significant act. The ideology of the parallel involved a belief in the essentially repetitive nature of history—a belief that there is nothing new under the sun.[62] There was a prevalent tendency to frame the events of the Civil War in classical and literary terms—a phenomenon that was not merely literary.[63] The continued fashion for the *Sortes Virgilianae*, in which the random choice of a verse from Virgil was used to tell one's fortune, illustrates its potency.[64] An apocryphal story attributed to John Wilkins of Wadham College, Oxford, relates an occasion on which Charles I "laid his finger upon that place toward the latter end of the fourth Eneid, which contains Dido's curse to Enêas," and discovered his fate:[65]

> at bello audacis populi vexatus et armis,
> finibus extorris, complexu avolsus Iuli,
> auxilium imploret videatque indigna suorum
> funera; nec, cum se sub leges pacis iniquae
> tradiderit, regno aut optata luce fruatur.
> sed cadat ante diem mediaque inhumatus harena.[66]

It is also claimed that the verses pricked by the king were loosely translated as follows by Abraham Cowley:

> By a bold peoples stubborn armes opprest,
> Forc'd to forsake the land which he possest,
> Torn from his dearest son, let him in vain
> Beg help, and see his friends unjustly slain:
> Let him to bold unequal Termes submit,
> In hopes to save his Crown, but loose both it
> And life at once: untimely let him dye
> And on an open stage unburied lye.[67]

A charming story! But while the attribution to Cowley is not implausible, the assignation of the translation to 1644 cannot be credited. Even so precocious a poet as Cowley could hardly predict with such chilling accuracy the precise circumstances of the execution of the royal actor.

As the royalist cause deteriorated, the search for parallels became increasingly desperate, and the execution of Charles forced many poets to give up the attempt altogether. Henry King, having announced in his *Elegy upon the most Incomparable King Charls the First* that "Our Story . . . through time's vast Kalendar / Must stand without Example or Repair," goes on to draw a series of strained scriptural parallels in a tone that veers wildly between elegiac dignity and scabrous invective.[68] The anonymous author of "The Times" is faced with the same problem of discursive practice: "What dialect or fashion / Shall I assume?"[69] With regard to the lack of parallels for the present times, he adopts a tone of weary resignation:

> Hence we confute thy tenant *Solomon*,
> *Vnder the Sun a new thing hath been done.*
> A thing before all pattern, all pretence
> Of rule or copy: Such a strange offence
> Of such original extract, that it bears
> Date only from the *Eden* of our years.[70]

He concludes with the despairing recognition that to speak about such times simply perpetuates their evil: "This only *Axiom* from ill *Times* increase / I gather, *There's a time to hold one's peace*."[71] In his own poem, written shortly after the execution of the king, Smith was to face the same hard choices.

"Mr. Smith, to Sir John Mennis upon the surrender of Conway Castle by the Ar, B Y," is dated from Pollard's house in King's Nympton on 15 February 1648[/9], and perhaps the most striking thing about it is that it makes no explicit mention of the execution. Instead, Smith chides Mennes for his part in the surrender of Conway Castle and for his appearance before the Committee for Compounding in 1646. Given that the previous epistle of May 1648 discusses events from 1645, it is clear that Mennes and Smith were still catching up on old news. But Smith's reluctance to respond directly to the king's death is by no means unique: Henry King's elegy, for example, dated "From my sad Retirement / March 11. 1648 [/9]," was not in fact completed until 1659.[72] There is, moreover, a surprising lack of tonal confidence in those elegies that have survived: even the garrulous Alexander Brome produced two elegies of extraordinarily unremitting bleakness.[73] There is no explicit reference to the king or his death in Smith's poem, but the description of the committeemen of Goldsmith's Hall as "those hungry Kings" registers the king's absence and the consequent natural disorder (such bureaucrats are now kings).[74] A number of other covert allusions permeate the poem.

Smith's evasive response is bewildered and nostalgic without being completely pessimistic. The centerpiece of the epistle is a reverie in which the poet recollects a vanished past, considers the present plight of himself and his friends, and, in a concluding couplet, reviews his hopes for the future:

> And now I call to mind the tale,
> How mounted in thy nights of ale
> Thou rod'st home duely to thy Den
> On back of resty Cittizen,
> Still pressing as the cattle grew
> Weary, at every stage, a new:
> Some thorough-pac'd, and sure of foot
> Some tripping, with string-halt to boot,
> Now 'tis their time, and thou art ore-
> Ridden by them, thou roadst before.
> So have I seen the flyes in Summer,
> Yellow as was the neighbouring scummer,
> With shambling thighs, each other back
> By turns, and traverse o're the rack.
> Ah! worthy friend, it makes me mad
> To count the dayes, that we have had;
> When we might freely meet and drink
> And each man speak what he did think.
> Now every step we doubt, and word
> As men to passe some unkown for'd.
> As Patridges devide their way
> When stoop'd at by the Birds of prey,
> And dare not from their coverts peep
> Till night's come on, and all's asleep,
> Then from their severall brakes they hast,
> And call together to repast.
> So frighted by these buzzards, flye
> Our scattered friends, and sculking lye

Till cover'd in the night, they chant
And call each other to the hant,
   Some trusty Taverne, where in bowles
They drown their feares, & chirp poore souls,
What sad plight are we in? what pickles?
That we must drink in conventicles?
Search all the Centuries, there's none
Like this fell Persecution;
But when Time sorts, do but command,
At noon I'le meet thee, here's my hand.
                        I. S.

The passage involves a series of delicate mood changes. The nostalgic recollection of the rituals of the Order of the Fancy—expressions of the stability of the Caroline social order—leads into the familiar topos of "the world turned upside down"—an inversion of order embodied in the collapse of the harmony between content and verse form (the broken word "ore- / Ridden"). The ensuing simile, satiric in tone, exhibits the way in which the burlesque tendency toward indiscriminate ridicule, so unproblematic in a stable context, becomes self-destructive in times of social disorder: as a fly on a dunghill, Mennes is tarred by the same brush as the resty citizens. The tone then reverts to nostalgia, as Smith bemoans the breakdown of the social bonds of trust and friendship. The simile of the partridges frightened by "the Birds of prey" registers natural disorder when it is confirmed that these are buzzards: here are no princely eagles.[75] As the poem draws to its close, the bleakness of tone gathers to a crescendo in the grim recognition that there are no parallels to be found "for this fell Persecution." At such moments, even the pretense at "drollery" has been dropped.

The poem is not entirely bleak, however. The final couplet picks up a hint dropped earlier about the cyclical nature of events ("Now 'tis their time") and expands it into a statement of faith in providentialism; an expectation of a future "when Time sorts." This providential view of events was a common royalist response and helps to explain their favoring of the genres of romance and tragicomedy during the Interregnum.[76] While there is little room for human agency in the wished-for resolution of providentialism, the poem does not entirely erase the need for individual and social action. Smith alludes to the preservation of the traditions of clubbing in dark days and looks forward to the time when his concluding pun will be righted—to a time when he will be able to offer Mennes his handshake, rather than merely his handwriting, in good earnest. In the dating of the poem, moreover, is a covert, but nonetheless potent, allusion to the seed of tragicomic renewal—the Perdita, as it were, of the piece—the young Charles II. The epistle is dated from Pollard's house in Kings

Nympton, "Where one drinks, and another pledges" (p. 45). To "drink" and "pledge" was to share a toast of mutual allegiance and support for a cause, which, given the date of the epistle, must surely have been "King Charles II."[77] The drinking of a health to Charles as "King" was an act of symbolic defiance that directly contravened the regicidal "Act prohibiting the proclaiming any person to be King of England."[78] Futile though it may seem, the gesture was regarded gravely by the authorities, being punishable by death. During the long years of Puritan rule, it would become one of the most important gestures of royalist solidarity.[79]

12

Drollery in Defeat

I

During the spring of 1648, many who had previously supported the Parliamentary cause (and even more who had not) became anxious about the progress of events in London—anxious about what they saw as the increasing sway over Westminster held by radicals and extremists. In the summer, a petition was delivered by a number of conservative Kentish gentlemen demanding the disbanding of the army (the main focus of radicalism) and a treaty with the king. A short-lived rising followed, which in turn set off a mutiny among parts of the Parliamentary fleet based on or near the Kentish coast. A small handful of rebel ships plied over to Holland where they made contact with the Prince of Wales, who took them under his personal command and sailed for England.[1] Mennes was apparently involved with this maneuver in some way, possibly as commander of one of the rebel ships. His naval experience and his Kentish connections would have been valuable assets for the rebel force.[2]

The absence of clear lines of responsibility or a coherent plan of action meant that the excursion was ultimately rather futile. By the time the rebel ships reached the Kentish coast, the rising had been crushed, and the rebels made themselves unpopular with local merchants by raiding trade ships. By the late summer supplies were running out, local support was dwindling, and mutiny was in the offing. Only the threat of being caught between the Parliamentary fleet under Warwick and a loyal squadron from Portsmouth enabled the royalist leaders to persuade their crews that it was best to slip back to Holland.[3]

The royal squadron anchored in the port of Helvoetsluys. Safe from direct attack, they awaited the arrival of Warwick. According to the Parliamentary agent in the Low Countries, this was announced by Mennes with typically mordant humor: "Uppon Tuesday night all the bloud-royall being att a play together about Ten a clock att night, a boatswaine came with Sir John Minch, and brought good newes from the Navy; being asked what good newes, hee said, Warwick was come with 20 shippes into

193

Goree."[4] The royal party's theatre visit emphasizes the importance of the cultural life of the exiled court and, in lieu of the recent closure of the theatres in England, suggests an element of open defiance—a defiance embodied also in Mennes's preservation of a tone of ironic detachment in the face of trouble.

While the royal squadron was relatively secure from direct damage, it was vulnerable in other ways. Blockaded inside the port, unable to take prizes, it had no income. As money ran out, forcing the pawning of ships' cannon, sailors deserted and mutinied, and they brawled in town taverns with members of Warwick's fleet.[5] The war of attrition dragged on through the autumn until late November when Warwick, having recaptured a number of ships and perhaps underestimating the resolve of the remaining crews, sailed for England. This was a serious error, and Rupert (now in command of the fleet) was quick to exploit it, capturing a number of English merchant ships before breaking out of Helvoetsluys with his small fleet in early January 1648/9 and heading for the south coast of Ireland.[6]

The appointment of the uncompromising Rupert was not universally welcomed by the exiled royalists, and it was probably hoped that Mennes, who was appointed rear admiral under him in the *Swallow*, would be a stabilizing and moderating influence.[7] Rupert's plan was characteristically bold. Basing his squadron at the well-fortified town of Kinsale and joining there with a force of Irish privateers, he preyed upon English shipping, thus inflicting damage on the enemy and providing the exiled court with a source of income. For a time Rupert's force enjoyed success, giving the exiles cause to rejoice. But the takings were of greater propaganda value than financial significance, and by the spring Rupert was blockaded inside Kinsale by a superior Parliamentary force. It was not until August that Rupert escaped, together with seven ships, to the relative sanctuary of Lisbon.[8]

Rupert was well received in Portugal and given assurances of good faith. But, with the arrival of the Parliamentary fleet in the spring of 1650, pressure was applied to the Portuguese to hand over the royalist leaders. Again the Parliamentarians adopted a policy of attrition, and again Rupert seized his opportunity and escaped with a handful of ships. This time, however, he was not so lucky: his squadron was captured and destroyed by Admiral Blake in November. Rupert himself managed to escape in his flagship, making his way out into the Atlantic.[9]

Mennes, meanwhile, had fallen sick in Lisbon and was left behind there. He became seriously ill, and for a time it was thought he might die. But by 1652 he was back in action, energetically administering business on behalf of the royal cause in Lisbon.[10] With the recovery of his health he returned once more to privateering, joining the community of exiles at Flushing by the end of 1653.[11]

Although Blake's defeat of Rupert's squadron removed any serious royalist threat to Commonwealth shipping, individual privateers like Mennes continued to score small victories, taking the odd prize ship here and there. On such occasions he was able to supply his impoverished wife and his friends at home with gifts and luxuries.[12] The importance of such gifts to those at home is implied in a verse epistle from Smith to Mennes that probably dates from late 1653, "To Sir John Mennis, on a rich prize which he took on the Seas." In this epistle Smith rails good-humoredly at Mennes for his failure to furnish his friends with bounty from his latest prize. A strategy of fanciful exaggeration is deployed to make the most of Mennes's success. Smith fancies Mennes as a jewel-encrusted sultan, "bristling" in his seraglio, and then as "the great *Leviathan*" (a topical allusion to the work that had caused such consternation among the exiles), devouring and spewing out ships like pilchards; and finally as the scriptural miser, Dives:

> One that nere thought upon his friends till then,
> When he was in the Devills frying pan.
> Then when it is too late thou wilt confesse,
> Thou hast more sinn'd in Friendship then
>   *I.S.*[13]

The element of admonition, enhanced by the return to a slightly more dignified decasyllabic line, runs throughout the poem and culminates in a cautionary note, reminding Mennes, in a not entirely frolic fashion, of the dangers of transgressing the unwritten laws of friendship.

II

A study of the cultural life of royalists in exile during the Interregnum is long overdue. There was a formidable array of talent among the exiles, and it is no surprise that intellectual life in their midst was lively and varied, stimulated by contact with Continental men of letters and science.[14] Among the poets and erstwhile club members based at the court of Henrietta Maria in Paris in the later 1640s were Sir William Davenant, John Denham, and William Crofts. Other poets and courtiers in exile included Abraham Cowley, Edmund Waller, Thomas Killigrew, and George Villiers, duke of Buckingham. Sir William Cavendish, his brother Charles, and his remarkable wife, Margaret, took a lively interest in the work of natural philosophers such as Hobbes, Descartes, and

Gassendi.[15] Like many exiles, the Cavendishes later gravitated toward Charles's court in the Low Countries, but contacts between the various different royalist groups remained strong, as did rivalries and policy disputes.

The English were vigorous consumers of the latest French literary fashions, including plays, poetry, and (then, as now) literary theory. Something of the temper of their activities is suggested by Davenant's ambitious fragmentary epic, *Gondibert* (1651), its lengthy theoretical *Preface*, and the response to this by Thomas Hobbes (1650). Not all literary activity took place on such a lofty plane. As will shortly be seen, several of Davenant's associates at the Louvre clubbed together and published a set of burlesque verses on *Gondibert*, scoffing at his literary and social pretensions.

The vogue for burlesque was widespread among the exiled courtiers, stimulated no doubt by the travesties and the weekly *Gazette Burlesque* published from 1655 by the French godfather of the mode, Paul Scarron, and by the interest of the younger members of the English royal family.[16] Charles and James appear to have been avid readers of Scarron's *Gazette*: in May 1655 Charles wrote requesting his brother to send him copies of the *Gazette* from Paris.[17] In 1646, Martin Lluellin had dedicated his strange collection of octosyllabic doggerel *Men-Miracles* (1646) to James, implying that the prince had already read some of them ("*Part* of these Papers being already destin'd to your Highnesse's Recreation").[18] It should not be forgotten that after the Restoration, the king—hardly the most bookish of monarchs—was so taken with *Hudibras* that he offered its author a substantial pension and was said to have carried a copy of the poem with him at all times.[19]

The influence of Scarron on the exiled court and therefore upon the development of English burlesque, however, has been seriously overestimated. Contrary to traditional assumptions, the vogue was not simply a French invention imported to England at the Restoration together with satire and licentious morals. Many of the burlesques produced and circulated by English poets during the Interregnum and Restoration were simply continuations of earlier English traditions that had flourished in clubs like the Order of the Fancy. It is even possible that the work of Mennes and Smith might actually have influenced Scarron.

Mennes and Smith anticipated most of the innovations generally attributed to the French poet. Smith's travesty, *The Innovation of Penelope and Ulysses* (ca. 1636), predates Scarron's *Virgile Travesti* (1648) by at least eight years.[20] Mennes's account of his visit to the wells, "To a friend upon a journey to Epsam Well," was written before December 1640, while Scarron's account of his visit to the baths, "La Premiere Legende de Bourbon," dates from October 1641.[21] Mennes, as will be soon seen, wrote a burlesque "diurnal" in late 1654 ("Verses upon an Entertainment"), while Scarron's burlesque diurnal, the *Gazette Burlesque*, first appeared in January 1655.[22] Finally, Smith's travesty of the tale of Hero and Leander dates from the mid-1630s and was published in 1651, while Scarron's burlesque ode, *Leandre et Hero*, was written in 1656.[23] Although these are noteworthy coincidences, they should not be pushed too far. There is no evidence that Scarron knew the work of Mennes or Smith, and there are only minimal similarities of form or tone between their works.[24]

The literary activities of royalists at home and in exile have traditionally been presented as escapist, consolatory, or quietist.[25] While there is a strong element of truth in this view, the politically engaged and frequently subversive character of the verse written, circulated, and published during the Interregnum has generally been overlooked. This is due to a failure of contextualization. A text that in itself appears innocuous, escapist, or merely nostalgic may involve an element of subversion or protest if one considers the medium and context in which it was produced and circulated. To take one obvious example, the very tune of "The Black-Smith," the popular ballad written by the Order of the Fancy in the 1630s, and its memorable refrain ("Which nobody can deny"), came to signal loyal cavalier values during the Interregnum. Both tune and refrain were employed with monotonous regularity in royalist songs of satire and protest—including one written by a "loyal blacksmith" himself.[26]

Of great importance in the production, circulation, and publication of verse during the Interregnum were the erstwhile members of the clubs of Caroline London. After the war, royalists both at home and abroad attempted to preserve the traditions of clubs like the Order of the Fancy, arranging convivial meetings where possible and circulating verses through correspondence networks. Since such networks were primarily conspiratorial, it is no surprise to find that such they were employed with equal vigour for literary communication and political subversion. Indeed, such activities were frequently inseparable, and Parliamentary propagandists such as John Hall of Durham expressed well-founded fears about the subversive potential of the clubs.[27] Parliament responded to such fears by clamping down on outlets for the circulation of literature by intercepting private correspondence, closing the theatres in 1648, and banning the sale of printed matter by streetsellers in 1649 (a sure way of curbing the circulation of ballads).[28] Throughout the Protectoral period, regular attempts were made to prohibit the circulation and publication of scurrilous or comic verse.

During the late 1640s and the 1650s several related clubs or circles based in the Low Countries attempted to continue the traditions of the prewar clubs, holding meetings and engaging in corporate literary activities. One such group was mentioned by Thomas Killigrew in his semi-autobiographical play *Thomaso, or, the Wanderer*. In his play, Killigrew alludes to a convivial pig-roast at the St John's Head Tavern in Rotterdam, which apparently took place in 1652: "Twas where we met Embassador *Will*, and Resident *Tom*, with M. Sheriffs Secretary, *John* the Poet with the Nose; all *Gondiberts* dire Foes."[29] A marginal note identifies these figures as William Murray, William Crofts, Killigrew himself, and John Denham. This gathering appears to represent a fusion of the rival prewar groups of Murray himself and Peter Apsley, in whose rival group both Crofts and Killigrew had been involved.

The St. John's Head group was only a part of a larger network of exiled wits. Two of its members, Crofts and Denham, were among those who clubbed together to publish the collection of attacks on *Gondibert*. Billed as the work of Davenant's "four best friends," this collection of burlesques, travestying Davenant and his poem, was published at London in April 1653 under the title *Certain Verses Written by Sevèrall of the Authors Friends: to be Re-Printed with the Second Edition of Gondibert*. The fact that Denham had arrived in London by the beginning of March 1652/3 makes one suspect that he may have brought the manuscript with him for publication.[30] Be that as it may, the volume claimed to be the production of a club of four wits, identified by burlesque nicknames in the title of a collection printed in response to *Certain Verses*, supposedly in Davenant's defense, *The Incomparable Poem Gondibert, Vindicated from the Wit-Combats of Four Esquires, Clinias, Dametas, Sancho, and Iack Pudding* ([n.p.], 1653).[31] The identities of the four members of this club have been the subject of some confusion, and various candidates have been identified, including Denham, Crofts, John Donne the younger, George Villiers, duke of Buckingham, Sir Alan Broderick, and Edmund Waller.[32] The involvement of Denham seems certain,[33] that of Crofts and that of Donne seem possible,[34] that of Broderick seems less likely,[35] and neither Buckingham nor Waller appear to have been involved.[36]

Both *Certain Verses* and *Gondibert Vindicated* continued the tradition of printing mockeries of an associate's work that flourished in the earlier clubs. The first collection includes the octosyllabic doggerel, the mock-heroic pieces, and the displays of bogus learning familiar to readers of the "Panegyricke Verses" on *Coryats Crudities*—*Gondibert Vindicated* even alludes to Coryate (p. 18). Indeed, like the "Panegyricke Verses," the collection claims in its title that it was intended to be printed along with the work it mocked. Wittingly or not, Davenant had taken up Coryate's mantle as the comic butt of the court. Although subsequent readers have been puzzled by the tone and purpose of the *Verses*, the highly conventional character of the collections was obvious to contemporaries.[37] Such mockeries were heavily ritualized "flytings" or "Wit-Combats" (as *Gondibert Vindicated* noted in its title)—competitive compositions of a kind in which the Mermaid Club and the Order of the Fancy had engaged. Their very composition possessed a positive subtext for the exiled court, asserting the continuity of the traditions and cultural practices of prewar London.

III

It has been suggested that Mennes was one of the contributors to *Certain Verses*.[38] Although this seems to be an error, Mennes may have written a poem on *Gondibert*.[39] During the early 1650s he was closely involved with members of the *Certain Verses* club. He was an intimate of Denham (whom he later claimed to have cured of the pox at this time) and, on at least one occasion during the early 1650s, was involved with him in a pig-roast akin to that of the St. John's Head group.[40] The event is memorialized in Denham's poem "To Sir John Mennis being Invited from Calice to Bologne to Eat a Pig." In a coarse, ballad form the poem recounts the journey from Calais to Boulogne:

> All on a weeping *Monday*,
>   With a fat *Bulgarian* Sloven,
>   Little Admiral *John*
>   To *Bologne* is gone
> Whom I think they call old *Loven*.
> . . . .
> A Knight by Land and Water
>   Esteem'd at such a high rate,
>   When 'tis told in *Kent*,
>   In a Cart that he went,
> They'll say now hang him Pirate.[41]

Along for the ride were other exiles, including Aubrey de Vere, earl of Oxford, and Charles Dormer, Viscount Ascot.[42]

Although Mennes almost certainly wrote a number of poems during this period, only one seems to have survived. It exists in a manuscript copy among the Clarendon papers in the Bodleian Library, Oxford, entitled "Verses upon an Entertainment given by the Chancellor."[43] It was written, like most of Mennes's verse, in comic octosyllabics. Like so much royalist poetry of the period, it was an occasional piece, memorializing for absent friends and for posterity a particular moment of conviviality and friendship. The poem celebrates the continuation in adversity of courtly rituals in the form of an entertainment given by Chancellor Hyde

late in 1654. Although the precise occasion of the entertainment is unclear (it may have been the arrival of funds from France or the chimerical
news of some royalist success at home), it was thrown to cheer up Charles
on his return to Cologne (where his court was now established) after a
tearful parting from his sister, Mary.[44] In addition to Hyde himself, those
present at the feast and mentioned in the poem included members of the
court and visiting dignitaries, such as secretary Nicholas ("the good old
pen man"), Lords Newburgh and Taaffe, and Lord Wentworth, sometime
patron of James Smith. Also mentioned is the French agent at Cologne,
Armand Frederick Schomberg.[45]

Both feast and poem illustrate the way in which the court employed social and cultural activities in order to keep up appearances during a
period of poverty and inactivity. The poverty of the court at this time is
legendary: on one occasion the Duchess of Newcastle was jokingly asked
by her husband to pawn her clothes in order to pay for a dinner. But
throughout the years of exile, the emphasis on saving face prevailed.[46] At
some point in the late 1640s or early 1650s, the Duke of Newcastle composed "A Prologe thatt shoulde have been spoken before an Intended
Pastorall at Antwerpe," which offered a witty apology for the poor fare
that was to be served:

> Since on vss, are the times moste fatall Curses,
> Nott feaste your taste, Itt is beyond our Purses
> Butt [we] doe Invite you, & before you Rise,
> Weel feaste your Vnderstandinges, Eares, & Eyes[47]

Attempts to keep up such entertainments and the search for novel ways
of making such apologies were recurrent. Thus, prior to the entertainment for which Mennes composed his poem, a master of the feast and six
attendants were chosen. There was talk of turning the feast into a potluck
affair, with each guest bringing his or her own meal, but Hyde—anxious
to preserve decorum—offered to foot the bill himself. Mennes made
much of this gesture in his poem:

> T'was mention'd each should bring his dish
> Where at the Chancellor Cry'd Pish
> Quoth he, though I haue little pelfe
> I'le rather pay for all my selfe
> To which wee quickly all agreed
> Such strifes with vs last not indeed

(lines 17–22)

The poem went on to give a jocular relation, against the background of
the feast, of two parallel "love contests" between Newburgh and Schom-

berg over a young virgin, and between Wentworth and Taaffe over an
elderly matron:

> Now Shcomberg 'gins the virgin Court
> Which quickly spoyles old Newbrugh's sport
> For he with Loue was soe besotted
> That for that tyme he long had plotted
> But seeing such a riuall there
> It bread both Ielouzie and feare
> To Cure the last with treble flute
> His riuall Home he doth salute
> Thinking there with to knock him downe
> (as then the Virgin were his owne)
> Shcombergh the charge receiued & stood
> as firme as Rock against a floud
>
> . . . .
>
> Wentworth & Taaffe by age Exempt
> From Loue and such like Complement
> Close yoaked with the good old woman
> Drank Rinco sang and troubled noeman,
> Yet something still of Loue remayns
> For while this Nectar warmes their Veyns
> They Court the Matron, first they dip
> her fingers in the wyne then sip.
> And like old Britaine Bards they sing
> And drinke healths to the Princess, King
> And all that Royall Tribe as fast
> As long as night and Rinco last
>
> (lines 71–82 and 104–15)

While the poem is on one level an occasional and inconsequential production, these love contests were expressive of deeper divisions in the
court. Relations between Hyde and Nicholas were poor, and various
courtiers mentioned by Mennes were currently squabbling with one
another.[48] In a letter to Nicholas of 1 January 1654/5 Lord Hatton alludes
to the tales that have reached Paris concerning "the divisions and quar-
rells of Fraiser and Wentworth, Fraiser and Newburgh, Wentworth and
Fleming, Newburgh and Taafe, all which are the great mirth of *the Pallais
Royall*."[49] Mennes, it seems, was attempting to heal rifts in the court by
donning the cap and bells, trivializing its divisions and emphasizing points
of agreement (like Hyde's decision to provide victuals for the feast). The
courtier's adoption of the role of clown for a court that could afford no
professional fool underlines the truth in Sir William Temple's association
of the rise of burlesque style with the adoption by courtiers of the discourse of foolery.[50]

The role of court jester or comic poet-in-residence was congenial, but,
during the middle 1650s, Mennes was to play other roles for the cause,

the most important of which was that of intelligencer. In the planning of the royalist rising of 1655 he was a vital link in the lines of communication between Charles in the Low Countries and his agents in England. The operation of this network reveals some surprising interconnections between the circulation of burlesque poetry and political subversion.

In February 1654/5 Mennes registered at "the signe of the Towne of Rouen" in Flushing under the pseudonym "William Thomas."[51] Like many of the disguises and covers adopted by royalists at this time it was a thin one: his true identity was well-known to the Commonwealth agent there.[52] From his tavern he passed information between Charles and royalist agents in England. On 8 March 1654/5, the morning of the planned rising, Daniel O'Neill (one of those agents) wrote to Charles from London. O'Neill reviewed the unpromising situation in England, holding out the hope that Lord Fairfax in the north was "very hearty" in the cause and would commit himself. To this observation he added a brief verse quotation:

I am assured by an express from Newett [*the north*] that Fowell [*lo: Fairfax*] is very hearty in your business. . . . if that be so as the Poet said

If this day thriue we'ele ride in Coatches;
If not, bonnes noches[53]

This is, of course, an inaccurate quotation of the concluding lines from Smith's epistle to Mennes on his marriage ("If this day smile, they'l ride in Coaches, / And, if it frown, then *Bonas Noches*") —lines that, in their original context presented a devil-may-care nonchalance in the face of the impending Parliamentary vote to abolish episcopacy.[54] O'Neill's employment of these lines in the context of another imminent royalist defeat indicates something of the serviceableness of the verse of Mennes and Smith to the culture of cavalier conspiracy during the Interregnum. His quotation of them in a letter that Mennes himself was to pass to Charles illustrates something of the clubby humor that permeated these cavalier networks: the identity of the unnamed poet would be no mystery to at least one reader of the letter.

IV

The fact that the first publication of Smith's poem to Mennes coincided so closely with O'Neill's visit to London raises the possibility that he may have acted as a middleman between Mennes and the publisher, Henry Herringman, carrying with him copy for the collection in which the poem appeared, the popular miscellany or "drollery" *Musarum Deliciae*. For this suggestion there is some additional circumstantial evidence. First, O'Neill was in London between February 1654/5 and June 1655; *Musarum Deliciae* was entered on the Stationers' Register on 1 June 1655.[55] Second, the collection contains poems by George Morley, whom O'Neill would have met at Hyde's entertainment in late 1654, and one poem possibly by Brian Duppa, with whom O'Neill may at this time have been in correspondence.[56] O'Neill's knowledge of Smith's poem, however, may simply be the result of coterie circulation among royalist exiles. The inclusion of poems by Morley and Duppa is inconclusive: these poems, like many others in the collection, were circulating widely in manuscript.[57] It is probably safe to assume that Herringman compiled the collection from such sources as came to hand and that these included single manuscript sheets and manuscript pamphlets containing "linked groups" of poems (such as those by Mennes and Smith, which appear at the opening and close of the collection).[58] Indeed, many of the poems in the collection appear to have been circulating in manuscript since the 1630s or 1640s, either in loose sheets (many of which were copied into personal commonplace books or miscellanies) or in "linked groups" of related poems. It is even possible that part of the collection may represent a complete manuscript miscellany.[59] Thus, there is no evidence to conclude that Mennes or Smith directly connived at the publication of their poetry in *Musarum Deliciae*, either via O'Neill or otherwise.[60] Further, there is the testimony of one contemporary that *"they never allowed of the publishing of their Copies."*[61] But in spite of their consistent ridiculing of print culture, they would not have been the first gentlemen to wink at the printing of their verses. There were, moreover, certain political advantages to appearing in print at this moment.

Up until this point, the circulation of the verse of Mennes and Smith seems to have been carefully restricted to the poets' immediate circle—the Order of the Fancy in the 1630s and courtly exiles and royalist conspirators in the 1640s and early 1650s. There were surprisingly few leaks, judging from the evidence of unauthorized manuscript copies in collections unconnected with the poets. Such tight control was undoubtedly appropriate in the clubs of 1630s London, when the promotion of distinct corporate identities and ideologies was at a premium; but, in the 1650s, with friends and associates separated by geographical distances and with erstwhile rival groups drawn together through common antipathies, a more public means of circulation was appropriate for broadcasting values, as public gestures of solidarity, and as foci for discontent.

This move toward the public presentation of verse that had previously circulated within a tiny coterie is expressed by the title page of *Musarum Deliciae* and of collections like it (the so-called "drolleries" of the 1650s), which almost invariably print the initials rather than the full names of the contributors.[62] This transparent device keeps up the pretense of disguising the authors, while simultaneously revealing them. It does so in a manner that flatters the reader, appealing to a desire for inclusion in the exclusive coterie of cognoscenti implied by the title page and prefatory material.[63] This construction of a readerly community of "knowing Gentleman" (as Humphrey Moseley put it in the preface to his edition of Suckling) is a gesture of aggressive inclusiveness: it implicates the reader in an alliance with Mennes, Smith, and the values of their circle.[64]

While it has long been recognized that the "drolleries" of the 1650s were political in import, it is less easy to pin down where, exactly, their politics resides.[65] Firm conclusions must await a fresh study of the drolleries—one that attends to their organizational principles and reception and to the role of stationers and printers such as Henry Herringman and Nathaniel Brook in their compilation, publication, and circulation.[66] One might, however, venture a few general suggestions about the politics of the drolleries on the basis of *Musarum Deliciae*.

The dominant feature of *Musarum Deliciae*—and one that it shares with the elegant collections of court poets published in the 1640s by Humphrey Moseley—is the politics of nostalgia. The volume includes many older, Caroline poems. These were popular pieces—lyrics, songs, epitaphs, ballads, and occasional poems, which had enjoyed wide manuscript circulation. Many of them emanated from an explicitly courtly milieu (such as the anonymous poem on Madame de Chevereuze swimming the Thames; p. 49). By grounding the volume in the verse of a vanished period, the drollery seeks, like Moseley's volumes, to memorialize a lost golden age of Stuart culture. Moseley in his publications explicitly associated the court writers of the 1630s (Carew, Suckling, Waller, and so forth) with the royalism of the 1640s, thereby turning, as Chernaik puts it, "the physical book into a statement of allegiance."[67] The drolleries do not inhabit the same rarefied courtly atmosphere as the Moseley volumes, but they share the monarchism inherent in such a self-consciously retrospective stance.[68]

The latent royalism of the collection is released by careful structuring. The Caroline pieces are situated between clusters of poems by Mennes and Smith and members of their circle (William Bagnall and Simeon Steward, for example). These pieces possess a more or less explicitly royalist emphasis: the volume opens with verse epistles dating from the Scots War, and it closes with Smith's recent poem to Mennes on his taking a prize ship, with its scoffing allusion to the Protector. This framing sets off some strangely polemical resonances in the earlier poems: "The Fart censured in the Parliament House" takes on the qualities of a generalized debunking of the institution itself (pp. 65–71), while the account of battling bishops and mated kings in the anonymous Jacobean poem "Vpon Chesse-play. To Dr. Budden" takes on a new poignancy in the mid-1650s (pp. 41–45). Thus, although the volume contains few explicitly royalist moments, its points of reference (Caroline literary society, the Scots War, royalist piracy) and its tone of cavalier bravado, libertinism, and antipuritanism amounted to a clear statement of allegiance. The recipe was clear enough, at least, to be imitated by compilers of the many drolleries issued in the wake of *Musarum Deliciae*—volumes that included *Wit and Drollery* (1656), *Sportive Wit* (1656), *Choyce Drollery* (1656), and *Wit Restor'd* (1658).

It is one thing to broadcast an appeal for solidarity, quite another to have it received and acted upon. The question of how effective the drolleries were as documents of subversion is unquantifiable. But the extent of government interest in the circulation of subversive poetry at this time suggests that it was hitting a raw nerve—reaching even those who were not in any sense cavaliers. Early in 1655, Colonel Robert Overton, a radical associated with Quakers and later with Fifth Monarchy Men, was arrested after the exposure of the so-called "Overton plot" (a rising of religious radicals in the Scottish army).[69] Overton was thought to be in secret communication with Charles Stuart, but a search of his rooms in Leith yielded nothing more incriminating than "severall unhandsome verses relateinge to his highnes the lord protector, written upon the backside of an old letter."[70] This "paper of verses, called the Character of a Protector" was a variant version of a poem once assigned to Cleveland.[71] Overton's servant explained that his master had copied the verses down after "hearinge a fidler's boy singe them in London."[72] Overton himself claimed rather desperately that he was given the verses by a friend who had told him that Cromwell himself "had seen them, and I believe laughed at them, as (to my knowledge) heretofore he hath done at papers and pamphlets of more personal and particular import or abuse."[73]

Overton was unlucky to be caught with an explicitly political libel in his possession, but even poems that were not explicitly political were often thought to imply a subversive stance. Such was the case with the drollery *Sportive Wit: the Muses Merriment* (1656), a volume fundamentally similar in tone and composition to *Musarum Deliciae*. In April 1656 Nathaniel Brook, the stationer responsible for *Sportive Wit*, was arrested and interrogated about the volume, described by the government informer (the stationer, Stephen Bowtell) as "scandalous and preiudiciall to the Comonnwealth." Questioned about the compilation of the volume, Brook claimed that he had compiled it himself from "sundry papers which he procured of seuerall persons" (including one Walter Wasse). He laid the blame for the introductory epistle at the door of "one John Phillips whoe liues about Westm[inster]" (the nephew of a recently retired government official, John Milton). With regard to the print run of the book, he claimed to have received 950 copies, no less than 700 of which he had sold at 18 pence each.[74] The investigators reported to the Council of State that *Sportive Wit* contained "much Scandalous, Lascivious, Scurrilous, and profane matter," and the Protector himself gave the order for the seizure and burning of the book and the fining of those involved in its publication.[75] A fortnight later a similar volume, *Choyce Drollery*, "being stufft with prophane and obscene matter, tending to the Corrupcion of manners," met with the same fate.[76] Although neither volume contains much in the way of explicitly political comment, both displayed a louche, drolling, libertine tone that bespoke royalism and subverted the Protector's attempt to build a lasting godly commonwealth upon the reformation of individual morality and manners.[77]

While the effectiveness of the drolleries as propaganda for the Stuart cause is unquantifiable, the success of *Musarum Deliciae* in bringing the names of Mennes and Smith to a wide reading public can hardly be doubted. Although little is yet known about the readership of such collections, one is probably safe in inferring that they appealed to young men about town, budding wits, anxious to assert their social and intellectual credentials—men not unlike those who had, three decades earlier, formed the Order of the Fancy. *Musarum Deliciae* quickly sold out and a second edition was issued in 1656. Other publishers, keen to capitalize on its success, hijacked the names of Mennes and Smith to endorse their own collections, even when, as in the case of *Wit and Drollery*, they contained little written by the two poets. Mennes and Smith rapidly became the benchmarks by which such collections were judged.[78] In the introductory epistle to *Sportive Wit*, John Phillips engaged in an aggressive marketing strategy, claiming that Mennes and Smith had never agreed to the publication of their poems (thus disparaging the authority of rival collections) and insisting that Mennes and Smith were, in any case, passé: "*there are other ingenuous persons in our little World* of Britain, *more youthfull, as familiar and joviall with the Muses as ever they were, and such as when they please to be right Drollers, can be as little in love as they*" (sig. A3).

The drolleries established Mennes and Smith as the social and stylistic models for a new generation of budding royalist wits. The mid-1650s witnessed a rapid increase in the number of productions exhibiting the characteristic features of their verse: the slipshod style, the use of octosyllabic doggerel, and the employment of such forms as the familiar epistle, the journey poem, and the classical travesty. In his invocation to *The Diarium, or Journall* (London, 1656), a poem advertized as being written in "Burlesque Rhime, or Drolling Verse" for the purpose of castigating those cavaliers "who never laughed since the King's death," Richard Flecknoe established his credentials by alluding to the stylistic models of

Mennes and Smith, whom he located in a tradition reaching back, via Scarron, Tassoni, and Cervantes, to Aristophanes and Plautus, only to reject them all in favor of his own muse, who *"For trifling yeildeth unto none"* (sigs. A2v, A4v). This was a burlesque strategy of ironic self-praise that Smith himself had earlier employed. Other productions exibiting the influence of Mennes and Smith include a mock-masque travestying the tale of Venus and Adonis printed in [Samuel Holland]'s *Wit and Fancy in a Maze* (London, 1656), John Lineall's journey poem *Itur Mediteraneum* (Stafford, 1658), and the journey poems and familiar epistles of Henry Bold, dating from 1656 and after.[79]

The vogue took particular hold in the legal community of London. In the last years of the decade Alexander Brome mastered the doggerel epistle, sending regular missives to friends in the provinces.[80] One of Brome's contacts was the Staffordshire gentleman, Charles Cotton, whose father was involved with members of Mennes and Smith's circle.[81] Cotton adopted the burlesque style himself to great effect, composing many epistles, journey poems, and one of the most popular travesties of the century, *Scarronides*.[82] It was at this time that an obscure Gray's Inn wit began work on a poem that eventually became *Hudibras*—but that is another story.[83] For the moment, it is important to return to the rising of 1655.

V

With hindsight it is clear that the rising of March 1654/5 was doomed. Planned by a small, dynamic faction at the exiled court, it lacked the wholehearted endorsement of Charles and the Sealed Knot, without whom little popular support could be expected. Only in the West Country, under John Penruddock, did any real rising take place. The rebels took Salisbury, but were soon overwhelmed by the Parliamentary army. Penruddock's men, pursued by the army, spent the night of 14 March at South Molton, Devon, a few miles from the home of Hugh Pollard at Kings Nympton. Pollard was in charge of royalist resistance in the area, and the rebels probably headed this way in the hope of gaining his support. Although Pollard did nothing to assist them, his refusal to commit himself was no doubt due to his realization of the futility of the attempt.[84]

It seems likely that James Smith—given his known sympathies, his closeness to Pollard, his residence in Kings Nympton, and his being rewarded after the Restoration—was an active conspirator in Pollard's western region. He certainly claims as much in his petition to Charles II after the Restoration, but no evidence of such activities survives. The only available evidence shows that, outwardly at least, Smith collaborated with the authorities, conforming to the Directory of Worship and retaining his benefice throughout the Interregnum.

Mennes's employment in Penruddock's rising marked the beginning of a period of employment by Hyde. Perhaps his bout of sickness in Lisbon had convinced him that he was too old for a life of piracy and for the reckless policies pursued by Rupert. Mennes was, after all, a man of Hyde's generation and temper, and the chancellor had a high regard for him. When Hyde was forced to send his wife away from Bruges in April 1656 he entrusted her to Mennes's care.[85] During the last years of the decade Mennes followed Hyde and became a permanent member of the prince's court, moving with the court to Cologne, to Brussels, and then to Bruges.[86] In spite of his advancing age, Mennes remained immensely energetic on behalf of the cause, hurling himself into a range of activities with vigor and attempting to clear up problems and disputes as they arose.[87]

Mennes was too valuable, by virtue of his extensive maritime experience, to be retained at court for long periods. He was frequently employed during the years prior to the Restoration as a roving adviser on maritime affairs. During the latter part of 1657 he organized the purchase of ships and gave advice on costings for fitting them out. On this business he was sent for a time to Holland, and in the spring of 1658 he was at Dort with Henry Coventry and with George Morley (the author of several poems in *Musarum Deliciae*).[88]

After the death of Cromwell and the collapse of the government of his son, Richard, royalist hopes rode high and conspiratorial activity was feverish. A rising in August 1659 was carefully monitored by Mennes from the coast of Holland, where he and the royal fleet awaited the opportunity to strike.[89] The opportunity never came, but hopes continued to soar. On 26 September/6 October, Mennes wrote to Hyde from Antwerp, where he had met with Lord Wentworth (Smith's erstwhile patron):

> I haue visited my Lord Wentwoorth whose lady ariued heere thursday last: she makes my lord in good humor, I hope in assuring him, and her selfe, of a better condicion in this change, which the rebbells are soe sencible of, that the king's last iorney gaue them such alarums that there were many searches after him being certainly perswaded he had been in England, whither God send him, though I waite on him in a footboys coat. . . . [90]

Mennes's desire for service, even in the anonymity of a footboy's coat, appears to have been granted, for, although he was clearly involved in assisting the Restoration of Charles, the exact part he played is not known.[91]

On 10/20 December 1659 John Heath wrote to Hyde from Calais requesting Mennes's services: "if hee can bee spared from other Imployment I had a hint this poast of some thing hee might bee vsefully imployed in about Chattam concerning the shipping, (besides the general of modelling the Country)."[92] A letter from secretary Nicholas to John Heath (who later married Mennes's niece) of 28 January/7 February 1659/60 concerns money paid by the king to send Mennes over (to England).[93] It is not clear whether Mennes actually crossed over to England early in 1660, nor, if he did, is it clear what he did there. Perhaps he had been sent, as Heath seems to suggest, to attempt to take control of the English fleet. If so, he failed. In mid-December the fleet had unexpectedly declared for Parliament.[94] Alternatively, Mennes may merely have been sent over in order to monitor the temper of the fleet. Whatever Mennes's involvement with the Navy, a shift occurred in March with the appointment of Monck and Montagu, men favorable to the idea of a restoration, to senior naval commands. Under their command the Navy was ideologically remodeled, accepting the Declaration of Breda in April and sailing to Holland to collect Charles in May. There is no evidence as to the whereabouts of Mennes at this time, but it is difficult to believe that he would not have been present on Charles's voyage to England and at his triumphal reception at Dover.[95]

Sir John Mennes and James Smith had served the Stuarts loyally throughout the Civil War and Interregnum. Charles did not forget this.

13

Restoration?

I

This chapter is, perforce, little more than a postscript. There is no surviving poetry by Mennes and Smith from the Restoration period, and information about them is either scarce or of little substantive interest. They ended their days in material comfort, incommoded only by the discomforts of old age and (in Mennes's case) the financial scars of the Civil War. If they were hoping for a Restoration of the halcyon days of the 1630s, in which they had cut their riotous swathe through London society, they were disappointed. The tone of Restoration society, conditioned by the long years of exile and poverty, involved an obscenity more vulgar, a cynicism more bitter, and a vandalism more fundamental and skeptical than anything ever dreamt up by the Order of the Fancy.

James Smith lived out his latter years in Devon, where he accumulated benefices in a leisurely fashion. After petitioning Charles Stuart shortly after his return to England, Smith was granted the archdeaconry of Barnstaple, which he held until 1662.[1] This was only the first of many tokens of favor. In July 1660 he was granted the canon residentiary's place at Exeter Cathedral—his qualifications being attested by two literary clerics associated with Exeter, John Earle, author of the influential collection of characters, *Microcosmography*, and George Morley, cousin of Denham and author of a number of poems printed along with Smith's in *Musarum Deliciae*. Perhaps his literary reputation helped secure him the post. While there, he apparently composed a number of anthems for the cathedral, although no record of them has survived.[2] Other places and tokens included the award of the degree of Doctor of Divinity by Oxford University on 3 July 1661, the rectory of Alphington in October 1662 (upon which he resigned from King's Nympton), the precentorship of Exeter Cathedral, perhaps in the same year, and the rectory of Exminster, Devon, in July 1664.[3] Smith's multiple benefices would have brought him a fair income, and he may have been wealthy enough by the mid-1660s to involve himself in a spot of property dealing.[4] Even a dispute with the crown over the appointment of a canon in 1663, which saw Smith briefly suspended as precentor, had no lasting effects.[5] He died in comfortable seclusion on 20 June 1667 and was buried in the church of King's Nympton, where he had weathered the grim days of the commonwealth.[6]

While Smith remained in rural retirement, Mennes rose to a position of considerable public prominence. On his return to England, Mennes set about reclaiming his sequestered estate and attempting to acquire new lands.[7] His petition to the king of August 1666 for rents due to the Crown on the Duchy of Lancaster during the Civil War and Interregnum and the lease and keepership of Hylin's Park, Staffordshire, makes much of his loyal service to two Stuart monarchs:

> for his constant loyaltie hee hath not only lost the benifitt of his estate during all the late R[ebel *MS torn*]lion, but also spent out of purse (For most whereof hee is still in debt) some thowsands of pounds, in raising forces, buyeing Armes, & holding correspondencies, For the service of the Crowne, And in mainteining himselfe at his ow[n *MS torn*] sole charge all that time in attending the persons, and businesse of your Royall Father, and your selfe.[8]

Mennes had a fair case. But one of the terms of Charles's return had been that sequestered properties should remain with their current owners. The figure of the impoverished "old cavalier" loomed large in the Restoration imagination, and laments about the king's ingratitude, such as Cowley's "Complaint," were legion.[9] Few of such petitions were successful, and there is no evidence that Mennes fared better than others.

In his search for lucrative places, Mennes met with more success. In 1660 he petitioned Charles to be reinstated as keeper of Walmer Castle, Kent. His petition was granted, and he immediately set about repairing it. But other demands fell upon him, and, in April 1663, the keepership was granted to Sir Thomas Ingram.[10]

In May 1661 he was appointed commander in chief in the Downs and Admiral of the Narrow Seas. His flagship was the *Henry*, one of the largest men-of-war built during the Protectorate.[11] Other places and benefits followed. He was appointed a gentleman of the Privy Council in 1660, master of the Trinity House and a member of the Council for Foreign Plantations in 1661, a member of the Tangier Committee in 1662 and a governor of the Chatham Chest (a fund for the support of disabled seamen) in 1662, and a member of the Fishery Corporation in 1664.[12] His most prestigious post, however, was that of comptroller of the Navy, which he held from November 1661 until his death on 18 February 1671.[13]

No sooner had Mennes received this appointment than he was committed, as Admiral of the Fleet, to undertaking a lengthy expedition to Tangier, recently acquired from Portugal as a part of Queen Catherine's marriage dowry.[14] Mennes returned briefly to his prewar role of ferrying important diplomats. Having deposited the new governor and his retinue, the fleet sailed for Lisbon to collect the queen herself. There they examined the jewels that formed part of the dowry, and Mennes was entrusted with their safekeeping—a task for which he appears to have been rewarded with a "great Portugall Iewell wherein are about One hundred and fourescore Diamonds sett in gold."[15] He had not been back in England long before he was off again, bringing over the queen mother from France.[16] During this period of absence, there was a domestic tragedy: on 23 July 1662, Mennes's wife, Jane, died at the home of John Boys and was buried at his expense in Nonnington Church, Kent. The bereaved husband erected a pious and handsome memorial tablet in the church.[17]

Following the death of his wife, Mennes began to search for new lodgings and a new wife, but, failing to find either, settled for a substantial redecoration of his official rooms in Seething Lane.[18] This did not satisfy him for long. He became increasingly crotchety, moaning about his accommodation to anyone who would listen. He berated Pepys and Sir William Carteret "in the most childish and most unbeseeming manner" that "everybody had a palace, and he had no house to lie in."[19]

Mennes's business life in these latter years was no happier than his domestic arrangements. His duties as Comptroller gave him a seat on the Navy Board (along with a treasurer, a surveyor, a clerk, and three commissioners). The board controlled the Navy's finances, looking after the payment of men and the provisioning of ships. The comptroller's role was to ensure efficiency by auditing accounts, supervising the payment of seamen, and keeping a check on the fluctuating prices of materials. The rapid expansion of naval bureaucracy after the Restoration made the job an impossible one.[20] And Mennes's own talents did not mark him out as a natural choice for such a post. The comptrollership demanded patient, methodical, and painstaking accounting. Although he was endowed with considerable managerial skills and was able to handle personnel problems with fairness and tact, the debit and credit of the balance sheet was something he could never master.[21] The post also imposed upon its incumbent a gruelling program of travel, which took its toll upon the ageing Mennes. He was repeatedly ill, suffering regular attacks of the stone and on one occasion collapsing in church.[22] The increasingly professional tone of the office meant that gentlemanly dilettantes like Mennes were expensive anachronisms. Pepys's observation that Mennes was esteemed at Whitehall as "an old good companion," as "a jester or a ballat-maker," rather than as a "man of business," reflects this changing ethos: these were the very qualities that had, in earlier life, aided his career.[23] All in all, Mennes was precisely the wrong man for the job.

That Mennes managed to cling on the comptrollership until his death in February 1670/1 is itself remarkable. That he managed to do so despite such disasters as the Medway incident and the continued machinations of his colleagues seems little short of miraculous, for throughout the later

1660s there were repeated attempts to dislodge him—attempts master-minded by his industrious subordinate, Samuel Pepys. Pepys was initially rather impressed by the old comptroller, whose company he found conge-nial and whose integrity he respected. But as the depth of Mennes's in-competence became apparent, Pepys and his colleagues became ever more determined to get rid of him.[24] Parliamentary complaints and words in the king's ear yielded no more than a compromise: in 1667 the comp-troller was forced to accept the appointment of two assistants.[25] While the refusal to dismiss Mennes was no doubt in part a refusal on Clarendon's part to bow to Parliamentary pressure, one suspects that Clarendon and his master were sensible of a long-standing debt to the old comptroller.

It was not only in the Navy Office that Mennes, after the Restoration, was out of place. In the social and literary life of the metropolis he appears to have played no part. If he kept up his verse correspondence with James Smith, there is no record of it. Perhaps, like his friend Den-ham, with whom he remained close, he made a conscious decision to forego poetry in favor of more serious business.[26] True, he whiled away many afternoons with his colleagues drinking, visiting plays, reading from his books of poetry, and recounting bawdy stories.[27] On one memorable occasion he engaged in an amicable "wit-combat" with John Evelyn, who caused great hilarity by outdoing the old poet at his own game, the im-promptu recitation of verses. Pepys records the incident with characteris-tic verve:

> Among other humours, Mr. Eveling's repeating of some verses made up of no-thing but the various acceptations of May and Can, and doing it so aptly, upon occasion of something of that nature, and so fast, did make us all die almost with laughing, and did so stop the mouth of Sir J. Mennes in the middle of all his mirth (and in a thing agreeing with his own manner of Genius) that I never saw any man so out-done in all my life; and Sir J. Mennes's mirth too, to see himself out-done, was the crown of all our mirth.[28]

But such occasions were notable in their rarity, and the bourgeois Pepys and the pious Evelyn can only have been pale shadows of his compatriots in the Order of the Fancy. Were it not for his advanced age, he might have had more in common with the wild young rakes of Charles's court. But even here, the tone of the young court involved cultural changes too great for him to stomach. While he might have looked with indulgence on such acts of high-spirited vandalism as the beating up of the watch or the smashing of the odd royal sundial, he viewed the fashionable libertinism of the court with distaste, complaining that "buggery is now almost grown as common among our gallants as in Italy, and that the very pages of the town begin to complain of their masters for it."[29]

To courtiers of the younger generation Mennes, like many of the "old cavaliers," was a figure of fun. They delighted in cruel jokes at his expense. On one occasion, while arguing with "a pretty Quaker woman," the king pointed at Mennes "as a man the fittest for her quaking religion, saying that his beard was the stiffest thing about him."[30] Mennes undoubtedly took such cracks with a good humor and made many at his own expense. On one occasion, when his grasp of the comptrollership was called into question, he told Clarendon "that he understands all his duty as easily as crack a nut; and easier . . . for his teeth are gone."[31] But the days in which a viable career at court or in the services might be made solely through the pursuit of wit or self-mockery were, at least for men of Mennes's generation, over.

Mennes died at his Navy Office lodgings in Seething Lane on 18 February 1670/1. He was buried in the nearby church of St. Olave Hart Street on 27 February: his handsome monument, recently restored, now adorns a pillar on the east chancel wall of the church.[32] The funeral was attended by many dignitaries, but few friends or family, most of them having died long before him.[33] The loss of his estate meant that he had little property to bestow on those who did survive him. To his nephew and niece, Francis and Elizabeth Hammon, he left the manor of Loughton in Essex and his claim to the rectory of Woodnesborrow in Kent. Various valuables and moderate sums of money were left for other friends and relatives: £100 went to the son of Anthony Moyle and Mennes's niece, Jane. Two jewels went to descendants of his half-brother, Matthew: to Matthew's daughter, Lady Heath, he bequeathed his great "Portugal Jewel," and to her daughter he left "a small Crosse of gold with seaven Diamonds in it" and moneys due on a bond. Other sums were left for servants and charities, including £50 for repairing the parish church of St. Peter in his home town of Sandwich.[34]

II

While Mennes and Smith may have been aliens in the new order of the 1660s, their legacy permeated the literary and social life of the age.

The Restoration marked the beginning of the great age of literary clubbing. Many of these bodies share striking similarities with the Order of the Fancy. In the 1670s and 1680s a club of Tory wits met at Barnard's Inn and composed burlesques and travesties of the latest translations. One member of the club, Alexander Radcliffe, guyed the author of a relentlessly obscene travesty of the Dryden translation of Ovid's *Epistles* with his own remarkable *Ovid Travestie* (1680).[35] Similar clubs flourished at the inns until well into the eighteenth century, when the young William Cowper and his associates formed the Nonsense Club, which specialized in the composition of facetious verse.[36] Nonsense and mock-learning were deployed to defend literary (and political) values against an advancing horde of dunces and scribblers in a manner reminiscent of *The Innovation* in the Scriblerus Club of Pope and Swift.[37]

In the literary marketplace the drolleries continued to enjoy great popularity. The drolleries in their Restoration manifestation were increasingly comprised of songs and prologues and epilogues from the plays. They retained, however, their antipuritan (now high-Tory) character, and they often printed pieces indebted to the verse of Mennes and Smith.[38]

It was above all in the burlesques and travesties that flourished after the Restoration that the legacy of Mennes and Smith is to be found. Their octosyllabic doggerel epistles had initiated a tradition that flourished with unprecedented obscenity among the wits and would-be wits of the Restoration court. Among the many who tried their hand at such epistles were George Etherege, the earl of Dorset, Lord Middleton, and the generally rather saturnine Dryden.[39] The Presbyterian Robert Wild even made a bid to claim the genre for the nonconformists.[40]

In the field of mock-poetry, Ovid's epistles remained favored texts for travesty, while Charles Cotton and his followers turned their attentions to Virgil, Lucian, and Homer.[41] The genial, playful tone of Cotton's burlesque verse is close to that of Mennes and Smith, and their influence on him seems certain.[42] With Cotton's *Scarronides*—as its title suggests— the influence in England of the French master of the mode began to wax, and, in the rush to imitate the success of Cotton's travesty, the native achievements of Mennes and Smith were soon forgotten.

One can also be confident of the influence of Mennes and Smith on the work of the unofficial laureate of the new regime, Samuel Butler.[43] *Hudibras* is distinguished from earlier efforts by the overarching satiric purpose for which the playful, drolling style is deployed. The resulting tone of the poem is thus complex and contradictory, frequently involving an incongruous blend of satiric denigration, gratuitous comedy, and indulgent celebration. While such features have their precedents in Smith's *Innovation*, this brief piece was overshadowed both in scope and popularity by Butler's monstrous creation. Butler's transformation of the drolling style into an instrument of satire was so influential that it left all subsequent writers of octosyllabic doggerel in his debt and all but erased the memory of Sir John Mennes and Dr. James Smith. Yet their contribution to the burlesque tradition was an important one. While they were not exactly the parents of the octosyllabic doggerel style, they were perhaps its midwives: they gave it its distinctive tone, and they popularized it, stimulating its adoption by others and thereby paving the way for the burlesques and travesties that, for better or worse, so dominated Restoration literary culture.

Appendix 1.
Mennes and Smith: The Canon

The bulk of the verse of Mennes and Smith was first published in three verse miscellanies (of a kind traditionally known as "drolleries") in the mid-1650s: *Musarum Deliciae* (1655; 2d ed. 1656), *Wit and Drollery* (1656; 2d ed. 1661; 3d ed. 1682), and *Wit Restor'd* (1658). The first and last of these collections are traditionally assumed to have been edited by Mennes and Smith. There is, however, no evidence for this assumption and much against it.

The assumption that Mennes and Smith edited *Musarum Deliciae* and *Wit Restor'd* has led to a tendency to assign to them any poems that appear therein—a practice that has led to much confusion. Like the posthumous Rochester collection, *Poems on Several Occasions* (1680), both *Musarum Deliciae* and *Wit Restor'd* contain a body of material by one or two central figures, while being miscellaneous in character. (On such issues, see Vieth, *Attribution in Restoration Poetry*; Mary Hobbs, *Early Seventeenth Century Verse Miscellany Manuscripts* [Aldershot: Scolar Press, 1992].)

My approach to the attribution of poems in these collections has been tentative. No work is assigned to Mennes or Smith without firm evidence. Poems that may on merely stylistic grounds be felt to be their work are relegated to sections entitled "dubia." I have also identified poems wrongly attributed to Mennes or Smith.

The Collections

Musarum Deliciae (1655; 2d ed. 1656)
Date and Publication: Entered in the Stationers' Register for its publisher, Henry Herringman, on 1 June 1655: "*Musarum Delitiae or the Muses recreation containing severall select pieces of sportive witt*, written by Sir John Mennis & F[athe]r Smith" (*A Transcript of the Registers of the Worshipful Company of Stationers 1640-1708 A.D.*, 2 vols. [London: privately printed, 1913], 1.484). The first edition appeared some three months later—Thomason dates his copy 28 August (*Catalogue of*

the Pamphlets, Newspapers, and Manuscripts Relating to the Civil War, the Commonwealth, and Restoration, Collected by George Thomason, 2 vols. [London: British Museum, 1908], 2.1.126).

Editor: In "The Stationer to the Ingenious Reader," Herringman implies that he himself edited the collection: "*I have therefore, to regal the curious Pallats of these Times, made a Collection of Sir* John Mennis, *and* Doctor Smiths *Drolish Intercourses*" (sigs. A3–A3v). The word "*made*" implies in this context more than just "printed." It is possible that Mennes and Smith may have provided copy for the volume.

Contents: Forty-five poems, just over half of which can be attributed: eight to Mennes and Smith, nineteen to others. Of the remaining seventeen, some are included as "dubia" in the Mennes/Smith canon on stylistic grounds.

Bibliography: "Achievement," pp. 244–56; *MD&WR*.

Wit and Drollery (1656; 2d ed. 1661; 3d ed. 1682)

Date and Publication: Entered on the Stationers' Register for its publisher, Nathaniel Brook, on 30 January 1655/6: "*Witt and drollery, Joviall poems* by Sir John Mince, James Smith, Sir W[illia]m Davenant, John Dunne and other admirable witts" (2.27). The first edition had already appeared by this time: Thomason dated his copy 18 January 1656 (*Thomason*, 2.1.138).

Editor: The government investigation into the collection makes clear that its editor was John Phillips, Milton's wayward nephew (Stokes, p. xii). Nothing suggests that Mennes or Smith were involved.

Contents: Ninety-four poems, almost half of which can be attributed. Despite the appearance of their initials on the title page, Mennes and Smith had next to nothing to do with the volume. Only the three opening poems—"The Preface to that most elaborate piece of Poetry entitled Penelope Ulysses," *The Innovation* itself, and "The Black-Smith" (here entitled "Song")—can be attributed to Smith, while nothing in the collection can be confidently assigned to Mennes.

Bibliography: Stokes; "Achievement," pp. 257–59.

Wit Restor'd (1658)

Date and Publication: Entered on the Stationers' Register for Nathaniel Brook and Thomas Dring on 8 July 1658 (2.186). It is not known when the volume appeared, although it was advertized at the end of *Naps upon Parnassus* (London, 1658), which was on sale by October 1658.

Editor: Unknown.

Contents: Out of 131 poems, 70 can be attributed. A substantial body of these are by Smith, Mennes and their circle. In addition to nineteen poems by Smith, there are contributions by Atkins, Massinger, and

Mennes; an anonymous crony contributed commendatory verses to *The Innovation*, and Bagnall's "Ballet" is printed in full, including three stanzas omitted from the text in *Musarum Deliciae*. Nothing suggests that Mennes or Smith were responsible for any other poem in the collection. About one-sixth of the poems in *Wit Restor'd* are associated with Mennes or Smith. It is primarily a miscellany.

Bibliography: "Achievement," pp. 260–64; *MD&WR*.

Mennes: Extant Poems

"Active Love."

Texts: BL MS Add. 53723, fol. 64; Henry Lawes, *The Second Book of Airs*, p. 10; *The Second Part of the Treasury of Musick* (London, 1669), p. 43.

Attribution: Assigned to "Sir *John Mennes*" in *Second Book of Ayres*. See Pamela J. Willetts, *The Henry Lawes Manuscript* (London: British Museum, 1969), no. 129. One of many contemporary lyrics with the opening "Tell me no more," the most famous of which is by Henry King. (On these poems, see Jeremy Treglown, "The Satirical Inversion of Some English Sources in Rochester's Poetry," *RES* 24 [1973]: 43.)

Date: Early to mid-1630s? The poem appears toward the beginning of the Lawes manuscript, which is, generally speaking, arranged chronologically.

"The Black-Smith" [written by The Order of the Fancy; Mennes a contributor].

Texts: This popular ballad was regularly altered and embellished in performances and printings, and it spawned a host of imitations. It therefore exists in many variant states. Broadsides: *The Bonny Black-Smith's Delight* [London, 1674–79] (Wing B3603A); *The bonny Black-smiths delight* [Magdalene College, Cambridge, Pepys Ballads, 4.264]; *A merry new Ballad: both pleasant and sweete* [London?, 1650] (Wing M1870A); Collections: *WD*, p. 6; *WR*, sig. L8v, p. 156; *The Second Part of Merry Drollery, or A Collection of Jovial Poems, Merry Songs, Witty Drolleries* (London, [1661?]) (Wing S2295), p. 40; N. D., *An Antidote Against Melancholy: Made up in Pills* (London, 1661) (Wing D66A), p. 20. For references to other versions of the ballad (including one by a genuine blacksmith), see *Merry Drollery Compleat*, pp. 387–89; Lister, *Loyal Blacksmith*, pp. 24–26.

Attribution: Assigned to "some of the Modern Familie of the Fancies" in *WR*, a reference to the Order of the Fancy, of which Mennes and Smith were members.

Date: Probably late 1620s or early 1630s, when the order flourished. H. E. Rollins assumes that it was entered on the Stationers' Register on 21 March 1635, *An Analytical Index to the Ballad Entries (1557–1709) in the Registers of the Company of Stationers* (Chapel Hill: University of North Carolina Press, 1924), no. 204. There seems, however, to be no evidence for this suggestion; Simpson, *British Broadside Ballad*, p. 247, n. 7.

"Gill upon Gill, or, Gills Asse uncas'd, unstript, unbound."
Text: HL, p. "75" (57).
Attribution: In a verse epistle to Mennes of 10 January 1640/1 ("In answer to this last, or some such like Letter"), Smith mentions the poems: "Seest thou not, *Ovid, Homer, Virgil*, / With Muse more needy, *John*, then your *Gill*" (*MD*, p. 12). The poem appears in *HL*, a volume containing verse by Smith. The attribution is complicated by the fact that the poem is preceded in *HL* by another ballad on Gill, "On Doctor Gill, Master of Pauls Schoole" (p. 54), but this ballad can be assigned to the royalist minister Thomas Triplett. Aubrey states that Triplett wrote a ballad on Gill and had it performed beneath the master's window (2.264). Although Aubrey quotes both pieces on Gill almost verbatim from *HL* (including the marginal notes, which have been misinterpreted as Aubrey's own annotations), there is no doubt that "On Doctor Gill" is Triplett's because it is a straightforward ballad for which a tune exists, while "Gill upon Gill" employs two voices, and requires footnotes to elucidate it (Simpson, *British Broadside Ballad*, p. 711, n. 1). It seems from Aubrey's holograph that he copied Triplett's ballad from *HL* and realizing the relevance of Mennes's, copied that too (Bodl. MS Aubrey 8, fols. 52–52v). Clark prints a bowdlerised version of the ballad in Aubrey, 1.263–66.
Date: Late 1620s or early 1630s. It alludes to the younger Gill's crying down of the king in 1628 (*CSPD, 1628–29*, p. 319): "*But now remaines the vilest thing / The Ale-House barking 'gainst the K.*" (p. 59), and apparently to the pardon granted Gill on 30 November 1630 (*CSPD, 1630*, pp. 362 and 393).

"In answer to certaine Letters, which he received from London, whilst he was engaged to follow the Camp."
Text: MD, p. 9.
Attribution: Signed "*J. M.*" (*MD*, p. 11). Wrongly ascribed to James Smith by Wedgwood, *Poetry and Politics*, p. 109.
Date: 1 January 1640/1: its opening line—"What, Letters two on, New-years-day?"—alludes to Smith's epistles of 24 and 27 December 1640 ("The same, To the same" ["My doubtie Squire of *Kentish* crew"] and "The same, to the same" ["My note which cost thee pennies Sixe"]).

"To a friend upon a journey to Epsam Well."
Text: MD, p. 3.
Attribution: Assigned to Mennes by Smith in "Mr. Smith, to Captain Mennis then commanding a Troop of Horse in the North." Smith rebukes Mennes for the failure of his muse:

> The Grecian prize; how did she earne?
> The bayes she brought from *Epsom* Fearne?
> There teem'd she freely as the hipps,
> The Hermit kist with trembling lipps.
>
> (*WR*, p. 1)

Smith alludes to the lines "Close by the Well, you may discerne / Small shrubs of *Eglantin* and *Fern*," and to the hemmit's plea, after witnessing Mennes's victory in a shitting contest, "dear, let me kisse those thighes" (*MD*, pp. 4 and 7).
Date: A terminal date of December 1640 is provided by Smith's poem. Smith's reference to the poem suggests that it was written long enough ago to be recalled as a past triumph, but recently enough to be topical. Mennes's period of unemployment between 1639 and 1640 seems a likely time for both the journey and the poem.

"To his Deare Friend Mr J. S. upon his quaint *Innovation of Penelope and Ulysses*."
Text: WR, sig. L2; p. 143.
Attribution: Signed "*J.M.*" No other known friend of Smith has such initials. In his *DNB* account of Smith, Sidney Lee attributes this poem, without foundation, to Jasper Mayne.
Date: Like *The Innovation*, mid to late 1630s.

"To Parson Weeks. An Invitation to London."
Text: MS: Yale University, Beinecke MS b104, p. 1, Collections: *MD*, p. 1; Chamberlain, *Harmony of the Muses*, p. 8; John Dryden, *The Sixth Part of Miscellany Poems* (London, 1716), p. 365.
Attribution: Assigned to Mennes in Beinecke MS b104 ("Io: Minees"), *Harmony of the Muses* ("Joh. Myns"), and Dryden's *Miscellany*, but there is no evidence that these are based on anything more substantial than the association of Mennes with *MD*.
Date: After 2 September 1642, by its reference to the Parliamentary prohibition of stage plays on that day (Firth & Rait, 1.26–27): "hath the Bishop, in a rage / Forbid thy comming on our Stage?" (p. 1).

"To the Youth of Cotswold, on Mr. Robert Dover, his annuall meetings."

Text: Annalia Dubrensia, sig. F4.
Attribution: Signed "Captaine Iohn Menese."
Date: Mid-1630s.

"Verses upon an Entertainment given by the Chancellor."
Text: Bodl. MS Clarendon 49, fols. 245–46.
Attribution: Assigned to "Ia: Mennes" by Hyde (fol. 246v).
Date: Late 1654. The sheets containing the poem are bound up at the end
of the 1654 section of the manuscript. The opening lines mention a
parting at "Santon" involving one "of more then humane race," surely
an allusion to Charles's farewell to his sister at Xancten or Santoigne
on 5 November 1654 (Clarendon, 5.357–60).

["What Man would sojourne heere"].
Texts: Bodl. MS Malone 13, fol. 10v (text only); BL MS Add. 53723, fol.
27 (first stanza only, with musical setting).
Attribution: Signed "I: Mennesse" in Bodl. MS Malone 13.
Date: Early 1630s. The first stanza appears toward the beginning of the
(generally) chronologically arranged Lawes manuscript (BL MS Add.
53723). See Willetts, *Lawes Manuscript*, no. 129; p. 2.

Mennes: Dubia

"A Gentleman on his being trim'd by a Cobler" [Mennes?].
Text: WD, p. 48.
Attribution: Assigned to Mennes by Stokes in his edition of *WD* on the
basis of its references to Wales, where Mennes was stationed during the
Civil War. The poem alludes to Carmarthen and "*Gally*'s Bridge,"
which Stokes regards as a misreading for "Towy," the river that runs
through Carmarthen (p. 222). It seems more likely that "*Gally*" is a
version of "Gwilli," a river northeast of Carmarthen, which was crossed
by the main road into the town; John Ogilby, *Britannia* (London,
1675), pp. 167–78 and plate 84. Although one might travel on this road
from North Wales, where Mennes was stationed in 1644, to Carmarthen, there is no evidence that Mennes did so. Biographical evidence
cannot determine the poem's authorship, nor can stylistic evidence.
Although, like Mennes's burlesque verse, the poem is a witty, occasional piece employing an informal style and comic double rhymes—
"monster"/"conster"—these similarities cannot determine Mennes's
authorship. The poem is, for example, written in regular pentameters
rather than the chaotic octosyllabics typical of Mennes's verse.

"An Elegy, offered to the Memory of that Incomparable Son of Apollo, Mr. John Cleaveland."

Text: J. Cleaveland Revived (London, 1660), p. 2.

Attribution: Signed "*J.M.*" Hilton Kelliher assumes that Mennes is the most likely author of the elegy in his facsimile edition of "*J. Cleaveland Revived," Second edition (1660)* (Aldershot: Scolar Press, 1990), p. xvi. But there were other poets with such initials—Jasper Mayne, for example. Without further evidence, therefore, the attribution must remain speculative.

"The Anglers Song."

Text: WD, p. 51.

Attribution: Signed "*J.N.*" Stylistic evidence—together with the signature (which Stokes suggests is a misreading for "J.M."; p. 223)—renders Mennes's authorship possible. The poem employs both octosyllabics and pentameters and contains a description of morning remarkably similar to that of an epistle from Smith to Mennes. Compare the couplet "Of Dew there was a gallant draught, / Which when the Sun arose he quaft" (p. 52), with Smith's "Or else as *Phoebus*, when full fraught, / And tipled with his mornings draught" (*WR*, p. 13). Finally, like other verse by Mennes and Smith, it contains proverbs and allusions to good fellowship.

"Upon a lame tired Horse."

Texts: MS: BL MS Add. 47111, fol. 5, Collection: *MD*, p. 27.

Attribution: It is assumed to be the work of Mennes in *Facetiae*, but there is only stylistic evidence for this assumption, and it is not entirely convincing (1.330). The poem exhibits the absurd similes and reductive tendencies typical of Mennes and Smith, but it employs pentameters, rather than their usual octosyllabics. The poem cannot be securely assigned to them. The poem on riding a lame or tired horse appears to have been a recognized subgenre of the journey poem in the seventeenth century: see, for example, Brome, *Poems*, 1.275.

Mennes: Lost Poems

Epistle to Smith on his journey with the Scots' money.

Attribution: Smith refers to an epistle relating Mennes's "journey to the foe with Coyne" in "The same, to the same" ("My note which cost thee pennies Sixe").

Date: Late December 1640, when Mennes made the journey to the Scots.

Epistle to Smith on his second journey with the Scots' money.

Attribution: Smith refers to an epistle relating a fight with a Scot in "The same, to the same" ("No sooner I from supper rose").

Date: January 1640/1, when Mennes made a second journey to the Scots army, but before 26 January, when Smith's epistle was written.

Epistle to Smith on the priest Goodman.

Attribution: Smith's "A letter to Sir John Mennis, when the Parliament denied the King Money" contains an explanatory headnote quoting a couplet from Mennes's epistle—"*What is't for him to hang an houre, / To give an Army strength and power?*" (*MD*, p. 63).

Date: Late January–early February 1640/1. The headnote dates Mennes's poem to the period "when the Parliament denied the King Money to pay the Army, unlesse a Priest, whom the King had reprieved, might be executed" (p. 63). This was the Catholic priest, John Goodman. On 22 January 1640/1, the House of Commons refused to authorize a loan by the City of London because Charles I had reprieved the death sentence passed on Goodman by Parliament. The debate lost its significance after 3 February 1640/1, when Parliament voted £30,000 worth of "brotherly assistance" for the Scots (Gardiner, 9.264–65 and 272).

Epistle to Smith on his adoption of the Directory of Worship.

Attribution: Smith wrote an epistle entitled "An answer to a Letter from Sr. John Mennis, wherein he jeeres him for falling so quickly to the use of the Directory."

Date: After August 1645, when the Directory of Worship was introduced (Firth & Rait, 1.755) and before May 1648, the date of Smith's epistle.

Mock-Poem on Gondibert.

Attribution: Wood assigns to Mennes "a mock poem on sir Will. Davenant and his *Gondibert*" (*Athenae*, 3.925). Laughton, in his *DNB* account of Mennes, assumes that this is a reference to the *Certain Verses* (1653), but this seems unlikely given that Wood discusses the volume elsewhere without mentioning Mennes (*Athenae*, 3.805 and 808).

Date: After 1650.

Mennes: Wrongly Attributed Poems

A Letter sent by Sir John Suckling from France.

Text:————. London, 1641. (Wing S6132A).

Attribution: Assigned to Mennes in the catalogues of the William A.

Clark and Henry E. Huntington libraries, presumably on the basis of its similarity to other ballads on Suckling that have been assumed to be by Mennes—"Upon Sir John Suckling," etc—a similarity noted by Thomas Seccombe in his *DNB* account of Suckling. Since these assignations are false, that of *A Letter* is presumably an error. It is unlikely that Mennes would have written so antiroyalist a ballad (it attacks Mennes's friends Davenant and Suckling for their involvement in the First Army Plot). The ballad is assigned to William Norris by W. Carew Hazlitt, *Collections and Notes 1867–1876* (London, 1876), p. 412.

"The loose Wooer."
Texts: MSS: BL MS Sloane 1446, fol. 26; Yale University, Beinecke MS b104, p. 114, Collections: *MD*, p. 46; *WD*, sig. K7 (p. "125").
Attribution: Assigned to Mennes (or Smith) by Stokes on the false assumption that *MD* is "almost entirely" their work (p. 301). Stylistic evidence does not suggest their authorship.

Merry Newes from Epsom-Wells.
Text:————. London, 1663. (Wing M1872).
Attribution: Wood assigns "*Epsom Wells, a Poem*—Printed in qu." to Mennes (*Athenae*, 3.925)—a perplexing attribution, since the poem bears little resemblance to other works by Mennes. The obvious explanation is that Wood is confusing the ballad with Mennes's epistle "To a friend upon a journey to Epsam Well" (printed in *MD*), but this is undermined by Wood's insistence that the ballad was printed in quarto, as this is.
Date: Early 1660s.

"To a friend upon his Marriage."
—See Smith.

"Upon Madam Chevereuze swimming over the Thames."
Texts: MSS: Bodl. MSS Eng. Poet. c. 53, fol. 1; Eng. Poet. f. 27, p. 245; Rawl. Poet. 65, fol. 73v: Collection: *MD*, p. 49.
Attribution: It is assumed in *Facetiae* (1817) that Mennes is its author, but nothing buttresses this assumption (1.xvii).
Date: Summer 1625, this being the date of the Duchess's scandalous swimming expedition; Michael Prawdin, *Marie de Rohan: Duchesse de Chevreuse* (London: Allen and Unwin, 1971), p. 36.

"Upon Sir John Suckling."
Text: WD, p. 44.

Attribution: Aubrey assigns both this and "Upon Sir John Sucklings most warlike preparations" to Mennes (2.242 and 245, n. 2). Clayton discredits the assignation of "Upon Sir John Suckling" on the grounds that Suckling could not have written its companion piece, "Sir John Sucklings Answer" (*WD*, p. 46), thus removing the mainstay of the argument—Aubrey's point that Suckling wrote this in answer to Mennes (Suckling, pp. 348–49). Clayton argues that Aubrey's attribution is based solely on the appearance of the poem in *WD*, a collection associated with Mennes.

"Upon Sir John Sucklings most warlike preparations for the Scotish Warre."
Text: MD, sig. χ6v; p. 82.
Attribution: Clayton argues that this piece may be attributed on similar grounds to the former: Mennes was associated with *MD*, in which the ballad appeared (Suckling, p. 352). Clayton concludes that Mennes is more likely to have been the author of this piece since the text in *MD* is sound and is the only known substantive version of the poem. But Aubrey's attribution is worthless, being based solely on his association of Mennes with *MD*. See my "Samuel Hartlib's Copy of 'Upon Sir John Suckling's hundred horse'," 445–47.

Vox Borealis, or the Northern Discoverie.
Text:———. [London], 1641. (Wing V712).
Attribution: Assigned to Mennes by H. E. Rollins in "Martin Parker, Ballad-Monger," *Modern Philology* 16 (1919): 461. This pamphlet contains another version of "Upon Sir John Sucklings most warlike preparations" and can be dismissed on the same grounds as that ballad.

Smith: Extant Poems

"A Letter to Sir John Mennis, when the Parliament denied the King Money to pay the Army" ("The Reply").
Text: MD, p. 63.
Attribution: Smith is Mennes's only known verse correspondent.
Date: Late January–early February 1640/1—see Mennes's lost epistle to Smith on the priest Goodman.

"Ad Johannuelem Leporem, Lepidissimum, Carmen Heroicum."
Texts: WR, p. 35; *WD1682*, p. 192.
Attribution: The poem is close to Smith's other mock-poems in its

travestying of classical sources and its use of mock-learned footnotes, and it appears at the beginning of a linked group of poems by Smith and his associates in *WR*, suggesting that the group circulated as a manuscript pamphlet. (On the phenomenon of "linked groups" circulating in manuscript form, see Vieth, *Attribution*, pp. 26–27, 76–79, and 322–52.) The "witty Johnny" of the title is presumably Mennes.

Date: After 1640, on the basis of footnote "(*h*)," "*Jansen. de praed. lib.* 22" (*WR*, p. 36), an allusion to Cornelius Jansen (1585–1638), whose writings were much concerned with predestination. It is reasonable to assume that Smith's knowledge of Jansen derived from his only published work, *Augustinus* ([Louvain], 1640). Smith's reference to "*de praed.*" is presumably bogus (like many such allusions in the poem), but *Augustinus* does contain a chapter entitled "Qui est de praedestinatione hominum & Angelorum" (p. 833; vol. 3, bk. 9).

"An answer to a Letter from Sr. John Mennis, wherein he jeeres him for falling so quickly to the use of the Directory."
Texts: *WR*, p. 46; *Rump*, 1.209; *WD1682*, p. 205.
Attribution: Signed "I. S." (p. 48).
Date: 4 May 1648. It is dated:

> The fourth of *May*; and dost thou heare,
> 'Tis as I take it, the eighth year
> Since *Portugall* by *Duke Braganza*
> Was cut from *Spaine* without a hand-saw.

(p. 48)

Portugal was liberated in 1640. The long gap between the date of the poem (8 May 1648) and the events discussed in it (the fall of Bristol and the issue of the Directory of Worship in the summer and autumn of 1645) is a little perplexing (for an even more striking anomaly, see below, "Mr. Smith, to Sir John Mennis, upon the surrender of Conway Castle by the Ar, B Y"). But it seems unlikely that the poem could have been written before 1648 because it alludes to the Parliamentary ordinance of 8 June 1647 abolishing Christmas, holidays, and festivals (Firth & Rait, 1.954). It is true that Christmas had been banned in 1644, but not holidays and festivals (Firth & Rait, 1.580). Sixteen forty-seven, moreover, appears to have been the year in which the Directory was forcibly imposed on Devon: this was the year of Herrick's expulsion from Dean Prior; Herrick, p. xvi.

"The Black-Smith." [Smith a contributor].
—See Mennes.

"Dr. Smiths Ballet."

Texts: MS: BL MS Harl. 3991, fols. 20v–22, 43v: Broadside: *An Invective against the Pride of Women* [London, 1657] (Wing I284): Collection: *MD*, sig. χ3v; p. "76."

Attribution: Title.

Date: 1630s. A reference to Booker's almanacs—"*Booker* hath no such Prognostications" (*MD*, sig. χ4; p. "77")—affords a *terminus a quo* of 1631, in which year Booker published his first almanac; Keith Thomas, *Religion and the Decline of Magic: Studies in Popular Beliefs in Sixteenth- and Seventeenth-Century England* (Harmondsworth: Penguin, 1973), p. 363. But the ballad was probably written not long after this because it is a contribution to a controversy over the affectation of masculine dress by women, which came to a head in 1620 with the publication of *Hic Mulier: or The Man Woman* (London, 1620) (*STC* 13374–75) and which fizzled on throughout the decade. For the social and ideological context of this debate see Wright, *Middle-Class Culture*, chap. 13, especially pp. 492–97; Woodbridge, *Women and the English Renaissance*, pp. 139–51. Smith's ballad imitates "Will Bagnalls Ballet," a piece printed alongside it in *MD* and a contribution to the same debate. It provoked a number of responses: see Thomas Jordan, *Wit in a Wildernesse* (London, [1665?]), sig. +2; Weaver, *Songs and Poems* (1654), p. 32; and Bold, *Poems* (1664), p. 110.

"In answer to this last, or some such like Letter."

Text: *MD*, p. 11.

Attribution: Signed "*James Smith*" (p. 13).

Date: 10 January 1640/1; it is dated—"The tenth of *January* day durty, / One thousand, hundreds six, and forty" (p. 13).

The Innovation of Penelope and Ulysses, A Mock-Poem.

—"The Author to the Author. To his worthy Friend J. S. upon his happy Translation of *Ulysses and Penelope.*" *WR*, sig. L2v; p. 144.

—"The Author to himselfe." *WR*, sig. L4; p. 147.

—"The Preface to that most elaborate piece of poetry, entituled, *Penelope and Ulysses.*" *WD*, p. 1.

Texts: *WD*, p. 1; *WR*, sig. K6. (The *WR* text, with its battery of prefatory materials, was presumably printed from a manuscript pamphlet that circulated in the 1630s.)

Attribution: Signed "*J. S.*" (*WR*, sig. K6).

Date: Mid-late 1630s. A terminal date of 1640 is afforded by the inclusion of a commendatory poem by Philip Massinger in the *WR* text, since Massinger was buried on 18 March 1639/40; Massinger, *Plays and*

Poems, 1.xliii. Edwards and Gibson suggest that Massinger's piece dates from the mid-1630s on the basis of its reference to the current fashion for "Strips and Gorgets" (4.421–22). Further evidence for dating Smith's poem to the mid-1630s is suggested by the probability that it travesties a translation of Ovid's *Heroides* published by Wye Saltonstall in 1636; for a full discussion of this issue see part 3, chapter 9 above.

The Loves of Hero and Leander. A mock Poem.
Texts: 1651 (Wing L3276); 1653 (two editions) (Wing L3277–78). Subsequent editions accompanied *Ovid De Arte Amandi, and the Remedy of Love Englished*, [trans. Thomas Heywood]: 1662 (Wing O648), 1662/7 (an edition not listed in Wing that has a preliminary title page dated 1662 and a title for *Hero and Leander* dated 1667—copies in Bodleian, Antiq. f. E. (94)2; BL 1068 a. 7; Folger O649), 1672, 1677, 1682, and 1684 (Wing O650–53). A second edition of 1684 is not listed by Wing. (Copies of the 1684 editions in the Bodleian and the Folger Shakespeare libraries—Bodl. Vet. A3. f. 702; Folger O653—have a number of variants against the copy in Beinecke Library at Yale University—Yale Gno. 8 Cg. 598h: the latter has a different title page and misprints page 113 as 313.) There were also editions in 1701 and 1705. Bibliographical details are given by Arthur E. Case in his *Bibliography of English Poetical Miscellanies 1521–1750* (Oxford: Oxford Bibliographical Society, 1935), no. 103, but this account is supplemented by "Achievement," pp. 237–43.
Attribution: Frank notes that Smith may have been its author without offering evidence in *Hobbled Pegasus*, p. 277, no. 490. The most important evidence is contained in "the Authors Prologue," which concludes

> *Know all, I value this rich Gem,*
> *With any peice of* C. J. M.
> *Nay more then so, Ile goe no lesse,*
> *Then any script of Freinds,* J. S.

(*HL*, p. 1)

No "J. S." other than Smith is known to have written mock-poems based on classical sources at this time. C. C. Smith suggests in "The Seventeenth Century Drolleries," that the initials "J. S." are inserted simply to balance the initials "C. J. M." (p. 58), but there is no reason for this interpretation. It makes perfect sense, given the context, to regard the final initials as the author's signature. The prologue also refers to a group of friends, including one C. J. M., who wrote in the style of *Hero and Leander*. Smith's circle, which included Mennes, is the most likely such group: the initials C. J. M. presumably stand for Captain John Mennes.

Date: Mid-1630's. In his preface to *The Innovation* Smith alludes to *The Loves of Hero and Leander*:

> This History deserves a grave translation;
> And if comparisons be free from slanders,
> I say, as well as *Hero* and *Leanders*.
>
> (*WR*, L4+O1; p. 148)

Farley-Hills assumes that this is a reference to Marlowe's *Hero and Leander (Rochester's Poetry*, pp. 94–95). It is more likely that Smith is referring humorously to his own *Loves of Hero and Leander*, which must, therefore, precede *The Innovation* (later 1630s).

"The Miller and the King's Daughter, by Mr. Smith." [Smith a contributor].

Text: Collections: *WR*, p. 51; *WD1682*, p. 87; Dryden, *The Third Part of Miscellany Poems* (London, 1716), p. 316. There was a broadside printed for Francis Grove in 1656, but I have failed to locate it; "'The Miller's Melody,' An Old Ballad," *N&Q*, 1st ser. 10 (1852): 591–92; *The English and Scottish Popular Ballads*, ed. Francis James Child, 5 vols. (Boston and New York, 1882), 1.118–41.

Attribution: The poem is a version of a traditional ballad and cannot therefore be entirely credited to Smith. Similar ballads entitled "The Barkshire Tragedy" and "The Drowned Lady" are quoted by [Thomas Hughes] in *The Scouring of the White Horse: or, The Long Vacation Ramble of a London Clerk* (Cambridge, 1859), pp. 174–78. It is suggested in *Facetiae* that Smith fused the two (1.337). It would perhaps be more accurate to observe that all three versions derive from a common archetype. The ballad assigned to Smith is not a complete version of the story. In "The Drowned Lady," for example, a harpist makes a fiddle out of a drowned woman and plays it in front of her parents, whereupon it tells the lady's story, but in Smith's version the instrument is for some reason made by a miller, and there is no explanation as to how it came to be played in front of the royal family. Since Smith did not write the ballad or create this version by simply combining the two earlier versions, its attribution to him is questionable. It may have been assigned in error, since it appears in a group of poems by Smith, but the editor of *WR* does not engage in casual attribution. Smith was probably responsible for the various twists given to this version of the story. The invention of musical uses for various parts of the body introduced the possibility of variation, and it is likely that we can detect Smith's taste for the absurd can be defected in some of the more fanciful suggestions, the most ridiculous of which is unique to Smith's version: "What did he doe with her two shinnes? . . . / Unto the violl they danc't *Moll Syms*" (p. 53).

"Mr. Smith's taking a Purge."
Texts: WR, p. 48; *WD1682*, p. 207; [William Hickes], *Oxford Drollery* (London, 1673), p. 105.
Attribution: Title.

"Mr. Smith, to Captain Mennis then commanding a Troop of Horse in the North, against the Scots."
Text: WR, p. 1.
Attribution: Title; signed "*I.S.*" (p. 2).
Date: 21 December 1640. It is dated from Lord Conway's house in Queen Street ("street / Of woman Royall"):

> The fourth precedent to Plum-porrage
> December moneth, and year of grace
> Sixteene hundred and forty to an Ace.
>
> (p. 2)

Since plum porridge was traditionally eaten at Christmas, the epistle can be dated to 21 December—four days before Christmas.

"Mr. Smith, to Sir John Mennis, upon the surrender of Conway Castle by the Ar, B Y."
Text: WR, p. 43.
Attribution: Title; signed "*I.S.*" (p. 45).
Date: 15 February 1648/9. It is dated 1648:

> The 15 of the month that's black,
> Forty eight yeares, and sixteen hundred
> Since that of Grace, away are squandred. . . .
>
> (p. 45)

The "month that's black" is presumably February, on the basis of the proverb "February fill-dike be it black or be it white" (Tilley F167). The events described in the poem took place over two years previously: Mennes compounded in July, and Conway Castle was surrendered by the archbishop of York in November 1646 (Phillips, *Memoirs of the Civil War in Wales*, 1.375 and 379). One might wish to suggest that the poem is misdated (perhaps as a result of a compositor misreading "46" for "48," yielding the reading "forty eight," but the concluding allusion to Pollard's house "Where one drinks, and another pledges, / I meane at meales" alludes to the dangers of drinking healths to "King Charles II" in the wake of the Parliamentary "Act prohibiting the proclaiming of any person to be King of England or Ireland, or the Dominions thereof," 30 January 1648/9 (Firth & Rait, 1.1263). For a similar anomaly, see above, "An answer to a Letter from Sr. John Mennis, wherein he jeeres him for falling so quickly to the use of the Directory."

"Mr. Smith, to Tom Pollard, and Mr. Mering."
Text: WR, p. 54.
Attribution: Title; signed "*IS*" (p. 55).
Date: 5 July 1640. It is dated "*Iuly* the fifth I wrote this letter / One thousand six hunderd, & somewhat better" (p. 55). Smith was in Scotland with the army—as this epistle states—in 1640.

["On Felton's Arraignment"].
Texts: MSS: Bodl. Ashmole 36, 37, fol. 31; Malone 23, p. 208: Print: *Poems and Songs Relating to Buckingham*, p. 71.
Attribution: Signed "Ia: Smith" in MSS Ashmole 36, 37.
Date: Fairholt notes that Smith's plea to Felton's judges dates the poem to the period between 23 August 1627 (the day of the murder) and 27 November, the day of Felton's trial (Gardiner, 6.349 and 359).

"The Pigg."
Text: HL, p. 49.
Attribution: In addition to its low burlesque style, three pieces of circumstantial evidence suggest Smith's authorship. First, it refers to "the swine-faced Maydens head, / Ith' *Netherlands* they say was bred" (p. 49). It seems that Smith knew the account of this freakish birth entitled, *A Certain Relation of the Hog-faced Gentlewoman called Mistris Tanakin Skinker* (London, 1640) (*STC* 22627) for he uses a phrase from it in an epistle of 10 January 1640/1. The apparently idiomatic expression used by Smith in an epistle to Mennes, "Known, as the ready way to *Rumford*" (*MD*, p. 12), was obviously uncommon: it is not noted by *ODEP* or Tilley, but it appears in *A Certain Relation*: "so long as I have known *Rumford*" (sig. B2v). This coincidence is not conclusive, but a second piece of evidence adds weight to the attribution. In "The Pigg," a woman named "*Besse*" prepares a feast (p. 52): Smith's wife was called Elizabeth. Finally, the feast consists of "a Tithe Pigg" (p. 50), which suggests that the host may have been a clergyman, like Smith.

"The Same, to the same" ("I must call from between thy thighs").
Text: WR, p. 8.
Attribution: Signed "*I.S.*" (p. 9).
Date: 29–31 January 1640/1. It is dated:

> *Janus* the moneth that holdes us tack,
> One, with a face behinde his back:
> Full sixteene hundred yeares wee score
> And fiftie, (bateing six, and fowr). . . .
>
> (p. 9)

The epistle must date from late January because Smith alludes to appointments of 29 January, such as the replacement of Sir John Banks by Edward Herbert as the king's attorney (Gardiner, 9.264).

"The same, To the same" ("My doubtie Squire of *Kentissh* crew").
Text: WR, p. 3.
Attribution: Signed "*J. Smith*" (p. 4).
Date: 24 December 1640. Dated—"Christmas day is ee'ne tomorrow" (p. 3). References to events of December 1640 allow us to determine the year. Sir John Finch, for example, fled to Holland in December 1640 (Clarendon, 1.232, note): "But I am told the *Finch* is warie / And fled after the Secretarie" (p. 3).

"The same, to the same" ("My note which cost thee pennies Sixe").
Text: WR, p. 5.
Attribution: Signed "*I.S.*" (p. 7).
Date: 27 December 1640. It is dated:

> *December* moneth, day of St. *John*
> . . . .
> Forty, (besides the sixteen hundred)
> We count yeares past since Fiend was foundred
>
> (p. 7)

"The same, to the same" ("No sooner I from supper rose").
Text: WR, p. 12.
Attribution: Signed "*I.S.*" (p. 13).
Date: 26 January 1640/1. It is dated; "Day twenty sixt, and when *John* saies, / *Faces about*, the Month obays" (p. 13)—an allusion to the two faces of Janus. A reference to Mennes's encounter with a Scot allows us to date it to 1640/1, since this was the period of the Scots Wars.

"The same, to the same" ("Thy wants wherewith thou long hast tug'd").
Text: WR, p. 10.

Attribution: Signed "*I.S.*" (p. 12).

Date: 30 January 1640/1. It is dated; "Day tenth thrice told, the morning fair, / The month still with a face to spare" (p. 12). The year can be established because this epistle alludes to Smith's epistle of 26 January 1640/1, which urged Mennes to come to London: "I lately thee from North did call" (p. 12).

"The same, to the same" ("Why how now friend, why com'st not hither").

Text: WR, p. 14.

Attribution: Signed "*S* that hath an *J* before" (p. 15).

Date: Mid to late February 1640/1. It is dated:

> tis the Moneth sirnamed *Fill-Dike*
> . . . .
> Full sixteen hundred yeares (I hold)
> And fifty (bating five twice told)
> Expired are since yeare of grace. . . .
>
> (p. 16)

February was proverbially known as "Fill Dyke" (Tilley F167). Smith's reference to Maxwell's arrest of Berkeley allows the epistle to be dated to soon after 12 February, when this took place (Gardiner, 9.289–90):

> Judge *Bartlet* sitting on his stall,
> In *Westminster* . . .
> Was there surpriz'd, and grip'd by th'wrist
> By *Maxwell*. . . .
>
> (p. 15)

"To a friend upon his Marriage."

Texts: MSS: BL MSS Add. 47111, fol. 14v; Eg. 2725, fol. 31v; Harl. 6917, fol. 87v: Collection: *MD*, p. 7.

Attribution: Assigned to Mennes by Aubrey (1.206), Wood (*Athenae*, 3.804), and BL MS Add. 47111 ("Captaine Mence," fol. 14v). These attributions are not reliable: Wood's derives directly from Aubrey's, which in turn is probably based only on the poem's appearance in *MD*. The MS attribution might predate *MD*, since the British Library's *Catalogue of Additions to the Manuscripts 1946–1950* (London: British Library, 1979) dates MS Add. 47111 to the period 1646–49 (pp. 229–31), but it might still be associational—Mennes was connected with the poem and was better known than its author. I have suggested that this was the case—that the epistle was written to Mennes by Smith—in my facsimile edition, *MD&WR* (pp. 16–18).

Various factors support my identification of Smith as the author and Mennes as the recipient. These depend upon my dating of the poem to the period 7 June to 1 July 1641. First, Mennes was married in the North around February 1640/1. Second, no known friend of Mennes was married at this time. Third, in two MS versions the recipient of the poem is identified as a Captain John—BL MSS Harl. 6917, fol. 88, and Eg. 2725, fol. 31v (I quote the former version):

> But now my muse to th' Captaine sends
> some news to entertaine his friends;
> Iohn knows I know what Cavaleers. . . .

Fourth, the poem refers to an ongoing verse correspondence— "Since last I writ, I heare deare honey, / Thou hast committed Matrimony" (*MD*, p. 7): the only known correspondent with Mennes is Smith. Fifth, the poet mentions his indebtedness—"From *London*, where we sit and muse, / And pay Debts when we cannot chuse" (p. 9): Smith complains to Mennes of this problem in a verse letter of 30 January 1640/1 (*WR*, p. 10). Finally, the poem was written "From *London*": it seems that at the time of compostion—7 June to 1 July 1641—Smith was in London and Mennes in the North. This requires some discussion. Mennes was out of London for part of this period: he traveled to London around 13 February 1640/1 and had returned to the North by 21 June. Smith was in Bromley in February 1640/1, but in Devon by late October 1641. If Smith did write the poem, he might have left London shortly after 12 February, when he sent an epistle from there to Mennes, since Mennes was traveling south on 13 February: had they both been in London, they would probably have met, and Smith would have been able to congratulate Mennes on his marriage then, rendering the epistle redundant. It is not unreasonable to posit this departure because Smith had been complaining about his pursuit by creditors: he may have left London in order to escape them. Perhaps, on the other hand, Smith was unable to leave Bromley during Mennes's visit to the capital. Wherever Smith was in the spring of 1641, it is likely that the epistle is his because it states that news of the marriage reached the poet after he had sent his last letter: Smith's last letter to Mennes was that of 12 February, and nothing suggests that there are any lost epistles from this period. In fact, if the marriage referred to is Mennes's, the material in the letter is arranged chronologically (the marriage, Davenant's arrest, and the Bishops' Bill) suggesting that this is the first correspondence since February.

Date: 7 June–1 July 1641. The poem refers to Davenant's arrest for complicity in the First Army Plot at Faversham, Kent on 12 May 1641; after being bailed on 9 July he was again arrested at Canterbury; Arthur H. Nethercot, *Sir William Davenant: Poet Laureate and Playwright-Manager* (Chicago: University of Chicago Press, 1938), pp. 189–98. Aubrey and Wood assume that the poem concerns the second arrest, but they must be mistaken: the final lines allow us to date the poem to before 1 July 1641:

> The day that Bishops, Deans and Prebends,
> And all their friends, wear mourning Ribbands;
> If this day smile, they'l ride in Coaches,
> And, if it frown, then *Bonas Noches*.

(MD, p. 9)

This refers to the "act for the utter abolishing and taking away of all archbishops, bishops . . . deans . . . prebendaries . . . and other under-officers, out of the Church of England." According to Clarendon this bill was first announced in Parliament on 27 May 1641. A second reading, planned for 7 June, did not occur until 11 June, whereupon it was debated for twenty days (1.314–15 and 362–63). Since the poem was written on the day on which these debates were expected to be concluded, it must have been written between 7 June and 1 July 1641.

"To Parson Weeks. An Invitation to London." [Smith?].
—See Mennes.

"To Sir John Mennis, on a rich prize which he took on the Seas."
Text: MD, sig. G3v; p. 84.
Attribution: Signed "*I.S.*" (sig. G4; p. 85).
Date: Around or after 14 December 1653. It contains a reference to the Protector—"We shall be free born people then (*Oh Hector*) / When we have nothing left but a ———." (sig. G4; p. 85). Cromwell was appointed Lord Protector on 14 December 1653 (Clarendon, 5.285).

["Upon Madam Mallett"].
Texts: BL MSS: Add. 10309, fol. 122; Eg. 2421, fol. 13; Sloane 1446, fol. 26v; Sloane 1792, fol. 24; Bodl. MSS: Don d. 58, fol. 41; Eng. Poet. e. 14, fol. 26; Rawl. Poet. 117, fol. 20v; Rawl. Poet. 142, fol. 40; Rawl. Poet. 199, p. 85; Folger Shakespeare Library MSS V. a. 103 Part 1, fol. 72 and V. a. 345, p. 122.
Attribution: The poem is most frequently assigned to Smith or "J. S." and is assigned to "Mr <I> Smith of Ch[rist] Ch[urch]" in the best text of the poem (Bodl. MS Eng. Poet. e. 14; see appendix 2)—not, as Crum

suggests, "F Smith" (S781). This attribution possesses authority because the manuscript containing it was compiled by an Oxford man
during Smith's student days: Falconer Madan and H. E. Craster's *Summary Catalogue of Western Manuscripts in the Bodleian Library at Oxford*, 6 vols. (Oxford: Clarendon Press, 1895–1937) notes that it was
compiled around 1620–30 (6.132). There other attributions to "J. S."—
BL MS Add. 10309, fol. 122; Folger MS V. a. 103 Part 1, fol. 72. It is
twice attributed to Corbett (Bodl. MSS Rawl. Poet. 142, fol. 40; and
Rawl. Poet. 199, p. 85), but these are dismissed by Bennett and
Trevor-Roper as confusions of this poem with Corbett's own piece on
Mallett (*Corbett*, p. 170). It is assigned to Brian Duppa in BL MS
Sloane 1446 (fol. 27) and, according to Bennett and Trevor-Roper, to
Jeremial Terrent in the same MS, but I have not found this attribution.
Its assignation to "I: stone" in Folger MS V. a. 345 (p. 122) probably
derives from a false interpretation of Smith's initials, but I am unsure
of the basis for Helen Gardner's attribution of it to the character writer
John Stephens in John Donne, *The Elegies, Songs and Sonnets* (Ox-
ford: Clarendon Press, 1965), pp. 119–20.

Smith: Dubia

Untitled: "Dear Coz: the want of thy sweet company." [Smith?].
Text: MD, sig. G2; p. 83.
Attribution: This quatrain is printed at the end of Sir William Spring's
   "Upon the naked Bedlams, and spotted Beasts" as though it were an
   epilogue to that poem. But it does not appear in any known MS version
   (BL MS Add. 18220, fol. 62; Bodl. MSS Eng. Poet. d. 152, fol. 105;
   Rawl. Poet. 65, fol. 70v; Rawl. Poet. 191, fol. 100v; Rawl. Poet. D.
   260, fol. 37v). Nor is the quatrain, with its relaxed cavalier concern
   with friendship and classical ritual, in keeping with Spring's frenetic indignation. I quote the quatrain in full:

> Dear Coz: the want of thy sweet company,
> Puts me upon this idle Poetry:
> May you returne with *Olive* in your hand,
> Bring thy deare selfe to me, peace to the Land.

This is so similar in tone to Herrick's "Farewell Frost" that it is tempting to assign it to one of Herrick's circle such as Smith. It would look
quite at home at the end of one of Smith's decasyllabic epistles to Mennes (such as the epistle that appears immediately afterward in *MD*),
but there is insufficient evidence to justify this assumption.

"On the praise of Fat Men."

Text: WD, sig. 2G6v (p. "76").

Attribution: Assigned to Smith by Stokes because of its "general tone" and the fact that, like much of Smith's work, it does not appear elsewhere (p. 277). John Wardroper assigns it to Mennes or Smith on stylistic grounds and because he claims that both men were fat; *Love and Drollery* (London: Routledge and Kegan Paul, 1969), p. 301. There is internal evidence for Smith's authorship in passages reminiscent of Smith's comic uses of excrement and purges in other poems. The grotesque account of fat women—

> Such whose large podes do roar as loude
> As wind doth in a tall Ships shroud;
> There blasts are such as you with wonder,
> If not beheld, would sweare were thunder.
>
> (sig. 2H5r; p. "89")

is remarkably similar to "Mr. Smith's taking a Purge"—

> At rumbling noyse the mastive growles
> The frighted mice forsake their holes,
> And Souldiers to my window come
> Invited thither by my drum. . . .
>
> (*WR*, p. 49)

There are also two details that occur both here and in Smith's *HL*: a reference to the aphrodisiac effect of the oyster—a word that is rhymed with "Cloyster" (*WD*, sig. 2H2v [p. "84"]; *HL*, pp. 7 and 18)— and the rhyming of "aslopen" with "open" (*WD*, sig. 2H4v [p. "88"]; HL, p. 13). These similarities are striking enough to suggest Smith's authorship.

"Upon a Surfeit caught by drinking evill Sack, at the George Tavern in Southwark."

Texts: MS: BL MS Harl. 6917, fol. 50v: Collection: *MD*, p. 28.

Attribution: Stylistic evidence suggests that the poem may be the work of Mennes or Smith because—although it is written in pentameters rather than octosyllabics—it employs a familiar, fanciful tone to give a witty account of physical discomfort (like "Mr. Smith's taking a Purge"). Circumstantial evidence suggests that, if it is their work, Smith is the more likely author. First, a reference to "the Laety" suggests that its author was a cleric (p. 29). Second, Smith was a frequenter of Southwark taverns. Third, the recipient of the poem is named "*Ned*" (p. 28), and Smith may have had a clerical friend named Edward (Layfield) who lived in the London area. Finally, the poet's intention to avoid sack "while *Severn*, and old *Avon* can / Afford a draught" (p. 29) would have a topical resonance were Smith the poet, for from 1639 his benefice was in the West Country. This mixture of stylistic and circumstantial evidence is not, however, substantial enough to determine Smith's authorship.

Smith: Lost Poems

Epistle to Mennes on the imprisonment of their friends.
Attribution: Smith's "The same, To the same" ("My doubtie Squire of *Kentish* crew") contains the couplet, "I hitherto have told, dear Captain, / Of prisons that our peeres are clapt in" (*WR*, p. 3).
Date: Before 24 December 1640, when the above epistle was written.

Epistle to Mennes on the priest Goodman.
Attribution: In "A letter to Sir John Mennis, when the Parliament denied the King Money," Smith writes, "By my last letter *Iohn* thou see'st / What I have done to soften Priest" (*MD*, p. 63).
Date: January 1640/1; see "A letter to Sir John Mennis.".

Religious Anthems.
Attribution: Wood assigns to Smith "Certain Anthems Not the musical, but the poetical part of them; which are to this day used and sung in the cath. ch. at Exeter" (*Athenae*, 3.776). Although there is no trace of these in Exeter Cathedral Library, there is no reason to doubt Wood's attribution.
Date: 1660–67.

Mennes and Smith: Dubia

This section considers unattributed poems that appear in collections which claim to contain verse by Mennes and Smith and which might, for various reasons, be the work of either Mennes or Smith.

"Description of three Beauties."
Text: MSS: BL MSS Add. 25303, fol. 137; Harl. 6057, fol. 10v; Folger Shakespeare Library MS V. a. 276 Part 2, fol. 10v: Collection: *MD*, p. 13.
Attribution: William A. Ringler, Jr. notes that it is "probably" the work of Mennes or Smith; *The Poems of Sir Philip Sidney* (Oxford:

Clarendon Press, 1962), p. 351, but this attribution is based only on its appearance in *MD*. Stylistic evidence suggests that it may be by Mennes or Smith. It employs light octosyllabics and a playful, drolling style (like their epistles), and it uses coarseness to reduce elevated literature (like Smith's mock-poems): the influence of Pamela and Philoclea—heroines of the *Arcadia*—is countered by Mopsa (p. 15).

"Hankins Heigh-hoa."
Text: MD, p. 23.
Attribution: It employs nonsense (the Order of the Fancy spoke nonsense) and, like Smith's "Ad Johannuelem Leporem," it contains a narrative of sorts: Hankins has been in love with Susan for three years, but she has broken her oath to him, as a result of which he resolves to impale himself on a cooking spit. This mingling of sense and nonsense is unusual, but is insufficient evidence to determine the authorship of Mennes or Smith.

"On Luce Morgan a Common-Whore."
Texts: MS: Yale University, Beinecke MS Osborn b197, p. 68: Collection: *WD*, sig. C2.
Attribution: Stokes assigns it to Mennes or Smith (p. 197), presumably on account of its coarse, octosyllabic style: "Here lies black Luce that Pick-hatch drab, / Who had a word for every stab." Although the few poems in *WD* written in this style are either probably the work of Mennes or Smith—"On the praise of fat Men" is probably by Smith—or associates of Mennes and Smith—"The long Vacation" is by Davenant, and "Epitaph on a Whore" by the younger Charles Cotton—this is not sufficient evidence to offer a definite attribution.

"Some Gentlemen shut out of their seats in Pauls, while they went to drinke."
Text: MD, p. 26.
Attribution: Like "Description of Three Beauties," the poem is written in light octosyllabics, and, like much of the verse of Mennes and Smith, it is urbane and conversational in tone. It also contains a sneering disdain for enthusiasm—"Must we, mix'd with the zealous rout, / Stand hoofeing on the vulgar stone"—which would not be conspicuous in their verse. But the octosyllabics of "Some Gentlemen" do not have the comic waywardness typical of those of Mennes and Smith. There is insufficient stylistic evidence for even a reasonably firm attribution.

Appendix 2.
Mennes and Smith: Unpublished Poems

JOHN MENNES, [*ON LIFE*]

What Man would sojourne heere
if ought wee cheifely prise
A thousand hasards rise
to make the purchase deare
and when with paine and care tis gott
wee hold itt and wee hold it not.

Our honors others breath
with them tis won and Lost
On seas of Cares wee are tost
In purchasing this wreath   10
yet never was ther one soe fitt
But Envy disproportion'd itt.

The rich mans head is full of feares
and Liues as much perplext
as is the poore man Vext
with necessary Cares,
and sigh them both in the Extreame
the seale hangs on an equall beame.

For Loue noe such things ment
the Elder brothers Ledd   20
with reason to the bedd
made sure by Argument
and when such Fuell makes the fyer,
noe wonder if it flame noe higher.

When Loue goes hand in hand
and soules together meete
with voluntary Feete
he doeth tryumphant stand
and when I meete that simpathy
I'le Liue againe, till then I dye.   30

Text: Bodl. MS Malone 13, fol. 10v.
Variants: 1 heere]—, 2 prise]—, 3 rise]—, 4 deare]—, 5 paine]—,

gott]—, 7 breath]—, 8 Lost]—, 9 tost]—, 10 wreath]—. 11 fitt]—, 13 feares]—, 14 perplext]—, 15 rent *altered to* Vext 17 sigh] ~~may~~ sigh Extreeme]—, 19 Loue]—, ment]—, 20 brother[s *added*] Ledd]—, 21 bedd]—, 22 Argument]—; 25 hand]—, 26 meete]—; 27 Feete]—; 28 stand]—: 29 simpathy]—, *Endorsement*: I: Mennesse

Commentary: Corrections and punctuation are inserted in a lighter ink, although possibly in the same hand. Since this corrected punctuation is excessively heavy for modern taste, I have shown it only in the notes. The poem does not seem to be in Mennes's hand (he never spells his name in this fashion).

JOHN MENNES, *ON AN ENTERTAINMENT GIVEN BY THE CHANCELLOR [EDWARD HYDE]*

Copy of Verses upon an Entertainment given by the Chancellor

Yee morning Muses and Nocturnall
giue Cleare aspects on our Diurnall
Noe more that parting sad at Santon
The very thought of that would dant one
Though he of more then Humane race
And with salt Teares ore flow the face
A nobler day did since appeare
Enlightning all our Hemispheare
And vsher'd in with starrs soe bright
Which twinckled all the former night   10
That every man had working Pate
This morrow how to Celebrate
'mongst which a Councell was decreed
To make our feast a feast indeed
Our Maister first of all being Chosen
And his attendants halfe a dozen
T'was mention'd each should bring his dish
Where at the Chancellor Cry'd Pish
Quoth he, though I haue little pelfe
I'le rather pay for all my selfe   20
To which wee quickly all agreed
Such strifes with vs last not indeed
But marke the impudence of youth
For I must tell the naked truth
The young men cry, 't will not appeare
a feast at all, Sans chere entiere
Which well how to accomodate
Was growne a business now of state
The matter was referr'd to Voice
And all agreed without more noise   30

A Beauty now there liu'd fast by
The Emulation of each Eye
strict Gaurded by a stricter Mother
a preying sister and a brother
shee must be woo'd but who shall doe't
wee put the good old pen man to't
For to his worth and Grauity
The mother nothing could deny
What Rhetorick he us'd, wee passe
But Mother, sister and the Lasse   40
Att House appointed meete aboue
In place For feasting and For Loue
The table's prest with Various store
Tall Flagons fill'd till they run o're
The Maister Sate, Commands each Guest
To take his Seate where hee lik's best
Onely the Virgin as t'was fitt
Must next vnto our Maister sitt
The good old Mother Sate below
The one Eye'd sister planted soe   50
That well she could not vpward see
vnlesse she turn'd vnmannerly
The Grauer plac'd the younger Frye
Take vp there Roome Promiscuously
Now German flutes begin to Crowne
your name with Honor and renowne
The olde grow young the younger wild
The Matron wanton as a Child
Meane while the virgin sitts as Mute
As tale vntold, or, vnstrung'd Lute   60
On Eyes she feastes, those on her fixt
Darte beames, on which Loue play's betwixt
But Scarce a touch of hand or lipps
Noe thought of motion of the Hipps
(Loue's Complement) but all in vayne
shape Cupid in Platonick strayne
yet now the Maister giue's consent
Each Guest vse his owne meeriment
They rise a while some sing and dance
Some wooe, and some the flute advance   70
Now Shcomberg 'gins the virgin Court
Which quickly spoyles old Newbrugh's sport
For he with Loue was soe besotted
That for that tyme he long had plotted
But seeing such a riuall there
It bread both Ielouzie and feare
To Cure the last with treble flute

His riuall Home he doth salute
Thinking there with to knock him downe
(as then the Virgin were his owne) `   80
Shcombergh the charge receiued & stood
as firme as Rock against a floud
But Newbrugh could not longer smother
The truth he was the weaker brother
Yet feirce he loues and faine would vtter
But now could nether speake nor stutter
His tounge rowles vp and downe, and faine,
It could say something but in vayne,
The which sad want, he to supply
Makes vse of Fingers and of Eye   90
Reeles his approaches, Courts her hand
And holds her fast, to help him stand
Gripes hard her wrists Hipps sids and Armes
As if that black and blue wer Charmes
Shee skreeks, his phansy strech'd soe farr
It made him thinke 'twas his Gittar
But yet att length to make amends
Kneels downe and sucks her fingers ends
Our Maister and the Grauer sort
Sitt by and Listen to the sport   100
Our good old penman he gan stare on't
And rather had beene writting warrant
To send them on some better arrant
    Wentworth & Taaffe by age Exempt
From Loue and such like Complement
Close yoaked with the good old woman
Drank Rinco sang and troubled noeman,
    Yet something still of Loue remayns
For while this Nectar warmes their Veyns
They Court the Matron, first they dip   110
her fingers in the wyne then sip.
And like old Britaine Bards they sing
And drinke healths to the Princess, King
And all that Royall Tribe as fast
As long as night and Rinco last
    But now the Cock foretells the Morne
And tappers dymm begin to burne
Our louers had their loues forgott
And Quenched those fires in pottle pott
All take theire leaues, Thats all that could   120
For some there could not Though they would
Cupid was mad cald Ceres whore
And Bacchus Knaue that did noe more. /

Text: Bodl. MS Clarendon 49, fols. 245–46.

Variants: 33–34 *lines interlineated*: Read next—strict Gaurd[ed] by a stricter Mother / a pre[y?]ing sister and a brother 57 wild] ~~weild~~ wild 59 while]
~~tyme~~ while 75 a riuall] ariuall 95 strech'd] streche'd 96 made] ~~m~~ made *Endorsement*: "Copy of Verses upon an Enter: / :tainment giuen by the /
Chancellor / Endorsed by him / "Ia: Mennes."

Commentary: The poem is written in one hand and is subscribed "Ia.
Mennes" in a script identified as Clarendon's in a second subscription (in
another hand). Neither hand resembles Mennes's.

JAMES SMITH, *ON MADAM MALLETT*

Mr. I Smith of Christ Church vpon the same

Skelton some rimes; good Elderton a ballett
Heere's theame enough for all, Madam Mallett
Whome Poetts all do scorne; but driuing Muse
Makes choyce of this occasion; & doth chuse
To write of her whom all the Towne admires
For going, speaking, looking, strange attires;
Made vp by Natures hasty handelinge
The Modell of whose witt, is scarce as big
As a fly-blow, Nitt, or kernell of a Fig
Her Eyes, are like 2 buttons set in clay   10
Her face is past-bord, & her hayre is Hay
Her writhled cheekes, her nosetrills & her Chinne
Stinke all withowt, are putrifyed within.
Yett wold this Trunke, this Coffin, nay this Grave
This living Sepulcher, a husband have;
A Husband? yes, yow shall, he must goe brave
And so must yow, that all the Towne may know
That Madam Mallett still can bravely goe:
Of Gownes, Coates, Petticoates thow has variety
Why? thow canst fitt thy selfe for all society   20
Were it to mowrne to morrow yow could fitt him
Butt he that mowrnes for thee, I say God quitt him.
    Come Goody fiddle strings, must yow have a Man?
A handsome husband? with some Lutheran?
Noe some old Fidler, who after two yeares space
Shall strip thy skin off, for his fiddle Case
Or to a Carryer, that may Scrape thy hide
Which yett, with Scabbs & Itch is fortifide
Ah, thow old Glew-pott! hast not yett enough?
Is not thy Taper yet burnt owt? Noe, there's a snuff   30

Foh! owt with it, for it stinkes I sweare
Worse then burnt Partridge feathers, or Goates hayre
What! are yow prowd? & must yow needs ingender
Gett thee a Baboone, or Ape, & with them blender.
Yow answerd one yow had no Chyld, no Motion
And have yow now drunke a provoking Potion?
Art thow not asham'd to be so impudent?
A Schollars Chamber often to frequent?
Sollicite College, Canons & a Deane
Provoke a virtuous Spiritt? Ah thow Queane!   40
Thow Citterne-head! oh thow painted Post!
Thow Puppett! Baby! Baggage! that dost boast
Of Gownes, of Smocks of Ruffs & bands
Of no obligations, Chattells, nor noe lands
For none thow hast: The Gentleman that dy'de
Hated thee living; therefore he denide
That thow showldst any thinge at all possess
But that, of which thow cowldst be Governess
Which was iust nothing; for thy senseless Braynes
Are giddy, Idle, & thy Lute-string veynes   50
Make such a discord, that Thow instrument
Art the Base Violl of thy Discontent
When thow art finest, bravest & at best
Thow art thy owne fine foole, the Peoples lest.

Text: Bodl. MS Eng. Poet. e. 14, fols. 26–26v.
Variants: title I] <I> Christ Church] Ch: Chu: 29 Taper] Tap[er] 35 provoking] p[ro]voking

NOTES

Introduction

1. Tim Raylor, "*Wits Recreations* not by Sir John Mennes or James Smith?" *N&Q*, n. s. 32 (1985): 2–3; *idem*, "The Source of 'He that fights and runs away,'" *N&Q*, n. s. 33 (1986): 465–66; Appendix 1, above. See also, "*Witts Recreations: Selected from the Finest Fancies of Moderne Muses" (1640)*, introd. Colin Gibson (Aldershot: Scolar Press, 1990), p. xv.

2. It is significant that the notable exceptions to this statement are historians, such as C. H. Firth and Christopher Hill.

3. See, for example, *Literature and the English Civil War*, ed. Thomas Healy and Jonathan Sawday (Cambridge: Cambridge University Press, 1990), the published proceedings of a conference held in 1986; Peter W. Thomas, "The Impact on Literature," in *The Impact of the English Civil War*, ed. John Morrill (London: Collins and Brown, 1991), pp. 123–42. Several studies are currently in progress.

4. See, for example, Lois Potter, *Secret Rites and Secret Writing: Royalist Literature 1640–1660* (Cambridge: Cambridge University Press, 1989), Raymond A. Anselment, *Loyalist Resolve: Patient Fortitude in the English Civil War* (Newark: University of Delaware Press, 1988), and R. Malcolm Smuts, *Court Culture and the Origins of a Royalist Tradition in Early Stuart England* (Philadelphia: University of Pennsylvania Press, 1987). The late Harold Brooks noted the need for such studies, especially of Mennes and Smith, in "English Verse Satire, 1640–1660: Prolegomena," *The Seventeenth Century* 3 (1988): 17.

5. There is a useful discussion of the term in *Cavalier Poets: Selected Poems*, ed. Thomas Clayton (Oxford: Oxford University Press, 1978), pp. xv–xvi.

6. See Anselment, *Loyalist Resolve*, and Earl Miner, *The Cavalier Mode from Jonson to Cotton* (Princeton: Princeton University Press, 1971). Robin Skelton's anthology, *The Cavalier Poets* (London: Faber, 1970), offers a broad and generous selection of cavalier verse, but his selection criteria are occasionally questionable (John Bunyan is hardly a cavalier poet in any traditional sense; p. 54).

7. See, for instance, C. V. Wedgwood, *Poetry and Politics under the Stuarts* (Cambridge: Cambridge University Press, 1960), p. 71.

8. See Nigel Smith's review of Potter's *Secret Rites*, "Secret Selves," *EIC* 41 (1991): 324–31.

9. *The New Cambridge Bibliography of English Literature*, vol. 1, ed. George Watson (Cambridge: Cambridge University Press, 1974), gives Smith his own entry, while Mennes appears only under the titles of the anthologies associated with him; pp. 1318 and 2028. See also Douglas Bush, *English Literature in the Earlier Seventeenth Century 1600–1660*, The Oxford History of English Literature, 2d ed. (Oxford: Clarendon Press, 1962), pp. 105–106 and 615, and J. W. Saunders, *A Biographical Dictionary of Renaissance Poets and Dramatists, 1520–1650* (Brighton: Harvester; Totowa, N.J. : Barnes and Noble, 1983), p. 112.

10. *MD* (the second edition) and *WR* were reprinted, along with *Wits Recrea-*

tions, in *Facetiae*, ed. Thomas Park and Edward Dubois (London, 1817). A revised edition was printed by John Camden Hotten (London, [1874]). A facsimile edition of *MD* and *WR*, with an introduction and attributions by the present author (unfortunately marred by a serious printing error that rendered the introductory material almost useless), was issued by Scholars' Facsimiles and Reprints (Delmar, N.Y. 1985).

11. Previous studies of Mennes and Smith include *Athenae* (3.775–76 and 925); *Facetiae*, 3–13; *Alumni*; J. K. Laughton, "Mennes, Sir John (1599–1671)," *DNB*; Sidney Lee, "Smith, James (1605–1667)," *DNB*; Geoffrey Callender, "Sir John Mennes," *Mariner's Mirror* 6 (1940): 276–85; Edgar K. Thompson, "Admiral Sir John Mennes 1599–1671," *Mariner's Mirror* 48 (1962): 227; Pepys, 10.243–44. Except where they are pertinent to my discussion, I have generally ignored the errors in these accounts (although I give occasional details in footnotes). Such matters are dealt with at length in my dissertation ("Achievement").

Chapter 1. John Mennes: "Markt for the True-wit of a Million"

1. Peter Laslett, "The Gentry of Kent in 1640," *Cambridge Historical Journal* 9 (1948): 151–55 and 160; Alan Everitt, *The Community of Kent and the Great Rebellion 1640–60* (Leicester: Leicester University Press, 1966), p. 14.

2. It may be that their local connection was an ancient one, the family name deriving from the Kentish place name "Minnis," on which see H. G. C., "'Minnis' in Place Names," *N&Q*, 6th ser. 1 (1880): 96; W.D. Parish, "Minnis," *N&Q*, 6th ser. 1 (1880): 245. There is no evidence for the suggestion that the family were of Scottish descent; J.M., "Earldom of Carric: Sir John Mennis: Endymion Porter," *N&Q*, 3d ser. 4 (1863): 144; "Mennes, Sir John (1599–1671)," *DNB*. The pronunciation of the name is clear from contemporary spellings of it.

3. William Boys, *Collections for an History of Sandwich in Kent* (Canterbury, 1792), pp. 207 and 350. Boys prints a useful genealogy of the family.

4. It is possible that Thomas Nashe's allusion to "the Mannies of Kent" in *Lenten Stuff* (1599) is an allusion to the Mennes family; *The Works of Thomas Nashe*, ed. Ronald B. McKerrow, 2d ed., rev. F. P. Wilson, 5 vols. (Oxford: Blackwell, 1958), 3.187.

5. Their first son, Matthew, was baptized on 22 August 1591. He probably died soon afterward because another son, christened on 14 January 1592/3, was also named Matthew (it was he who inherited the family estates). On 30 June 1594, a third son, Thomas, was christened. He died without issue in 1632, four years after his wife; Boys, *Collections*, p. 350; Canterbury Cathedral Archives, U3/12/1/1 (Parish Registers of Sandwich St. Peter).

6. Frances (christened 22 January 1597/8), Nicholas (10 May 1601), Mary (6 November 1603) and Andrew (6 April 1606); Boys, *Collections*, p. 350; Canterbury Cathedral Archives, U3/12/1/1. The Blechendens were also a Kentish family; *Facetiae*, 1.3.

7. Tim Raylor, "Sir Matthew Mennes," *Historical Research: The Bulletin of the Institute of Historical Research* 61 (1988): 118–22.

8. Canterbury Cathedral Archives, U3/12/1/1.

9. The family had contributed handsomely to its foundation. The poet's elder brother, Matthew, studied at Lincoln College, Oxford, which had links (in the form of scholarships) with the Manwood school; Boys, *Collections*, p. 200; *Alum-*

ni. Unfortunately the school registers for the period do not appear to have survived; John Cavell and Brian Kennett, *A History of Sir Roger Manwood's School, Sandwich, 1563–1963* (London: Cory, Adams and Mackay, 1963), p. 16.

10. The statutes are printed by Boys, *Collections*, pp. 222–32. The original documents are in the Kent Archives Office (Cavell and Kennett, *Manwood's School*, p. 41). M. L. Clarke, *Classical Education in Britain 1500–1900* (Cambridge: Cambridge University Press, 1959), pp. 3–7; T. W. Baldwin, *William Shakespere's Small Latine & Lesse Greeke*, 2 vols. (Urbana: University of Illinois Press, 1944), 1.77 and 2.69.

11. Baldwin, *Shakespere's Small Latine*, 1.441; Boys, *Collections*, pp. 220–29.

12. Baldwin, *Shakespere's Small Latine*, 1.342; Boys, *Collections*, pp. 230–31.

13. Although Knolles was asked repeatedly by the citizens of Sandwich to resign his post (on the grounds that he had not "intended with that diligence as was meet he should") he does not appear to have done so. He died at Sandwich in 1610; Boys, *Collections* pp. 271–72; "Knolles, Richard (1550?–1610)," *DNB*. Anthony Wood gives a rather more glowing account of Knolles's career than seems to have been warranted; *Athenae*, 2.80–81.

14. Boys, *Collections*, pp. 230–32.

15. *Chaucer: The Critical Heritage*, ed. Derek Brewer, 2 vols. (London: Routledge and Kegan Paul, 1978), 1.13–14, 23, and 153–54.

16. Pepys, 4.184, 200, and note. The book was perhaps a collection of Skeltonic "flytings."

17. Pepys, 8.141; see also 6.237.

18. Joan Thirsk, "Younger Sons in the Seventeenth Century," in idem, *The Rural Economy of England: Collected Essays* (London: Hambledon, 1984), pp. 335–57; John Earle, *Microcosmography*, ed. Alfred West (Cambridge, 1897), p. 70.

19. Despite the wide practice of "gavelkind," or partible inheritance, in Kent, the Mennes family do not appear to have employed it; Everitt, *Community of Kent*, p. 35.

20. Anthony Wood suggested that he went to Corpus Christi College, Oxford at the age of about seventeen; but Wood seems to have confused Mennes with John Mynne of Surrey, who entered Corpus Christi in 1615, aged seventeen. The details Wood gives about Mennes's supposed career at Corpus are merely formulaic: "continuing for some years [*he*] did advance himself much in several sorts of learning, especially in humanity and poetry, and something in history"; *Athenae*, 3.925–26. For Wood's use of such formulae, see Baldwin, *Shakespere's Small Latine*, 1.31. There is only Wood's unreliable testimony that Mennes went to Oxford, and against this can be set the following facts: first, he was at sea by 1616, and, second, few of his gentlemanly naval colleagues—men like John Burley, Sir George Carteret, and Sir Robert Slingsby—went to university; "Carteret, Sir George (1611–1661)," *DNB*; "Burley or Burleigh, Sir George (d. 1648)," *DNB*.

21. D. E. Kennedy, "Naval Captains at the Outbreak of the English Civil War," *Mariner's Mirror* 46 (1960): 192–93; G. V. Scammell, "The Sinews of War: Manning and Provisioning English Fighting Ships *c* 1550–1650," *Mariner's Mirror* 73 (1987): 363.

22. Phineas Pett, *The Autobiography of Phineas Pett*, ed. W. G. Perrin, Navy Records Society, 51 (London, 1918), pp. 14–126.

23. Michael M. Oppenheim, *A History of the Administration of the Royal Navy and of Merchant Shipping in Relation to the Navy from MDIX to MDCLX* (London, 1896), pp. 184–96.

24. Roger Lockyer, *Buckingham* (London: Longman, 1981), p. 274.

25. PRO SP 16/24/87; *CSPD, 1625–26*, p. 311.

26. Monson was removed from the post of Admiral of the Narrow Seas on 12 January 1615/16 and held no further naval employment for twenty years; "Monson, Sir William (1569–1643)," *DNB*.

27. Brett may be mistaken, but it seems an odd mistake to make in this context. Brett may have been using the term "father in law" in the then current sense of "step-father," but, although Mennes's father was probably dead by the 1620s, I have no evidence that his mother ever remarried.

28. Thomas Lediard notes in *The Naval History of England* (London, 1735) that there are contemporary accounts of the incident in Captain John Smith's *Generall Historie of Virginia* (London, 1624), 4.128–30, and in Samuel Purchas's *Purchas his Pilgrimes* (London, 1625), 4.1780–82. It seems to me that both of these accounts are abridgements of an earlier printed account, *A true relation of a wonderfull sea fight between two great and well appointed Spanish ships. and a small English ship* (London, 1621), an abbreviated version of which was printed contemporaneously under the title *A notable and wonderfull sea fight between two great and wel-mounted Spanish shipps* (Amsterdam, 1621). These works were based in turn upon a damaged manuscript account by Thomas Hothewall, an eyewitness (PRO SP 14/120/29; *CSPD, 1619–23*, p. 236). The various accounts agree on all but the most minor details.

29. Hothewall says 19 March 1620[/1]; PRO SP 14/120/29.

30. PRO SP 14/120/29. Mennes's name is absent from the printed accounts.

31. The Spanish ships were men of war, weighing about 300 tons and carrying about 20 guns each, while the English ship was merely a merchantman of 160 tons armed with only 4 functioning guns.

32. His funeral monument in St. Olave's Hart Street, London, isolates this quality.

33. The cause of the quarrel is not known. PRO SP 14/162/17; *CSPD, 1623–25*, p. 208.

34. Oppenheim, *Royal Navy*, pp. 195–96 and 236. Lockyer offers a sympathetic account of Buckingham's handling of the Navy in *Buckingham*.

35. G. E. Aylmer, *The King's Servants: The Civil Service of Charles I, 1625–1642* (London: Routledge and Kegan Paul, 1961), p. 60.

36. PRO SP 16/21/31; *CSPD, 1625–26*, p. 257. It can be deduced from Brett's letter that Mennes was given command of the *Seahorse* some time after the accession of Charles I (3 April 1625) because he states that Mennes was given this charge "in his Maiesties service," as opposed to "in the late kinges seruice."

37. It is possible that prior to this, Mennes had taken over the prize ship *Esperance* for a short time; *DNB*. I have found no evidence for this suggestion in contemporary references to the ship; *CSPD, 1625–26*, pp. 309 and 418; *CSPD, 1627–28*, p. 59.

38. It carried 48 seamen and 160 soldiers. Mennes's name—spelt "Mince"—appears in "A Catalogue of all the Kinges Shipps," Folger Shakespeare Library, MS V. a. 275, p. 55. See Suckling, p. xlii.

39. Conrad Russell, *Parliaments and English Politics 1621–1629* (Oxford: Clarendon Press, 1979), p. 265.

40. Herrick, Smith, and Weeks served as chaplains (Herrick to Buckingham himself, Smith to Henry Rich, earl of Holland, and Weeks perhaps to Endymion Porter); Herrick, p. xiv; Smith's involvement is noted in the following chapter, and Weeks's is posited (without evidence) by Marchette Chute in *Two Gentle Men: The Lives of George Herbert and Robert Herrick* (London: Secker and Warburg, 1960), pp. 195–96. It is possible that Weeks was serving under Endymion

Porter, whom he served as chaplain in 1629 and 1633 (Herrick, p. 528). Suckling probably served as a horseman under Edward, Lord Conway, while Davenant's involvement has never been proved; Suckling, p. xlii; William Davenant, *The Shorter Poems and Songs from the Plays and Masques*, ed. A. M. Gibbs (Oxford: Clarendon Press, 1972), p. xxii; Mary Edmond, *Rare Sir William Davenant* (Manchester: Manchester University Press, 1987), pp. 34–36.

41. For this and similar groups, see part 2.

42. Gardiner, 6.197–200.

43. There were at this stage no knights in the family, and seventeenth-century Englishmen were acutely conscious of divisions within the upper echelons of society; Keith Wrightson, *English Society 1580–1680* (London: Hutchinson, 1982), pp. 19–21.

44. The title page of *Annalia Dubrensia* (London, 1636), to which Mennes contributed a poem, suggests not. The title page lists thirty-three contributors whose status is assured by university affiliations or by the designations "Esq." and "Gent." Mennes's is one of only four names to appear without such a guarantee. Although this derives in part from the decision to style him "CAPTAINE," rather than John, "MENESE," this decision is itself significant.

45. PRO SP 16/98/43. Captain "Mintz" is identified as Mennes in *CSPD, 1628–29*, p. 39—a reasonable inference since no other captain of this name seems to have serving in the King's Navy at this time.

46. One might infer from Mennes's threat to bring in his men that his business concerned the payment of wages.

47. Felton had traveled down to Portsmouth with an explanation to this effect sewn inside his hat; Gardiner, 6.353. On Felton and his background, see my "Providence and Technology in the English Civil War: Edmond Felton and his Engine," *Renaissance Studies* 7 (1993). On the assassination generally, see James Holstun, "'God bless thee, little David!': John Felton and his Allies," *ELH* 59 (1992): 513–52.

48. James Howell, *Epistolae Ho-Elianae: The Familiar Letters of James Howell*, ed. Joseph Jacobs, 2 vols. (London, 1890), 1.254. The letter, of 23 August, is misdated 5 August (2.743). Annabel Patterson has warned against taking Howell's letters too much at face value: they are at least partly fictitious productions; *Censorship and Interpretation: The Conditions of Writing and Reading in Early Modern England* (Madison: University of Wisconsin Press, 1984), pp. 210–18.

49. Gardiner, 6.343 and 372.

50. PRO SP 16/121/40; *CSPD, 1628–29*, p. 391.

51. Gardiner, 6.372; G. M. D. Howat, *Stuart and Cromwellian Foreign Policy* (London: Black, 1974), p. 36.

52. *The Barrington Family Letters 1628–1632*, ed. Arthur Searle, Camden Society, 4th ser. 28 (London, 1983), p. 41.

53. PRO SP 16/131/33; *CSPD, 1628–29*, p. 446.

54. Howat, *Stuart and Cromwellian Foreign Policy*, p. 36.

55. *CSPD, 1628–29*, pp. 456 and 470.

56. PRO SP 16/140/68; *CSPD, 1628–29*, p. 521.

57. PRO SP 16/141/13; *CSPD, 1628–29*, p. 524.

58. *CSPD, 1628–29*, p. 541.

59. *CSPD, 1628–29*, p. 524.

60. PRO SP 16/142/110; *CSPD, 1628–29*, pp. 553 and 557; Gardiner, 7.102.

61. He was instructed to return to Chatham docks in late October; *CSPD, 1629–31*, p. 80.

62. On Mennes's scientific and medical interests, see his funeral monument (transcribed in "Achievement," pp. 127–28); Pepys, 4.39, 40, 143, 218, 329, and 334 and 5.242.

63. Philip Edwards, et al. *The Revels History of Drama in English, Volume IV, 1613–1660* (London: Methuen, 1981), p. 76.

64. Pepys was later to remark that Mennes would have made a fine actor; Pepys, 7.1–2.

65. For details of this club and its membership, see part 2, chapters 7 and 8.

66. The original is attributed to Posidipus or Plato the Comic Poet, *The Greek Anthology*, trans. W. R. Paton, 5 vols. (London: Heinemann, 1916–18), 3.192. See, for example, Francis Bacon's rather more successful imitation of it, "The world's a bubble."

67. Bodl. MS Malone 13, fol. 10v (the poem appears here without Lawes's setting). A full text of the poem is printed in appendix 2.

68. Henry Lawes, *The Second Book of Ayres and Dialogues* (London, 1653), p. 10.

69. The Mennes family's relationship with Porter was not an entirely happy one: Sir Matthew Mennes was involved in a dispute with Porter: see Raylor, "Sir Matthew Mennes."

70. Dorothea Townshend, *Life and Letters of Mr. Endymion Porter* (London, 1897), chap. 8; Gervas Huxley, *Endymion Porter: The Life of a Courtier 1587–1649* (London: Chatto and Windus, 1959), pp. 126, 137, 159–60, and 163. On the Rhé expedition Mennes would have met Porter's brother, who commanded a ship, and possibly Porter himself; Huxley, *Endymion Porter*, p. 147.

71. On Mennes's interest in painting, see Pepys, 4.187, 191, and 319 and 8.403. On his portrait, which may even be the work of Van Dyck himself, see Robin Gibson, *Portraits from the Collection of the Earl of Clarendon* ([London]: Paul Mellon Centre for Studies in British Art, 1977), p. 94.

72. Uncertainty exists over the date of the journey. Gibbs surveys the evidence in Davenant, *Shorter Poems*, pp. 352–53, and suggests that it may have taken place over Whitsun 1630 or 1636 (Gibbs favors the latter). Edmond, however, proposes a date in the late 1620s (*Davenant*, p. 44). Sixteen-thirty is one of the few occasions on which Mennes could have visited the Cotswold Games, for he was normally at sea over Whitsuntide and could not have attended in 1636.

73. Gibbs concludes that there is no positive evidence for identifying the captain; Davenant, *Shorter Poems*, p. 353.

74. Davenant, *Shorter Poems*, p. 25.

75. Mennes may himself have written a poem upon riding a lame horse, suggesting that this was a conventional burlesque topos; see appendix 1, "Upon a Lame Tired Horse," *MD*, p. 27.

76. Christopher Whitfield, *Robert Dover and the Cotswold Games* (Evesham: distributed by Henry Sotheran, London, 1962), pp. 1–57; *Athenae*, 4.222.

77. Whitfield, *Robert Dover*, pp. 16–17 and 41; *Constitutional Documents of the Puritan Revolution*, ed. Samuel Rawson Gardiner, 3d ed. (Oxford: Clarendon Press, 1906), pp. 99–103.

78. Peter Stallybrass, "'Wee feaste in our Defense': Patrician Carnival in Early Modern England and Robert Herrick's *Hesperides*," *ELR* 16 (1986): 243–44; see also, Leah S. Marcus, *The Politics of Mirth: Jonson, Herrick, Marvell, and the Defense of Old Holiday Pastimes* (Chicago and London: University of Chicago Press, 1986), chap. 5.

79. *Annalia Dubrensia*, sig. F4.

80. Warren Chernaik, *The Poetry of Limitation: A Study of the Poetry of Edmund Waller* (New Haven: Yale University Press, 1968), p. 61.

81. Herrick, p. 194.

82. For the Gills, see Donald Lemen Clark, *John Milton at St. Paul's School: A Study of Ancient Rhetoric in English Renaissance Education* (New York: Columbia University Press, 1948), pp. 70–98.

83. He apparently suggested that James and Buckingham were together with the Devil in hell and added, with casual blasphemy, "if there were a hell and a devil"; *CSPD, 1628–29*, pp. 319 and 338; Clark, *Milton at St. Paul's*, pp. 83–98.

84. *HL*, p. 59.

85. *HL*, p. 58.

86. Clark, *Milton at St. Paul's*, p. 94; David Norbrook, *Poetry and Politics in the English Renaissance* (London: Routledge and Kegan Paul, 1984), p. 240. Gill's son was a friend of the self-conscious inheritor of this Spenserian tradition, Milton.

87. In the masque, Jonson defends the royal edict forbidding discussion of state affairs. He attacks obliquely, associating the antilaureate Wither with the religious and political factiousness of those who would discuss matters of state (metonymically, Parliament) and with the social disorder found among meaner inhabitants of the city: he is the laureate of Billingsgate; Ben Jonson, *Ben Jonson: The Complete Masques*, ed. Stephen Orgel (New Haven: Yale University Press, 1969), pp. 390–408, especially lines 97–117 and 142–48.

88. *Ben Jonson*, 8.410, 9.253, and 11.346.

89. Zouch Townley was one such defendant who was forced to flee to the Hague to escape investigation. In his poem "To Mr. Ben Johnson" he emphasizes the solidarity of the Jonson circle and equates literary with political values. The poem adopts an ad hominem strategy, establishing Gill's sentence for disloyalty as a disenfranchisement from literary judgement "Itt cannott moue thy frind<s> firme Ben, that hee / whome the Starr Chamber censur'd Rayles att thee"; *Ben Jonson*, 11.348.

90. Mennes's association with the King's Company, the Blackfriars Theatre, and a Jonsonian tradition is discussed in full in part 2.

91. Gill was a butt for jokes and ballads among the tavern wits of London, who presumably recalled their own sufferings at the hands of humanist grammarians; Clark, *Milton at St. Paul's*, pp. 70–80. The coarse character of these squibs can be illustrated by the ballad assigned to Thomas Triplett that is printed alongside Mennes's in *HL*. In this ballad, Gill's liberality with the lash is alluded to in a series of comic incidents involving stock-types such as Frenchmen, Welshmen, and porters. According to Aubrey it was performed by a singer under Gill's window (2.264).

92. *HL*, p. 57. The elder Gill would have been odious to Mennes because of his dismissal of Chaucer as a result of Chaucer's failure to preserve linguistic purity; Alexander Gill, *Logonomia Anglica*, ed. Bror Danielsson and Arvid Gabrielson, 2 vols. (Stockholm: Almqvist and Wiksell, 1972), 1.x.

93. *HL*, pp. 58–59.

94. PRO SP 16/173/46; *CSPD, 1629–31*, p. 344.

95. *CSPD, 1629–31*, pp. 392, 415, 420, 474, 479, 503, and 510; Gardiner, 7.170 and 176.

96. On writing as an entry to state employment, see J. W. Saunders, *The Profession of English Letters* (London: Routledge and Kegan Paul, 1964), pp. 38–44.

97. In both 1633 and 1637 the poet and pamphleteer, Wye Saltonstall, dedi-

cated a translation of Ovid's *Tristia* to Kenelm Digby, in a bid for patronage on behalf of his brother Charles, an unemployed naval officer, Wye Saltonstall, *Picturae Loquentes*, ed. C. H. Wilkinson (Oxford: Luttrell Society, 1946), p. x; *Ovids Tristia*, translated by W[ye] S[altonstall] (London, 1637) (*STC* 18980), sigs A3–A4; "Saltonstall, Wye (*fl.* 1630–1640)," *DNB*.

98. Oppenheim, *Royal Navy*, pp. 286–87.

99. Charles Wilson, *Profit and Power: A Study of England and the Dutch Wars* (London: Longman, 1957), pp. 2–38.

100. Charles Carlton, *Charles I: The Personal Monarch* (London: Routledge and Kegan Paul, 1984), pp. 176–79; B. W. Quintrell, "Charles I and His Navy in the 1630s," *The Seventeenth Century* 3 (1988): 159–79. My account of the 1630s is indebted to Quintrell's study. Kenneth R. Andrews's *Ships, Money and Politics: Seafaring and Naval Enterprise in the Reign of Charles I* (Cambridge: Cambridge University Press, 1991) appeared too late for me to take account of it here.

101. Quintrell, "Charles I and his Navy," 161.

102. PRO SP 12/237, fols. 100v–102; *CSPD, 1629–31*, p. 547. These were notes extracted from Monson's letter of 1616 to Lord Elsmore and Francis Bacon "concerning the insolences of the Dutch"; *A Collection of Voyages and Travels*, ed. Awnsham and John Churchill, 4 vols. (London, 1704), 3.239–46; *DNB*. Monson was renowned for his anti-Dutch views; Wilson, *Profit and Power*, p. 39. For Mennes's anti-Dutch stance see also, PRO SP 16/140/68; *CSPD, 1628–29*, p. 521.

103. PRO SP 12/237, fol. 102.

104. It seems unlikely that there was a prominent religious dimension to Mennes's advocacy of an anti-Dutch policy, despite Monson's possible Catholic sympathies; Quintrell, "Charles I and his Navy," 168.

105. Quintrell, "Charles I and his Navy," 162 and 165.

106. The post, to be fair, went to the highly capable George Carteret; *CSPD, 1629–31*, pp. 409, 413, and 523.

107. The *Garland* was offered to Captain Pennington in March 1631/2; *CSPD, 1631–33*, p. 283. It is possible that Mennes commanded another ship in 1632: there is a warrant of 4 February 1632/3 ordering Captain "Mince" them to hand over some cloth taken from a foreign ship; *CSPD, 1631–33*, p. 527.

108. *CSPD, 1633–34*, p. 232. Denbigh had visited India in 1631 and may have entertained ideas of returning himself or organizing an expedition there; "Feilding, William, First Earl of Denbigh (*d.* 1643)," *DNB*.

109. Quintrell, "Charles I and his Navy," 163–64.

110. *CSPD, 1634–35*, p. 603; *CSPD, 1635*, p. 171; Oppenheim, *Royal Navy*, p. 202; Quintrell, "Charles I and his Navy," 163.

111. *CSPD, 1635*, pp. 287 and 314.

112. *CSPD, 1635*, pp. 417 and 429.

113. Quintrell, "Charles I and his Navy," 169–70.

114. Quintrell, "Charles I and his Navy," 168–69.

115. *CSPD, 1635*, p. 384; *CSP Ireland, 1633–47*, pp. 105 and 110; *CSPD, 1636–37*, p. 379.

116. Quintrell, "Charles I and his Navy," 170.

117. Quintrell, "Charles I and his Navy," 171.

118. PRO SP 16/321/45, fol. 90v; *CSPD, 1635–36*, p. 436.

119. Oppenheim, *Royal Navy*, p. 238; Gerald Brenan, *A History of the House of Percy*, 2 vols. (London: Freemantle, 1902), 2.221–22; Carlton, *Charles I*, pp. 154–90.

120. The fleet was, as usual, divided into three squadrons. Mennes, in the admiral's squadron, was given the names of rendezvous points and an order of

battle; but even this is qualified by the appallingly self-evident caveat that "The uncertainty of a sea fight is such, that no certaine instruccions can be giuen by reason till wee come to [it *MS damaged*] wee know not how the Enemy will worke"; PRO SP 16/321/46, fol. 94v.

121. Quintrell, "Charles I and his Navy," 170–71; *CSPD, 1636–37*, p. 251.
122. *CSPD, 1636–37*, p. 511.
123. Brenan, *Percy*, 2.225.
124. *CSPD, 1636–37*, p. 307.
125. *CSPD, 1637–38*, p. 366; *CSPD, 1638–39*, p. 11; Oppenheim, *Royal Navy*, p. 207.
126. Walmer was part of the new breed of coastal defenses commissioned by Henry VIII. Despite the fact that it was worth £138 a year on paper, it was ill-equipped, and Mennes was forced to make a formal complaint about lack of ammunition; PRO SP 3/11 (Signal Office Records), Nov. 1637; Thomas Rymer, *Foedera, Conventiones, Literae et Cujusque Generis*, 20 vols. (London, 1735), 20.202; Edward Hasted, *The History and Topographical Survey of the County of Kent*, 4 vols. (Canterbury, 1778–79), 4.173, note *m*; *CSPD, 1637–38*, p. 344.
127. Oppenheim, *Royal Navy*, p. 239–40.
128. *CSPD, 1638–39*, p. 537.
129. PRO SP 16/415/49; *CSPD, 1638–39*, p. 615.
130. Oppenheim, *Royal Navy*, p. 240.
131. Quintrell, "Charles I and his Navy," 174.
132. Brenan, *Percy*, 2.231–32; *CSPD, 1639*, p. 303.

Chapter 2. James Smith: "A man much given to excessive drinking"

1. *Marston Morteyne, 1602–1812*, ed. F. G. Emmison, Bedfordshire Parish Registers, 44 (Bedford, 1953).
2. In his will he left at least three houses to his eldest son, Thomas, a meadow called Whitson Leyes in Kennington, Berkshire, and a house in St. Aldates, Oxford, to his younger sons, and £180 to his daughters. All this was in addition to the lands in Marston and nearby Wootton that he left to his wife, Mary; "Smith, James (1605-1667)," *DNB*; PRO Prob. 11/113/64; *The Victoria County History of the County of Bedford*, 3 vols. (Westminster: Constable, 1904–14), 3.307.
3. Middle-ranking clergy and those entitled to sign themselves "Gent." were regarded by contemporaries as members of the gentry, albeit of a minor order; Wrightson, *English Society*, pp. 21, 25.
4. The eldest son, Thomas, must have been born sometime before 1602—probably in late 1601. Another son, Samuel, was baptized on 25 September 1602. James, the poet, was baptized on 25 July 1605. Over the next eleven years there followed William, John, Oliver, and Richard. In addition there were three daughters, Helen, Elizabeth and Mary, whose dates of birth are not known; *Marston Morteyne*, ed. Emmison. Thomas is not mentioned in the registers, but he must have been born in late 1601 because he was seventeen in 1619. It is unlikely that the Thomas Smith buried on 14 September 1602 was a son of the parson of Marston (would he really have named two sons, Thomas?). This entry is of dubious status: Emmison notes that it is interlined in a different hand (p. 51).
5. Having taken his B.A. on 7 November 1622 and his M.A. on 27 June 1625, he proceeded as Bachelor and Doctor of Medicine and was licensed to practice on

24 July 1633; *Alumni*. Anthony Wood states that he was "sometimes an eminent physician of Brasen. coll." (*Athenae*, 3.776), but I have found no Brasenose connection.

6. Nicholas North, the recipient of this drubbing, describes the scuffle in excruciating detail: "taking me by the ear and hair of the head with one hand, he pluckt out a cudgel that was under his gown and breaking into the chamber upon me and struck me with the cudgel upon the head. About the third blow it broke in two, and then he struck half a dozen blows with the piece that was left in his hand"; Lincoln College, "Vetus Registrum," fols. 104–9, 115, and 120; quoted in Vivian Green, *The Commonwealth of Lincoln College 1427-1977* (Oxford: Oxford University Press, 1979), pp. 178–80.

7. Green, *Commonwealth*, pp. 179–80.

8. See, for example, Earle, *Microcosmography*, p. 70.

9. Nicholas Carlisle, *A Concise Description of the Endowed Grammar Schools in England and Wales*, 2 vols. (London, 1818), 1.26–27.

10. *Alumni*; *Athenae*, 3.776; Herrick, p. 528. Smith later alluded to his residence at Lincoln in a verse epistle to Mennes: "Soe thou shalt not blush to acknowledge / Him that was once of *Lincolne*-College"; *WR*, p. 4.

11. This unfortunate figure has been identified as the widow of the vice-chancellor's servant; Richard Corbett, *The Poems of Richard Corbett*, ed. J. A. W. Bennett and H. R. Trevor-Roper (Oxford: Clarendon Press, 1955), p. xv. A text of Smith's poem is printed above, appendix 2.

12. Corbett, *Poems of Corbett*, p. 106; Henry Knight Miller, "The Paradoxical Encomium with Special Reference to its Vogue in England, 1600-1800," *MP* 53 (1956): 145.

13. For examples and a survey, see John Collop, *The Poems of John Collop*, ed. Conrad Hilberry (Madison: University of Wisconsin Press, 1962), pp. 19–26. See also, Philip Sidney, *The Poems of Philip Sidney*, ed. William A. Ringler Jr. (Oxford: Clarendon Press, 1962), p. 384.

14. John Carey, however, argues otherwise in his *John Donne: Life, Mind and Art* (London: Faber, 1981), p. 236.

15. Lines 50–51. Further references, to the text of the poem printed in appendix 2 are given parenthetically within the text.

16. John Skelton, *The Complete English Poems*, ed. John Scattergood (Harmondsworth: Penguin, 1983), p. 128.

17. The term "carnivalesque" is, of course, Mikhail Bakhtin's. He uses it to describe an inclusive, communal, festive laughter—a laughter of "gay relativity"— that is distinguished from the closed, superior laughter of modern satire, in which an object of scorn is uniformly denigrated; see his *Rabelais and his World*, trans. Helene Iswolsky (1968; reprint, Bloomington: Indiana University Press, 1984), pp. 10–12. The presence of a "carnival spirit" in Skelton's verse is discussed by Douglas Gray in "Rough Music: Some Early Invectives and Flytings," in *English Satire and the Satiric Tradition*, ed. Claude Rawson (Oxford: Blackwell, 1984), pp. 21–43 (first published, *YES* 14 [1984]).

18. Robert C. Elliott, *The Power of Satire: Magic, Ritual, Art* (Princeton: Princeton University Press, 1960), pp. 3–48; Gilbert Burnet, *Some Passages of the Life and Death of Rochester* (1680), quoted in *Rochester, The Critical Heritage*, ed. David Farley-Hills (London: Routledge and Kegan Paul, 1972), p. 54.

19. Corbett, *Poems of Corbett*, pp. xviii and xx; William Cartwright, *The Plays and Poems of William Cartwright*, ed. G. Blakemore Evans (Madison: University of Wisconsin Press, 1951), pp. 10–11.

20. On elite involvement in popular culture, see Peter Burke, *Popular Culture in Early Modern Europe* (1978; reprint, Aldershot: Wildwood House, 1988), pp. 24–28 and 104.

21. Aubrey, 1.184–85.

22. *WR*, pp. 35–39 and [139]–62.

23. Smith notes in an epistle to Mennes of 27 December 1640 that he has been married to "*Bettie*" for fourteen years; *WR*, p. 6. Wood notes that Smith's wife was named Elizabeth, but on what authority I do not know; *Athenae*, 3.776. Whether Smith's marriage was the cause or the consequence of his move to London is not clear.

24. Gardiner, 6.191; PRO SP 29/7/68; *CSPD, 1660–61*, p. 114 (Smith's petition to Charles II); *Athenae*, 3.776.

25. Earle, *Microcosmography*, p. 70.

26. One of Charles I's earliest naval reforms had been to ensure the regular provision of naval chaplains; Walter F. Scott, "The Naval Chaplain in Stuart Times" (D.Phil. diss., University of Oxford, 1935), p. 16. The increasing competetiveness of the church at this time is noted by Thirsk, "Younger Sons."

27. John Louis Beatty, *Warwick and Holland: being the Lives of Robert and Henry Rich* (Denver: Alan Swallow, 1965), pp. 230–48; Clarendon, 1.79; R. M. Smuts, "The Puritan Followers of Henrietta Maria in the 1630s," *EHR* 93 (1978): 31–33; Charles Webster, *The Great Instauration, 1626-1660: Science, Medicine and Reform* (London: Duckworth, 1975), pp. 36 and 40; "Rich, Henry, Earl of Holland (1590-1649)," *DNB*; Lockyer, *Buckingham*, p. 188.

28. Gardiner. 6.191–200.

29. The strategies and political complexities of these poems are discussed by Gerald Hammond, *Fleeting Things: English Poets and Poems. 1616–1660* (Cambridge and London: Harvard University Press, 1990), pp. 49–66, and by Holstun, "God bless thee, little David!," 513–52.

30. Bodl. MS Malone 23, p. 209.

31. It is still strained even if one treats the terminal "-tion" as two syllables —an increasingly outmoded pronunciation at the time; E. J. Dobson, *English Pronunciation 1500–1700*, 2 vols. (Oxford: Clarendon Press, 1957), 2.957–58.

32. Corbett, *Poems of Corbett*, pp. xvii–xviii.

33. *Athenae*, 3.776.

34. "Wentworth, Sir Thomas, fourth Baron Wentworth of Nettleshead and first Earl of Cleveland (1591–1667)," *DNB*; Allan Fea, *The Loyal Wentworths* (London: Bodley Head, 1928), pp. 4–5 (the portrait is reproduced opposite p. 220); Clare Stuart Wortley, "Van Dyck and the Wentworths," *Burlington Magazine* 59 (1931): 102–7.

35. Fea, *Loyal Wentworths*, pp. 50–51; *DNB*.

36. By 1633, he had mortgaged his holdings in Hackney and Stepney, and, by 1641, he had sold them. In 1636 a settlement was drawn to clear his debts, some of which were later estimated at £19,200. *CSPD, 1636–37*, p. 310; PRO SP 16/377/ 169; *CSPD, 1637–38*, p. 130; BL MS Add. 25302, fols. 119–25; BL MS Eg. 3006, fols. 4–33. The dismal tale of the family finances can be unravelled from *CCC*, 3.2156–68.

37. HMC, *8th Report*, appendix 4a.

38. Laurence Stone, *The Causes of the English Revolution 1529–1642*, 2d ed. (London: Routledge and Kegan Paul, Ark Paperbacks, 1986), pp. 83–86.

39. *Suffolk in the XVIIth. Century: The Breviary of Suffolk by Robert Reyce, 1618*, ed. Lord Francis Hervey (London: John Murray, 1902), p. 76.

40. A sixteenth-century plan of the house (BL MS Add. 38065) is printed by

James Boutwood in "A Vanished Elizabethan Mansion: Toddington Manor House, Bedfordshire," *Country Life* 129 (1961): 640. Boutwood also prints a scale plan.

41. Historians such as Sharpe and Smuts have warned of the danger of taking the court/country dichotomy at face value. The conflict was in an important sense a myth that permeated all ranks of socety and not a fact of economic or social history; Kevin Sharpe, *Criticism and Compliment: The Politics of Literature in the England of Charles I* (Cambridge: Cambridge University Press, 1987); Smuts, *Court Culture.*

42. He wrote a forceful letter to the collector in 1637 threatening to "appeale for reparacions unto the Lords of the Councell" and was clearly less than diligent in enforcing the unpopular tax; Perez Zagorin, *The Court and the Country: The Beginning of the English Revolution* (London: Routledge and Kegan Paul, 1968), chaps. 2–4 (esp. p. 41); *CSPD, 1629–31*, p. 116; *CSPD, 1640*, p. 206; "The Ship Money Papers of Hen. Chester and Sir Will. Boteler, 1637–1639," ed. F. G. and Margaret Emmison, *Publications of the Bedfordshire Historical Record Society* 18 (1936): 57. Zagorin notes that Bedfordshire was one of the most reluctant counties to yield up ship money (p. 115), and it is clear from Emmison's list of arrears in 1638 that many of these occur in the hundred containing Wentworth's estates of Toddington, Tingrith, and Harlington.

43. *Athenae*, 3.776.

44. They held the manor on lease after their aunt's death in 1614 (despite Wentworth's ownership of it) until the mid-1640s; Fea, *Loyal Wentworths*, pp. 9–10, 45–50, and 73.

45. Thomas Carew, *The Poems of Thomas Carew*, ed. Rhodes Dunlap (Oxford: Clarendon Press, 1949), pp. xxxii, 225, 242–43, 254, and 270.

46. Davenant, *Shorter Poems*, p. 369; Herrick, p. 267.

47. *CSPD, 1629–31*, p. 516; *CSPD, 1636–37*, p. 66; *CSPD, 1639–40*, p. 171.

48. Paul S. Seaver, *The Puritan Lectureships: The Politics of Religious Dissent 1560–1662* (Stanford, Calif.: Stanford University Press, 1970), pp. 246 and 351; "Bishops Visitation Book 1628," Guildhall Library MS 9537/13, fol. 64v; Consistory Court of London Office Act Book 1627–1629/30, Greater London Record Office MS DL/C/317, fol. 14. By 1638 Cleveland's chaplain was one William Witton; Carew, *Poems of Carew*, p. 270.

49. "List of Lecturers in London 1629," Lambeth Palace Library MS 942, no. 16.

50. PRO SP 16/240/25; *CSPD, 1633–34*, p. 86.

51. *WR*, sig. L8v.

52. The identification of James Smith the poet with the James Smith of this brief has been assumed (without recourse to this evidence) by Martin Butler in *Theatre of Crisis 1632–42* (Cambridge: Cambridge University Press, 1984), p. 113.

53. PRO SP 16/240/25, fol. 1. Subsequent references to this document are given as folio numbers within the text.

54. PRO Prob. 11/148/14.

55. PRO Prob. 11/148/14.

56. John Earle characterizes them as places where fewer bowls are thrown than curses, *Microcosmography*, p. 75.

57. *WR*, sig. LIv; Philip Massinger, *The Plays and Poems of Philip Massinger*, ed. Philip Edwards and Colin Gibson, 5 vols. (Oxford: Clarendon Press, 1976), 1.xxii–xxiii and 4.421–23; "Mr. Smith, to Tom Pollard and Mr. Mering," *WR*, p. 54. Bentley warns that Pollard was a common name at the time and that at least

two men of this name lived in St Botolph's Bishopsgate in the early seventeenth century (2.532–35).

58. Edwards et al., *Revels History*, pp. 75–76, 96, and 98. Bentley notes that Pollard received his patent around 1635 (2.535).

59. Edwards et al., *Revels History*, pp. 6, 43, 45, 74–76, and 99.

60. Butler, *Theatre of Crisis*, pp. 100–33.

61. See Burke, *Popular Culture*, pp. 24–28, 104, and 134.

62. He alludes on occasion to both *Tamburlaine* and *Dr Faustus; WR*, pp. 11 and 38; Edwards et al., *Revels History*, pp. 165 and 168.

63. *WR*, pp. 51–54.

64. Smith's and Bagnall's ballads are printed alongside one another in *MD*, sigs χ1v ("F4[v]")-χ5v; pp. "72–81." For the debate over women, see, Louis B. Wright, *Middle-Class Culture in Elizabethan England* (Chapel Hill: University of North Carolina Press, 1935), pp. 492–97; Linda Woodbridge, *Women and the English Renaissance: Literature and the Nature of Womankind, 1540–1620* (Brighton: Harvester, 1984), pp. 139–51.

65. See appendix 1.

66. *MD*, sig. χ5v; p. "80."

67. We cannot be certain of the date of Smith's expulsion since the statement given in the brief may have been copied verbatim from the deposition of William Hawkins, a deposition that may predate the brief by some time, but it seems likely that the lawyer would have adjusted this statement were it incorrect on 3 June 1633.

68. Seaver, *Puritan Lectureships*, p. 193.

69. *Alumni*; Charles Edward Mallet, *A History of the University of Oxford*, 3 vols. (London: Methuen, 1924–27), 1.188, 195, and 325; C. W. Foster, "Institutions to Benefices in the Diocese of Lincoln," *Associated Architectural Society Reports and Papers* 39 (1928–29): 214.

70. Clive Holmes, *Seventeenth-Century Lincolnshire*, History of Lincolnshire (Lincoln: Society for Lincolnshire History and Archaeology, 1980), pp. 117–19.

71. I have failed to trace the previous incumbent.

72. PRO SP 16/271/82; *CSPD, 1634–35*, p. 149.

73. His successor was appointed on 19 December 1639; Foster, "Institutions," 214.

74. *WR*, pp. 16–19.

75. "Murray, William, first Earl of Dysart (1600?–1651)," *DNB*; Doreen Cripps, *Elizabeth of the Sealed Knot: A Biography of Elizabeth Murray Countess of Dysart* (Kineton: Roundwood Press, 1975), pp. 1–7. Murray was involved in a duel in 1624/5 (Bentley, 7.58). My identification of *"Willmott"* as Henry, viscount Wilmot (father of the poet, John Wilmot) is buttressed by his involvement with Goring, Pollard, and Wentworth in the Army Plot; see the statements of those involved in HMC, *13th Report*, appendix part 1, pp. 15–23. Other named members are Cave, Cornwallis, Stradling, George Symonds, and Weston.

76. *WR*, p. 17.

77. Apsley's career is outlined in *Alumni*; details of his misdemeanours are given by Brenan in *Percy*, 2.217–18. The identification of *"Crofts and Kelligrew"* as William Crofts and Thomas Killigrew is reinforced by the fact that the two men were related by Killigrew's marriage to Crofts's aunt Cecilia (a maid of honor to the queen) in 1636: they were thus both related to Thomas Wentworth; Fea, *Loyal Wentworths*, genealogical table 3; Thomas Gage, *The History and Antiquities of Suffolk. Thingoe Hundred* (Bury St. Edmunds, 1838), p. 134. Crofts was

a member of the Queen's Bedchamber and, like other members of these groups, was an inveterate dueler; Thomas Birch, *The Court and Times of Charles I*, 2 vols. (London, 1848), 2.89; William S. Powell, *John Pory / 1572–1636: The Life and Letters of a Man of Many Parts* (Chapel Hill: University of North Carolina Press, 1977), microfiche supplement, pp. 260, 264, and 312. He appears to have been involved in a series of brawls with [George?] Digby between 1634 and 1636 (including a scuffle at the Blackfriars Theatre); Bentley, 1.47; *CSPD, 1634–35*, pp. 81 and 129; *CSPD, 1635*, pp. 463 and 523 (the christian names of the duelers are rarely specified). But there can be no truth in the tale—recounted in R. T. Petersson's *Sir Kenelm Digby: The Ornament of England 1603–1665* (London: Cape, 1956), p. 237—that he was killed in 1644 during a duel with Jeffrey Hudson, the queen's dwarf (whom he faced armed with a water pistol) since he did not die until 1672. Henrietta Maria identities the dueler as "Croft's brother" in a letter to Cardinal Mazarin of 20 October 1644 (*The Letters of Queen Henrietta Maria*, ed. Mary Anne Everett Green [London, 1857], p. 260), and Fea identifies this brother as Charles, but on what grounds I do not know. Thomas Killigrew was certainly involved with Crofts and Murray (along with Sir John Denham, Mennes, and other royalist exiles) during the Interregnum; see Alfred Harbage, *Thomas Killigrew: Cavalier Dramatist 1612–83* (Philadelphia: University of Pennsylvania Press, 1930), pp. 99–100; Brendan O Hehir, *Harmony from Discords: A Life of Sir John Denham* (Berkeley and Los Angeles: University of California Press, 1968), pp. 89–93. Other named members of this group are "*George* Generall of Guenifrieds," Geoffrey Peters, and Harry Wind.

78. *WR*, p. 19.

79. PRO SP 16/240/25, fol. 13.

80. Wentworth, Crofts, and Killigrew were kinsmen, and Murray and Killigrew are associated in a ballad by Sidney Godolphin; "The Ballad of Tom and Will," in his *The Poems of Sidney Godolphin*, ed. William Dighton (Oxford: Clarendon Press, 1931), pp. 70–72.

81. Sir William Pole, *Collections Towards a Description of the County of Devon* (London, 1791), p. 435; Devon Bishops' Registers, Devon Record Office, 23.15.

82. Thomas Westcote, *A View of Devonshire in MDCXXX*, ed. Rev. George Oliver and Pitman Jones (Exeter, 1845), p. 72; John Prince, *The Worthies of Devon* (London, 1810), p. 642; "Pollard, Sir Hugh (*d.*1666)," *DNB*.

83. Sir Hugh's grandfather's first wife was Dorothy, daughter of Sir John Chichester of Raleigh; Pole, *Collections*, pp. 407–9; Westcote, *View of Devonshire*, pp. 494 and 607. One wonders whether there was perhaps a connection between the Devon Pollards and Thomas, the King's Company actor.

84. Herrick, p. 528; F. W. Moorman, *Robert Herrick: A Biographical and Critical Study* (London: Nelson, 1910), pp. 71–93.

Introduction to Part 2

1. *The Spectator*, ed. Donald F. Bond, 5 vols. (Oxford: Clarendon Press, 1955), 1.39 (no. 9).

2. See especially, John Timbs, *Club Life of London*, 2 vols. (London, 1866); Robert J. Allen, *The Clubs of Augustan London* (Cambridge: Harvard University Press, 1933); I. A. Shapiro, "The Mermaid Club," *MLR* 45 (1950): 6–17; Lance Bertelsen, *The Nonsense Club: Literature and Popular Culture, 1749–64* (Oxford: Clarendon Press, 1986).

3. Martin Butler, *Theatre of Crisis*; idem, "*Love's Sacrifice*: Ford's Metatheatrical Tragedy," in *John Ford: Critical Re-Visions*, ed. Michael Neill (Cambridge: Cambridge University Press, 1988), pp. 201–31; Sandra A. Burner, *James Shirley: A Study of Literary Coteries and Patronage in Seventeenth-Century England* (Lanham, Md.: University Press of America, 1988).

4. Allen, *Clubs of Augustan London*, p. 4.

5. "Club," *OED*.

Chapter 3. Precursors

1. Oswyn Murray, "The Greek Symposion in History," in *Tria Corda: Scritti in onore di Arnaldo Momigliano*, ed. E. Gabba, Biblioteca di Athanaeum (Como: Edizioni New Press, 1983), p. 259. I am indebted in much of what follows to conversations with Dr. Murray.

2. Oswyn Murray, "The Affair of the Mysteries: Democracy and the Drinking Group," in *Sympotica: A Symposium on the "Symposion,"* ed. Oswyn Murray (Oxford: Clarendon Press, 1990), pp. 149–61; Nicholas R. E. Fisher, "Greek Associations, Symposia, and Clubs," in *Civilization of the Ancient Mediterranean*, ed. Michael Grant and Rachel Kitzinger, 3 vols. (New York: Scribners, 1988), 2.1167–97.

3. Nicholas R.E. Fisher, "Roman Associations, Dinner Parties, and Clubs," in *Civilization of the Ancient Mediterranean*, ed. Michael Grant and Rachel Kitzinger, 3 vols. (New York: Scribners, 1988), 2.1199–225.

4. *Clubs of Augustan London*, p. 6; Timbs, *Club Life of London*, 1.3; Thomas Hoccleve, *Selections from Hoccleve*, ed. M.C. Seymour (Oxford: Clarendon Press, 1981), p. 111.

5. *Ben Jonson*, 1.49; Michael Strachan, *The Life and Adventures of Thomas Coryate* (London: Oxford University Press, 1962), p. 146; Timbs, *Club Life of London*, 1.8 and 10; Baird W. Whitlock, *John Hoskyns Serjeant-At-Law* (Washington, D.C.: University Press of America, 1982), pp. 392–93.

6. Louise Brown Osborn, *The Life, Letters, and Writings of John Hoskyns, 1566–1638* (New Haven: Yale University Press, 1937), pp. 196–99 and 288–91; Strachan, *Coryate*, pp. 147–48. Whitlock questions the attribution of this poem to Hoskyns; *Hoskyns*, pp. 91–93.

7. Corbett, *Poems of Corbett*, pp. xvii–xviii.

8. Shapiro, "The Mermaid Club," 8 and 13.

9. *Ben Jonson*, 8.653–57; Michael Strachan, "The Mermaid Club: A New Discovery," *History Today* 17 (1967): 538. Coryate's letter is dated to 1615 by Strachan, *Coryate*, p. 146.

10. I quote from the contemporary translation by Henry Reynolds; Osborn, *Hoskyns*, p. 288.

11. Strachan, *Coryate*, p. 13.

12. Osborn, *Hoskyns*, p. 289.

13. *Ben Jonson*, 11.296.

14. Whitlock, *Hoskyns*, pp. 287–88.

15. *MD*, p. 65.

16. *Ben Jonson*, 11.375–76. The attribution of this poem to Beaumont is questioned by Shapiro, "Mermaid Club," 14.

17. *Ben Jonson*, 8.396. The sending of verse epistles is discussed further below in part 3, chap. 8, and part 4.

18. Herrick, p. 289. It has been suggested that Alexander Brome, poet and lawyer, was involved with Jonson's club on the basis of his translation of the "Leges Convivales," but it seems equally likely that Brome's translation and his song "The Club," illustrate the continuation of a Jonsonian tradition after the laureate's death: Brome was only seventeen when Jonson died; Alexander Brome, *Poems*, ed. Roman R. Dubinski, 2 vols. (Toronto: University of Toronto Press, 1982), 1.341–42.

19. James Howell gives a (possibly fictitious) account of a dinner of wits in 1636, ruined by Jonson's immoderate self-congratulation, see his *Epistolae Ho-Elianae*, 1.403–4.

20. The few discussions of these groups are Walton B. McDaniel, "Some Greek, Roman and English Tityretus," *American Journal of Philology* 35 (1914): 52–66; Thornton Shirley Graves, "Some Pre-Mohock Clansmen," *SP* 20 (1925): 395–421; Annabel Patterson, *Pastoral and Ideology: Virgil to Valery* (Berkeley and Los Angeles: University of California Press, 1987), pp. 144–45.

21. The existence of youth groups in France was established by Natalie Zemon Davis in "The Reasons of Misrule," in her *Society and Culture in Early Modern France* (Stanford, Calif.: Stanford University Press, 1975), pp. 97–123. Bernard Capp has found evidence of similar organisations in England, "English Youth Groups and *The Pinder of Wakefield*," *P&P* 76 (1977): 127–33.

22. In one of his many gestures of conciliation, James I gave the Spanish ambassador permission to raise a regiment for Spanish use in the Low Countries in early 1622. The regiment, under the command of the Catholic Lord Vaux, was active between April 1622 and July 1624, when the conclusion of a Dutch treaty saw Vaux's grant revoked; Graves, "Clansmen," 402, n. 23.

23. John Chamberlain, *The Letters of John Chamberlain*, ed. Norman Egbert McClure, 2 vols. (Philadelphia: American Philosophical Society, 1939), 2.530.

24. "Bugle," 1; *OED*.

25. Many contemporary allusions to such societies are noted by Graves ("Clansmen," 401–21) and McDaniel ("Tityretus").

26. Walter Yonge, *The Diary of Walter Yonge, Esq.*, ed. George Roberts, Camden Society, 41 (London, 1848), p. 70.

27. McDaniel, "Tityretus," 62–66.

28. Bentley, 1.10–12; Margot Heinemann, *Puritanism and Theatre: Thomas Middleton and Opposition Drama under the Stuarts* (Cambridge: Cambridge University Press, 1980), chap. 10.

29. Patterson, *Pastoral and Ideology*, pp. 144–45. Patterson's conclusion that the Tityretus were pan-Protestant in sentiment is directly opposed to my own (and that of contemporary commentators).

30. Michael Leslie, *Spenser's "Fierce Warres and Faithfull Loves": Martial and Chivalric Symbolism in "The Faerie Queene"* (Cambridge: Brewer, 1983), chap. 8; Roy Strong, *The Cult of Elizabeth: Elizabethan Portraiture and Pageantry* (London: Thames and Hudson, 1977), chap. 6. Frances Yates draws attention to the Hapsburg satires on the deposed king of Bohemia that scoff at the loss of his garter; see her *The Rosicrucian Enlightenment* (London: Routledge and Kegan Paul, 1972), p. 23 (see also pp. 3–4, 8–10, and 31–35).

31. Graves, "Clansmen," 402, n. 23; *CSPD, 1619–23*, pp. 180, 199, and 272.

32. PRO SP 14/155/56. I quote from the original manuscript because the transcript printed by Graves ("Clansmen," 400–1) contains a number of inaccuracies. I have not shown the many deletions and insertions in this hastily compiled document. Although the significance of wearing "orange tawny" is not clear, it was

apparently associated with pride; Francis Markham, *Five Decades of Epistles of Warre* (London, 1622), p. 75.

33. Carlton, *Charles I*, p. 44.

34. PRO SP 14/155/56; subsequent citations to this document are given within the text.

35. PRO SP 14/155/57.

36. "Herbert, Thomas (1597–1642)," *DNB*.

37. Mansfeld received his commission on 4 November 1624; the regiment began to assemble at Dover later in the year, but it did not leave for the continent before January. By July it was reduced to a half its intended size by disease and, presumably, desertion: Howat, *Stuart and Cromwellian Foreign Policy*, p. 33; Gardiner, 5.271–72, 282–88, and 335–36.

38. *CSPD, 1623–25*, p. 404.

39. *CSPD, 1623–1625*, pp. 408 and 456.

40. John Adair, *Roundhead General: A Military Biography of Sir William Waller* (London: Macdonald, 1969), p. 30.

41. "Underhill, John (*d.* 1672)," *DNB*.

42. I drew attention to it in my 1986 dissertation, and John Kerrigan has recently discussed the reference in his "Thomas Carew," *Proceedings of the British Academy* 74 (1988): 312–13.

43. Carew, *Poems of Carew*, pp. xxx–xxxv.

44. Edward Sherburne, *The Poems and Translations of Sir Edward Sherburne (1616–1702) excluding Seneca and Manilius*, ed. F. J. Van Beeck, SJ (Amsterdam: Te Assen, 1961), p. xxxviii.

45. Sharpe's is one of the most interesting recent accounts of this poem; see his *Criticism and Compliment*, pp. 146–47.

46. Carew, *Poems of Carew*, p. 77.

47. Sharpe, *Criticism and Compliment*, pp. 146–47. For a more extensive reading along these lines, see Raymond A. Anselment, "Thomas Carew and the 'Harmelesse Pastimes' of Caroline Peace," *Philological Quarterly* 62 (1983): 201–19.

48. Ben Jonson, *The Fortunate Isles* (1625), line 189, in his *Complete Masques*, p. 442.

49. *WR*, p. 29.

50. See Burke, *Popular Culture*, p. 40.

51. PRO SP 14/155/57.

52. McDaniel, "Tityretus," 59.

53. For the problem of younger sons as sources of discontent, see Stone, *Causes of the English Revolution*, p. 112; Thirsk, "Younger Sons."

54. On this distinction, see Patterson, *Pastoral and Ideology*, pp. 144–45.

55. Scammell, "The Sinews of War," 360–61. Felton was also "the younger son of a minor gentry family"; Lockyer, *Buckingham*, pp. 458–59.

56. Christopher Hill, *The Century of Revolution 1603–1714*, 2d ed. (Wokingham: Van Nostrand Reinhold, 1980), pp. 48–49.

57. Ben Jonson, "*No State-affaires, nor any politique* Club"; "Prologue" to *Tale of a Tub* (1634), in *Ben Jonson*, 3.10.

58. Joseph Mede, letter to Sir Martin Stuteville, 25 January 1622/3, BL MS Harl. 389, fol. 274r.

59. *WR*, p. 29. The authorship and underlying ideology of the ballad are difficult to pin down. The attribution to Chambers is undermined by the fact that the relationship between Windsor and him is presented in the unflattering terms of an analogy to the homosexual relationship that was widely thought to exist between

Charles ("the prince") and Buckingham (the "favorite"); Carlton, *Charles I*, p. 108. The prevailing tone of the ballad is, however, one of support for Chambers's group and disdain for the investigating authorities. Archbishop Abbot, who exposed them, is dealt a double blow. An allusion to his accidental slaughter of a keeper on a hunting trip (Hugh Trevor-Roper, *Archbishop Laud, 1573-1645*, 3d ed. [London: Macmillan, 1988], p. 58) develops the homosexual subtext of the ballad with delicate obscenity:

> If hee were but behind mee now,
> And should this ballad heare;
> Sure he'd revenge with bended bow
> And I die like a Deere.
>
> (WR, p. 30)

The term "deer" was much used in a sexual context in the Renaissance; see Eric Partridge, *Shakespeare's Bawdy* (London: Routledge and Kegan Paul, 1968), p. 91. Whoever actually wrote it, the ballad employs a form and style felt to be appropriate to the fraternity.

Chapter 4. Membership

1. *WR*, sig. L8v (p. 156).
2. *MD*, p. 10
3. *WR*, sigs. K8–L4.
4. Butler, *Theatre of Crisis*, p. 113. For Massinger's circle and its relation to other theatrical and literary circles at the time, see Burner, *James Shirley*, pp. 60–69, and Butler, *"Love's Sacrifice,"* pp. 201–5.
5. "Atkine, Atkins, or Etkins, James (1613?–1687)," *DNB*.
6. *WR*, p. 54.
7. Bentley, 2.532–35 and 4.755.
8. *MD*, sigs χ1v–χ6r (pp. 72–75). In the 1655 edition of *Musarum Deliciae*, the ballad is assigned "Tom Bagnalls Ballet," but this is corrected in the 1656 edition to "Will Bagnalls Ballet." For these ballads (and responses to them), see appendix 1.
9. Donald S. Lawless, "Massinger, Smith, Horner and Selden," *N&Q*, n. s. 4 (1957): 55–56. It is tempting to suggest that Thomas Smith may have been James's roguish older brother, but there is no evidence that he was ever based in London.
10. Massinger, *Plays and Poems*, 1.217–18 and 314, and 5.118.
11. Bentley, 2.634.
12. Massinger, *Plays and Poems*, 1.xxxviii. Gray's Inn was a center for literary activity at the time; for this issue in general and Harvey in particular see Burner, *Shirley*, chap. 2.
13. Herrick, p. 528; John Venn and J.A. Venn, *Alumni Cantabrigienses. Part 1. From the Earliest Times to 1751*, 4 vols. (Cambridge: Cambridge University Press, 1922–27). *CSPD, 1629–31*, p. 5, *CSPD, 1633–34*, pp. 230, 316, and 445.
14. Huxley, *Porter*, pp. 169–78; Townshend, *Porter*, pp. 131–43.
15. Anthony Wood, *Fasti Oxonienses*, ed. Philip Bliss, 2 vols. (London, 1815–20), 2.68.
16. *MD*, pp. 2–3.

17. Herrick, pp. 132, 194, 233, and 321.

18. Herrick, p. 484.

19. Robert Herrick, *The Complete Poetry of Robert Herrick*, ed. J. Max Patrick (New York: Norton, 1968), p. 173, n. 3.

20. Herrick, *Complete Poetry*, ed. Max Patrick, p. 401, n. 1.

21. Herrick, pp. 528–29.

22. Davenant, *Shorter Poems*, pp. xx–xxv; Suckling, pp. xxx–xxxiv; Petersson, *Digby*, pp. 74–82; Andrews, *Ships*, chap. 5; *CSPD, 1633–34*, p. 501.

23. Edmond, *Davenant*, p. 31; Huxley, *Porter*, pp. 169–78; Townshend, *Porter*, pp. 131–39.

24. Bentley, 3.201–25; Davenant, *Shorter Poems*, pp. 125–30 and 403.

25. Davenant, *Shorter Poems*, pp. 37 and 364; Stephen Orgel and Roy Strong, *Inigo Jones: The Theatre of the Stuart Court*, 2 vols. (London: Sotheby Parke Bernet, 1973), 2.665.

26. Davenant, *Shorter Poems*, pp. xlvi–xlix; Aubrey, 2.242–44; Edmond, *Davenant*, pp. 63–64.

27. Aubrey, 1.204; William Davenant, *Sir William Davenant's "Gondibert,"* ed. David F. Gladish (Oxford: Clarendon Press, 1971), p. 286; Edmond, *Davenant*, pp. 36–37.

28. George Bas, "James Shirley, et 'Th'Untun'd Kennell': Une petite guerre des théâtres vers 1630," *Etudes Anglaises* 16 (1963): 11–22; Peter Beal, "Massinger at Bay: Unpublished Verses in a War of the Theatres," *YES* 10 (1980): 190–203; Colin Gibson, "Another Shot in the War of the Theatres," *N&Q*, n. s. 34 (1987): 308–9; Burner, *Shirley*, pp. 66–70.

29. Andrew Gurr, "Singing through the Chatter: Ford and Contemporary Theatrical Fashion," in *John Ford: Critical Re-Visions*, ed. Michael Neill (Cambridge: Cambridge University Press, 1988), pp. 85–89. Gurr perhaps underemphasizes the presence of divisions based on playhouse allegiance and mistakenly attributes Suckling's "Session of the Poets" to Carew (p. 89).

30. Beal, pp. 201–3. Martin Butler also depicts the War of the Theatres as a fight between members of a circle; *"Love's Sacrifice,"* p. 202.

31. Petersson, *Digby*, pp. 83–87 and 106–12; *Conway Letters: The Correspondence of Anne, Viscountess Conway, Henry More, and Their Friends, 1642–1684*, ed. Marjorie Hope Nicolson, rev. Sarah Hutton (Oxford: Clarendon Press, 1992), pp. 23–28.

32. *WR*, p. 7.

33. Petersson, pp. 66–112.

34. *WR*, p. 7; *MD*, p. 11.

35. Petersson, p. 154; BL MS Add. 41846, fol. 116v.

36. There are four main bases for positing a connection between Suckling and Mennes, the first three of which are broadly literary. First, Anthony Wood states that Mennes "did assist, as I have been credibly informed, Sir John Suckling in the composition of some of his poetry" (*Athenae*, 3.925–26). Unfortunately Wood's credible informant remains unidentified (it was not, on this occasion, Aubrey), and, in the absence of any other evidence, the claim is unverifiable. Second—and perhaps relatedly—Mennes may have been the "Friend" who provided copy for the posthumous collection of Suckling's works, *Fragmenta Aurea* (1646). It is not impossible that Mennes was involved in this publication, since *Fragmenta Aurea* was entered on the Stationers' Register on 24 July 1646, and it happens that Mennes was in London earlier in July for what was probably his last visit before 1660. But Thomas Clayton, in his fine edition of Suckling's poetry and prose, concludes that the available information points to Frances, Lady Dorset as

the friend in question: any claim for Mennes's editorship will thus need to offer new evidence (Suckling, pp. lxxxiii–iv). Third, there are the lampooning ballads that Mennes is supposed to have written about the lavishly clad troop of horse that Suckling raised for the First Scots War. But the evidence for these attributions has been called into question. The fact that these pieces are attacks on Suckling would in any case be of limited use in demonstrating his friendship with Mennes (Suckling, pp. 347–52; Timothy Raylor, "Samuel Hartlib's Copy of 'Upon Sir John Suckling's hundred horse'," N&Q, n. s. 36 [1989]: 445–47). This leaves only one firm biographical link between Mennes and Suckling. Clayton has found a demonstrable connection between Mennes and Suckling in their association with the Bulkeley family of Beaumaris, Anglesey (Mary Bulkeley being Suckling's "Aglaura"). He dates Suckling's association with the family to the period 1634–39 and identifies the addressees of a short letter by Mennes as Anne and Mary Bulkeley, suggesting that the letter is contemporary with Suckling's association with the Bulkeleys, dating from [1634–38?] (Suckling, pp. xli–ii). The problem with this argument is that there is no external evidence for any connection between Mennes and the Bulkeleys prior to 1644, when he became governor of Anglesey. By this time, of course, Suckling was dead. I would guess that the letter in question dates from 1644/5, for in it Mennes mentions a trip to the university. He is known to have spent some time at Oxford while it was held by royalists, between 1642 and 1646, and the phrasing of the letter—"My sudden and vnexpected departure for the vniuersity"—implies that he was acting upon orders, rather than upon whim or pleasure. He does apppear to have been absent from Beaumaris over Christmas 1644 as there is a gap in his otherwise regular correspondence at this time. But this is no more than a guess, and it could be countered by the argument that Mennes would not have addressed the girls as "Mrs. Anne and Mrs. Mary" as late as 1644, when Mary, at least, was married. The evidence for associating Suckling with Mennes remains largely circumstantial.

37. The fact that they received their commissions on the same day suggests the possibility of a group enrolment similar to that I have posited for the Rhé expedition; Suckling, p. xxx; CSPD, 1639–40, p. 481.

38. Bentley, 1.131–32; Suckling, p. xxxvii.

39. Suckling, pp. 153–54 and 330. Smith actually calls his tavern "the Beare and Wheel-barrow on the Bank-side" (WR, sig. K7r), which, in the absence of any evidence that there was such a tavern, I take to be the Bear. It is possible that Smith was involved with a group of court wits that met here in the 1630s.

40. The Sucklingtonian Faction: or (Sucklings) Roaring Boyes (London, 1641) (Wing S6133).

41. Suckling, pp. 153–54; MD, pp. 3–7.

42. Suckling, p. 70; Hales was a friend and relative of Thomas Carew; Carew, Poems, p. xli.

43. Such "invitation" poems derive, via Ben Jonson, from Martial. For examples of similar poems, many of which are written in octosyllabics, see Ben Jonson, "Inviting a Friend to Supper"; Mildmay Fane, "An Invitation to R[obert] H[errick]," [ca. 1626] (quoted by T. G. S. Cain in "Robert Herrick, Mildmay Fane, and Sir Simeon Steward," ELR 15 [1985]: 312–17); Mildmay Fane, "An Inuitation to R.H.: to change the Citty life for this in the Cuntry" (quoted by Eleanor Withington in "The Fugitive Poetry of Mildmay Fane," (HLB 9 [1955]: 66–68); Richard Flecknoe, "To Colonell Jos. Rutter. Inviting him to a Feast in Lisbon" (in his Miscellania, or, Poems [London, 1653], pp. 55–57 [the Jonson connection here is direct: Rutter was a son of Ben; see Ben Jonson, 8.414–15 and 11.459–60]); Henry Vaughan, "To His Retired Friend, an Invitation to Brecknock"; Ale-

xander Brome, "To his Friend W.C." (in his *Poems*, 1.254); and Henry Colman, "The Invitation" (a sacred parody) in his *Divine Meditations (1640)*, ed. Karen E. Steanson (New Haven and London: Yale University Press, 1979), p. 131.

44. Suckling, p. 70. There is no reason to connect Hales with the Order of the Fancy.

45. Suckling, p. 39; Clayton clearly does not regard this piece as an epistle; Suckling, p. 265.

46. *Athenae*, 3.925–26.

47. John Denham, *The Poetical Works of Sir John Denham*, ed. Theodore Howard Banks, 2d ed. ([Hamden, Conn.]: Archon, 1969), pp. 100–2; Aubrey 1.220; Bentley, 1.120; O Hehir, *Harmony*, pp. 4, 26, and 38–42. Aubrey assigns Denham's burlesque to post-1652 (1.218), but recent scholars assign it to ca. 1636; O Hehir, *Harmony*, pp. 12–13, and 101–2.

48. Sheffield University Library, Hartlib Papers, 29/2, sigs. G-H 14 ("Ephemerides" 1634).

49. Clarendon, 1.186.

50. HMC, *14th Report*, appendix part 2, p. 52. Mukkle John and Jeffrey [Hudson] are the court dwarves.

51. PRO SP 16/519/123; *CSPD, 1636–37*, pp. 437–38; *CSPD, 1648–49*, p. 10; *CSPD, 1651*, p. 85; *CSPD, 1631–33*, p. 213.

52. *CSPD, 1633–34*, p. 63, *CSPD, 1635–36*, pp. 272 and 296; *CSPD, 1644–45*, p. 206; *CSPD, 1652–53*, p. 449; *CSPD, 1653–54*, pp. 35, 43, and 85.

53. PRO SP 16/372/111; *CSPD, 1637*, p. 582; HMC, *14th Report*, appendix part 2, pp. 50, 186, and 192–204; *CSPD, 1640*, p. 190; Ian Roy, "The Libraries of Edward, 2nd Viscount Conway, and Others: an Inventory and Valuation of 1643," *Bulletin of the Institute of Historical Research* 41 (1968): 43–44; *Conway Letters*, pp. ix–x.

54. *Conway Letters*, p. 19; HMC, *14th Report*, appendix part 2, pp. 186, 193, and 197.

55. *The Correspondence of Bishop Brian Duppa and Sir Justinian Isham 1650–1660*, ed. Sir Gyles Isham, Publications of the Northamptonshire Record Society, 17 (Lamport Hall, Northamptonshire: Northamptonshire Record Society, 1955), pp. 68–69 (letter from Duppa at Richmond, 21 September 1653).

56. Butler, *Theatre of Crisis*, p. 112.

57. The list (PRO SP 16/478/16, fol. 27) is printed without identification by John Curtis Reed, in his "Humphrey Moseley, Publisher," *Oxford Bibliographical Society Proceedings and Papers* 2 (1927–30): 132–33. My calculations are based on the figures given by Bentley (7.95–123). Publications containing more than one play are counted as single works:

Year	Conway purchases	Total published
1634	4	17
1635	7	16
1636	9	14
1637	11	21
1638	9	30
1639	15	35
1640	11	41
Total	66	174

58. *Conway Letters*, pp. 23–28; *CSPD, 1634–35*, p. 185; HMC, *14th Report*, appendix part 2, pp. 34–49.

59. *CSPD, 1633–34*, p. 256; *CSPD, 1635*, p. 463; *CSPD, 1639*, p. 393.
60. PRO SP 16/372/111, fols. 210r and 211r; PRO SP 16/450/20, fol. 33v.
61. *Conway Letters*, pp. 17–18.
62. PRO SP 16/372/111, fol. 210v; *Conway Letters*, pp. 22–23.
63. PRO SP 16/372/111, fol. 208r, Richard Braithwait, *Ar't Asleepe Husband? A Boulster Lecture* (London, 1640); Huntington Library, MS HM 16522.

Chapter 5. Character

1. For the possibility that Carew wrote for the King's Company, see Gurr, "Singing Through the Chatter," p. 85; Bentley, 3.104–11.
2. It is set to the tune of "Greensleeves"; C. M. Simpson, *The British Broadside Ballad and its Music* (New Brunswick, N.J.: Rutgers University Press, 1966), pp. 273–78.
3. *WR*, sig. L1v (p. 142).
4. Thomas Coryate, *Coryats Crudities* (London, 1611), sig. e6r. According to Aubrey, Hoskyns also wrote a "nonsense discourse, which is very good"; Aubrey, 1.424.
5. Corbett, *Poems of Corbett*, pp. 95–96.
6. *WR*, p. 38.
7. *WR*, sig. K8r (p. 139). Strachan questions the existence of this feud, suggesting that it may have been a marketing stunt on Taylor's part; *Coryate*, pp. 149–56.
8. *WD*, pp. 8–10; *WR*, sigs. L8v–M3v (pp. 156–62).
9. *WR*, sig. L8v (p. 156); *The Aeneid*, 8.416–32.
10. *Metamorphoses*, 4.168–90; *WR*, sig. M1v (p. 158); Henry B. Wheatley, *London Past and Present*, 3 vols. (London, 1891), 3.52–53.
11. *WR*, sig. M3r (p. 161).
12. See appendix 1.
13. On Jonson's incongruousness, see Richard Helgerson, *Self-Crowned Laureates: Spenser, Jonson, Milton and the Literary System* (Berkeley, Los Angeles, and London: University of California Press, 1983), pp. 101–84.
14. Pepys, 3.243, 4.278 and 346, 7.1–2, and 8.566–67; Alexander Pope, *The Correspondence of Alexander Pope*, ed. George Sherburn, 5 vols. (Oxford: Clarendon Press, 1956), 3.108.
15. Michael A. Hogg and Dominic Abrams use this term to describe the means by which subordinate groups can avoid direct competition with dominant groups on the latter's terms. Such strategies include (1) the setting up of alternative standards for comparison, (2) redefinition of the value assigned to certain faculties, and (3) the use of other subordinate groups for comparison; see their *Social Identifications: A Social Psychology of Intergroup Relations and Group Processes* (London: Routledge, 1988), pp. 26–29 and 56–58.
16. Suckling, p. xxx; Edmond, *Davenant*, chap. 2 (Davenant did not inherit his estate until 1638/9). Discontent among younger sons is regarded by Thirsk as a contributing factor to the outbreak of war; see her "Younger Sons," p. 352. See also, Mark H. Curtis, "The Alienated Intellectuals of Early Stuart England," in *Crisis in Europe 1560–1660*, ed. Trevor Aston (London: Routledge and Kegan Paul, 1965), pp. 295–316.
17. Herrick was the born into a family of prosperous goldsmiths (and served as an apprentice in his uncle's business); Moorman, *Herrick*, pp. 15–29 and 249–50.

A sense of the financial standing of Herrick's uncle can be gleaned from the catalogue prepared for the sale of the Herrick Papers by Sotheby's on 15 December 1988; Sotheby's, *English Literature and History* (London: Sotheby, 1988), pp. 12–33. Despite his anxieties about his origins, Davenant was the son of a wealthy and influential vintner; Edmond, *Davenant*, chaps. 1 and 2 (pp. 1–26).

18. T. A. Dunn, *Philip Massinger: The Man and the Playwright* (Edinburgh: University College of Ghana, 1957), pp. 21–24; Edwards, et al., *Revels History of Drama*, p. 35.

19. Increasing competition for posts in the church is noted by Thirsk, "Younger Sons," pp. 344–45.

20. The creation of strong fraternal bonds in the patriarchal family is discussed by Emmanuel Todd in *The Explanation of Ideology: Family Structures and Social Systems*, trans. David Garrioch (Oxford: Blackwell, 1985), p. 8.

21. Murray, "Greek Symposion," pp. 259–62.

22. Louis Adrian Montrose, "'The Place of a Brother' In *As You Like It*: Social Process and Comic Form," *Shakespeare Quarterly* 32 (1981): 45.

23. James I, *The Trew Law of Free Monarchies* (1598), and *A Speech to the Lords and Commons of the Parliament at White-Hall* (1610), extracts in *Divine Right and Democracy: An Anthology of Political Writing in Stuart England*, ed. David Wootton (Harmondsworth: Penguin, 1986), pp. 99–100 and 107. The order may even have been, in broad social terms, an anxious, conservative response to the breakdown of the old family structure, the extended "open lineage family," with its attendant network of support: both Mennes and Smith appear to have been brought up in the emergent "restricted patriachal family;" Laurence Stone, *The Family, Sex and Marriage in England 1500–1800*, abr. ed. (Harmondsworth: Penguin, 1979), pp. 93–146.

24. *WR*, p. 44.

25. "Citizen," 1d; *OED*; Sir Thomas Smith, *De Republica Anglorum*, ed. Mary Dewar (Cambridge: Cambridge University Press, 1982), p. 73.

26. "Resty," 1, and 2; *OED*; Zagorin, *Court and Country*, pp. 119–20; *Rump: or An Exact Collection of the Choycest Poems and Songs Relating to the Late Times*, 2 vols. (1662; reprint, [London], [1874]), 1.114.

27. *WR*, p. 44.

28. Davis, "Reasons of Misrule," pp. 115–16; Capp, "English Youth Groups," 133.

29. It is a "performative" rather than a "constative" statement, in Austin's terms; J. L. Austin, *How to Do Things with Words*, 2d ed. J. O. Urmson and Marina Sbisa (Oxford: Clarendon Press, 1975).

30. Sigmund Freud, *Jokes and Their Relation to the Unconscious*, trans. James Strachey, ed. Angela Richards, The Pelican Freud Library (Harmondsworth: Penguin, 1976), pp. 133 and 174–76.

31. Although this nonsense lacks the truly open and communal basis of the carnivalesque as Bakhtin defines it in *Rabelais and his World*, p. 11, the term may still be appropriate.

32. This does not mean that such events are always or inevitably successfully contained. Much has been written in recent years on the containment/subversion issue in early modern culture. Stephen Greenblatt emphasizes containment in "Invisible Bullets," in his *Shakespearean Negotiations: The Circulation of Social Energy in Renaissance England* (Oxford: Clarendon Press, 1988), pp. 21–65. Those who have emphasized the possibility of genuine subversion through carnival include Burke, *Popular Culture*, pp. 199–204; Michael D. Bristol, *Carnival and Theater: Plebeian Culture and the Structure of Authority in Renaissance England*

(London: Methuen, 1985), pp. 26–39 and 50; Peter Stallybrass and Allon White, *The Politics and Poetics of Transgression* (London: Methuen, 1986), pp. 6–26 and passim. For important discussions of subversion in general, see Jonathan Dollimore, *Radical Tragedy: Religion, Ideology and Power in the Drama of Shakespeare and his Contemporaries* (Brighton: Harvester, 1984), pp. 25–28; and James Holstun, "Ranting at the New Historicism," *ELR* 19 (1989): 189–225.

33. Unfortunately we have no examples of the nonsense actually spoken by the Order of the Fancy, but at least one nonsense poem associated with it appears to contain a degree of tendentiousness, being employed as a code for political satire; see the discussion of "Ad Johannuelem Leporem" in part 4, chap. 11, below.

34. "The process, and the faculty, of forming mental representations of things not present to the senses, chiefly applied to the so-called creative or productive imagination, which frames images of objects, events, or conditions that have not occurred in actual experience"; "Fancy," 4 and 7; *OED*.

35. Michael Neill, "'Wits most accomplished Senate': The Audience of the Caroline Private Theatres," *SEL* 18 (1978): 359.

36. William Rossky, "Imagination in the English Renaissance Psychology and Poetic," *Studies in the Renaissance* 5 (1958): 49–73; Thomas Middleton and William Rowley, *The Changeling*, ed. N. W. Bawcutt (Manchester: Manchester University Press, 1977), p. 54 (3.3.193–98).

37. Orgel and Strong, *Inigo Jones*, 2. 546–51.

38. 1.118, and 3.293, in Abraham Cowley, *The Collected Works of Abraham Cowley*, ed. Thomas O. Calhoun, et al., 6 vols. (Newark: University of Delaware Press, 1989–), 1.117 and 153; Davenant, *Gondibert*, pp. 19 and 22.

39. Hogg and Abrams, *Social Identifications*, pp. 56–58.

40. An exile in Paris in the Interregnum, she had been involved in discussions with her husband and his brother about the Davenant-Hobbes prefaces to *Gondibert*; Douglas Grant, *Margaret the First: A Biography of Margaret Cavendish Duchess of Newcastle 1623–1673* (London: Rupert Hart-Davis, 1957), pp. 113–15 and 124–26.

41. *MD*, pp. 2–3.

42. *WR*, pp. 5–6.

43. Zagorin, *Court and Country*; Stone, *Causes of the English Revolution*.

44. Sharpe, *Criticism and Compliment*, especially chap. 1; Smuts, *Court Culture*.

45. See, for instance, Hugh Trevor-Roper's "Three Foreigners: The Philosophers of the Puritan Revolution," a seminal account of the aspirations underlying the "country" ideology of men like the earls of Pembroke and of Warwick, John Pym, and Oliver St John, in his *Religion, the Reformation, and Social Change* (London: Macmillan, 1967), chap. 5.

46. Smuts, "Puritan Followers," 31.

47. Zagorin, pp. 54 and 61–63; Michael G. Brennan, *Literary Patronage in the English Renaissance: The Pembroke Family* (London; Routledge, 1988), chap. 9; Heinemann, *Puritanism and Theatre*, pp. 264–83. Brennan questions Massinger's proximity to the Herberts, p. 196.

48. Smuts, "Puritan Followers," 27.

49. Davenant, *Shorter Poems*, pp. xxvi–xxvii; Sharpe, *Criticism and Compliment*, pp. 94–103; Suckling, pp. liii–lix.

50. Butler, *Theatre of Crisis*; Michael P. Parker, "'All are not born (Sir) to the Bay': 'Jack' Suckling, 'Tom' Carew, and the Making of a Poet," *ELR* 12 (1982): 341–69; Sharpe, *Criticism and Compliment*.

51. Bentley, 1.60–61; Butler, *Theatre of Crisis*, pp. 49–52; Heinemann, *Puritanism and Theatre*, pp. 213–21. The fact that Massinger's play was brought to the king's attention (bypassing the royal censor) by William Murray may, given Smith's possible association with Murray, be further evidence of the close connections between the clubs of Caroline London.

52. Sharpe, *Criticism and Compliment*, pp. 62–69.

53. Parker, "Making of a Poet," 344–45; Parker does not treat Suckling's use of such forms as simply oppositional or anticourtly.

54. John Suckling, *The Works of Sir John Suckling: The Plays*, ed. L. A. Beaurline (Oxford: Clarendon Press, 1971), pp. 132 (and 280), 150 (and 286), 192–93 (and 295), 209–13, 289–90, and 304; Butler, *Theatre of Crisis*, p. 76.

55. The literary and biographical evidence for Massinger's Catholicism is inconclusive; Donald S. Lawless, *Philip Massinger and His Associates*, Ball State Monograph, 10 (Muncie, Ind.: Ball State University, 1967), pp. 8–9 and 63; Heinemann, *Puritanism and Theatre*, p. 220, n. 33.

56. The only notable exceptions are Philip Massinger, who died before the war, and Eliardt Swanston, who became a Presbyterian and a Parliamentarian; Bentley, 2.587 and 4.757.

57. David Aers and Gunther Kress offer a similar reading of the career and social position of Donne, in "Darke Texts need Notes: Versions of Self in Donne's Verse Epistles," in David Aers, Bob Hodge, and Gunther Kress, *Literature. Language and Society in England 1580–1680* (Dublin and Totowa, N.J.: Gill and Macmillan, 1981), pp. 34–40.

Chapter 6. Critical Contexts

1. A.F.B. Clark, *Boileau and the French Classical Critics in England (1660–1750)*, Bibliothèque de la Revue de littérature comparée (Paris: Éduoard Champion, 1925), p. 327; George Saintsbury, "The Prosody of the Seventeenth Century," *Cambridge History of English Literature*, ed. A. W. Ward and A. R. Waller, 15 vols. (Cambridge: Cambridge University Press, 1907–27), 8.231–32; *Hudibras*, p. xxxiii.

2. "Burlesque," B1; *OED* ("That species of composition, or of dramatic representation, which aims at exciting laughter by caricature of the manner or spirit of serious works, or by ludicrous treatment of their subjects").

3. Richmond P. Bond, *English Burlesque Poetry 1700–1750* (Cambridge: Harvard University Press, 1932); John Jump, *Burlesque*, The Critical Idiom (London: Methuen, 1972).

4. Bond, *English Burlesque*, p. 4. Bond's definition is retained by Jump and by Raman Selden, *English Verse Satire 1590–1765* (London: Allen and Unwin, 1978), p. 100.

5. The distinction between mode and genre is often difficult to retain. By genre, I mean a literary kind, with distinctive formal rules and conventions, and by mode, a style or manner that may be employed in different genres.

6. "Burlesque," A1, *OED*; Randall Cotgrave, *A Dictionarie of the French and English Tongues* (London, 1611); Thomas Blount, *Glossographia* (London, 1656). I have, however, found an earlier usage; see below, note 14.

7. "Droll," "Drollery," *OED; WR*, p. 2.

8. Jacob Rosenberg, Seymour Slive, and E. H. Ter Kuile, *Dutch Art and*

Architecture 1600–1800 (Harmondsworth: Penguin, 1966), pp. 101 and 110–12; John Evelyn, *The Diary of John Evelyn*, ed. E. S. de Beer, 6 vols. (Oxford: Clarendon Press, 1955), 2.39; Bond, *English Burlesque*, p. 19.

9. Richard Flecknoe, *The Diarium, or Journall* (London, 1656), sig. A3r.

10. Orgel and Strong, *Inigo Jones*, 2.770–71.

11. Bond, *English Burlesque*, p. 19; Montagu Bacon, "A Dissertation on Burlesque Poetry," in Zachary Grey, *Critical, Historical, and Explanatory Notes Upon "Hudibras"* ([London], 1752), pp. 14–15.

12. Several contributors to the 1986 Le Mans colloquium on burlesque and parody argue to this effect: see especially, Zygmunt Marzys, "Le burlesque et les fondateurs de la langue classique," and Nicholas Cronk, "La defense du dialogisme: vers une poetique du burlesque," in *Burlesque et Formes Parodiques dans la Litterature et les Arts: Actes du Colloque de l'Université du Maine, Le Mans (du 4 au 7 decembre 1986)*, ed. Isabelle Landy-Houillon and Maurice Menard (Paris, Seattle, and Tubingen: Biblio 17, 1987), pp. 121–22 and 322.

13. For these, see Bond, *English Burlesque*, chap. 5.

14. The two exceptions I have found fall within the temporal development I have discussed. The term "burlesque" is used in the generic sense by 1651 by Sir Theodore Turquet de Mayerne in a letter to Edward, viscount Conway, of 17 October 1651 (*Conway Letters*, p. 22). Mayerne was, however, familiar with continental travesties such as that of Lalli. Even toward the end of the century, John Dryden retains the modal definition of the term "burlesque," using it to describe a comic manner in "A Discourse Concerning the Original and Progress of Satire" (1693), in his *Of Dramatic Poesy and Other Critical Essays*, ed. George Watson, 2 vols. (London: Dent, 1962), 2.147.

15. Jean Serroy, introduction to Paul Scarron, *Le Virgile Travesti* (Paris: Garnier, 1988), pp. 2–9.

16. Bond, *English Burlesque*, p. 5; Ian Jack, *Augustan Satire: Intention and Idiom in English Poetry 1660–1750* (Oxford: Clarendon Press, 1952), p. 25.

17. J. E. Spingarn, ed., *Critical Essays of the Seventeenth Century*, 3 vols. (Oxford: Clarendon Press, 1908–1909), 3.102.

18. Spingarn, ed., *Critical Essays*, 3.101.

19. *Of Dramatic Poesy*, 2.147.

20. *Of Dramatic Poesy*, 2.147.

21. John Dennis distinguishes gentlemanly Butlerian burlesque from coarse Scarronic ridicule; see his *The Critical Works*, ed. E. N. Hooker, 2 vols. (Baltimore: Johns Hopkins University Press, 1939–43), 1.6–10.

22. See Marzys, "Le Burlesque," and Cronk, "La Defense du Dialogisme."

23. As is noted by Paul Hartle, "Charles Cotton's *Burlesque upon Burlesque: Or, The Scoffer Scoft*," *Restoration* 11 (1987): 4.

24. Cronk, "La Defense du Dialogisme," especially pp. 337–38.

25. Michael McKeon, "Historicizing *Absalom and Achitophel*," in *The New Eighteenth Century: Theory, Politics, English Literature*, ed. Felicity Nussbaum and Laura Brown (New York and London: Methuen, 1987), p. 25.

26. Michael Bakhtin, "From the Prehistory of Novelistic Discourse," in his *The Dialogic Imagination: Four Essays*, ed. Michael Holquist, trans. Caryl Emerson and Michael Holquist (Austin: University of Texas Press, 1981), p. 53.

27. Mallet, *History of the University of Oxford*, 2.131–32, 326, 395, 401, and 439; Anthony Wood, *The Life and Times of Anthony Wood, Antiquary of Oxford, Described by Himself*, ed. Andrew Clark, 5 vols. (Oxford: Oxford Historical Society, 1891–1900), 2.266–67 and 563–64 and 5.150–52; F[alconer] M[adan], un-

titled notes, *Bodleian Quarterly Record* 3 (1920–22): 123–24, Thomas Hearne, *Remarks and Collections by Thomas Hearne*, 11 vols. (Oxford: Oxford Historical Society, 1895–1921), 1.188–91. Among the known *Terrae Filii* were John Hoskyns of the Mitre club (1592) (Osborn, *Hoskyns*, p. 19), and Robert Whitehall (1655), tutor to John Wilmot, earl of Rochester (Wood, *Life and Times*, 2.563).

28. See Elliott's discussion of the function of the Washington "Gridiron Club" in the 1950s, in his *The Power of Satire*, pp. 82–84.

29. Marzys, "Le Burlesque," p. 122; Serroy, introduction to Scarron, *Virgile Travesti*, pp. 2–4.

30. Keith Thomas, "The Place of Laughter in Tudor and Stuart England," *TLS*, 21 January 1977, 77–81.

31. Sturgis E. Leavitt, "Paul Scarron and English Travesty," *SP* 16 (1919): 108–20.

32. For example, Edward Ames Richards, *"Hudibras" in the Burlesque Tradition* (New York: Columbia University Press, 1937).

33. Douglas Bush, *Mythology and the Renaissance Tradition in English Poetry* (Minneapolis: University of Minnesota Press, 1932), p. 287. A similar view of the function of burlesque and travesty is adopted by Margaret Anne Doody, *The Daring Muse: Augustan Poetry Reconsidered* (Cambridge: Cambridge University Press, 1985), pp. 49–51.

34. See, Hartle, "Charles Cotton's *Burlesque upon Burlesque*," 5–7; Scarron, *Le Virgile Travesti*, p. 1; Ulrich Broich, *The Eighteenth-Century Mock-Heroic Poem* (Cambridge: Cambridge University Press, 1990), p. 14.

35. David Farley-Hills, *Rochester's Poetry* (London: Bell and Hyman, 1978), p. 8.

36. In an earlier study, *The Benevolence of Laughter: Comic Poetry of the Commonwealth and Restoration* (London and Basingstoke Macmillan, 1974), Farley-Hills commented on the absence in their work of any serious skepticism: "The farcical verse of Mennes and Smith remains unconvincing, local, not a general expression of the absurdity of things" (p. 40). For their verse to appear unconvincing in this respect presupposes that they were attempting to convince someone of the absurdity of existence—a supposition that seems to be unwarranted.

37. Despite his discontent with Bond's classification—particularly with regard to *Hudibras*—Farley-Hills continues to use Butler's poem as "a touchstone" for his own attempt (unsuccessful, in my view) at generic definition; *Rochester's Poetry*, pp. 89–92.

38. *HL*, sig. A2r; *WR*, sig. K5r.

Chapter 7. Sources

1. This has been noted by, for instance, John Bakeless, in *The Tragicall History of Christopher Marlowe*, 2 vols. (Cambridge: Harvard University Press, 1942), 2.141.

2. Elizabeth Story Donno, introduction to her *Elizabethan Minor Epics* (London: Routledge and Kegan Paul, 1963), p. 10.

3. Brian Gibbons, "Comic Method in Marlowe's *Hero and Leander*," in *Christopher Marlowe*, ed. Brian Morris (London: Benn, 1968), pp. 115–31.

4. Ballads on the subject are not uncommon; see, for example, *An Excellent*

Sonnet of the Unfortunate Loves, of Hero and Leander, The Tragedy of Hero and Leander; The Euing Collection of English Broadside Ballads, ed. John Holloway (Glasgow: University of Glasgow Publications, 1971), nos. 8 and 347, pp. 131 and 574.

5. Nashe, *Works*, 3.195 and 199–200.

6. *Ben Jonson*, 6.125.

7. Strachan, *Coryate*, p. 127.

8. Coryate, *Coryats Crudities*, sig. d8v; subsequent references are given in the text.

9. "αρμα," Henry George Liddell and Robert Scott, *Greek-English Lexicon* (Oxford: Clarendon Press, 1929).

10. Here, as elsewhere, I employ the succinct definitions of rhetorical terms offered by Richard A. Lanham in *A Handlist of Rhetorical Terms* (Berkeley, Los Angeles, and Oxford: University of California Press, 1968).

11. Sigs. e1r, g1v, and g5v; *Hudibras*, p. 62 (1.3.1–2). The comic potential of the rhyme is too obvious to determine an influence.

12. William K. Wimsatt, "Rhetoric and Poems: The Example of Swift," in *The Author in his Work: Essays on a Problem in Criticism*, ed. Louis L. Martz and Aubrey Williams (New Haven and London: Yale University Press, 1978), pp. 231–32.

13. Martin Ingram has uncovered a manuscript lampoon of 1617 originating from Nottingham that exhibits an octosyllabic doggerel style; the form is also used in a chapbook of 1686 contained in the Pepys Collection; Martin Ingram, "Ridings, Rough Music and Mocking Rhymes in Early Modern England," in *Popular Culture in Seventeenth-Century England*, ed. Barry Reay (1985; reprint, London: Routledge, 1988), pp. 181–82 and 185; J. W., *Vinegar and Mustard: or Wormwood Lectures for Every Day of the Week* ([n.p.], 1686), quoted in Samuel Pepys, *Samuel Pepys' Penny Merriments*, ed. Roger Thompson (London: Constable, 1976), pp. 295–96.

14. John Norton-Smith, "The Origins of Skeltonics," *EIC* 23 (1973): 57–62. On the involvement of the elite in popular culture, see Burke, *Popular Culture*, pp. 24–27.

15. Gabriel Harvey, *The Letter-Book of Gabriel Harvey, A.D. 1573–1580*, ed. Edmund John Long Scott, Camden Society, n. s. 33 (London, 1884), pp. 90–91.

16. Nicholas Breton, *Poems: Not Hitherto Reprinted*, ed. Jean Robertson (Liverpool: Liverpool University Press, 1967), pp. 135–48.

17. *The Arundel Harington Manuscript of Tudor Poetry*, ed. Ruth Hughey, 2 vols. (Columbus: Ohio State University Press, 1960), 1.226.

18. See, for example, the anonymous "On the Duke's Going to Dover, in December 1626," in Buckingham, *Poems and Songs Relating to George Villiers, Duke of Buckingham*, ed. F. W. Fairholt, Percy Society, 90 (London, 1850), pp. 6–8.

19. John Milton, *Original Papers Illustrative of the Life of John Milton*, ed. W. Douglas Hamilton, Camden Society, 75 (London, 1859), p. 67; *CSPD, 1628–29*, p. 240.

20. Sharpe, *Criticism and Compliment*, p. 19.

21. James I, *The Poems of King James VI. of Scotland*, ed. James Craigie, 2 vols. (Edinburgh: Scottish Text Society, 1955 and 1958), 2.182–91.

22. Reprinted as *Antient Drolleries*, no. 2, with a preface by A. H. Bullen (Oxford, 1891). See also *Cobbes Prophecies, his Signes and Tokens* (London, 1614), reprinted as *Antient Drolleries*, no. 1, with a preface by A. H. Bullen (London, 1890).

23. *Ben Jonson*, 5.53 (2.2.120). Jonson also wrote a bizarre mock-poem, "The Famous Voyage," on a grisly journey down the Fleet Ditch (an open sewer).

24. Strachan, *Coryate*, p. 272.

25. The poem was first published in 1621 and went through six editions by 1639 (*STC* 23050.5–54). A further twelve editions appeared between 1641 and the end of the century (Wing S4890–99). It has not been noted that *A New Droll: or, the Counter-Scuffle* (London, 1663) (Wing J1050), which is assigned on its title page to J.[Thomas?] Jordan, is also a text of Speed's poem.

26. Bond, *English Burlesque*, p. 147.

27. *The Counter-Scuffle* (London, 1653) (Wing S4891A), sig. A2r.

28. *Counter-Scuffle*, sig. D3v; *Hudibras*, p. 10 (1.1.311–14).

29. "Lloyd, David (1597–1663)," *DNB*.

30. Thomas, "The Place of Laughter," 77.

31. *The Legend of Captaine Jones* (London, 1648) (Wing L2630), sig. A4r.

32. *Captaine Jones*, sigs. A4v, B2r, and C3r.

33. See Bernard Capp, "Popular Literature," in *Popular Culture*, pp. 206–12.

34. PRO SP 16/372/111, fol. 208r.

35. A warning given by Roger Chartier in *The Culture of Print: Power and the Uses of Print in Early Modern Europe*, ed. Roger Chartier, trans. Lydia G. Cochrane (Cambridge and Oxford: Polity Press, 1988), p. 4, and by Reay, *Popular Culture*, p. 14.

36. Burke argues that this awareness developed during the seventeenth and eighteenth centuries in his *Popular Culture*, pp. 271–81.

37. The epistle, entitled "Captaine Mortons Answere out of Breda to Sir Ferdinando Careys Letter," appears in BL MS Harl. 367, fols. 174–75. It is dated from Breda, 23 November 1624 (fol. 175r). I have no information about Morton, but since the epistle notes that Carey was a corpulent man, he can probably be identified as the Sir Ferdinando Carey who died "suddenly of a lethargy" in 1638. This Carey was, notes George Garrard, "a Lieutenant-Colonel of the Low-Countries . . . a most overgrown man with Fat;" Thomas Wentworth, *The Earle of Straffordes Letters and Dispatches*, ed. William Knowler, 2 vols. (London, 1739), 2.164. He was once shot by a bullet that passed right through him and killed a man behind him; Fea, *The Loyal Wentworths*, pp. 32–37, genealogical table 2.

38. BL MS Harl. 367, fol. 174r. Subsequent references are given in the text.

39. This group included Mildmay Fane and Sir Simeon Steward. On the date and composition of these poems see Daniel H. Woodward, "Herrick's Oberon Poems," *Journal of English and Germanic Philology* 64 (1965): 270–84; Cain, "Robert Herrick, Mildmay Fane, and Sir Simeon Steward," 312–17; Valerie Letcher, "Herrick or Steward 'Oberons Clothing' in the Grey Collection," *Seventeenth Century News* 48 (1991): 58–59. The composition of poems in this manner was more widespread than has been recognized; see, for instance, Margaret Cavendish, *Poems and Fancies* (London, 1653), pp. 148–55. Leonard Willan, a friend of Herrick, composed "A Citie-Mous and Field-Mous" (a version of the Aesopean fable of the country and the city mouse) that is clearly a contribution to the tradition; it was printed in *The Phrygian Fabulist* (London, 1650); see *Rare Poems of the Seventeenth Century*, ed. L. Birkett Marshall (Cambridge: Cambridge University Press, 1936), p. 208. It seems reasonable to associate with these fairy poems the octosyllabic celebration of minuteness in "Fuscara; or the Bee Errant" by another Cambridge poet, John Cleveland.

40. *MD*, p. 2; Cain, "Herrick, Fane, and Steward," 315.

41. Woodward, "Herrick's Oberon Poems," 282–84; *MD*, p. 32.

Chapter 8. John Mennes and the Burlesque Verse Epistle

1. Herrick, p. 194; "Circumcised," "Civil," "Clean"; *OED*.

2. Slightly after Mennes wrote his poem, Paul Scarron wrote two poems on trips to the baths at Bourbon, *La Premiere* and *La Seconde Legende de Bourbon* (October 1641 and July 1642); *Poésies Diverses*, ed. Maurice Cauchie, 2 vols. (Paris: Société des Textes Français Modernes, 1947 and 1960), 1.127–77. For English examples of such poems, see Edmund Gayton, *To Mr Robert Whitehall at the Wells at Astrop* [Oxford, 1666], and Whitehall's manuscript "Answeare"; Bodl. MS Wood 416, fols. 114–18 (as Whitehall was the tutor of John Wilmot, earl of Rochester, it is interesting that Rochester himself later wrote a poem in this tradition, "Tunbridge Wells"); "A Letter to Julian from Tunbridge" [1685], in *Court Satires of the Restoration*, ed. John Harold Wilson (Columbus: Ohio State University Press, 1976), pp. 141–48. Many ballads and journey poems on Tunbridge Wells dating from the 1680s are collected in BL MS Harl. 7319, e.g. fols. 11, 106, 149, 175, 178, 204, 220, 351, and 369, and ballads on wells appear in many contemporary printed anthologies, e.g. *WD*, 1682, pp. 99 and 101. A closely related subgenre is the octosyllabic doggerel poem on the visit to a hothouse; see "The Virtue of a Hot-house," in C.F., *Wit at a Venture, or Clio's Privy Garden* (London, 1674), p. 65.

3. A number of English imitations of Horace's satire are listed by Bennett and Trevor-Roper in Corbett, *The Poems of Richard Corbett*, pp. 118–19. Corbett's influence on Smith has been discussed above.

4. Horace, *Satires, Epistles and Ars Poetica*, trans. H. Rushton Fairclough, rev. ed. (Cambridge: Harvard University Press; London: Heinemann, 1970), pp. 64–67 (lines 1–23).

5. *MD*, pp. 4–5; subsequent references to this poem are given parenthetically in the text.

6. Emrys Jones has discussed the element of geniality and delight that informs even Pope's excremental comedy in "Pope and Dulness," *Proceedings of the British Academy* 54 (1968): 231–63. For Pope's knowledge of Mennes's verse, see Joseph Spence, *Observations, Anecdotes, and Characters of Books and Men*, ed. James M. Osborn, 2 vols. (Oxford: Clarendon Press, 1966), 1.196 (no. 455); Owen Ruffhead, *The Life of Alexander Pope* (London, 1769), p. 426. The fact that Pope mentions "Tom Baynal" alongside Mennes as precursors of *Hudibras* implies his knowledge of the first edition of *MD*: Tom Bagnall exists only as a misprint in this edition; *MD*, sig. "F4v" [F5v]; p. "72."

7. For discussions of this theory, see Victor Harris, *All Coherence Gone: A Study of the Seventeenth Century Controversy over Disorder and Decay in the Universe* (Chicago: University of Chicago Press, 1949); Richard Foster Jones, *Ancients and Moderns: A Study of the Rise of the Scientific Movement in Seventeenth-Century England*, rev. ed. (St. Louis, Mo.: Washington University Press, 1961), especially chap. 2.

8. *Chaucer: The Critical Heritage*, ed. Brewer, 1.13–14, 23, 110, 127, 153–54, 157–58, and 165 (the quotation is from Milton's nephew and pupil, Edward Phillips). Mennes's love of Chaucer has been discussed above.

9. Baldwin, *Shakespere's Small Latine*, 2.251; J. W. Binns, "The Letters of Erasmus," in *Erasmus*, ed. T. A. Dorey (London: Routledge and Kegan Paul, 1970), p. 72. On the familiar epistle in literature, see Patterson, *Censorship and Interpretation*, chap. 5, and Miner, *Cavalier Mode from Jonson to Cotton*, chap. 6.

10. Katherine Gee Hornbeak, *The Complete Letter-Writer in English 1568–1800*, Smith College Studies in Modern Languages, 15 (3–4), (Hanover, N.H.: Smith College, 1934), p. 21; Erasmus, *Opera Omnia*, 10 vols. ([Leyden], 1703–1706), 1.350.

11. Baldwin, *Shakespere's Small Latine*, 1.91 and 2.242–43; Erasmus, *Opera*, 1.527.

12. Carey's epistle is discussed in the preceding chapter.

13. Angel Day, *The English Secretorie* (London, 1586), p. 22.

14. James Howell, for instance, adopts Day's schema; *Epistolae Ho-Elianiae*, 1.18.

15. Thomas Sprat, "An Account of the Life and Writings of Mr. Abraham Cowley" (1668), in Spingarn, ed., *Critical Essays of the Seventeenth Century*, 2.137. The paucity of manuscript copies of the verse of Mennes and Smith indicates small-scale circulation.

16. Angel Day defines the epistle as "the familiar and mutuall talke of one absent friend to another"; *English Secretorie*, p. 8.

17. "Cavalier," 2 and 3; *OED*.

18. *The Picture of an English Antick* [London, 1646] (Wing P2155).

19. Herrick, p. 194.

Chapter 9. James Smith and the Mock-Poem

1. *English Songs 1625–1660*, trans. and ed. Ian Spink, 2d ed., Musica Britannica: A National Collection of Music, 33 (London: Stainer and Bell, 1977), pp. 12–21. Spink doubts that the piece was written this early (p. 193).

2. *The Loves of Hero and Leander. A mock Poem* (London, 1651). For the date of the poem and a bibliography, see appendix 1.

3. Freud, *Jokes and their Relation to the Unconscious*, p. 133.

4. Richard Levin, *The Multiple Plot in English Renaissance Drama* (Chicago: University of Chicago Press, 1971), p. 144.

5. Trevor-Roper, *Archbishop Laud*, pp. 364–65.

6. Even Olivia's oft-quoted maxim from *Twelfth Night* that "there is no slander in an allowed fool" (1.5.189) is perhaps more double-edged than is generally allowed, implying restriction as much as license—there's no slander in an allowed fool because (despite his railing) he *may not* slander.

7. PRO SP 16/240/25, fol. 13.

8. *Conway Letters*, p. 22; see above, p. 97.

9. *HL*, p. 1. Quotations are taken from the 1651 edition. Subsequent references are given in the text.

10. At least one other contemporary song, printed in *Choyce Drollery* (1656) has the same refrain; *Choyce Drollery: Songs & Sonnets*, ed. J. Woodfall Ebsworth (Boston, Lincs., 1876), pp. 31 and 285. For similar refrains, see Thomas Middleton, *A Chaste Maid in Cheapside*, ed. R. B. Parker (London: Methuen, 1969), pp. 22 and 143–44.

11. For ballads on this subject, see William Shakespeare, *Love's Labours Lost*, ed. Richard David (London: Methuen, 1951), pp. 66–67, n.; Pepys, *Samuel Pepys' Penny Merriments*, p. 64.

12. Musaeus, *Hero and Leander*, ed. and trans. by E. H. Blakeney (Oxford: Blackwell, 1935).

13. Christopher Marlowe, *The Complete Poems and Translations*, ed. Stephen Orgel (Harmondsworth: Penguin, 1971), pp. 27–30 (Sestiad 1, lines 385–484), 35–38 (Sestiad 2, lines 155–226), and 88–89 (Sestiad 5, lines 274–93).

14. Christopher Marlowe, *The Poems*, ed. Millar Maclure (London: Methuen, 1968), p. xxiv.

15. Donno, ed., *Elizabethan Minor Epics*, p. 9.

16. p. 14; Marlowe, *Poems and Translations*, pp. 35 (Sestiad 2, line 153) and 68 (Sestiad 5, line 62).

17. Erasmus, *The Collected Works of Erasmus*, vol. 3, *Adages Ii1–Iv100*, trans. Margaret Mann Phillips (Toronto: University of Toronto Press, 1982), pp. 3–15.

18. Natalie Zemon Davis, "Proverbial Widsom and Popular Errors," in her *Society and Culture in Early Modern France*, pp. 245–57; Burke, *Popular Culture*, pp. 271–81.

19. Woodward, "Herrick's Oberon Poems," 282.

20. Sig. B1. See George Puttenham, *The Art of English Poesie*, ed. Gladys Doidge Willcock and Alice Walker (Cambridge: Cambridge University Press, 1936), p. 258.

21. *Scarronides, or, Virgile Travestie* (London, 1678), p. 37.

22. On the circulation of manuscript pamphlets, see my discussion of the attribution of Smith's "Ad Johannuelem Leporem, Lepidissimum, Carmen Heroicum" in appendix 1.

23. *WR*, sigs. K6r–M3v. Subsequent references to this poem are given parenthetically in the text.

24. Bush, *Mythology*, p. 289.

25. See Gregory T. Dime, "The Difference between 'Strong Lines' and 'Metaphysical Poetry'," *SEL* 26 (1986): 54; George Williamson, "Strong Lines," in his *Seventeenth Century Contexts* (London: Faber, 1960), pp. 120–31.

26. Clark, *Milton at St. Paul's*, pp. 161–62; "The Lords Censures of Mr Prynne for his Histriomastix" [1633/4], Sheffield University Library, Hartlib Papers, 68/10/3a.

27. Murray Tolmie, *The Triumph of the Saints: The Separate Churches of London 1616–1649* (Cambridge: Cambridge University Press, 1977), p. 34.

28. Christopher Hill, *Society and Puritanism in Pre-Revolutionary England* (London: Secker and Warburg, 1964), chap. 3; Curtis, "Alienated Intellectuals," pp. 308–11. For a more balanced view, see Seaver, *Puritan Lectureships*.

29. Richard Helgerson finds a similar movement within the career of Ben Jonson, *Self-Crowned Laureates*, pp. 117–19.

30. Roger Pooley, "Language and Loyalty: Plain Style at the Restoration," *Literature and History* 6 (1980): 2–18; Brome, *Poems*, 1.9–10.

31. Zagorin, *The Court and the Country*, chap. 5. Many royalists were later to regard London (not entirely inaccurately) as one of the main instigators of the Civil War; Valerie Pearl, *London and the Outbreak of the Puritan Revolution: City Government and National Politics, 1625–43* (Oxford: Oxford University Press, 1961), p. 1; *Rump*, 1.114.

32. On Taylor, see Wallace Notestein, "John Taylor," in his *Four Worthies* (New Haven: Yale University Press, 1957), pp. 169–208.

33. On these attempts, see Richard C. Newton, "Jonson and the (Re-) Invention of the Book," in *Classic and Cavalier: Essays on Jonson and the Sons of Ben*, ed. Claude J. Summers and Ted-Larry Pebworth (Pittsburgh: University of Pittsburgh Press, 1982), pp. 31–55; Stallybrass and White, *Politics and Poetics of Transgression*, pp. 66–77.

34. J. W. Saunders, "The Stigma of Print: A Note on the Social Bases of

Tudor Poetry," *EIC* 1 (1951): 139–64; J. W. Saunders, *The Profession of English Letters*, pp. 31–64 and 133; David Margolies, *Novel and Society in Elizabethan England* (Totowa: Barnes and Noble, 1985), chap. 2; John Taylor, *All the Workes of Iohn Taylor* (London, 1630), sigs. A3v–A4r ("Epistle Dedicatory").

35. It may be significant that Taylor claimed that he took up poetry after being visited by the muses while he sat in his boat telling the story of Hero and Leander; *Workes*, sig. 2E6r (2nd sequence, p. 55).

36. Taylor excused this style by claiming that it was (like the burlesque) intentionally inept: "If any where my lines do fall out lame, / I made them so, in merriment and game"; Taylor, *Workes*, sig. 2E6v (p. "58"). It may even be that the travesty represents a continuation of the battle between Taylor and the earlier clubs, a battle that incorporated a degree of social antagonism; Strachan, *Coryate*, pp. 149–57.

37. *Ovids Heroicall Epistles*, trans. W[ye] S[altonstall] (London, 1636). On earlier and later translations of the *Heroides*, see Caroline Jameson, "Ovid in the Sixteenth Century," in *Ovid*, ed. J. W. Binns (London: Routledge and Kegan Paul, 1973), pp. 210–42; and Rachel Trickett, "The Heroides and the English Augustans," in *Ovid Renewed: Ovidian Influences on Literature and the Arts from the Middle Ages to the Twentieth Century*, ed. Charles Martindale (Cambridge: Cambridge University Press, 1988), pp. 191–204.

38. His grandfather had been Lord Mayor of London and governor of the Merchant Adventurers company, and his cousin was the staunch Puritan (and later Parliamentarian general), Sir Thomas Myddleton; "Saltonstall, Wye (*fl.* 1630–1640)," *DNB*; "Myddleton, Sir Thomas (1586–1666)," *DNB*.

39. All these attributions are noted in *DNB* with the exception of *The Complaint of Time against the Tumultuous and Rebellious Scots* (London, 1639) (*STC* 21643.5) and *A Description of Time: Applied to this present Time* (London, 1638) (*STC* 21643), both of which have been ascribed to Saltonstall in *STC*.

40. *Ovids Tristia* (London, 1637), sig. A3; *Ovid De Ponto* (London, 1639), sig. A2.

41. On the notion of a cultural division at this time, see P. W. Thomas's controversial article, "Two Cultures? Court and Country under Charles I," in *The Origins of the English Civil War*, ed. Conrad Russell (London and Basingstoke: Macmillan, 1973), pp. 168–93.

42. Wye Saltonstall, *Picturae Loquentes*, ed. C. H. Wilkinson (Oxford: Luttrell Society, 1946), pp. 29-30. Maren Sofie Røstvig, *The Happy Man: Studies in the Metamorphosis of a Classical Ideal*, 2d ed., 2 vols. (Oslo: Norwegian University Presses, 1962), 1.103–5. On Puritan melancholy, see my "Providence and Technology."

43. Country folk, writes Saltonstall, "will not be perswaded from dancing after Service; for they say tis an old custome, and therefore lawfull. Thus they live in stubborne ignorance. . . ." *Picturae Loquentes*, pp. 67, vii. For the declaration and the surrounding controversy, see my discussion of the Cotswold Games, above, chap. 1.

44. On Sparke, see *Biographical Dictionary of British Radicals in the Seventeenth Century*, ed. Richard L. Greaves and Robert Zaller, 3 vols. (Brighton: Harvester, 1982–84). During the *Histriomastix* trial, Sparkes was described as "a Comon publisher of vnlicenced & vnlawfull Bookes"; "The Lords Censure," Sheffield University Library, Hartlib Papers, 68/10/8a.

45. *Ovid's Heroicall Epistles*, trans. W[ye] S[altonstall] (London, 1639), sigs. A3–A4. Further references to this edition of the poem are given parenthetically in the text. Suzanne W. Hull takes seriously Saltonstall's claim that the poem is

aimed at an elite female audience; *Chaste, Silent & Obedient: English Books for Women 1475–1640* (San Marino, Calif.: Huntington Library, 1982), pp. 14, 16, and 190. My own sense is that the vast numbers in which the work sold suggests a broader audience; see below note 49.

46. Howard Jacobson, *Ovid's Heroides* (Princeton: Princeton University Press, 1974), pp. 243–56.

47. Ovid, *Heroides and Amores*, trans. Grant Showerman, 2d ed. (Cambridge: Harvard University Press, 1977), pp. 12–13.

48. *Ovid's Heroicall Epistles*, trans. S[altonstall], p. 5.

49. It was reprinted in 1636, 1639 (*STC* 18945.5–46), 1653, 1656, 1663, 1671, 1673, 1677, 1686, and 1695 (Wing O67A–672).

50. "Sherburne, Sir Edward (1618–1702)," *DNB*; Sherburne, *Poems and Translations*, pp. xix–xx.

51. Bodl. MS Top. Oxon. c. 160, fols. 9–10; quoted in Galbraith Miller Crump, "Edward Sherburne's Acquaintances," *TLS*, 19 March 1958, 139.

52. *Ovids Heroical Epistles*, trans. John Sherburne (London, 1639), sigs. A3v–A4r.

53. Hill, *Society and Puritanism*, chap. 2, pp. 124–44; Michael Walzer, *The Revolution of the Saints: A Study in the Origins of Radical Politics* (Cambridge: Harvard University Press, 1965), chap. 6, especially pp. 199–219. Classic examples of this popular association are the hypocritical Puritan of Ben Jonson's *Bartholomew Fair* (1614), Zeal-of-the-Land Busy, and Samuel Butler's Hudibras (e.g. *Hudibras* 1.1.187–204).

54. On the involvement of issues of social hierarchy and property ownership in the construction of a "classic," see Ernst Robert Curtius, *European Literature and the Latin Middle Ages*, trans. Willard R. Trask (London: Routledge and Kegan Paul, 1953), pp. 249–50; Stallybrass and White, *Politics and Poetics*, pp. 1–4, 59–61, and 66–79; Newton, "Jonson," pp. 45–46.

55. *Epistles*, trans. Sherburne, sig. A4v.

56. His translation is impressive, not least for its attempt (not wholly successful) to imitate Ovid's rhetorical elegance within a "*verse for verse traduction*" (a method wisely avoided by Dryden and his team in their version of the *Heroides*); *Epistles*, trans. Sherburne, sig. A4v.

57. Aubrey, 2.228. The prolific translator, John Davies of Kidwelly (a moderate Presbyterian) concurred in this estimate.

58. PRO SP 16/540/428, fols. 204–15 (fol. 204).

59. On this market, see Wright, *Middle-Class Culture in Elizabethan England*, pp. 349–54. But note the devastating attack on the idea of a "rising middle class" by J. H. Hexter, "The Myth of the Middle Class in Tudor England," in his *Reappraisals in History* (London: Longman, 1961), pp. 71–116.

60. Richard Flecknoe, "Of Translation of Authors," in his *Miscellania, or Poems* (1653), p. 114.

61. Ovid, *Heroides and Amores*, pp. 132–33.

62. See, for example, Farley-Hills, *Benevolence of Laughter*, p. 46.

63. *Rump*, 1.114.

64. See Hexter, "Myth of the Middle Class."

65. Massinger's plays exhibit much the same endorsement of traditional aristocratic and courtly values at the expense of the middle class; see Nancy S. Leonard, "Overreach at Bay," in *Philip Massinger: A Critical Reassessment*, ed. Douglas Howard (Cambridge: Cambridge University Press, 1985), pp. 171–72; Michael Neill, "Massinger's Patriarchy: The Social Vision of *A New Way to Pay Old Debts*," *Renaissance Drama* 10 (1979): 185–213.

Chapter 10. War with Scotland

1. Sheffield University Library, Hartlib Papers, 13/19 and 13/25 (letters to Hartlib, 5 and 27 December 1643).

2. Aubrey, 2.242.

3. Edmond, *Davenant*, p. 77.

4. "Upon Sir John Suckling" and "Upon Sir John Sucklings most warlike preparations for the Scotish Warre"; see appendix 1.

5. *CSPD, 1639–40*, pp. 138 and 321.

6. Brenan, *Percy*, 2.233–34.

7. *CSPD, 1639–40*, p. 481. Because Wood gave the date of Mennes's appointment as 1639 (*Athenae*, 3.925) and because Aubrey attributed the lampoon on Suckling's part in the First Scots War to Mennes (2.242), it is often mistakenly assumed that Mennes took part in the First Scots War.

8. Suckling, p. xlii, n. 3. A letter from Conway to Northumberland of 29 April 1640, notes the arrival of Mennes's and Sir John Digby's troops on the previous day (*CSPD, 1640*, p. 83). Sir John Digby (Suckling's rival) was the brother of Mennes's friend, Sir Kenelm.

9. PRO SP 16/452/61; *CSPD, 1640*, pp. 122–23.

10. *CSPD, 1640*, p. 182–83.

11. *CSPD, 1640*, p. 441.

12. *WR*, p. 54. Subsequent references to this poem are given parenthetically within the text.

13. Bernard Capp, *Astrology and the Popular Press: English Almanacs 1500–1800* (London: Faber, 1979), p. 56.

14. *CSPD, 1640*, pp. 189, 332, 470, 476, and 496.

15. See, for example, Herrick, "To the King," "Farewell Frost, or welcome the Spring" (pp. 25 and 224); Carew, "To my Friend G. N. from Wrest"; Cowley, "The Civill Warre," 1.94, 149, and 188 (in his *Collected Works*, 1.116–18). Winter was also used as a metaphor for war in Renaissance military manuals: James A. Freeman, *Milton and the Martial Muse: "Paradise Lost" and European Traditions of War* (Princeton: Princeton University Press, 1980), p. 24, n. 15.

16. See Richard Cust, "News and Politics in Early Seventeenth-Century England," *P&P* 112 (1986): 60–90; Patterson, *Censorship and Interpretation*, p. 8.

17. Gardiner, 9.193; BL MS Add. 4207, fols. 165–74. The latter document (Lord Conway's justification for his conduct during the campaign) reveals the total unpreparedness of the northern forces.

18. Gardiner, 9.200.

19. Gardiner, 9.211.

20. *CSPD, 1640–41*, p. 302.

21. *CSPD, 1640–41*, p. 318. Wilmot had been another member of the London club world; see above, p. 66.

22. PRO SP 16/473/74; *CSPD, 1640–41*, p. 321.

23. *MD*, p. 11.

24. *WR*, p. 1. Subsequent references to this poem are given parenthetically within the text.

25. *WR*, p. 4.

26. *WR*, p. 16.

27. Bromley Hall was one of two manors in Bromley. Nothing seems to be known about it between 1625, when William Ferrers died seised of it, and 1661, when it was purchased from the Ferrers family; James Dunstan, *History of the Parish of Bromley St. Leonard, Middlesex* (London, 1862), pp. 36 and 151–53.

28. In an epistle of 30 January he mentions a trip to Barking, undertaken in order "To mend my commons" (*WR*, p. 11). Layfield, a relative of Laud, may have been on the fringes of the Smith and Mennes circle. Smith and he were at Oxford together in the 1620s, and after the Restoration there was talk of Mennes marrying his daughter; see below, p. 292, n. 18. Layfield himself seems to have engaged in verse correspondency; A. G. Matthews, *Walker Revised* (Oxford: Clarendon Press, 1948); Thomas Pestell, *The Poems of Thomas Pestell*, ed. Hannah Buchan (Oxford: Blackwell, 1940), pp. 57 and 120.

29. PRO SP 16/476/4; *CSPD, 1640–41*, p. 404. Many officers went to London to jump the queue for pay. This was, perhaps, Mennes's desire; Conrad Russell, "The First Army Plot of 1641," *Transactions of the Royal Historical Society* 38 (1988): 99.

30. *WR*, p. 9.

31. *CSPD, 1640–41*, p. 457.

32. "The Journal of John Aston, 1639," *Six North Country Diaries*, Surtees Society, 118 (Durham, 1910), p. 4.

33. Richard Welford, *History of Newcastle and Gateshead*, 3 vols. (London, 1884–87), 3.388. Durham County Record Office contains documents relating to his ownership of lands south of the Tyne, including a one-eighth share of the Lordship of Winlaton and the colliery which fell within it (D/CG 19/12, 16, and 17). One such document of 23 March 1639/40 records Anderson's conveyance of his share of the lordship of Winlaton to his wife after his death (D/CG 19/21), and another document contains the probate of his will in which the conveyance is effected—the probate is dated 6 July 1640, the will 6 May 1640 (D/CG 19/22).

34. *CSPD, 1640–41*, p. 459; *CSPD, 1641–43*, pp. 21, 50, 71, 92, and 97.

35. *WR*, p. 8. Subsequent references to this poem are given parenthetically within the text.

36. Potter, *Secret Rites and Secret Writing*, pp. 191–92.

37. Gardiner, 9.264.

38. "The Fart" was frequently reused by royalist writers; see *Rump*, 1.61.

39. *WR*, p. 4; *MD*, p. 10.

40. Gardiner, 9.264–65, 269, and 272.

41. *MD*, p. 63. Subsequent references to this poem are given parenthetically within the text.

42. Despite the regular employment of apes in proverbial adages (and their appearance in Brueghelian painting), I am not aware of a specific source for Smith's simile. See H. W. Janson, *Apes and Ape Lore: in the Middle Ages and the Renaissance* (London: Warburg Institute, 1952); F. Grossman, *Pieter Bruegel: Complete Edition of the Paintings* (London: Phaidon, 1973), p. 56 (no. 29).

43. In his fine account of the poem, Michael P. Parker dates it to the period of the First Scots War; "'To my friend G.N. from Wrest': Carew's Secular Masque," in *Classic and Cavalier*, ed. Summers and Pebworth, pp. 171–91 (note 4).

44. *MD*, p. 12.

45. *WR*, p. 11.

46. Anselment, *Loyalist Resolve*.

47. J. C. Drummond and Anne Wilbraham, *The Englishmans Food: A History of Five Centuries of English Diet*, rev. Dorothy Hollingsworth (London: Cape, 1957), pp. 102, 110–11, and 125.

48. *MD*, p. 11.

49. *WR*, p. 5.

50. See, Timothy Raylor, "Samuel Hartlib and the Commonwealth of Bees," in *Culture and Cultivation in Early Modern England: Writing and the Land*, ed.

Michael Leslie and Timothy Raylor (Leicester: Leicester University Press, 1992), pp. 91–129.

51. The examinations of the conspirators are calendared in HMC, *13th Report*, appendix part 1, pp. 15–23. The most complete and cogent account of the plot and its significance is that of Russell, "The First Army Plot."

52. HMC, *13th Report*, appendix part 1, p. 17.

53. *MD*, p. 8. Although this verse has been quoted by Aubrey, Wood, and many subsequent biographers of Davenant (e.g., Edmond, *Davenant*, p. 88) its author and source have seldom been identified.

54. On the associations of the term, see C. V. Wedgwood, *The King's War 1641–1647* (London: Collins, 1958), pp. 53 and 165; Joyce Lee Malcolm, *Caesar's Due: Loyalty and King Charles 1642–1646* (London: Royal Historical Society, 1983), chap. 6; Thomas Osborne Calhoun, "Cowley's Verse Satire, 1642–1643, and the Beginnings of Party Politics," *YES* 21 (1991): 194-206.

55. *MD*, p. 8.

56. Herrick, p. 124; above, chap. 1.

57. PRO SP 16/485/15; *CSPD, 1641–43*, p. 144.

58. *MD*, p. 9.

Chapter 11. Civil War

1. PRO SP 16/489/54; *CSPD, 1641–43*, p. 290. Since Mennes was knighted on the very day that the queen arrived at the Hague (25 February), he cannot have escorted them, as Wedgwood claims (*King's War*, pp. 68–69); *Letters of Queen Henrietta Maria*, p. 50.

2. Wedgwood, *The King's War*, pp. 68–69; Malcolm, *Caesar's Due*, p. 131; J. R. Powell, *The Navy in the English Civil War* (Hamden, Conn.: Archon, 1962), p. 129.

3. Clarendon, 2.215 and 225. My account of the loss of the fleet is based primarily upon Clarendon, 2.214–26.

4. There is conflicting evidence about which ship Mennes commanded: *The True List of his Majesties Navie Royall* (London, [1642]) (Wing T2717), gives the *Rainbow*, while *CSPD, 1641–43* gives the *Victory* (pp. 313, 314, and 350).

5. Wedgwood, *King's War*, pp. 103–5; Carlton, *Charles I*, p. 243.

6. Pepys, 4.124.

7. Andrews, *Ships*, pp. 184–87.

8. *CSPD, 1641–43*, p. 349.

9. *A Letter sent from the Right Honourable Robert Earle of Warwik* (London, 1642), sigs. A1v–A2r.

10. Clarendon, 2.218, n. 1.

11. *Journals of the House of Commons*, 2.650, 658, and 674.

12. HMC, *13th Report*, appendix part 1, p. 43.

13. *MD*, p. 2. Subsequent references to this poem are given parenthetically within the text.

14. The main Parliamentary objections to episcopacy were encapsulated in the Root and Branch Petition of December 1640; Gardiner, ed., *Constitutional Documents of the Puritan Revolution*, pp. 137–44. On Puritan factiousness in Somerset and its prevalence in Weeks's parish of Banwell, see David Underdown, *Revel, Riot and Rebellion: Popular Politics and Culture in England 1603–1660* (Oxford: Clarendon Press, 1985), pp. 77–78, 130, 140, and 218.

15. Gardiner, ed., *Constitutional Documents of the Puritan Revolution*, p. 247.

16. Aristotle, *The Ethics of Aristotle: The Nicomachean Ethics*, trans. J. A. K. Thompson, rev. Hugh Treddenick (Harmondsworth: Penguin, 1976), pp. 259 and 273–79.

17. On the importance of friendship in cavalier poetry see Miner, *The Cavalier Mode*, chap. 6.

18. Plays were forbidden by an act of 2 September 1642; Firth & Rait, 1.26.

19. Howell, *Epistolae Ho-Elianae*, 1.15.

20. Wedgwood, *King's War*, p. 157.

21. P. W. Thomas, *Sir John Berkenhead 1617–1679: A Royalist Career in Politics and Polemics* (Oxford: Clarendon Press, 1969), chap. 2.

22. H. E. Rollins, ed., *Cavalier and Puritan: Ballads and Broadsides Illustrating the Period of the Great Rebellion 1640–1660* (New York: New York University Press, 1923), p. 14; Malcolm, *Caesar's Due*, pp. 131 and 146; Thomas, *Berkenhead*, chap. 2.

23. "Andrew Mennes," P. R. Newman, *Royalist Officers in England and Wales 1642–1660: A Biographical Dictionary* (New York and London: Garland, 1981).

24. Ronald Hutton, *The Royalist War Effort 1642–1646* (London: Longman, 1982), p. 63; Eliot Warburton, *Memoirs of Prince Rupert and the Cavaliers*, 3 vols. (London, 1849), 1.159. In a letter from Capel of 26 May, Mennes was referred to as "Generall of the Ordinance to his Highness" and was authorized to defend Shrewsbury; "The Ottley Papers Relating to the Civil War," ed. William Phillips, *Transactions of the Shropshire Archaeological and Natural History Society*, 2d ser. 8 (1895): 321–23.

25. John Roland Phillips, *Memoirs of the Civil War in Wales and the Marches, 1642–1649*, 2 vols. (London, 1874), 2.30–31; Malcolm, *Caesar's Due*, p. 125.

26. Hutton, *Royalist War Effort*, p. 131.

27. BL MS Add. 18981, fol. 25; Phillips, *Memoirs*, 2.136.

28. BL MS Add. 18981, fols. 28 and 62.

29. Hutton, *Royalist War Effort*, p. 137.

30. Bodl. MS Carte 10, fol. 601.

31. Bodl. MS Carte 11, fol. 46; Malcolm, *Caesar's Due*, p. 116.

32. Norman Tucker, *North Wales in the Civil War* (Denbigh: Gee, 1961), p. 177.

33. Hutton, *Royalist War Effort*, pp. 147–48; William Williams, "History of the Bulkeley Family," ed. E. Gwynne Jones, *Transactions of the Anglesey Antiquarian Society and Field Club* (1948): 73–74; Bodl. MS Carte 11, fol. 246 (Williams to Ormonde, 19 June 1644), printed in Phillips, *Memoirs*, 2.168–70; Bodl. MS Carte 12, fol. 519 (the same to the same, 30 October 1644), printed Phillips, *Memoirs*, 2.214.

34. Bodl. MS Carte 13, fol. 5 (21 Nov 1644).

35. Bodl. MS Carte 14, fol. 609v (25 May 1645); Phillips, *Memoirs*, 2.89.

36. Bodl. MS Carte 11, fol. 287; Thomas Carte, *A Collection of Original Letters and Papers Concerning the State of England, from the Year 1641–1660*, 2 vols. (London, 1739), 1.54.

37. "Penington, Sir John (1568?–646)," *DNB*; Hutton, *Royalist War Effort*, p. 179.

38. Mennes's name does not appear on any of the lists painstakingly assembled by Peter Young in *Naseby 1645: The Campaign and the Battle* (London: Roundwood, 1985).

39. *The Chatto Book of Nonsense Poetry*, ed. Hugh Haughton (London: Chatto and Windus, 1988), pp. 122–23 (by omitting the burlesque footnotes, this ver-

sion loses much of the wit of the poem); Gavin Ewart, "A sixpence short of a shilling," *The Sunday Times*, 20 November 1988, G12. Ewart is himself no mean writer of comic verse.

40. See the full arguments for date and attribution in appendix 1.

41. See above, p. 100; John Cleveland, "The Mixt Assembly," in his *The Poems of John Cleveland*, ed. Brian Morris and Eleanor Withington (Oxford: Clarendon Press, 1967), p. 27 (lines 36–40); *Hudibras*, 2.2.29–32.

42. *WR*, pp. 38–39. Subsequent references to this poem are given within the text.

43. *Lucans Pharsalia: or the Civil Warres of Rome*, trans. Thomas May, 3d ed. (London, 1635), sig. A1v.

44. Potter, *Secret Rites and Secret Writings*.

45. Malcolm, *Caesar's Due*, p. 151; Henry King, *The Poems of Henry King*, ed. Margaret Crum (Oxford: Clarendon Press, 1965), p. 121; *Rump*, 1.198–99.

46. Cowley, *Collected Works*, 1.373–78.

47. *A True Relation of the Victory obtained over the King's Forces* (London, 1645) (Wing T2895), sig. A3.

48. Antonia Fraser, *Cromwell Our Chief of Men* (London: Weidenfeld and Nicolson, 1973), p. 14; "The Protecting Brewer" and "The Brewer," in *Rump*, 1.331 and 336, are both set to the tune of Smith's "The Black-Smith." Other Parliamentary leaders suffered similar slurs on their social status; Malcolm, *Caesar's Due*, pp. 44–45.

49. John Woodward, *Heraldry British and Foreign*, 2 vols. (London and Edinburgh, 1896), 1.123, 156, 416, and 497.

50. M. A. Gibb, *The Lord-General: A Life of Sir Thomas Fairfax* (London: Lindsay Drummond, 1938), pp. 13–14; Young, *Naseby*, p. 31.

51. Clarendon, 4.198; Young, *Naseby*, p. 358.

52. Chernaik, *Poetry of Limitation*, p. 61; Anselment, *Loyalist Resolve*, pp. 22 and 41–42.

53. After Naseby even the irrepressible John Berkenhead interrupted publication of *Mercurius Aulicus* for nine weeks; Thomas, *Berkenhead*, pp. 71–72 and 124.

54. On the instability of Cowley's epic, see Anselment, *Loyalist Resolve*, pp. 160–65. Smith's allusions to Lucan and the comically fragmentary state of his text make one wonder whether he is alluding to Cowley's incomplete work.

55. Mennes was one of the three royalist commissioners responsible for the treaty; Warburton, *Memoirs*, 3.176–78.

56. *CCC*, 1.42. Mennes's brother Andrew was also apparently at the fall of Oxford; *CCAM*, 1.193; Paul H. Hardacre, *The Royalists During the Puritan Revolution* (The Hague: Nijhoff, 1956), p. 23.

57. On the distinction between raillery and railing, which hardened in the later seventeenth-century, see P. K. Elkin, *The Augustan Defence of Satire* (Oxford: Clarendon Press, 1973), pp. 15–19.

58. *WR*, p. 46. Subsequent references to this poem are given parenthetically within the text.

59. Firth & Rait, 1.954. On "churching," see the discussion by Hammond in *Fleeting Things*, pp. 217–18, 221–24, and 263–66.

60. *Hudibras*, 1.1.225–29 (p. 8). Compare also Marchamont Nedham's verses on the abolition of Christmas reprinted from *Mercurius Pragmaticus* in his *A Short History of the English Rebellion Compiled in Verse* (London, 1680), p. 9; quoted in Wedgwood, *Poetry and Politics*, p. 95.

61. Thomas, *Berkenhead*, p. 188. But see also, King, *Poems*, p. 103.

62. John Dryden, "The Life of Plutarch," in *Of Dramatic Poesy*, 2.4; Seneca, *Epistles*, 108.

63. Potter, *Secret Rites*, p. 73.

64. On the *Sortes Virgilianae*, see Sir Philip Sidney, *An Apology for Poetry*, ed. Geoffrey Shepherd (London: Nelson, 1965), pp. 98 and 151.

65. BL MS Birch 4460, fol. 69.

66. *Aeneid*, 4.615–20; quoted from *Virgil*, trans. H. Rushton Fairclough, rev. ed., 2 vols. (Cambridge: Harvard University Press; London: Heinemann, 1935), 1.436–38.

67. Abraham Cowley, *The Mistress with Other Select Poems of Abraham Cowley*, ed. John Sparrow (London: Nonesuch Press, 1926), pp. 192 and 206; Arthur H. Nethercot, *Abraham Cowley: The Muse's Hannibal* (London: Oxford University Press, 1931), pp. 86–88.

68. King, *Poems*, pp. 117–32 (especially lines 5–6 and 19–20); Potter, *Secret Rites*, pp. 184–93.

69. *Rump*, 1.200.

70. *Rump*, 1.203.

71. *Rump*, 1.204.

72. King, *Poems*, pp. 132 and 214.

73. Potter, *Secret Rites*, p. 184; Brome, *Poems*, 1.294-98. Poetic responses to the king's death are discussed by Wedgwood in *Poetry and Politics*, pp. 98–103.

74. *WR*, p. 44. Subsequent references to this poem are given parenthetically within the text.

75. The strategy of registering natural disorder is not dissimilar to that of Cleveland in "The Kings Disguise: The Princely Eagle shrunke into a Bat," see *Poems of Cleveland*, p. 7 (line 48).

76. Potter, *Secret Rites*, pp. 107–21.

77. *OED*, "Pledge," 4; "Drink," 13b.

78. Firth & Rait, 1.954.

79. On the practice and symbolism of drinking healths to Charles II during the Interregnum, see Hardacre, *Royalists During the Puritan Revolution*, pp. 74 and 122; Potter, *Secret Rites*, p. 148; Anselment, *Loyalist Resolve*, p. 135; Brome, *Poems*, 1.134; Charles Cotton, *Poems of Charles Cotton 1630–1687*, ed. John Beresford (London: Cobden-Sanderson, 1923), pp. 360–61; *Rump*, 2.176. For Puritan objections to the practice prior to the regicide, see Timothy Gunton, *An Extemporary Answer to a cluster of drunkards met together at Schiedam, by Timothy Gunton, who was compelled thereto, upon his refusall to drink the King's health* ([London], [1648]).

Chapter 12. Drollery in Defeat

1. Bernard Capp, *Cromwell's Navy: The Fleet and the English Revolution 1648–1660* (Oxford: Clarendon Press, 1989), pp. 15–33. My account of naval activities during the Interregnum is indebted to Capp's fine study.

2. *CCAM*, 1.893; M[atthew] C[arter], *A Most True and Exact Relation of that as Honourable as Unfortunate Expedition of Kent, Essex, and Colchester* ([London], 1650), pp. 51 and 64–66; Warburton, *Memoirs*, 3.249–51.

3. Capp, *Cromwell's Navy*, pp. 33–37.

4. William Clarke, *The Clarke Papers Selections from the Papers of William Clarke*, ed. C. H. Firth, vol. 2, Camden Society, n. s. 104 (London, 1894), p. 41.

5. Powell, *The Navy*, pp. 182–83; Warburton, *Memoirs*, 3.265–273.

6. Capp, *Cromwell's Navy*, pp. 37–40; Powell, *The Navy*, pp. 184–88.

7. Capp, *Cromwell's Navy*, p. 38; Warburton, *Memoirs*, 3.266.

8. Capp, *Cromwell's Navy*, pp. 61–64; Bodl. MS Carte 24, fol. 265; Warburton, *Memoirs*, 3.281–82 and 298. The journal kept by Mennes at Kinsale is apparently lost; *CSPD, 1671*, p. 97.

9. Capp, *Cromwell's Navy*, pp. 64–66; Warburton, *Memoirs*, 3.301–4 and 312.

10. BL MS Add. 18982, fols. 206–7 (Rupert's Journal); Bodl. MS Clarendon 41, fol. 80v; HMC, *Ormonde*, n. s. 1.258.

11. *CSPD, 1653–54*, p. 295.

12. On 11 December 1653, Luke Whittington wrote to Ralph Parker at Flushing requesting the tobacco that Mennes had promised him; *CSPD, 1653–54*, p. 297. Mennes's wife was currently attempting to reclaim parts of her northern estate; *CCC*, 3.1805–6; *CSPD, 1655*, p. 141.

13. *MD*, sigs. G2v-G3r (pp. "84–85").

14. P. H. Hardacre offers a brief survey in "The Royalists in Exile During the Puritan Revolution, 1642–1660," *HLQ* 16 (1953): 353–70.

15. James R. Jacob and Timothy Raylor, "Opera and Obedience: Thomas Hobbes and *A Proposition for Advancement of Moralitie* by Sir William Davenant," *The Seventeenth Century* 6 (1991): 205–50.

16. Naomi Forsythe Phelps, *The Queen's Invalid: A Biography of Paul Scarron* (Baltimore: Johns Hopkins University Press, 1951), p. 232.

17. Hardacre, "Royalists," 362.

18. *Men-Miracles* ([Oxford], 1646), sig. A3r.

19. Like many such pensions, it was only irregularly paid; Aubrey, 1.136; *Hudibras*, pp. xix–xxi; Samuel Butler, *The Posthumous Works of Mr Samuel Butler* (London, 1732), "The Dedication," sig. π2r.

20. See above, part 2, chap. 4.

21. Scarron, *Poésies Diverses*, 1.129, n. 2.

22. Phelps, *Queen's Invalid*, p. 232.

23. Phelps, *Queen's Invalid*, p. 247.

24. Scarron's epistle on his trip to the baths is an elegant social satire, rather than a coarse piece of doggerel; his diurnal is written in prose rather than verse; and his version of the Hero and Leander story drew on an earlier French attempt; Phelps, *Queen's Invalid*, p. 247.

25. See especially Wedgwood, *Poetry and Politics*, chap. 4; Anselment, *Loyalist Resolve*, passim; Miner, *Cavalier Mode*, passim.

26. See, for instance, *Rump*, 1.39, 111, 153, 308, 331, 336, and 369, and 2.1, 4, 22, 54, 69, 89, 108, 115, 119, and 168; Raymond Lister, *The Loyal Blacksmith* (Cambridge: Golden Head Press, 1957), pp. 24–26.

27. Potter, *Secret Rites*, p. 138; John Davies, *An Account of the Author of this Translation and his Works*, prefaced to J[ohn] Hall, *Hierocles upon the Golden Verses of Pythagoras* (London, 1657), sig. b3v. See also, Lucy Hutchinson, *Memoirs of the Life of Colonel Hutchinson*, ed. James Sutherland (London: Oxford University Press, 1973), pp. 210 and 227.

28. C. H. Firth, "The Royalists under the Protectorate," *EHR* 52 (1937): 634–48.

29. Killigrew, *Comedies and Tragedies* (London, 1664), p. 456; Harbage, *Killigrew*, pp. 99–100; O Hehir, *Harmony from Discords*, p. 94, n. 25.

30. Davenant, *Gondibert*, p. 279. Thomason dates his copy of the volume 30 April 1653; O Hehir, *Harmony from Discords*, pp. 92 and 98.

31. The 1653 edition is extremely rare and is not listed in Wing (I have a copy in my possession). All quotations are taken from the 1655 edition (Wing W2130). The anonymous author alludes on several occasions to the involvement of the wits of *Certain Verses* in a number of "Clubbs o'th'Town," as does Anthony Wood; *Gondibert Vindicated*, pp. 4 and 23; *Athenae*, 3.808. Strangely, this collection is not mentioned by Gladish, and its authorship is not certainly known. Wood attributes it to Davenant himself, but the correct attribution is likely to be that of Wing, which assigns it to the Presbyterian royalist, Robert Wild. An allusion in *Gondibert Vindicated* helps establish the author's identity. A gloss upon the word "Mundungus" (here abbreviated to "Dungus") explains that the author writes that he "*doth not put in* Mun—*because it is the abreviation, or nick of his own name*" (p. 7). While "Mun" is not an abbreviation for Wild, there is a possible line of derivation in the fact that one of the seventeenth-century fraternities was known as "the Muns." Since such groups were renowned for their wild behavior, it may be that Wild, was given the nickname "Mun" by virtue of his surname. Although the earliest citation of the word given by *OED* dates from 1691, the citation itself refers to the earlier part of the century when the Muns flourished; it is taken from Shadwell's *The Scowrers* in which an elderly Scowrer reminisces—"Why I knew the Hectors, and before them the Muns and the Titire Tu's" (1.1.3). The former group is alluded to in [Edmund Prestwich]'s play, *The Hectors* (London, 1656), as "a certain Order, more famous then that of *Malta*, the Garter, Saint *Esprit*, or the Golden-fleece, a race of Adventurers" (p. 13).

32. *Gondibert Vindicated*, pp. 3, 14, and 27; Aubrey, 1.207 and 221; *Athenae*, 3.805 and 808; Isaac Disraeli, "D'Avenant and a Club of Wits," in his *Casualties and Quarrels of Authors*, 2d ed. (London, 1882), pp. 403–14; *Choyce Drollery*, ed. Ebsworth, pp. 378–80; Alfred Harbage, *Sir William Davenant: Poet Venturer 1606–1668* (Philadelphia and London: University of Pennsylvania Press, 1935), pp. 133–34; Denham, *Poetical Works*, pp. 311–12; O Hehir, *Harmony*, p. 92.

33. Aubrey's identification of Denham as the chief contributor was buttressed by the discovery of copies of several of the poems in the collection in Denham's hand; Denham, *Poetical Works*, appendix A.

34. Like Denham, Crofts and Donne are mentioned in *Gondibert Vindicated* (pp. 3, 14, and 15).

35. The inference that Broderick is meant by the abbreviation "-*De*-" in *Gondibert Vindicated* (p. 27) is perhaps a little stretched. No other evidence firmly corroborates his involvement with this group at the time, and later in the decade there appears to have been a certain enmity between Broderick and Denham; David Underdown, *Royalist Conspiracy in England 1649–1660* (New Haven: Yale University Press, 1960), pp. 243 and 305.

36. Buckingham's involvement has been discounted by Arthur Mizener in "George Villiers, Second Duke of Buckingham: A Life and a Canon of his Works" (Ph.D. diss., Princeton University, 1934), pp. 340–42. Although Waller is alluded to in *Gondibert Vindicated* (p. 27), his temperament and his authorship of a commendatory poem to *Gondibert* make him an unlikely contributor.

37. Disraeli describes the volume as "playful, sarcastic, malicious"; *Casualties and Quarrels*, p. 410. More recent critics have begun to suspect that the attack was not as severe as it might appear, *Gondibert*, ed. Gladish, p. ix; Potter, *Secret Rites*, p. 94.

38. Laughton, "Mennes," *DNB*; Harbage, *Davenant*, p. 134. This suggestion is presumably based on Wood's attribution to Mennes of a "mock poem" on Davenant and *Gondibert*; *Athenae*, 3.925.

39. It is presumably lost, unless it is the piece entitled "How Daphne payes his debts," which appears, unattributed, in *Sportive Wit* (London, 1656), sig. 2H4v.

40. Denham was abroad between 1648 and early 1653, and Mennes was at Lisbon in February 1651/2 and in Flushing by December 1653; Pepys, 5.242; O Hehir, *Harmony*, pp. 91 and 95.

41. Denham, *Poetical Works*, p. 100.

42. Denham, *Poetical Works*, pp. 100–1; O Hehir, *Harmony*, p. 127, n. 26.

43. Bodl. MS Clarendon 49, fols. 245–46. Quotations (cited by line numbers) are from the text printed in appendix 2.

44. Clarendon, 5.357–60; Ronald Hutton, *Charles the Second: King of England, Scotland, and Ireland* (Oxford: Clarendon Press, 1989), pp. 86–87.

45. On these figures, see Bodl. MS Clarendon 49, fol. 107; Clarendon, 5.356.

46. Margaret, Duchess of Newcastle, *The Life of William Cavendish, Duke of Newcastle*, ed. C. H. Firth, 2d ed. (London: Routledge, [1906]), pp. 46 and 50.

47. Portland Papers, Nottingham University Library, PwV 24, p. 30.

48. Donald Nicholas, *Mr. Secretary Nicholas (1593–1669): His Life and Letters* (London: Bodley Head, 1955), p. 270.

49. Edward Nicholas, *The Nicholas Papers: Correspondence of Edward Nicholas*, ed. George F. Warner, vol. 2, Camden Society, n. s. 50 (London, 1892), p. 156.

50. See above, part 2, chap. 4.

51. Nicholas, *Papers*, 2.226.

52. John Thurloe, *A Collection of the State Papers of John Thurloe*, ed. Thomas Birch, 7 vols. (London, 1742–45), 3.39 and 190; Firth, "Royalists under the Protectorate," 647.

53. BL MS Eg. 2535, fol. 75v; Nicholas, *Papers*, 2.221.

54. *MD*, p. 9; above, pp. 173.

55. Appendix 1; Underdown, *Royalist Conspiracy*, pp. 133–37 and 161.

56. Nicholas, *Papers*, 2.156; John, Viscount Mordaunt, *The Letter Book of John Viscount Mordaunt*, ed. Mary Coate, Camden Society, 3d ser. 59 (London, 1945), p. 32. For a different identification of O'Neill's correspondent, see Underdown, *Royalist Conspiracy*, p. 287.

57. "The Nightingale," "Epitaph on Mistresse Mary Prideaux," "Upon Drinking in the Crown of a Hat," and "An Epitaph on Doctor Prideaux's Son," *MD*, pp. 76–80. For attributions, see *MD&WR*, pp. 15–16. For manuscript copies see, for instance, BL MS Sloane 1792, fols. 41v, 89, and 19.

58. On "linked groups," see David Vieth, *Attribution in Restoration Poetry: A Study of Rochester's "Poems" of 1680* (New Haven: Yale University Press, 1963), pp. 26–27, 76–79, and 322–52.

59. On the conditions of manuscript circulation at this time, see Mary Hobbs, "Early Seventeenth-Century Verse Miscellanies and Their Value for Textual Editors," *English Manuscript Studies*, 1 (Oxford: Blackwell, 1989): 182–210; Harold Love, "Scribal Publication in Seventeenth-Century England," *Transactions of the Cambridge Bibliographical Society* 9 (1987): 130-54; idem, "Scribal Texts and Literary Communities: The Rochester Circle and Osborn b. 105," *Studies in Bibliography* 42 (1989): 219–35; Arthur F. Marotti, *John Donne, Coterie Poet* (Madison and London: University of Wisconsin Press, 1986), pp. 3–24.

60. Nor does *Musarum Deliciae* contain texts of the standard one would expect were the author of those texts involved in its compilation. The evidence is reviewed at length in "Achievement," pp. 252–56.

61. This claim, however, is made in the preface to another drollery in order to

undermine the authenticity of rival collections; *Sportive Wit* (London, 1656), sig. A3.

62. See, for example, *MD, WD, Sportive Wit.*

63. In the case of *MD*, a preface actually spells out the full names of Mennes and Smith, for those unable to infer them from the title (sig. A3v).

64. On Moseley's use of this technique, see Warren Chernaik, "Books as Memorials: The Politics of Consolation," *YES* 21 (1991): 212–13.

65. One only needs to notice the anomalies between different attempts at classification. In *Hobbled Pegasus: A Descriptive Bibliography of Minor English Poetry 1641–1660* (Albuquerque: University of New Mexico Press, 1968), Joseph Frank classes *WD* as nonpolitical and nonreligious (no. 618). Rollins, however, argues that *WD* is decidely antiParliamentarian; *Cavalier and Puritan*, p. 65.

66. The best studies remain those of Courtney Craig Smith: "The Seventeenth Century Drolleries" (Ph.D. diss., Harvard University, 1944); idem, "The Seventeenth-Century Drolleries," *HLB* 6 (1952): 40–51. See also, John Wardroper, *Love and Drollery* (London: Routledge and Kegan Paul, 1969).

67. Chernaik, "Books as Memorials," 210.

68. The drolleries advertized themselves as retrospective collections; see, for example, *"The Harmony of the Muses" by Robert Chamberlain (1654)*, introd. by Ernest W. Sullivan, II (Aldershot: Scolar Press, 1990), sig. A2; *"Parnassus Biceps, or Severall Select Pieces of Poetry" by Abraham Wright (1656)*, introd. by Peter Beal (Aldershot: Scolar Press, 1990), sig. A1.

69. On Overton, see Greaves and Zaller, eds., *A Biographical Dictionary of British Radicals*.

70. Thurloe, *Papers*, 3.197.

71. Thurloe, *Papers*, 3.75. It was first published in *J. Cleaveland Revived* (1660), pp. 78–79; *"J. Cleaveland Revived" Second edition (1660)*, introd. by Hilton Kelliher (Aldershot: Scolar Press, 1990); John Cleveland, *The Poems of John Cleveland*, ed. John M. Berdan (New Haven: Yale University Press, 1911), p. 185.

72. The text of the poem in Overton's possession bears the signs of memorial reconstruction and would be consonant with the servant's account of Overton copying it after hearing it sung. Differences between it and the version later published in *Cleaveland Revived* suggest the possibility that distinct versions of the poem were in circulation, one for singing and one for reading. Here are the opening lines of each text: "A Protector what's that? 'Tis a stately thing, / That confesseth itself but the ape of a king"; "What's a Protector? He's a stately thing, / That apes it in the non-age of a King." While the former is written in a rollicking ballad meter, suitable for singing, the latter adopts a more stately iambic form.

73. Thurloe, *Papers*, 3.111.

74. Bodl. MS Rawl. A 37, fols. 558–64; *CSPD, 1655–56*, p. 298; Thurloe, *Papers*, 4.717–18.

75. PRO SP 25/77, pp. 80 and 83.

76. PRO SP 25/77, p. 108; *CSPD, 1655–56*, p. 314; Smith, "Drolleries," 46–47.

77. On the government's interest in reforming morality, see Jacob and Raylor, "Opera and Obedience."

78. Appendix 1; "Achievement," pp. 233–67.

79. "To W.M. Esq; I being in a Course of Physick and newly recoverd of a Squinancy, February 1659," "A Journey from Oxon, 1656"; *Poems Lyrique Macaronique Heroique, &c.* (London, 1664), pp. 149–58. The collection betrays the influence of both Smith and Martin Lluellin, since it includes both a mock-song in imitation of Smith's ballad on women and "An Allusion to Doctor Lluel-

lin's Shon Price"; pp. 110–15 and 158–63. Another, similar collection which predates the publication of *MD* is Thomas Weaver's *Songs and Poems of Love and Drollery* ([London], 1654), which includes both a doggerel epistle and a response to Smith's ballad on women (pp. 32–36 and 46–49). The epistle, sent to Sir Evan Lloyd from Llangiby Castle, Monmouthsire, may date from the Civil War period, when Mennes was in Wales: it appears in a manuscript of Weaver's poetry dated 1646; Bodl. MS Rawl. Poet. 211, fols. 69–70.

80. Brome, *Poems*, 1.227–44 and 246–55.

81. Herrick wrote a poem to him (Herrick, p. 297), while Davenant dedicated the final canto of *Gondibert* to him (*Gondibert*, p. 253). The evidence for the longstanding assumption that Mennes was familiar with the younger Cotton has been discredited; see Aubrey, 2.38; Everitt, *Community of Kent*, p. 278.

82. Cotton, *Poems*, pp. 251–72 and 293–318. Most of Cotton's burlesques appear to date from after the Restoration, although an interesting version of his burlesque "Epitaph on M.H." was printed in *WD* (sig. C2). Paul Hartle is currently preparing a much-needed edition of Cotton.

83. *Hudibras*, pp. xlv-xlvi.

84. Underdown, *Royalist Conspiracy*, pp. 137, 150–55, and 205; A.H. Woolrych, *Penruddock's Rising 1655* (London: Historical Association, 1955).

85. Bodl. MS Clarendon 51, fol. 171.

86. *CSPD, 1657–58*, p. 201.

87. Amos C. Miller, *Sir Richard Grenville of the Civil War* (London and Chichester: Phillimore, 1979), p. 156 (PRO SP 18/67/4, fol. 11); *CSPD, 1656–57*, p. 288; Bodl. MS Clarendon 55, fol. 319v.

88. Bodl. MS Clarendon 55, fol. 266v; MS Clarendon 56, fols. 184 and 321; MS Clarendon 58, fol. 55.

89. Bodl. MS Clarendon 64, fols. 4 and 38; Capp, *Cromwell's Navy*, pp. 339–41; Underdown, *Royalist Conspiracy*, chap. 12.

90. Bodl. MS Clarendon 65, fol. 58.

91. He is not even mentioned in Ronald Hutton's *The Restoration: A Political and Religious History of England and Wales 1658–1667* (Oxford: Clarendon Press, 1985).

92. Bodl. MS Clarendon 67, fol. 200v.

93. *CSPD, 1659–60*, p. 333.

94. Clarendon, 6.159; Capp, *Cromwell's Navy*, p. 347.

95. Clarendon, 6.186, 208, 216, 228–29, and 233; Capp, *Cromwell's Navy*, pp. 355–70.

Chapter 13. Restoration?

1. PRO SP 29/7/68; *Alumni*.

2. Exeter Cathedral Library, D&C Exeter 3499/182; *CSPD, 1660–61*, p. 114; *Athenae*, 3.776.

3. Devon Bishops' Registers, Devon Record Office, 24.39, 51, and 74; George Oliver, *Ecclesiastical Antiquities in Devon*, 3 vols. (Exeter, 1840–42), 1.76; *CSPD, 1663–64*, p. 597; *Alumni*. Wood's contention that Smith became chaplain to Clarendon at this time is presumably an error.

4. In 1664, a Dr. James Smith was involved, along with Sir Thomas Prestwich and Sir Henry Bennet, in the purchase of a lease of some land known as King's Bridleway in Middlesex; *CSPD, 1664–65*, p. 52.

5. HMC, *Report on Manuscripts in Various Collections*, 4.92.

6. *Athenae*, 3.776–77. Smith's funeral monument is on the north wall of the chancel in the church.

7. In August 1661, he and Robert Phillips, Groom of the Bedchamber, were given Cannington Priory, Somerset, along with the vicarage and other church lands, at a rent of £100 a year; *CSPD, 1660–61*, p. 531; *CSPD, 1661–62*, p. 59.

8. PRO SP 29/169/13; *CSPD, 1666–67*, p. 68. The petition was referred to Sir Thomas Ingram, chancellor of the Duchy, who recommended payment should it be possible to calculate the amount due; PRO SP 29/169/13.1.

9. Abraham Cowley, *The English Writings of Abraham Cowley: Poems*, ed. A. R. Waller (Cambridge: Cambridge University Press, 1905), pp. 435–40. See also, *Merry Drollery Compleat*, ed. J. Woodfall Ebsworth (Boston, Lincs., 1875), pp. 52–56.

10. *CSPD, 1660–61*, p. 90; *CSPD, 1661–62*, pp. 457 and 573; *CSPD, 1663–64*, p. 113. Wood mistakes Walmer for Dover; *Athenae*, 3.925.

11. *CSPD, 1660–61*, p. 590.

12. Pepys, 10.59–60 and 243–44; BL MS Add. 9317, fol. 1; HMC, *8th Report*, 250a and 251a.

13. John M. Collinge, *Navy Board Officials 1680–1832*, Office Holders in Modern England, 7 (London: Institute of Historical Research, 1978), p. 122; *CSPD, 1661–62*, p. 144.

14. *CSPD, 1661–62*, pp. 121 and 148; Pepys, 10.407–9; Edward Mountagu, *The Journal of Edward Mountagu, First Earl of Sandwich . . . 1659–1665*, ed. R. C. Anderson, Navy Records Society, 64 (London, 1929), p. xxxix.

15. Mountagu, *Journal*, pp. 121, 125, and 127, n. 1; F. R. Harris, *The Life of Edward Montagu, K.G. First Earl of Sandwich (1625–1675)*, 2 vols. (London: John Murray, 1912), 1.208–9. Mennes bequeathed such a jewel in his will, PRO Prob. 11/335/38.

16. Mountagu, *Journal*, p. 217; Pepys, 3.139, 143, and 148.

17. For transcriptions of the tablet, see "Achievement," pp. 116–17; *Facetiae*, 1.8.

18. Pepys, 3.111 and 262; *CSPD, 1661–62*, p. 571. Wood claims that Mennes married the daughter of Dr. Edward Layfield and that she later married Jeremiah Wells—author of a collection of *Poems upon Divers Occasions* (London, 1667), which includes a burlesque journey poem ("Iter Orientale," p. 75); *Athenae*, 3.1199. Although he was expecting to remarry early in 1663, there is, however, no evidence that Mennes ever did so; HMC, *Heathcote*, p. 70. For details of Wells's wife, see "Achievement," p. 118.

19. Pepys, 5.278.

20. Pepys, 10.282–99.

21. Mennes's shortcomings drove Pepys to distraction; Pepys, 5.7 and 326. His ability to handle personnel problems is illustrated by his handling of a mutiny of ropemakers in 1665; see *CSPD, 1664–65*, pp. 463, 464, 465, 468, 475, 481, and 484; PRO SP 29/126/59; "Achievement," pp. 121–22.

22. Pepys, 3.283–84, 5.268, 7.253, 8.296, 298, 314, and 324; *CSPD, 1663–64*, p. 351.

23. Pepys, 5.218 and 4.196.

24. Pepys, 2.206 and 210, 6.226, 4.67, 98, 194, and 205, 8.571, and 9.100.

25. *CSPD, 1663–64*, p. 35; Pepys, 4.61 and 66; 8.570 and 586, and 9.408.

26. O Hehir, *Harmony from Discords*, p. 174; Pepys, 4.437. Mennes claimed to have translated a Dutch pamphlet into English at this time, although Pepys

doubted him; Pepys, 5.235. For the attribution to him of *Merry Newes from Epsom-Wells* (1663), see appendix 1.

27. Pepys, 3.112, 4.184 and 200, 6.119, 193 and 220, 8.220 and 566–67, and 9.269–70.

28. Pepys, 6.220.

29. Pepys, 4.210.

30. Pepys, 5.12.

31. Pepys, 4.61. See also, Pope, *Correspondence*, 3.108.

32. *Athenae*, 3.926; Alfred Povah, *The Annals of the Parishes of St. Olave Hart Street and Allhallows Staining in the City of London* (London, 1894), p. 81. The transcription of the monument in "Achievement" (pp. 127–28) supercedes the inaccurate transcripts in Boys's *History of Sandwich* (p. 352), and *Facetiae* (1.8).

33. *CSPD, 1671*, p. 106; Evelyn, *Diary* 3.570.

34. PRO Prob. 11/335/38, "Achievement," pp. 126–27.

35. Alexander Radcliffe, *The Works of Alexander Radcliffe (1696)*, introd. by Ken Robinson (Delmar, N.Y.: Scholars' Facsimiles and Reprints, 1981), pp. viii–xiv.

36. Allen, *Clubs of Augustan London*, pp. 283–84.

37. Allen, *Clubs of Augustan London*, pp. 260–78.

38. On the Restoration drolleries, see *Covent Garden Drollery: A Miscellany of 1672*, ed. G. Thorn-Drury (London: Dobell, 1928); Smith, "The Seventeenth-Century Drolleries," *HLB*. *Covent Garden Drollery* includes an attack on "a Fanatick Knave" (p. 29); *Holborn Drollery* (London, 1673) includes an octosyllabic doggerel version of the tale of Romulus and Remus (p. 93); *Wit at a Venture* (London, 1674) includes a comic seduction poem related to the tradition of wells poems (p. 65); and [William Hickes]'s *Grammatical Drollery* (London, 1682) prints two octosyllabic journey poems (p. 88).

39. Charles Sackville, *The Poems of Charles Sackville, Sixth Earl of Dorset*, ed. Brice Harris (New York and London: Garland, 1979), pp. 105–17; George Etherege, *The Poems of Sir George Etherege*, ed. James Thorpe (Princeton: Princeton University Press, 1963), pp. 35–53. For a possible instance of direct borrowing, compare Etherege's "But the next morning, fresh and gay" (*Poems*, p. 39, line 31), with Smith's "*LEANDER* being fresh and gay" (*HL*, p. 1). For other contemporary examples of such verse, see Wilson ed., *Court Satires of the Restoration*, pp. 131–48.

40. Robert Wild, *Poems by Robert Wilde D.D.*, ed. John Hunt (London, 1870), pp. 96–108.

41. Bond, *English Burlesque Poetry*, chap. 5.

42. Cotton's badinage with his muse in the "Epistle to Sir Clifford Clifton" (*Poems*, p. 265) may have been influenced by Smith's coarser battle with his muse in the preface to *The Innovation*; while Cotton's account in *Scarronides* of Aeolus sousing the Trojans may derive from similar scatalogical elements in Smith's verse; *Scarronides or, Virgile Travestie* (London, 1678), pp. 5–10; *WR*, pp. 148–49, 11, and 48–51.

43. Aside from the "inviron"/"iron" rhyme used by both Smith and Butler (above, pp. 123, 140), there appears to be only one possible instance of direct borrowing. Butler's comparison of Hudibras's horse to Caesar's, "who, as fame goes, / Had Corns upon his feet and toes" (1.1.427–28) may derive from a line in "Upon a lame tired Horse" (a poem in *MD*, which may be the work of Mennes or Smith)—"his Horse has Corns upon his Toes" (p. 28).

Select Bibliography

In order to keep this bibliography within manageable proportions, I have taken some liberties. In the case of manuscripts, reference numbers only are given (no descriptions). In the case of printed material, I have omitted standard reference works such as *OED*, *DNB* (except in cases of particular importance), HMC reports, and the calendars *CCAM, CCC, CSPD,* and *CSP Ireland.* Also omitted are cases where a commonly known text is mentioned, but no specific edition is cited. Wing and *STC* numbers are given only where this seems necessary as a finding aid.

Manuscripts

Bodleian Library, Oxford. MS Ashmole 36, 37; MS Aubrey 8; MSS Carte: 10–14, and 24; MSS Clarendon: 41, 49, 51, 55, 56, 58, 64, 65, and 67; MS Don d. 58; MSS Eng. Poet.: c. 53, d. 152, e. 14, and f. 27; MSS Malone: 13 and 23; MS Rawl. A 37; MS Rawl. Poet. D. 260; MSS Rawl. Poet.: 65, 117, 142, 191, 199, and 211; MS Top. Oxon. c. 160; MS Wood 416.

British Library, London. MSS Add.: 4207, 9317, 10309, 18220, 18981, 18982, 25302, 25303, 38065, 41846, 47111, and 53723; MS Birch 4460; MSS Eg.: 2421, 2535, 2725, and 3006; MSS Harl.: 367, 389, 3991, 6057, 6917, and 7319; MSS Sloane: 1446 and 1792.

Canterbury Cathedral Archives. U3/12/1/1.

Devon Record Office, Exeter. Devon Bishops' Registers, 23–24.

Durham County Record Office. D/CG 19/12,16,17, 21, and 22.

Exeter Cathedral Library. D&C Exeter 3499/182.

Folger Shakespeare Library, Washington, D.C.. MSS V. a. 103, 275, 276, and 345.

Greater London Record Office. DL/C/317.

Guildhall Library, London. MS 9537/13.

Huntington Library, San Marino, California. MS HM 16522.

Lambeth Palace Library, London. MS 942, no. 16.

Nottingham University Library. Portland Papers, PwV 24.

Public Record Office, London. Prob. 11/113/64; Prob. 11/148/14; Prob. 11/335/38; SP 3/11 (Signal Office Records), Nov. 1637; SP 12/237; SP 14/120/29; SP 14/155/56; SP 14/155/57; SP 14/162/17; SP 16/21/31; SP 16/24/87; SP 16/98/43; SP 16/121/40; SP 16/131/33; SP 16/140/68; SP 16/141/13; SP 16/142/110; SP 16/173/46; SP 16/240/25; SP 16/271/82; SP 16/321/45; SP 16/321/46; SP 16/372/111; SP 16/377/169; SP 16/415/49; SP 16/450/20; SP 16/473/74; SP 16/476/4; SP 16/478/16;

SP 16/485/15; SP 16/489/54; SP 16/519/123; SP 16/540/428; SP 25/77; SP 29/7/68; SP 29/126/59; and SP 29/169/13.

Sheffield University Library. Hartlib Papers: 13/19, 13/25, 29/2, and 68/10.

Yale University Library. Beinecke MSS: b104 and Osborn b197.

Primary Sources

Annalia Dubrensia. London, 1636.

Aristotle. *The Ethics of Aristotle: The Nicomachean Ethics*. Translated by J. A. K. Thompson. Revised by Hugh Treddenick. Harmondsworth: Penguin, 1976.

The Arundel Harington Manuscript of Tudor Poetry. Edited by Ruth Hughey. 2 vols. Columbus: Ohio State University Press, 1960.

Aston, John. "The Journal of John Aston, 1639." In *Six North Country Diaries*, pp. 1–34. Surtees Society, 118. Durham, 1910.

Aubrey, John. *"Brief Lives," chiefly of Contemporaries, set down by John Aubrey, between the Years 1669 & 1696*. Edited by Andrew Clark. 2 vols. Oxford, 1898.

The Barrington Family Letters 1628–1632. Edited by Arthur Searle. Camden Society, 4th ser. 28. London, 1983.

Blount, Thomas. *Glossographia*. London, 1656.

Bold, Henry. *Poems Lyrique Macaronique Heroique, &c*. London, 1664.

The Bonny Black-Smith's Delight. London, 1674–79. (Wing B3603A).

The bonny Black-smiths delight. Magdalene College, Cambridge, Pepys Ballads, 4.264.

Braithwait, Richard. *Ar't Asleepe Husband? A Boulster Lecture*. London, 1640.

Breton, Nicholas. *Poems: Not Hitherto Reprinted*. Edited by Jean Robertson. Liverpool: Liverpool University Press, 1967.

Brome, Alexander. *Poems*. Edited by Roman R. Dubinski. 2 vols. Toronto: University of Toronto Press, 1982.

Buckingham. *Poems and Songs Relating to George Villiers, Duke of Buckingham*. Edited by F. W. Fairholt. Percy Society, 90. London, 1850.

Burnet, Gilbert. *Some Passages of the Life and Death of Rochester* (1680). In *Rochester, The Critical Heritage*, edited by David Farley-Hills, pp. 47–92. London: Routledge and Kegan Paul, 1972.

Butler, Samuel. *Hudibras*. Edited by John Wilders. Oxford: Clarendon Press, 1967.

Butler, Samuel. *The Posthumous Works of Mr Samuel Butler*. London, 1732.

Carew, Thomas. *The Poems of Thomas Carew*. Edited by Rhodes Dunlap. Oxford: Clarendon Press, 1949.

Carte, Thomas. *A Collection of Original Letters and Papers Concerning the State of England, from the Year 1641–1660*. 2 vols. London, 1739.

C[arter], M[atthew]. *A Most True and Exact Relation of that as Honourable as Unfortunate Expedition of Kent, Essex, and Colchester*. [London], 1650.

Cartwright, William. *The Plays and Poems of William Cartwright*. Edited by G. Blakemore Evans. Madison: University of Wisconsin Press, 1951.

Cavendish, Margaret. *Poems and Fancies*. London, 1653.

[Cavendish], Margaret, Duchess of Newcastle. *The Life of William Cavendish, Duke of Newcastle*. Edited by C. H. Firth. 2d ed. London: Routledge, [1906].

A Certain Relation of the Hog-faced Gentlewoman called Mistris Tanakin Skinker. London, 1640. (STC 22627).

Chamberlain, John. *The Letters of John Chamberlain*. Edited by Norman Egbert McClure. 2 vols. Philadelphia: American Philosophical Society, 1939.

Chamberlain, Robert. *"The Harmony of the Muses" by Robert Chamberlain (1654)*. Introduction by Ernest W. Sullivan, II. Aldershot: Scolar Press, 1990.

Chester, Henry. "The Ship Money Papers of Hen. Chester and Sir Will. Boteler, 1637–1639." Edited by F. G. and Margaret Emmison. *Publications of the Bedfordshire Historical Record Society* 18 (1936): 43–88.

Child, Francis James, ed. *The English and Scottish Popular Ballads*. 5 vols. Boston and New York, 1882.

Choyce Drollery: Songs & Sonnets. Edited by J. Woodfall Ebsworth. Boston, Lincs., 1876.

Churchill, Awnsham, and John Churchill. *A Collection of Voyages and Travels*. 4 vols. London, 1704.

Clarendon, Edward Hyde, Earl of. *The History of the Rebellion and Civil Wars in England*. Edited by W. Dunn Macray. 6 vols. Oxford, 1857.

Clarke, William. *The Clarke Papers: Selections from the Papers of William Clarke*. Edited by C. H. Firth. Vol. 2, Camden Society, n. s. 104. London, 1894.

Clayton, Thomas, ed. *Cavalier Poets: Selected Poems*. Oxford: Oxford University Press, 1978.

Cleveland, John. *"J. Cleaveland Revived" Second edition (1660)*. Introduction by Hilton Kelliher. Aldershot: Scolar Press, 1990.

———. *The Poems of John Cleveland*. Edited by John M. Berdan. New Haven: Yale University Press, 1911.

———. *The Poems of John Cleveland*. Edited by Brian Morris and Eleanor Withington. Oxford: Clarendon Press, 1967.

Cobbes Prophecies, his Signes and Tokens. London, 1614. Reprinted as *Antient Drolleries*, no. 1, with a preface by A. H. Bullen. London, 1890.

Collop, John. *The Poems of John Collop*. Edited by Conrad Hilberry. Madison: University of Wisconsin Press, 1962.

Colman, Henry. *Divine Meditations (1640)*. Edited by Karen E. Steanson. New Haven and London: Yale University Press, 1979.

Conway Letters: The Correspondence of Anne, Viscountess Conway, Henry More, and Their Friends, 1642–1684. Edited by Marjorie Hope Nicolson. Revised by Sarah Hutton. Oxford: Clarendon Press, 1992.

Corbett, Richard. *The Poems of Richard Corbett*. Edited by J. A. W. Bennett and H. R. Trevor-Roper. Oxford: Clarendon Press, 1955.

Coryate, Thomas. *Coryats Crudities*. London, 1611.

———. *Mr. Thomas Coriate to his Friends sendeth Greeting from Agra*. London, 1618.

Cotgrave, Randall. *A Dictionarie of the French and English Tongues*. London, 1611.

Cotton, Charles. *Poems of Charles Cotton 1630–1687*. Edited by John Beresford. London: Cobden-Sanderson, 1923.

———. *Scarronides, or, Virgile Travestie*. London, 1678.

Covent Garden Drollery: A Miscellany of 1672. Edited by G. Thorn-Drury. London: Dobell, 1928.

Cowley, Abraham. *The Collected Works of Abraham Cowley*. Edited by Thomas O. Calhoun, et al. 6 vols. Newark: University of Delaware Press, 1989–.

———. *The English Writings of Abraham Cowley: Poems*. Edited by A. R. Waller. Cambridge: Cambridge University Press, 1905.

———. *The Mistress with Other Select Poems of Abraham Cowley*. Edited by John Sparrow. London: Nonesuch Press, 1926.

D., N. *An Antidote Against Melancholy: Made up in Pills*. London, 1661. (Wing D66A).

Davenant, Sir William. *Sir William Davenant's "Gondibert."* Edited by David F. Gladish. Oxford: Clarendon Press, 1971.

———. *The Shorter Poems and Songs from the Plays and Masques*. Edited by A. M. Gibbs. Oxford: Clarendon Press, 1972.

Davies, John. *An Account of the Author of this Translation and his Works*. Prefaced to J[ohn] Hall, *Hierocles upon the Golden Verses of Pythagoras*. London, 1657.

Day, Angel. *The English Secretorie*. London, 1586.

Denham, John. *The Poetical Works of Sir John Denham*. Edited by Theodore Howard Banks. 2d ed. [Hamden, Conn.]: Archon, 1969.

Dennis, John. *The Critical Works*. Edited by E. N. Hooker. 2 vols. Baltimore: Johns Hopkins University Press, 1939–43.

Donne, John. *The Elegies, Songs and Sonnets*. Edited by Helen Gardner. Oxford: Clarendon Press, 1965.

Dryden, John. *Of Dramatic Poesy and Other Critical Essays*. Edited by George Watson. 2 vols. London: Dent, 1962.

———. *The Third Part of Miscellany Poems*. London, 1716.

———. *The Sixth Part of Miscellany Poems*. London, 1716.

Duppa, Brian. *The Correspondence of Bishop Brian Duppa and Sir Justinian Isham 1650–1660*. Edited by Sir Gyles Isham. Publications of the Northamptonshire Record Society, 17. Lamport Hall, Northamptonshire: Northamptonshire Record Society, 1955.

Earle, John. *Microcosmography*. Edited by Alfred West. Cambridge, 1897.

Erasmus. *The Collected Works of Erasmus*. Vol. 3, *Adages Ii1–Iv100*. Translated by Margaret Mann Phillips. Toronto: University of Toronto Press, 1982.

———. *Opera Omnia*. 10 vols. [Leyden], 1703–1706.

Etherege, George. *The Poems of Sir George Etherege*. Edited by James Thorpe. Princeton: Princeton University Press, 1963.

Euing. *The Euing Collection of English Broadside Ballads*. Edited by John Holloway. Glasgow: University of Glasgow Publications, 1971.

Evelyn, John. *The Diary of John Evelyn*. Edited by E. S. de Beer, 6 vols. Oxford: Clarendon Press, 1955.

F., C. *Wit at a Venture, or Clio's Privy Garden*. London, 1674.

Facetiae. "*Musarum Deliciae*" . . . "*Wit Restor'd*" . . . "*Wits Recreations.*" Edited by [Thomas Park and Edward Dubois]. London, 1817.

——. Edited by J. C. Hotten. 2 vols. London, [1874].

Firth, C. H., and R. S. Rait, eds. *Acts and Ordinances of the Interregnum, 1646–1660.* 3 vols. London: HMSO, 1911.

Flecknoe, Richard. *The Diarium, or Journall.* London, 1656.

——. *Miscellania, or, Poems.* London, 1653.

Gayton, Edmund. *To Mr Robert Whitehall at the Wells at Astrop.* [Oxford, 1666].

Gill, Alexander. *Logonomia Anglica.* Edited by Bror Danielsson and Arvid Gabrielson. 2 vols. Stockholm: Almqvist and Wiksell, 1972.

Godolphin, Sidney. *The Poems of Sidney Godolphin.* Edited by William Dighton. Oxford: Clarendon Press, 1931.

Gondibert. Certain Verses Written by Severall of the Authors Friends: to be Re-Printed with the Second Edition of Gondibert. London, 1653.

The Greek Anthology. Translated by W. R. Paton. 5 vols. London: Heinemann, 1916–18.

Gunton, Timothy. *An Extemporary Answer to a cluster of drunkards met together at Schiedam, by Timothy Gunton, who was compelled thereto, upon his refusall to drink the King's health.* [London, 1648].

Harvey, Gabriel. *The Letter-Book of Gabriel Harvey, A.D. 1573–1580.* Edited by Edmund John Long Scott. Camden Society, n. s. 33. London, 1884.

Haughton, Hugh, ed. *The Chatto Book of Nonsense Poetry.* London: Chatto and Windus, 1988.

Hearne, Thomas. *Remarks and Collections by Thomas Hearne.* 11 vols. Oxford: Oxford Historical Society, 1895–1921.

Henrietta Maria. *The Letters of Queen Henrietta Maria.* Edited by Mary Anne Everett Green. London, 1857.

Herrick, Robert. *The Complete Poetry of Robert Herrick.* Edited by J. Max Patrick. New York: Norton, 1968.

——. *The Poetical Works of Robert Herrick.* Edited by L. C. Martin. Oxford: Clarendon Press, 1956.

Hic Mulier: or The Man Woman. London, 1620. (*STC* 13374–75).

[Hickes], [William]. *Grammatical Drollery.* London, 1682.

——. *Oxford Drollery.* London, 1673.

Hoccleve, Thomas. *Selections from Hoccleve.* Edited by M. C. Seymour. Oxford: Clarendon Press, 1981.

Holborn Drollery. London, 1673.

[Holland, Samuel]. *Wit and Fancy in a Maze.* London, 1656.

Horace. *Satires, Epistles and Ars Poetica.* Translated by H. Rushton Fairclough. Rev. ed. Cambridge: Harvard University Press; London: Heinemann, 1970.

Howell, James. *Epistolae Ho-Elianae: The Familiar Letters of James Howell.* Edited by Joseph Jacobs. 2 vols. London, 1890.

Hutchinson, Lucy. *Memoirs of the Life of Colonel Hutchinson.* Edited by James Sutherland. London: Oxford University Press, 1973.

An Invective against the Pride of Women. [London, 1657]. (Wing I284).

James I. *The Poems of King James VI, of Scotland.* Edited by James Craigie. 2 vols. Edinburgh: Scottish Text Society, 1955 and 1958.

Jansen, Cornelius. *Augustinus.* [Louvain], 1640.

Jonson, Ben. *Ben Jonson.* Edited by C. H. Herford, Percy and Evelyn Simpson. 11 vols. Oxford: Clarendon Press, 1925–1952.

———. *Ben Jonson: The Complete Masques.* Edited by Stephen Orgel. New Haven: Yale University Press, 1969.

Jordan, J. [Thomas?]. *A New Droll: or, the Counter-Scuffle.* London, 1663. (Wing J1050).

Jordan, Thomas. *Wit in a Wildernesse.* London, [1665?].

Killigrew, Thomas. *Comedies and Tragedies.* London, 1664.

King, Henry. *The Poems of Henry King.* Edited by Margaret Crum. Oxford: Clarendon Press, 1965.

Lawes, Henry. *The Second Book of Ayres and Dialogues.* London, 1653.

———. *The Second Part of the Treasury of Musick.* London, 1669.

A Letter sent from the Right Honourable Robert Earle of Warwik. London, 1642.

Lineall, John. *Itur Mediteraneum.* Stafford, 1658.

Lister, Raymond. *The Loyal Blacksmith.* Cambridge: Golden Head Press, 1957.

Lluellin, Martin. *Men-Miracles.* [Oxford], 1646.

Lloyd, David. *The Legend of Captaine Jones.* London, 1648. (Wing L2630).

The Loves of Hero and Leander. A mock Poem. London, 1651. (Wing L3276).

———. London, 1653. (Wing L3277).

———. London, 1653. (Wing L3278).

Lucans Pharsalia: or the Civil Warres of Rome. Translated by Thomas May. 3d ed. London, 1635.

Markham, Francis. *Five Decades of Epistles of Warre.* London, 1622.

Marlowe, Christopher. *The Complete Poems and Translations.* Edited by Stephen Orgel. Harmondsworth: Penguin, 1971.

———. *The Poems.* Edited by Millar Maclure. London: Methuen, 1968.

Marshall, L. Birkett, ed. *Rare Poems of the Seventeenth Century.* Cambridge: Cambridge University Press, 1936.

Marston Morteyne, *Marston Morteyne, 1602–1812.* Edited by F. G. Emmison. Bedfordshire Parish Registers, 44. Bedford, 1953.

Massinger, Philip. *The Plays and Poems of Philip Massinger.* Edited by Philip Edwards and Colin Gibson. 5 vols. Oxford: Clarendon Press, 1976.

Merry Drollery Compleat. Edited by J. Woodfall Ebsworth. Boston, Lincs., 1875.

Merry Drollery. The Second Part of Merry Drollery, or A Collection of Jovial Poems, Merry Songs, Witty Drolleries. London, [1661?]. (Wing S2295).

A merry new Ballad; both pleasant and sweete. [London?], 1650. (Wing M1870A).

Merry Newes from Epsom-Wells. London, 1663. (Wing M1872).

Middleton, Thomas. *A Chaste Maid in Cheapside.* Edited by R. B. Parker. London: Methuen, 1969.

Middleton, Thomas, and William Rowley. *The Changeling.* Edited by N. W. Bawcutt. Manchester: Manchester University Press, 1977.

Milton, John. *Original Papers Illustrative of the Life of John Milton.* Edited by W. Douglas Hamilton. Camden Society, 75. London, 1859.

Mordaunt, John. *Thé Letter Book of John Viscount Mordaunt*. Edited by Mary Coate. Camden Society, 3d ser. 59. London, 1945.

Mountagu, Edward. *The Journal of Edward Mountagu. First Earl of Sandwich . . . 1659–1665*. Edited by R. C. Anderson. Navy Records Society, 64. London, 1929.

Musaeus. *Hero and Leander*. Edited and translated by E. H. Blakeney. Oxford: Blackwell, 1935.

Musarum Deliciae. London, 1655.

———. 2d ed. London, 1656.

"Musarum Deliciae" (1655) and "Wit Restor'd" (1658). Introduction by Tim Raylor. Delmar, N.Y.: Scholars' Facsimiles and Reprints, 1985.

Naps upon Parnassus. London, 1658.

Nashe, Thomas. *The Works of Thomas Nashe*. Edited by Ronald B. McKerrow. 2d ed. Revised by F. P. Wilson. 5 vols. Oxford: Blackwell, 1958.

Nedham, Marchamont. *A Short History of the English Rebellion Compiled in Verse*. London, 1680.

Nicholas, Edward. *The Nicholas Papers: Correspondence of Edward Nicholas*. Edited by George F. Warner. Vol. 2. Camden Society, n. s. 50. London, 1892.

A notable and wonderfull sea fight between two great and wel-mounted Spanish shipps. Amsterdam, 1621.

Ogilby, John. *Britannia*. London, 1675.

Orgel, Stephen, and Roy Strong. *Inigo Jones: The Theatre of the Stuart Court*. 2 vols. London: Sotheby Parke Bernet, 1973.

Osborn, Louise Brown. *The Life, Letters, and Writings of John Hoskyns, 1566–1638*. New Haven: Yale University Press, 1937.

Ottley. "The Ottley Papers Relating to the Civil War." Edited by William Phillips. *Transactions of the Shropshire Archaeological and Natural History Society*, 2d ser. 8 (1895): 241–360.

Ovid De Arte Amandi, and the Remedy of Love Englished, Translated by Thomas Heywood. London, 1662. (Wing O648).

———. London, 1662/1667.

———. London, 1672. (Wing O650).

———. London, 1677. (Wing O651).

———. London, 1682. (Wing O652).

———. London, 1684. (Wing O653).

———. London, 1684. (Another, unlisted, edition).

———. London, 1701.

———. London, 1705.

Ovid. *Heroides and Amores*. Translated by Grant Showerman. 2d ed. Cambridge: Harvard University Press, 1977.

Ovid's Heroicall Epistles. Translated by W[ye] S[altonstall]. London, 1636 and 1639.

Ovids Heroical Epistles. Translated by John Sherburne. London, 1639.

Ovid De Ponto. Translated by Wye Saltonstall. London, 1639.

Ovids Tristia. Translated by W[ye] S[altonstall]. London, 1637. (*STC* 18980).

Pepys, Samuel. *The Diary of Samuel Pepys*. Edited by Robert Latham and William Matthews. 11 vols. London: Bell and Hyman, 1970–83.

———. *Samuel Pepys' Penny Merriments*. Edited by Roger Thompson. London: Constable, 1976.

Pestell, Thomas. *The Poems of Thomas Pestell*. Edited by Hannah Buchan. Oxford: Blackwell, 1940.

Pett, Phineas. *The Autobiography of Phineas Pett*. Edited by W. G. Perrin. Navy Records Society, 51. London, 1918.

The Picture of an English Antick. [London, 1646]. (Wing P2155).

Pimlyco, or, Runne Red-Cap. London, 1609. Reprinted as *Antient Drolleries*, no. 2, with a preface by A. H. Bullen. Oxford, 1891.

Pope, Alexander. *The Correspondence of Alexander Pope*. Edited by George Sherburn. 5 vols. Oxford: Clarendon Press, 1956.

[Prestwich, Edmund]. *The Hectors*. London, 1656.

Purchas, Samuel. *Purchas his Pilgrimes*. London, 1625.

Puttenham, George. *The Art of English Poesie*. Edited by Gladys Doidge Willcock and Alice Walker. Cambridge: Cambridge University Press, 1936.

Radcliffe, Alexander. *The Works of Alexander Radcliffe (1696)*. Introduction by Ken Robinson. Delmar, N.Y.: Scholars' Facsimiles and Reprints, 1981.

Reyce, Robert. *Suffolk in the XVIIth. Century: The Breviary of Suffolk by Robert Reyce, 1618*. Edited by Lord Francis Hervey. London: John Murray, 1902.

Rollins, H. E., ed. *Cavalier and Puritan: Ballads and Broadsides Illustrating the Period of the Great Rebellion 1640–1660*. New York: New York University Press, 1923.

Rump: or An Exact Collection of the Choycest Poems and Songs Relating to the Late Times. 2 vols. 1662; reprint. [London], [1874].

Rymer, Thomas. *Foedera, Conventiones, Literae et Cujusque Generis*. 20 vols. London, 1735.

Sackville, Charles. *The Poems of Charles Sackville, Sixth Earl of Dorset*. Edited by Brice Harris. New York and London: Garland, 1979.

Saltonstall, Wye. *Clavis Ad Portam*. London, 1634.

———. *Picturae Loquentes*. Edited by C. H. Wilkinson. Oxford: Luttrell Society, 1946.

[Saltonstall, Wye]. *The Complaint of Time against the Tumultuous and Rebellious Scots*. London, 1639. (STC 21643.5).

[———]. *A Description of Time: Applied to this present Time*. London, 1638. (*STC* 21643).

Scarron, Paul. *Poésies Diverses*. Edited by Maurice Cauchie. 2 vols. Paris: Société des Textes Français Modernes, 1947 and 1960.

———. *Le Virgile Travesti*. Edited by Jean Serroy. Paris: Garnier, 1988.

Shakespeare, William. *Love's Labours Lost*. Edited by Richard David. London: Methuen, 1951.

Sherburne, Edward. *The Poems and Translations of Sir Edward Sherburne (1616–1702) excluding Seneca and Manilius*. Edited by F. J. Van Beeck, SJ. Amsterdam: Te Assen, 1961.

Sidney, Philip. *An Apology for Poetry*. Edited by Geoffrey Shepherd. London: Nelson, 1965.

————. *The Poems of Sir Philip Sidney*. Edited by William A. Ringler Jr. Oxford: Clarendon Press, 1962.

Skelton, John. *The Complete English Poems*. Edited by John Scattergood. Harmondsworth: Penguin, 1983.

Skelton, Robin, ed. *The Cavalier Poets*. London: Faber, 1970.

Smith, Captain John. *Generall Historie of Virginia*. London, 1624.

Smith, Sir Thomas. *De Republica Anglorum*. Edited by Mary Dewar. Cambridge: Cambridge University Press, 1982.

The Spectator. Edited by Donald F. Bond. 5 vols. Oxford: Clarendon Press, 1955.

Speed, Robert. *The Counter Scuffle*. London, 1653. (Wing S4891A).

Spence, Joseph. *Observations, Anecdotes, and Characters of Books and Men*. Edited by James M. Osborn. 2 vols. Oxford: Clarendon Press, 1966.

Spingarn, J. E, ed. *Critical Essays of the Seventeenth Century*. 3 vols. Oxford: Clarendon Press, 1908–1909.

Spink, Ian, transcriber and ed. *English Songs 1625–1660*. 2d ed. Musica Britannica: A National Collection of Music, 33. London: Stainer and Bell, 1977.

Sportive Wit. London, 1656.

Stationers' Company. *A Transcript of the Registers of the Worshipful Company of Stationers 1640–1708 A.D.* 2 vols. London: privately printed, 1913.

Stokes, Joseph Morgan. "*Wit and Drollery* 1656." Ph.D. diss., Yale University, 1935.

Strafford, Earl of. *The Earle of Straffordes Letters and Dispatches*. Edited by William Knowler. 2 vols. London, 1739.

Suckling, Sir John. *A Letter sent by Sir John Suckling from France*. London, 1641. (Wing S6132A).

————. *The Works of Sir John Suckling: The Plays*. Edited by L. A. Beaurline. Oxford: Clarendon Press, 1971.

————. *The Works of Sir John Suckling: The Non-Dramatic Works*. Edited by Thomas Clayton. Oxford: Clarendon Press, 1971.

The Sucklingtonian Faction: or (Sucklings) Roaring Boyes. London, 1641. (Wing S6133).

Taylor, John. *All the Workes of Iohn Taylor*. London, 1630.

Thurloe, John. *A Collection of the State Papers of John Thurloe*. Edited by Thomas Birch. 7 vols. London, 1742–45.

The True List of his Majesties Navie Royall. London, [1642]. (Wing T2717).

A true relation of a wonderfull sea fight between two great and well appointed Spanish ships, and a small English ship. London, 1621.

A True Relation of the Victory obtained over the King's Forces. London, 1645. (Wing T2895).

Virgil. Translated by H. Rushton Fairclough. Rev. ed. 2 vols. Cambridge: Harvard University Press; London: Heinemann, 1935.

Vox Borealis, or the Northern Discoverie. [London], 1641. (Wing V712).

W., J. *Vinegar and Mustard; or Wormwood Lectures for Every Day of the Week*. [n.p.], 1686.

Wardroper, John. *Love and Drollery*. London: Routledge and Kegan Paul, 1969.

Weaver, Thomas. *Songs and Poems of Love and Drollery*. [London], 1654.

Wells, Jeremiah. *Poems upon Divers Occasions*. London, 1667.

Westcote, Thomas. *A View of Devonshire in MDCXXX*. Edited by Rev. George Oliver and Pitman Jones. Exeter, 1845.

Wild, Robert. *Poems by Robert Wilde D.D.* Edited by John Hunt. London, 1870.

[Wild?, Robert]. *The Incomparable Poem Gondibert, Vindicated*. [n.p.], 1653.

———. *The Incomparable Poem Gondibert, Vindicated*. [n.p.], 1655. (Wing W2130).

Willan, Leonard. *The Phrygian Fabulist*. London, 1650.

Williams, William. "History of the Bulkeley Family." Edited by E. Gwynne Jones. *Transactions of the Anglesey Antiquarian Society and Field Club* (1948): 1–99.

Wilson, John Harold, ed. *Court Satires of the Restoration*. Columbus: Ohio State University Press, 1976.

Wit and Drollery. London, 1656.

———. 2d ed. London, 1661.

———. 3d ed. London, 1682.

Wit at a Venture. London, 1674.

Wit Restor'd. London, 1658.

"Witts Recreations: Selected from the Finest Fancies of Moderne Muses" (1640). Introduction by Colin Gibson. Aldershot: Scolar Press, 1990.

Wood, Anthony. *Athenae Oxonienses*. Edited by Philip Bliss. 4 vols. London, 1813–20.

———. *Fasti Oxonienses*. Edited by Philip Bliss. 2 vols. London, 1815–20.

———. *The Life and Times of Anthony Wood, Antiquary of Oxford, Described by Himself*. Edited by Andrew Clark. 5 vols. Oxford: Oxford Historical Society, 1891–1900.

Wright, Abraham. *"Parnassus Biceps, or Severall Select Pieces of Poetry" by Abraham Wright (1656)*. Introduction by Peter Beal. Aldershot: Scolar Press, 1990.

Yonge, Walter. *The Diary of Walter Yonge. Esq.* Edited by George Roberts. Camden Society, 41. London, 1848.

Secondary Sources

Adair, John. *Roundhead General: A Military Biography of Sir William Waller*. London: Macdonald, 1969.

Aers, David, and Gunther Kress. "Darke Texts need Notes: Versions of Self in Donne's Verse Epistles." In David Aers, Bob Hodge, and Gunther Kress, *Literature, Language and Society in England 1580–1680*, pp. 23–48. Dublin and Totowa, N.J.: Gill and Macmillan, 1981.

Allen, Robert J. *The Clubs of Augustan London*. Cambridge: Harvard University Press, 1933.

Andrews, Kenneth R. *Ships, Money and Politics: Seafaring and Naval Enterprise in the Reign of Charles I*. Cambridge: Cambridge University Press, 1991.

Anselment, Raymond A. *Loyalist Resolve: Patient Fortitude in the English Civil War*. Newark: University of Delaware Press, 1988.

———. "Thomas Carew and the 'Harmelesse Pastimes' of Caroline Peace." *Philological Quarterly* 62 (1983): 201–19.

Austin, J. L. *How to Do Things with Words*. 2d ed. Edited by J. O. Urmson and Marina Sbisa. Oxford: Clarendon Press, 1975.

Aylmer, G. E. *The King's Servants: The Civil Service of Charles I 1625–1642*. London: Routledge and Kegan Paul, 1961.

Bacon, Montagu. "A Dissertation on Burlesque Poetry." In Zachary Grey, *Critical, Historical, and Explanatory Notes Upon "Hudibras,"* pp. 1–16. [London], 1752.

Bakeless, John. *The Tragicall History of Christopher Marlowe*. 2 vols. Cambridge: Harvard University Press, 1942.

Bakhtin, Mikhail. *The Dialogic Imagination: Four Essays*. Edited by Michael Holquist. Translated by Caryl Emerson and Michael Holquist. Austin: University of Texas Press, 1981.

———. *Rabelais and his World*. Translated by Helene Iswolsky. 1968; reprint, Bloomington: Indiana University Press, 1984.

Baldwin, T. W. *William Shakespere's Small Latine & Lesse Greeke*. 2 vols. Urbana: University of Illinois Press, 1944.

Bas, George. "James Shirley, et 'Th'Untun'd Kennell': Une petite guerre des théâtres vers 1630." *Etudes Anglaises* 16 (1963): 11–22.

Beal, Peter. "Massinger at Bay: Unpublished Verses in a War of the Theatres." *YES* 10 (1980): 190–203.

Beatty, John Louis. *Warrick and Holland: being the Lives of Robert and Henry Rich*. Denver: Alan Swallow, 1965.

Bedford. *The Victoria County History of the County of Bedford*. 3 vols. Westminster: Constable, 1904–14.

Bentley, Gerald Eades. *The Jacobean and Caroline Stage*. 7 vols. Oxford: Clarendon Press, 1941–68.

Bertelsen, Lance. *The Nonsense Club: Literature and Popular Culture, 1749–64*. Oxford: Clarendon Press, 1986.

Binns, J. W. "The Letters of Erasmus." In *Erasmus*, edited by T. A. Dorey, pp. 55–79. London: Routledge and Kegan Paul, 1970.

Birch, Thomas. *The Court and Times of Charles I*. 2 vols. London, 1848.

Bond, Richmond P. *English Burlesque Poetry 1700–1750*. Cambridge: Harvard University Press, 1932.

Boutwood, James. "A Vanished Elizabethan Mansion: Toddington Manor House, Bedfordshire." *Country Life* 129 (1961): 638–40.

Boys, William. *Collections for an History of Sandwich in Kent*. Canterbury, 1792.

Brennan, Michael G. *Literary Patronage in the English Renaissance: The Pembroke Family*. London: Routledge, 1988.

Bristol, Michael D. *Carnival and Theater: Plebeian Culture and the Structure of Authority in Renaissance England*. London: Methuen, 1985.

Broich, Ulrich. *The Eighteenth-Century Mock-Heroic Poem*. Cambridge: Cambridge University Press, 1990.

Brenan, Gerald. *A History of the House of Percy*. 2 vols. London: Freemantle, 1902.

British Library. *Catalogue of Additions to the Manuscripts 1946–1950*. London: British Library, 1979.

Brooks, Harold. "English Verse Satire, 1640-1660: Prolegomena." *The Seventeenth Century* 3 (1988): 17–46.

Burke, Peter. *Popular Culture in Early Modern Europe*. 1978; reprint, Aldershot: Wildwood House, 1988.

Burner, Sandra A. *James Shirley: A Study of Literary Coteries and Patronage in Seventeenth-Century England*. Lanham, Md.: University Press of America, 1988.

Bush, Douglas. *English Literature in the Earlier Seventeenth Century 1600–1660*. The Oxford History of English Literature. 2d ed. Oxford: Clarendon Press, 1962.

———. *Mythology and the Renaissance Tradition in English Poetry*. Minneapolis: University of Minnesota Press, 1932.

Butler, Martin. *"Love's Sacrifice*: Ford's Metatheatrical Tragedy." In *John Ford: Critical Re-Visions*, edited by Michael Neill, pp. 201–31. Cambridge: Cambridge University Press, 1988.

———. *Theatre of Crisis 1632–1642*. Cambridge: Cambridge University Press, 1984.

C., H. G. "'Minnis' in Place Names." *N&Q*, 6th ser. 1 (1880): 96.

Cain, T. G. S. "Robert Herrick, Mildmay Fane, and Sir Simeon Steward." *ELR* 15 (1985): 312–17.

Calhoun, Thomas Osborne. "Cowley's Verse Satire, 1642–1643, and the Beginnings of Party Politics." *YES* 21 (1991): 194–206.

Callender, Geoffrey. "Sir John Mennes." *Mariner's Mirror* 6 (1940): 276–85.

Capp, Bernard. *Astrology and the Popular Press: English Almanacs 1500–1800*. London: Faber, 1979.

———. *Cromwell's Navy: The Fleet and the English Revolution 1648–1660*. Oxford: Clarendon Press, 1989.

———. "English Youth Groups and *The Pinder of Wakefield*." *P&P* 76 (1977): 127–33.

———. "Popular Literature." In *Popular Culture in Seventeenth-Century England*, edited by Barry Reay, pp. 198–243. 1985; reprint, London: Routledge, 1988.

Carey, John. *John Donne: Life, Mind and Art*. London: Faber, 1981.

Carlisle, Nicholas. *A Concise Description of the Endowed Grammar Schools in England and Wales*. 2 vols. London, 1818.

Carlton, Charles. *Charles I: The Personal Monarch*. London: Routledge and Kegan Paul, 1984.

Case, Arthur E. *Bibliography of English Poetical Miscellanies 1521–1750*. Oxford: Oxford Bibliographical Society, 1935.

Cavell, John, and Brian Kennett. *A History of Sir Roger Manwood's School, Sandwich, 1563–1963*. London: Cory, Adams and Mackay, 1963.

Chartier, Roger. *The Culture of Print: Power and the Uses of Print in Early Mod-

ern Europe. Edited by Roger Chartier. Translated by Lydia G. Cochrane. Cambridge and Oxford: Polity Press, 1988.

Chaucer: The Critical Heritage. Edited by Derek Brewer. 2 vols. London: Routledge and Kegan Paul, 1978.

Chernaik, Warren. "Books as Memorials: The Politics of Consolation." *YES* 21 (1991): 207–17.

————. *The Poetry of Limitation: A Study of the Poetry of Edmund Waller*. New Haven: Yale University Press, 1968.

Chute, Marchette. *Two Gentle Men: The Lives of George Herbert and Robert Herrick*. London: Secker and Warburg, 1960.

Clark, A. F. B. *Boileau and the French Classical Critics in England (1660–1750)*. Bibliothèque de la Revue de littérature comparée. Paris: Éduoard Champion, 1925.

Clark, Donald Lemen. *John Milton at St. Paul's School: A Study of Ancient Rhetoric in English Renaissance Education*. New York: Columbia University Press, 1948.

Clarke, M. L. *Classical Education in Britain 1500–1900*. Cambridge: Cambridge University Press, 1959.

Collinge, John M. *Navy Board Officials 1680–1832*. Office Holders in Modem England, 7. London: Institute of Historical Research, 1978.

Cripps, Doreen. *Elizabeth of the Sealed Knot: A Biography of Elizabeth Murray Countess of Dysart*. Kineton: Roundwood Press, 1975.

Cronk, Nicholas. "La Defense du Dialogisme: Vers une Poetique du Burlesque." In *Burlesque et Fommes Parodiques dans la Litterature et les Arts: Actes du Colloque de l'Université du Maine. Le Mans (du 4 au 7 decembre 1986)*, edited by Isabelle Landy-Houillon and Maurice Menard, pp. 321–38. Paris, Seattle, and Tubingen: Biblio 17, 1987.

Crump, Galbraith Miller. "Edward Sherburne's Acquaintances." *TLS*, 19 March 1958, 139.

Curtis, Mark H. "The Alienated Intellectuals of Early Stuart England." In *Crisis in Europe 1560–1660*, edited by Trevor Aston, pp. 295–316. London: Routledge and Kegan Paul, 1965.

Curtius, Ernst Robert. *European Literature and the Latin Middle Ages*. Translated by Willard R. Trask. London: Routledge and Kegan Paul, 1953.

Cust, Richard "News and Politics in Early Seventeenth-Century England." *P&P* 112 (1986): 60–90.

Davis, Natalie Zemon. *Society and Culture in Early Modern France*. Stanford, Calif.: Stanford University Press, 1975.

Dime, Gregory T. "The Difference between 'Strong Lines' and 'Metaphysical Poetry.'" *SEL* 26 (1986): 47–57.

Disraeli, Isaac. "D'Avenant and a Club of Wits." In his *Casualties and Quarrels of Authors*. 2d ed. London, 1882.

Dobson, E. J. *English Pronunciation 1500–1700*. 2 vols. London: Clarendon Press, 1957.

Dollimore, Jonathan. *Radical Tragedy: Religion, Ideology and Power in the Drama of Shakespeare and his Contemporaries*. Brighton: Harvester, 1984.

Donno, Elizabeth Story, ed. *Elizabethan Minor Epics*. London: Routledge and Kegan Paul, 1963.

Doody, Margaret Anne. *The Daring Muse: Augustan Poetry Reconsidered*. Cambridge: Cambridge University Press, 1985.

Drummond, J. C., and Anne Wilbraham. *The Englishmans Food: A History of Five Centuries of English Diet*. Revised by Dorothy Hollingsworth. London: Cape, 1957.

Dunn, T. A. *Philip Massinger: The Man and the Playwright*. Edinburgh: University College of Ghana, 1957.

Dunstan, James. *History of the Parish of Bromley St. Leonard, Middlesex*. London, 1862.

Edmond, Mary. *Rare Sir William Davenant*. Manchester: Manchester University Press, 1987.

Edwards, Philip, et al. *The Revels History of Drama in English, Volume IV, 1613–1660*. London: Methuen, 1981.

Elkin, P. K. *The Augustan Defence of Satire*. Oxford: Clarendon Press, 1973.

Elliott, Robert C. *The Power of Satire: Magic, Ritual, Art*. Princeton: Princeton University Press, 1960.

Everitt, Alan. *The Community of Kent and the Great Rebellion 1640–60*. Leicester: Leicester University Press, 1966.

Ewart, Gavin. "A sixpence short of a shilling." *The Sunday Times*, 20 November 1988, G12.

Farley-Hills, David. *The Benevolence of Laughter: Comic Poetry of the Commonwealth and Restoration*. London and Basingstoke: Macmillan, 1974.

——. *Rochester's Poetry*. London: Bell and Hyman, 1978.

Fea, Allan. *The Loyal Wentworths*. London: Bodley Head, 1928.

Firth, C. H. "The Royalists under the Protectorate." *EHR* 52 (1937): 634–48.

Fisher, Nicholas R. E. "Greek Associations, Symposia, and Clubs." In *Civilization of the Ancient Mediterranean*, edited by Michael Grant and Rachel Kitzinger, 2.1167–97. 3 vols. New York: Scribners, 1988.

——. "Roman Associations, Dinner Parties, and Clubs." In *Civilization of the Ancient Mediterranean*, edited by Michael Grant and Rachel Kitzinger, 2: 1199–225. 3 vols. New York: Scribners, 1988.

Foster, C. W. "Institutions to Benefices in the Diocese of Lincoln." *Associated Architectural Society Reports and Papers* 39 (1928–29): 179–216.

Foster, Joseph. *Alumni Oxonienses, 1500–1714*. 4 vols. Oxford, 1891–92.

Frank, Joseph. *Hobbled Pegasus: A Descriptive Bibliography of Minor English Poetry 1641–1660*. Albuquerque: University of New Mexico Press, 1968.

Fraser, Antonia. *Cromwell Our Chief of Men*. London: Weidenfeld and Nicolson, 1973.

Freeman, James A. *Milton and the Martial Muse: "Paradise Lost" and European Traditions of War*. Princeton: Princeton University Press, 1980.

Freud, Sigmund. *Jokes and Their Relation to the Unconscious*. Translated by James Strachey. Edited by Angela Richards. The Pelican Freud Library. Harmondsworth: Penguin, 1976.

Gage, Thomas. *The History and Antiquities of Suffolk. Thingoe Hundred*. Bury St. Edmunds, 1838.

Gardiner, Samuel Rawson, ed. *Constitutional Documents of the Puritan Revolution*. 3d ed. Oxford: Clarendon Press, 1906.

————. *History of England from the Accession of James I. to the Outbreak of the Civil War 1603–42*. 10 vols. London, 1883–84.

Gibb, M. A. *The Lord-General: A Life of Sir Thomas Fairfax*. London: Lindsay Drummond, 1938.

Gibbons, Brian. "Comic Method in Marlowe's *Hero and Leander*." In *Christopher Marlowe*, edited by Brian Morris, pp. 115–31. London: Benn, 1968.

Gibson, Colin "Another Shot in the War of the Theatres." *N&Q*, n. s. 34 (1987): 308–9.

Gibson, Robin. *Portraits from the Collection of the Earl of Clarendon*. [London]: Paul Mellon Centre for Studies in British Art, 1977.

Grant, Douglas. *Margaret the First: A Biography of Margaret Cavendish Duchess of Newcastle 1623–1673*. London: Rupert Hart-Davis, 1957.

Graves, Thornton Shirley. "Some Pre-Mohock Clansmen." *SP* 20 (1925): 395–421.

Gray, Douglas. "Rough Music: Some Early Invectives and Flytings." In *English Satire and the Satiric Tradition*, edited by Claude Rawson, pp. 21–43. Oxford: Blackwell, 1984. First published in *YES* 14 (1984).

Greaves, Richard L., and Robert Zaller, eds. *Biographical Dictionary of British Radicals in the Seventeenth Century*. 3 vols. Brighton: Harvester, 1982–84.

Green, Vivian. *The Commonwealth of Lincoln College 1427–1977*. Oxford: Oxford University Press, 1979.

Greenblatt, Stephen. *Shakespearean Negotiations: The Circulation of Social Energy in Renaissance England*. Oxford: Clarendon Press, 1988.

Grossman, F. *Pieter Bruegel: Complete Edition of the Paintings*. London: Phaidon, 1973.

Gurr, Andrew. "Singing Through the Chatter: Ford and Contemporary Theatrical Fashion." In *John Ford: Critical Re-Visions*, edited by Michael Neill, pp. 81–96. Cambridge: Cambridge University Press, 1988.

Hammond, Gerald. *Fleeting Things: English Poets and Poems, 1616–1660*. Cambridge and London: Harvard University Press, 1990.

Harbage, Alfred. *Sir William Davenant: Poet Venturer 1606–1668*. Philadelphia and London: University of Pennsylvania Press, 1935.

————. *Thomas Killigrew: Cavalier Dramatist 1612–83*. Philadelphia: University of Pennsylvania Press, 1930.

Hardacre, Paul H. *The Royalists During the Puritan Revolution*. The Hague: Nijhoff, 1956.

Hardacre, P. H. "The Royalists in Exile During the Puritan Revolution, 1642–1660." *HLQ* 16 (1953): 353–70.

Harris, F. R. *The Life of Edward Montagu, K. G. First Earl of Sandwich (1625–1675)*. 2 vols. London: John Murray, 1912.

Harris, Victor. *All Coherence Gone: A Study of the Seventeenth Century Controversy over Disorder and Decay in the Universe*. Chicago: University of Chicago Press, 1949.

Hartle, Paul. "Charles Cotton's *Burlesque upon Burlesque: Or, The Scoffer Scoft.*" *Restoration* 11 (1987): 3–17.

Hasted, Edward. *The History and Topographical Survey of the County of Kent*. 4 vols. Canterbury, 1778–79.

Hazlitt, W. Carew. *Collections and Notes 1867–1876*. London, 1876.

Healy, Thomas, and Jonathan Sawday, eds. *Literature and the English Civil War*. Cambridge: Cambridge University Press, 1990.

Heinemann, Margot. *Puritanism and Theatre: Thomas Middleton and Opposition Drama under the Stuarts*. Cambridge: Cambridge University Press, 1980.

Helgerson, Richard. *Self-Crowned Laureates: Spenser, Jonson, Milton and the Literary System*. Berkeley, Los Angeles, and London: University of California Press, 1983.

Hexter, J. H. "The Myth of the Middle Class in Tudor England." In his *Reappraisals in History*, pp. 71–116. London: Longman, 1961.

Hill, Christopher. *The Century of Revolution 1603–1714*. 2d ed. Wokingham: Van Nostrand Reinhold, 1980.

———. *Society and Puritanism in Pre-Revolutionary England*. London: Secker and Warburg, 1964.

Hobbs, Mary. "Early Seventeenth-Century Verse Miscellanies and their Value for Textual Editors." In *English Manuscript Studies*, 1, pp. 182–210. Oxford: Blackwell, 1989.

———. *Early Seventeenth Century Verse Miscellany Manuscripts*. Aldershot: Scolar Press, 1992.

Hogg, Michael A., and Dominic Abrams. *Social Identifications: A Social Psychology of Intergroup Relations and Group Processes*. London: Routledge, 1988.

Holmes, Clive. *Seventeenth-Century Lincolnshire*. History of Lincolnshire. Lincoln: Society for Lincolnshire History and Archaeology, 1980.

Holstun, James. "'God bless thee, little David!': John Felton and His Allies." *ELH* 59 (1992): 513–52.

———. "Ranting at the New Historicism." *ELR* 19 (1989): 189–225.

Hornbeak, Katherine Gee. *The Complete Letter-Writer in English 1568–1800*. Smith College Studies in Modern Languages, 15 (3–4). Hanover, N.H.: Smith College, 1934.

Howat, G. M. D. *Stuart and Cromwellian Foreign Policy*. London: Black, 1974.

[Hughes, Thomas]. *The Scouring of the White Horse: or, The Long Vacation Ramble of a London Clerk*. Cambridge, 1859.

Hull, Suzanne W. *Chaste, Silent & Obedient: English Books for Women 1475–1640*. San Marino, Calif.: Huntington Library, 1982.

Hutton, Ronald. *Charles the Second: King of England, Scotland, and Ireland*. Oxford: Clarendon Press, 1989.

———. *The Restoration: A Political and Religious History of England and Wales 1658–1667*. Oxford: Clarendon Press, 1985.

———. *The Royalist War Effort 1642–1646*. London: Longman, 1982.

Huxley, Gervas. *Endymion Porter: The Life of a Courtier 1587–1649*. London: Chatto and Windus, 1959.

Ingram, Martin. "Ridings, Rough Music and Mocking Rhymes in Early Modern England." In *Popular Culture in Seventeenth-Century England*, edited by Barry Reay, pp. 166–97. 1985; reprint, London: Routledge, 1988.

Jack, Ian. *Augustan Satire: Intention and Idiom in English Poetry 1660–1750*. Oxford: Clarendon Press, 1952.

Jacob, James R., and Timothy Raylor. "Opera and Obedience: Thomas Hobbes and *A Proposition for Advancement of Moralitie* by Sir William Davenant." *The Seventeenth Century* 6 (1991): 205–50.

Jacobson, Howard. *Ovid's Heroides*. Princeton: Princeton University Press, 1974.

Jameson, Caroline. "Ovid in the Sixteenth Century." In *Ovid*, edited by J.W. Binns, pp. 210–42. London: Routledge and Kegan Paul, 1973.

Janson, H. W. *Apes and Ape Lore: in the Middle Ages and the Renaissance*. London: Warburg Institute, 1952.

Jones, Emrys. "Pope and Dulness." *Proceedings of the British Academy* 54 (1968): 231–63.

Jones, Richard Foster. *Ancients and Moderns: A Study of the Rise of the Scientific Movement in Seventeenth-Century England*. Rev. ed. St. Louis, Mo.: Washington University Press, 1961.

Jump, John. *Burlesque*. The Critical Idiom. London: Methuen, 1972.

Kennedy, D. E. "Naval Captains at the Outbreak of the English Civil War." *Mariner's Mirror* 46 (1960): 181–98.

Kerrigan, John. "Thomas Carew." *Proceedings of the British Academy* 74 (1988): 311–50.

Lanham, Richard. *A Handlist of Rhetorical Terms*. Berkeley, Los Angeles, and Oxford: University of California Press, 1968.

Laslett, Peter. "The Gentry of Kent in 1640." *Cambridge Historical Journal* 9 (1948): 148–64.

Laughton, J. K. "Mennes, Sir John (1599–1671)." *DNB*.

Lawless, Donald S. "Massinger, Smith, Horner and Selden." *N&Q*, n. s. 4 (1957): 55–56.

———. *Philip Massinger and His Associates*, Ball State Monograph, 10. Muncie, Ind.: Ball State University, 1967.

Leavitt, Sturgis E. "Paul Scarron and English Travesty." *SP* 16 (1919): 108–20.

Lediard, Thomas. *The Naval History of England*. London, 1735.

Lee, Sidney. "Smith, James (1605–1667)." *DNB*.

Leonard, Nancy S. "Overreach at Bay." In *Philip Massinger: A Critical Reassessment*, edited by Douglas Howard, pp. 171–72. Cambridge: Cambridge University Press, 1985.

Leslie, Michael. *Spenser's "Fierce Warres and Faithfull Loves": Martial and Chivalric Symbolism in "The Faerie Queene."* Cambridge: Brewer, 1983.

Letcher, Valerie. "Herrick or Steward 'Oberons Clothing' in the Grey Collection." *Seventeenth Century News* 48 (1991): 58–59.

Levin, Richard. *The Multiple Plot in English Renaissance Drama*. Chicago: University of Chicago Press, 1971.

Lockyer, Roger. *Buckingham*. London: Longman, 1981.

Love, Harold. "Scribal Publication in Seventeenth-Century England." *Transactions of the Cambridge Bibliographical Society* 9 (1987): 130–54.

———. "Scribal Texts and Literary Communities: The Rochester Circle and Osborn b. 105." *Studies in Bibliography* 42 (1989): 219–35.

M. J. "Earldom of Carric: Sir John Mennis: Endymion Porter." *N&Q*, 3d ser. 4 (1863): 144.

McDaniel, Walton B. "Some Greek, Roman and English Tityretus." *American Journal of Philology* 35 (1914): 52–66.

McKeon, Michael. "Historicizing *Absalom and Achitophel.*" In *The New Eighteenth Century: Theory. Politics. English Literature,* edited by Felicity Nussbaum and Laura Brown, pp. 23–40. New York and London: Methuen, 1987.

M[adan], F[alconer]. [Untitled notes]. *Bodleian Quarterly Record* 3 (1920–22): 123–24.

Madan, Falconer, and H. E. Craster. *Summary Catalogue of Western Manuscripts in the Bodleian Library at Oxford.* 6 vols. Oxford: Clarendon Press, 1895–1937.

Malcolm, Joyce Lee. *Caesar's Due: Loyalty and King Charles 1642–1646.* London: Royal Historical Society, 1983.

Mallet, Charles Edward. *A History of the University of Oxford.* 3 vols. London: Methuen, 1924–27.

Marcus, Leah S. *The Politics of Mirth: Jonson, Herrick, Milton, Marvell, and the Defense of Old Holiday Pastimes.* Chicago and London: University of Chicago Press, 1986.

Margolies, David. *Novel and Society in Elizabethan England.* Totowa, N.J.: Barnes and Noble, 1985.

Marotti, Arthur F. *John Donne, Coterie Poet.* Madison and London: University of Wisconsin Press, 1986.

Marzys, Zygmunt. "Le Burlesque et les Fondateurs de la Langue Classique." In *Burlesque et Formes Parodiques dans la Litterature et les Arts: Actes du Colloque de l'Université du Maine, Le Mans (du 4 au 7 decembre 1986),* edited by Isabelle Landy-Houillon and Maurice Menard, pp. 115–23. Paris, Seattle, and Tubingen: Biblio 17, 1987.

Matthews, A. G. *Walker Revised.* Oxford: Clarendon Press, 1948.

Miller, Amos C. *Sir Richard Grenville of the Civil War.* London and Chichester: Phillimore, 1979.

Miller, Henry Knight. "The Paradoxical Encomium with Special Reference to its Vogue in England, 1600–1800." *MP* 53 (1956): 145–78.

"'The Miller's Melody,' An Old Ballad." *N&Q,* 1st ser. 10 (1852): 591–92.

Miner, Earl. *The Cavalier Mode from Jonson to Cotton.* Princeton: Princeton University Press, 1971.

Mizener, Arthur. "George Villiers, Second Duke of Buckingham: A Life and a Canon of his Works." Ph.D. diss., Princeton University, 1934.

Montrose, Louis Adrian. "'The Place of a Brother' In *As You Like It*: Social Process and Comic Form." *Shakespeare Quarterly* 32 (1981): 28–54.

Moorman, F. W. *Robert Herrick: A Biographical and Critical Study.* London: Nelson, 1910.

Murray, Oswyn. "The Greek Symposion in History." In *Tria Corda: Scritti in onore di Arnaldo Momigliano,* edited by E. Gabba, pp. 257–72. Biblioteca di Athanaeum. Como: Edizioni New Press, 1983.

———. "The Affair of the Mysteries: Democracy and the Drinking Group." In *Sympotica: A Symposium on the "Symposion,"* edited by Oswyn Murray, pp. 149–161. Oxford: Clarendon Press, 1990.

Neill, Michael. "Massinger's Patriarchy: The Social Vision of *A New Way to Pay Old Debts.*" *Renaissance Drama* 10 (1979): 185–213.

———. "'Wits most accomplished Senate': The Audience of the Caroline Private Theatres." *SEL* 18 (1978): 341–60.

Nethercot, Arthur H. *Abraham Cowley: The Muse's Hannibal*. London: Oxford University Press, 1931.

————. *Sir William Davenant: Poet Laureate and Playwright-Manager*. Chicago: University of Chicago Press, 1938.

Newman, P. R. *Royalist Officers in England and Wales 1642–1660: A Biographical Dictionary*. New York and London: Garland, 1981.

Newton, Richard C. "Jonson and the (Re-)Invention of the Book." In *Classic and Cavalier: Essays on Jonson and the Sons of Ben*, edited by Claude J. Summers and Ted-Larry Pebworth, pp. 31–55. Pittsburgh: University of Pittsburgh Press, 1982.

Nicholas, Donald. *Mr. Secretary Nicholas (1593–1669): His Life and Letters*. London: Bodley Head, 1955.

Norbrook, David. *Poetry and Politics in the English Renaissance*. London: Routledge and Kegan Paul, 1984.

Norton-Smith, John. "The Origins of Skeltonics." *EIC* 23 (1973): 57–62.

Notestein, Wallace. *Four Worthies*. New Haven: Yale University Press, 1957.

O Hehir, Brendan. *Harmony from Discords: A Life of Sir John Denham*. Berkeley and Los Angeles: University of California Press, 1968.

Oliver, George. *Ecclesiastical Antiquities in Devon*. 3 vols. Exeter, 1840–42.

Oppenheim, Michael M. *A History of the Administration of the Royal Navy and of Merchant Shipping in Relation to the Navy from MDIX to MDCLX*. London, 1896.

Parish, W. D. "Minnis." *N&Q*, 6th ser. 1 (1880): 245.

Parker, Michael P. "'All are not born (Sir) to the Bay': 'Jack' Suckling, 'Tom' Carew, and the Making of a Poet." *ELR* 12 (1982): 341–69.

————. "'To my friend G.N. from Wrest': Carew's Secular Masque." In *Classic and Cavalier: Essays on Jonson and the Sons of Ben*, edited by Claude J. Summers and Ted-Larry Pebworth, pp. 171–91. Pittsburgh: University of Pittsburgh Press, 1982.

Partridge, Eric. *Shakespeare's Bawdy*. London: Routledge and Kegan Paul, 1968.

Patterson, Annabel. *Censorship and Interpretation: The Conditions of Writing and Reading in Early Modern England*. Madison: University of Wisconsin Press, 1984.

————. *Pastoral and Ideology: Virgil to Valery*. Berkeley and Los Angeles: University of California Press, 1987.

Pearl, Valerie. *London and the Outbreak of the Puritan Revolution: City Government and National Politics, 1625–43*. Oxford: Oxford University Press, 1961.

Petersson, R. T. *Sir Kenelm Digby: The Ornament of England 1603–1665*. London: Cape, 1956.

Phelps, Naomi Forsythe. *The Queen's Invalid: A Biography of Paul Scarron*. Baltimore: Johns Hopkins University Press, 1951.

Phillips, John Roland. *Memoirs of the Civil War in Wales and the Marches, 1642–1649*. 2 vols. London, 1874.

Pole, Sir William. *Collections Towards a Description of the County of Devon*. London, 1791.

Pollard, A. W., and G. R. Redgrave. *A Short-Title Catalogue of Books Printed in England, Scotland, & Ireland . . . 1475–1640*. 2d ed., revised by W. A. Jackson, F. S. Ferguson, and Katharine F. Pantzer. 3 vols. London: Bibliographical Society, 1976–91.

Pooley, Roger. "Language and Loyalty: Plain Style at the Restoration." *Literature and History* 6 (1980): 2–18.

Potter, Lois. *Secret Rites and Secret Writing: Royalist Literature 1640–1660*. Cambridge: Cambridge University Press, 1989.

Povah, Alfred. *The Annals of the Parishes of St. Olave Hart Street and Allhallows Staining in the City of London*. London, 1894.

Powell, J. R. *The Navy in the English Civil War*. Hamden, Conn.: Archon, 1962.

Powell, William S. *John Pory / 1572–1636: The Life and Letters of a Man of Many Parts*. Chapel Hill: University of North Carolina Press, 1977.

Prawdin, Michael. *Marie de Rohan: Duchesse de Chevreuse*. London: Allen and Unwin, 1971.

Prince, John. *The Worthies of Devon*. London, 1810.

Quintrell, B. W. "Charles I and his Navy in the 1630." *The Seventeenth Century* 3 (1988): 159–79.

Raylor, Timothy. "The Achievement of Sir John Mennes and Dr. James Smith." D.Phil. diss., University of Oxford, 1986.

———. "Providence and Technology in the English Civil War: Edmond Felton and his Engine." *Renaissance Studies* 7 (1993).

———. "Samuel Hartlib and the Commonwealth of Bees." In *Culture and Cultivation in Early Modern England: Writing and the Land*, edited by Michael Leslie and Timothy Raylor, pp. 91–129. Leicester: Leicester University Press, 1992.

———. "Samuel Hartlib's Copy of 'Upon Sir John Suckling's hundred horse'." *N&Q*, n. s. 36 (1989): 445–47.

———. "Sir Matthew Mennes." *Historical Research: The Bulletin of the Institute of Historical Research* 61 (1988): 118–22.

———. "The Source of 'He that fights and runs away'." *N&Q*, n. s. 33 (1986): 465–66.

———. "*Wits Recreations* not by Sir John Mennes or James Smith?" *N&Q*, n. s. 32 (1985): 2–3.

Reed, John Curtis. "Humphrey Moseley, Publisher." *Oxford Bibliographical Society Proceedings and Papers* 2 (1927–30): 57–142.

Richards, Edward Ames. *"Hudibras" in the Burlesque Tradition*. New York: Columbia University Press, 1937.

Rollins, H. E. *An Analytical Index to the Ballad Entries (1557–1709) In the registers of the Company of Stationers*. Chapel Hill: University of North Carolina Press, 1924.

———. "Martin Parker, Ballad-Monger." *Modern Philology* 16 (1919): 449–74.

Rosenberg, Jacob, Seymour Slive, and E. H. Ter Kuile. *Dutch Art and Architecture 1600–1800*. Harmondsworth: Penguin, 1966.

Rossky, William. "Imagination in the English Renaissance Psychology and Poetic." *Studies in the Renaissance* 5 (1958): 49–73.

Røstvig, Maren Sofie. *The Happy Man: Studies in the Metamorphosis of a Classical Ideal*. 2d ed. 2 vols. Oslo: Norwegian University Presses, 1962.

Roy, Ian. "The Libraries of Edward, 2nd Viscount Conway, and Others: an Inventory and Valuation of 1643." *Bulletin of the Institute of Historical Research* 41 (1968): 35–46.

Ruffhead, Owen. *The Life of Alexander Pope*. London, 1769.

Russell, Conrad. "The First Army Plot of 1641." *Transactions of the Royal Historical Society* 38 (1988): 85–106.

———. *Parliaments and English Politics 1621–1629*. Oxford: Clarendon Press, 1979.

Saintsbury, George. "The Prosody of the Seventeenth Century." In *Cambridge History of English Literature*, edited by A. W. Ward and A. R. Waller, 8.222–40. 15 vols. Cambridge: Cambridge University Press, 1907–27.

Saunders, J. W. *A Biographical Dictionary of Renaissance Poets and Dramatists, 1520–1650*. Brighton: Harvester; Totowa, N.J.: Barnes and Noble, 1983.

———. *The Profession of English Letters*. London: Routledge, and Kegan Paul, 1964.

———. "The Stigma of Print: A Note on the Social Bases of Tudor Poetry." *EIC* 1 (1951): 139–64.

Scammell, G. V. "The Sinews of War: Manning and Provisioning English Fighting Ships *c*. 1550–1650." *Mariner's Mirror* 73 (1987): 351–67.

Scott, Walter F. "The Naval Chaplain in Stuart Times." D.Phil. diss., University of Oxford, 1935.

Seaver, Paul S. *The Puritan Lectureships: The Politics of Religious Dissent 1560–1662*. Stanford, Calif.: Stanford University Press, 1970.

Selden, Raman. *English Verse Satire 1590–1765*. London: Allen and Unwin, 1978.

Shapiro, I. A. "The Mermaid Club." *MLR* 45 (1950): 6–17.

Sharpe, Kevin. *Criticism and Compliment: The Politics of Literature in the England of Charles I*. Cambridge: Cambridge University Press, 1987.

Simpson, Claude M. *The British Broadside Ballad and its Music*. New Brunswick, N.J.: Rutgers University Press, 1966.

Smith, Courtney Craig. "The Seventeenth Century Drolleries." Ph.D. diss., Harvard University, 1944.

———. "The Seventeenth-Century Drolleries." *HLB* 6 (1952): 40–51.

Smith, Nigel. "Secret Selves." *EIC* 41 (1991): 324–31.

Smuts, R. Malcolm. *Court Culture and the Origins of a Royalist Tradition in Early Stuart England*. Philadelphia: University of Pennsylvania Press, 1987.

Smuts, R. M. "The Puritan Followers of Henrietta Maria in the 1630s." *EHR* 93 (1978): 26–45.

Sotheby's. *English Literature and History*. London: Sotheby, 1988.

Stallybrass, Peter. "'Wee feaste in our Defense': Patrician Carnival in Early Modern England and Robert Herrick's *Hesperides*." *ELR* 16 (1986): 234–52.

Stallybrass, Peter, and Allon White. *The Politics and Poetics of Transgression*. London: Methuen, 1986.

Stone, Laurence. *The Causes of the English Revolution 1529–1642*. 2d ed. London: Routledge and Kegan Paul, Ark Paperbacks, 1986.

———. *The Family, Sex and Marriage in England 1500–1800*. Abr. ed. Harmondsworth: Penguin, 1979.

Strachan, Michael. "The Mermaid Club: A New Discovery." *History Today* 17 (1967): 533–38.

———. *The Life and Adventures of Thomas Coryate*. London: Oxford University Press, 1962.

Strong, Roy. *The Cult of Elizabeth: Elizabethan Portraiture and Pageantry*. London: Thames and Hudson, 1977.

Thirsk, Joan. "Younger Sons in the Seventeenth Century." In her *The Rural Economy of England: Collected Essays*, pp. 335–57. London: Hambledon, 1984.

Thomas, Keith. "The Place of Laughter in Tudor and Stuart England." *TLS*, 21 January 1977, 77–81.

———. *Religion and the Decline of Magic: Studies in Popular Beliefs in Sixteenth- and Seventeenth-Century England*. Harmondsworth: Penguin, 1973.

Thomas, P. W. *Sir John Berkenhead 1617–1679: A Royalist Career in Politics and Polemics*. Oxford: Clarendon Press, 1969.

———. "Two Cultures? Court and Country under Charles I." In *The Origins of the English Civil War*, edited by Conrad Russell, pp. 168–93. London and Basingstoke: Macmillan, 1973.

Thomas, Peter W. "The Impact on Literature." In *The Impact of the English Civil War*, edited by John Morrill, pp. 123–42. London: Collins and Brown, 1991.

Thomason, George. *Catalogue of the Pamphlets, Newsfapers, and Manuscripts Relating to the Civil War, the Commonwealth, and Restoration, Collected by George Thomason*. 2 vols. London: British Museum, 1908.

Thompson, Edgar K. "Admiral Sir John Mennes 1599–1671." *Mariner's Mirror* 48 (1962): 227.

Timbs, John. *Club Life of London*. 2 vols. London, 1866.

Todd, Emmanuel. *The Explanation of Ideology: Family Structures and Social Systems*. Translated by David Garrioch. Oxford: Blackwell, 1985.

Tolmie, Murray. *The Triumph of the Saints: The Separate Churches of London 1616–1649*. Cambridge: Cambridge University Press, 1977.

Townshend, Dorothea. *Life and Letters of Mr. Endymion Porter*. London, 1897.

Treglown, Jeremy. "The Satirical Inversion of Some English Sources in Rochester's Poetry." *RES* 24 (1973): 42–48.

Trevor-Roper, Hugh. *Archbishop Laud, 1573–1645*. 3d ed. London: Macmillan, 1988.

———. *Religion, the Reformation, and Social Change*. London: Macmillan, 1967.

Trickett, Rachel. "The Heroides and the English Augustans." In *Ovid Renewed: Ovidian Influences on Literature and the Arts from the Middle Ages to the Twentieth Century*, edited by Charles Martindale, pp. 191–204. Cambridge: Cambridge University Press, 1988.

Tucker, Norman. *North Wales in the Civil War*. Denbigh: Gee, 1961.

Underdown, David. *Revel, Riot and Rebellion: Popular Politics and Culture in England 1603–1660*. Oxford: Clarendon Press, 1985.

———. *Royalist Conspiracy in England 1649–1660*. New Haven: Yale University Press, 1960.

Venn, John, and J. A. Venn. *Alumni Cantabrigienses. Part 1. From the Earliest Times to 1751*. 4 vols. Cambridge: Cambridge University Press, 1922–27.

Vieth, David. *Attribution in Restoration Poetry: A Study of Rochester's "Poems" of 1680*. New Haven: Yale University Press, 1963.

Walzer, Michael. *The Revolution of the Saints: A Study in the Origins of Radical Politics*. Cambridge: Harvard University Press, 1965.

Warburton, Eliot. *Memoirs of Prince Rupert and the Cavaliers*. 3 vols. London, 1849.

Watson, George, ed. *The New Cambridge Bibliography of English Literature*. Vol. 1. Cambridge: Cambridge University Press, 1974.

Webster, Charles. *The Great Instauration, 1626–1660: Science, Medicine and Reform*. London: Duckworth, 1975.

Wedgwood, C. V. *The King's War 1641–1647*. London: Collins, 1958.

——. *Poetry and Politics under the Stuarts*. Cambridge: Cambridge University Press, 1960.

Welford, Richard. *History of Newcastle and Gateshead*. 3 vols. London, 1884–87.

Wheatley, Henry B. *London Past and Present*. 3 vols. London, 1891.

Whitfield, Christopher. *Robert Dover and the Cotswold Games*. Evesham: distributed by Henry Sotheran, London, 1962.

Whitlock, Baird W. *John Hoskyns, Serjeant-At-Law*. Washington, D.C.: University Press of America, 1982.

Willetts, Pamela J. *The Henry Lawes Manuscript*. London: British Museum, 1969.

Williamson, George. *Seventeenth Century Contexts*. London: Faber, 1960.

Wilson, Charles. *Profit and Power: A Study of England and the Dutch Wars*. London: Longman, 1957.

Wimsatt, William K. "Rhetoric and Poems: The Example of Swift." In *The Author in his Work: Essays on a Problem in Criticism*, edited by Louis L. Martz and Aubrey Williams, pp. 229–44. New Haven and London: Yale University Press, 1978.

Wing, Donald F. *Short-Title Catalogue of Books Printed In England, Scotland, Ireland, Wales, and British America . . . 1641–1700*. 2d ed. 3 vols. New York: MLA, 1972–88.

Withington, Eleanor. "The Fugitive Poetry of Mildmay Fane." *HLB* 9 (1955): 61–78.

Woodbridge, Linda. *Women and the English Renaissance: Literature and the Nature of Womankind, 1540–1620*. Brighton: Harvester, 1984.

Woodward, Daniel H. "Herrick's Oberon Poems." *Journal of English and Germanic Philology* 64 (1965): 270–84.

Woodward, John. *Heraldry British and Foreign*. 2 vols. London and Edinburgh, 1896.

Woolrych, A. H. *Penruddock's Rising 1655*. London: Historical Association, 1955.

Wootton, David. *Divine Right and Democracy: An Anthology of Political Writing in Stuart England*. Harmondsworth: Penguin, 1986.

Wortley, Clare Stuart. "Van Dyck and the Wentworths." *Burlington Magazine* 59 (1931): 102–7.

Wright, Louis B. *Middle-Class Culture in Elizabethan England*. Chapel Hill: University of North Carolina Press, 1935.

Wrightson, Keith. *English Society 1580–1680*. London: Hutchinson, 1982.

Yates, Frances. *The Rosicrucian Enlightenment*. London: Routledge and Kegan Paul, 1972.

Young, Peter. *Naseby 1645: The Campaign and the Battle*. London: Roundwood, 1985.

Zagorin, Perez. *The Court and the Country: The Beginning of the English Revolution*. London: Routledge and Kegan Paul, 1968.

Index